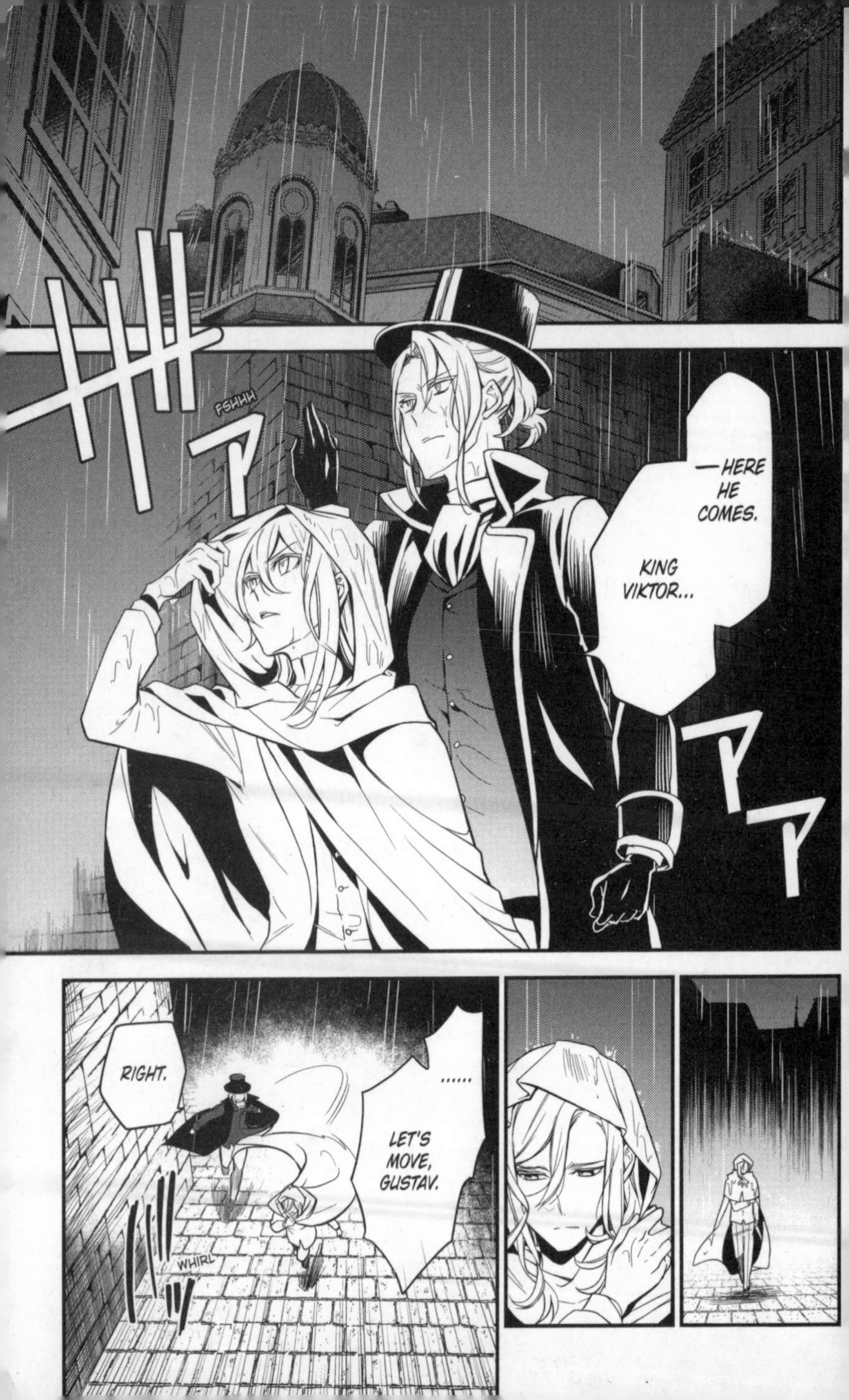
—HERE HE COMES.
KING VIKTOR...
FSHHH
......
LET'S MOVE, GUSTAV.
RIGHT.
WHIRL

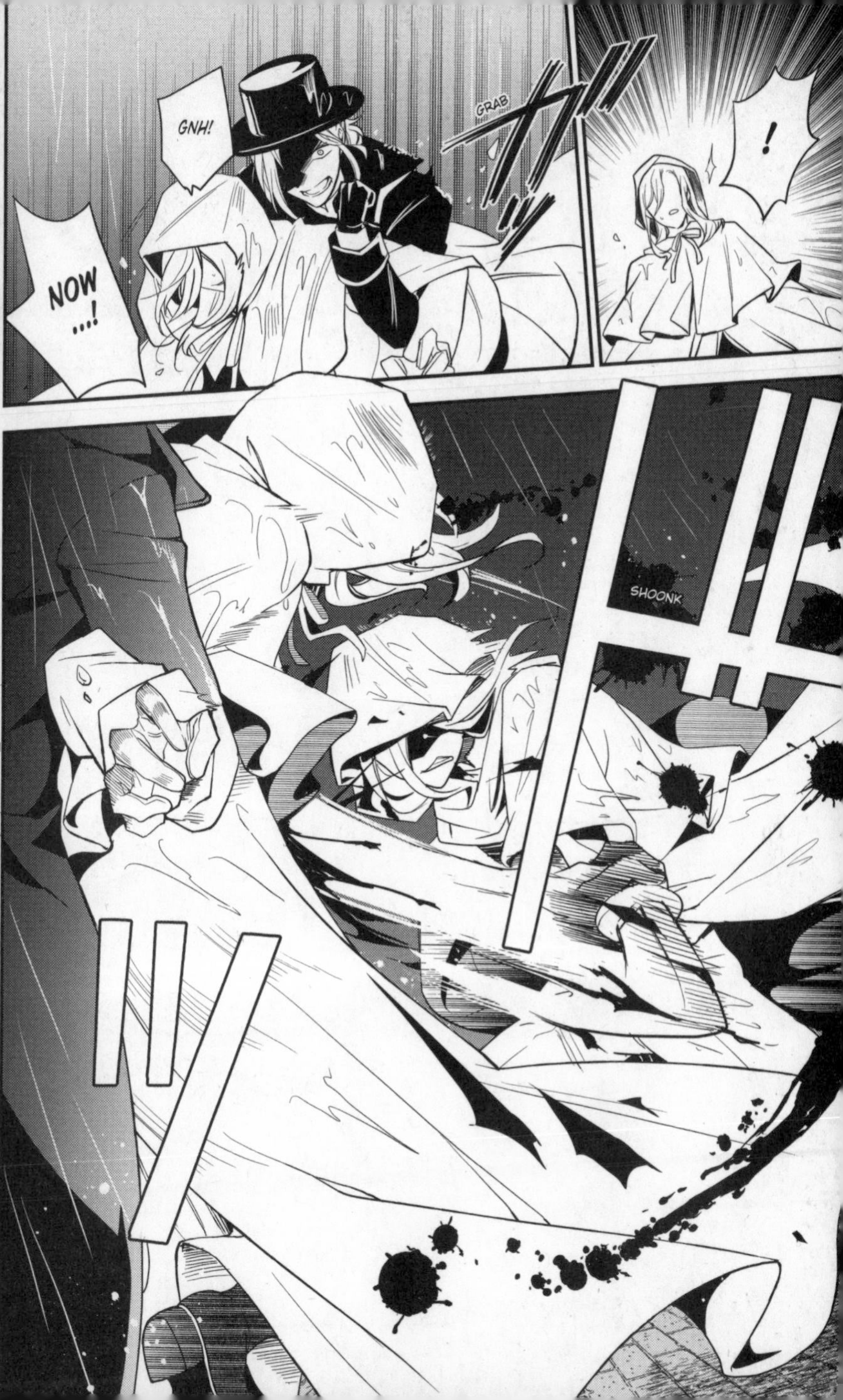
!
GRAB
GNH!
NOW ...!
SHOONK

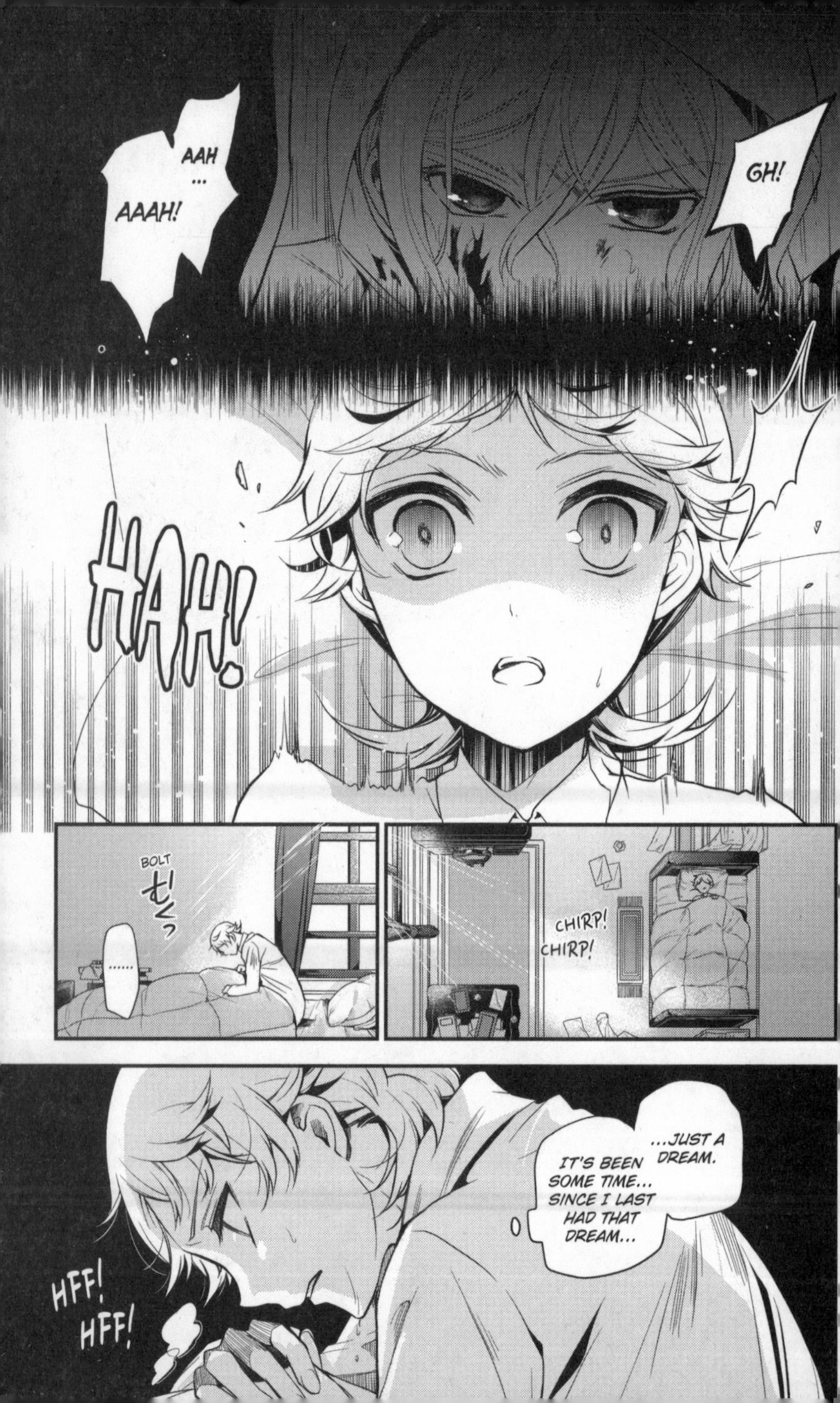
GH!
AAH ... AAAH!
HAH!
CHIRP! CHIRP!
BOLT むくっ
......
...JUST A DREAM.
IT'S BEEN SOME TIME... SINCE I LAST HAD THAT DREAM...
HFF! HFF!

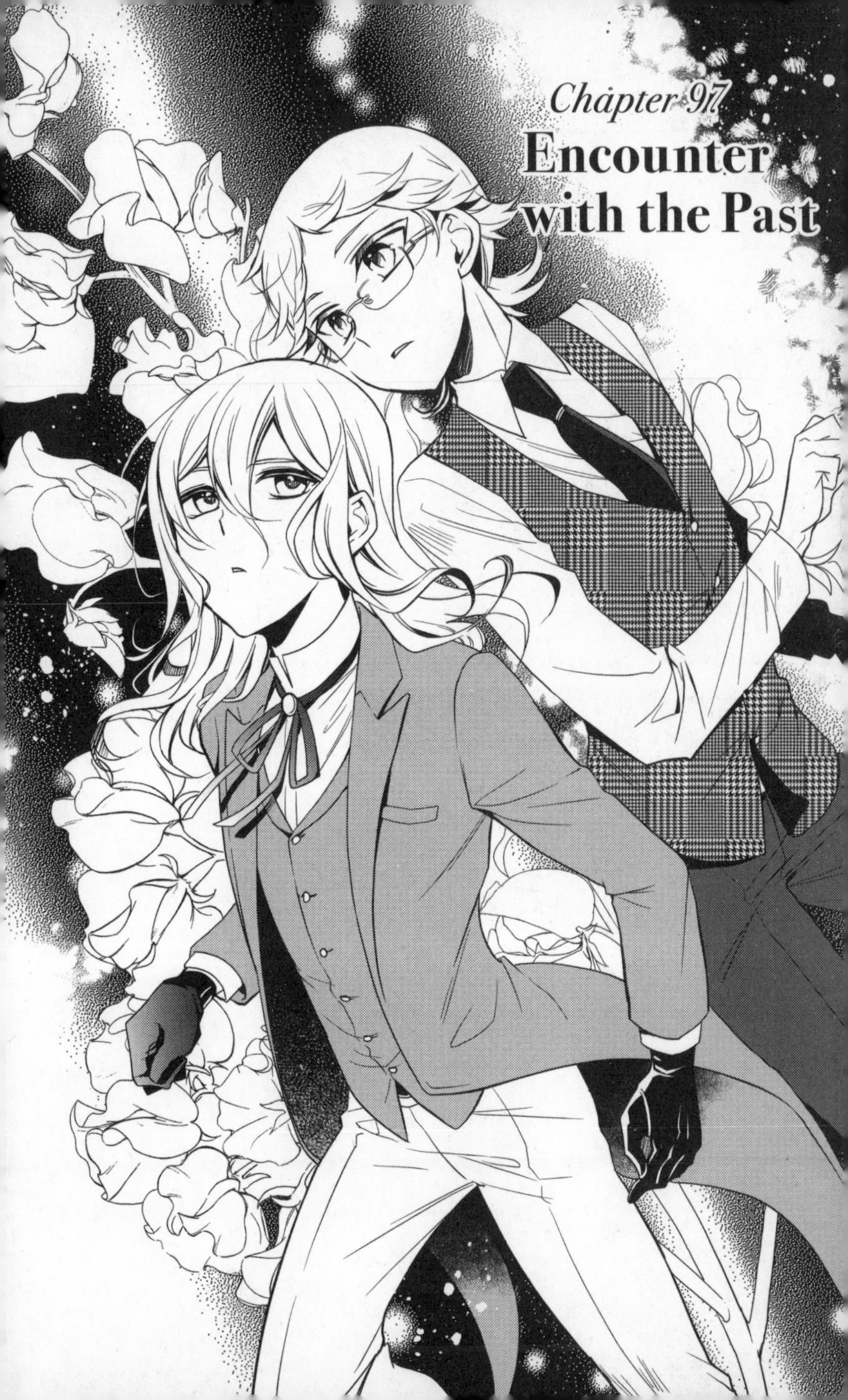
Chapter 97
Encounter with the Past

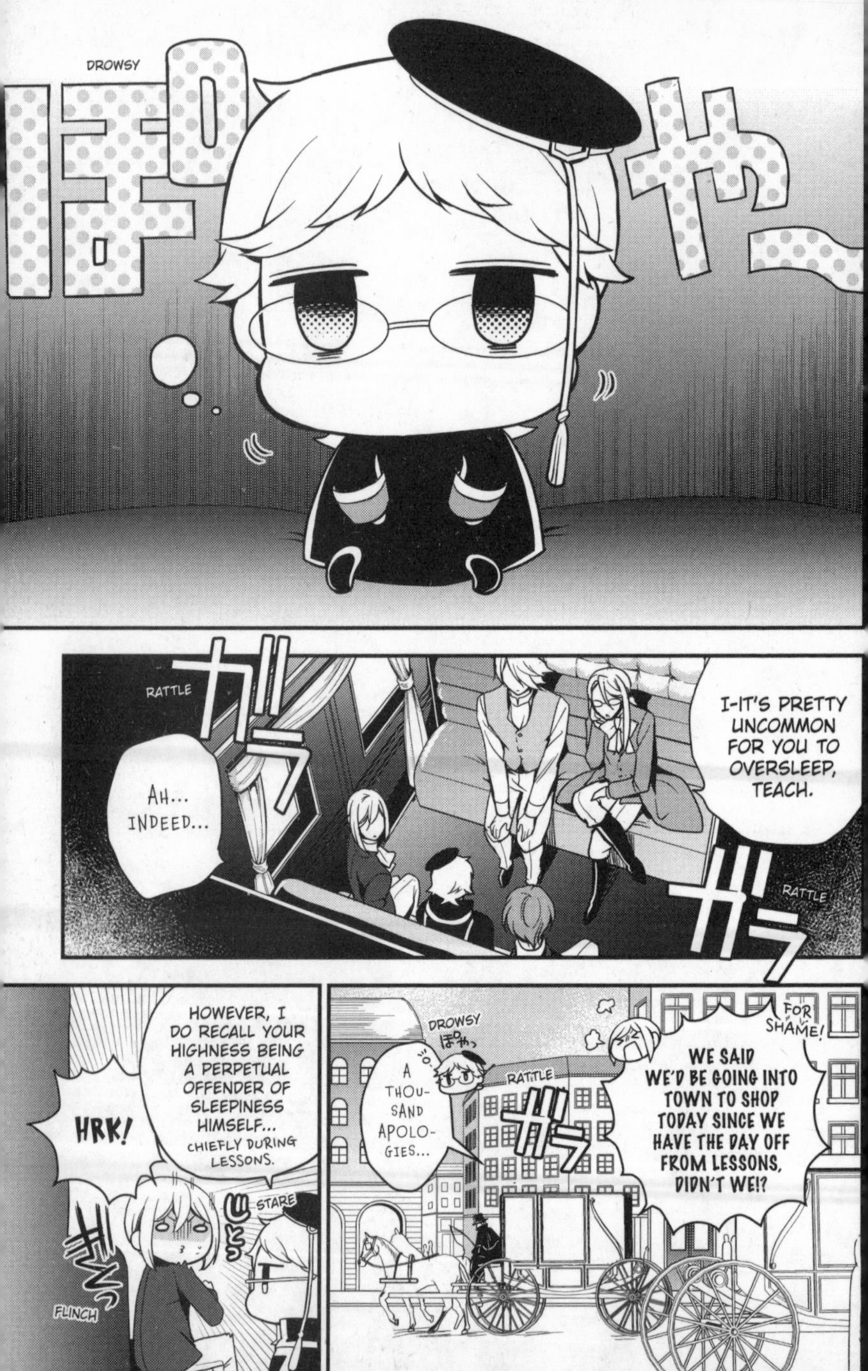
DROWSY
ぽやっ～
I-IT'S PRETTY UNCOMMON FOR YOU TO OVERSLEEP, TEACH.
RATTLE
AH... INDEED...
RATTLE
FOR SHAME!
WE SAID WE'D BE GOING INTO TOWN TO SHOP TODAY SINCE WE HAVE THE DAY OFF FROM LESSONS, DIDN'T WE!?
DROWSY
A THOU-SAND APOLO-GIES...
RATTLE
HOWEVER, I DO RECALL YOUR HIGHNESS BEING A PERPETUAL OFFENDER OF SLEEPINESS HIMSELF... CHIEFLY DURING LESSONS.
HRK!
STARE
FLINCH

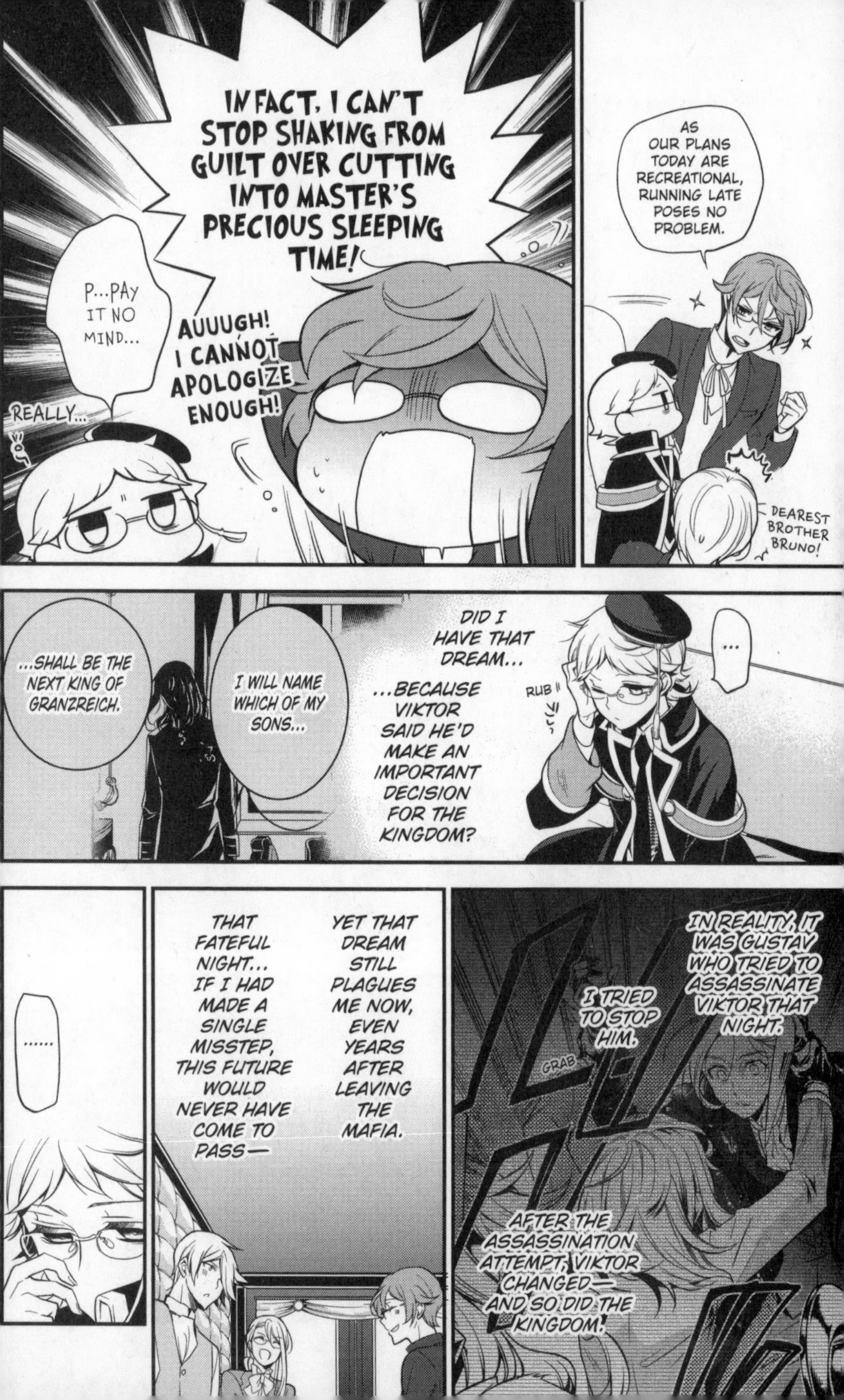
AS OUR PLANS TODAY ARE RECREATIONAL, RUNNING LATE POSES NO PROBLEM.
DEAREST BROTHER BRUNO!
IN FACT, I CAN'T STOP SHAKING FROM GUILT OVER CUTTING INTO MASTER'S PRECIOUS SLEEPING TIME!
AUUUGH! I CANNOT APOLOGIZE ENOUGH!
P...PAY IT NO MIND...
REALLY...
...
DID I HAVE THAT DREAM...
...BECAUSE VIKTOR SAID HE'D MAKE AN IMPORTANT DECISION FOR THE KINGDOM?
RUB
I WILL NAME WHICH OF MY SONS...
...SHALL BE THE NEXT KING OF GRANZREICH.
IN REALITY, IT WAS GUSTAV WHO TRIED TO ASSASSINATE VIKTOR THAT NIGHT.
I TRIED TO STOP HIM.
GRAB
AFTER THE ASSASSINATION ATTEMPT, VIKTOR CHANGED—AND SO DID THE KINGDOM.
YET THAT DREAM STILL PLAGUES ME NOW, EVEN YEARS AFTER LEAVING THE MAFIA.
THAT FATEFUL NIGHT... IF I HAD MADE A SINGLE MISSTEP, THIS FUTURE WOULD NEVER HAVE COME TO PASS—
......

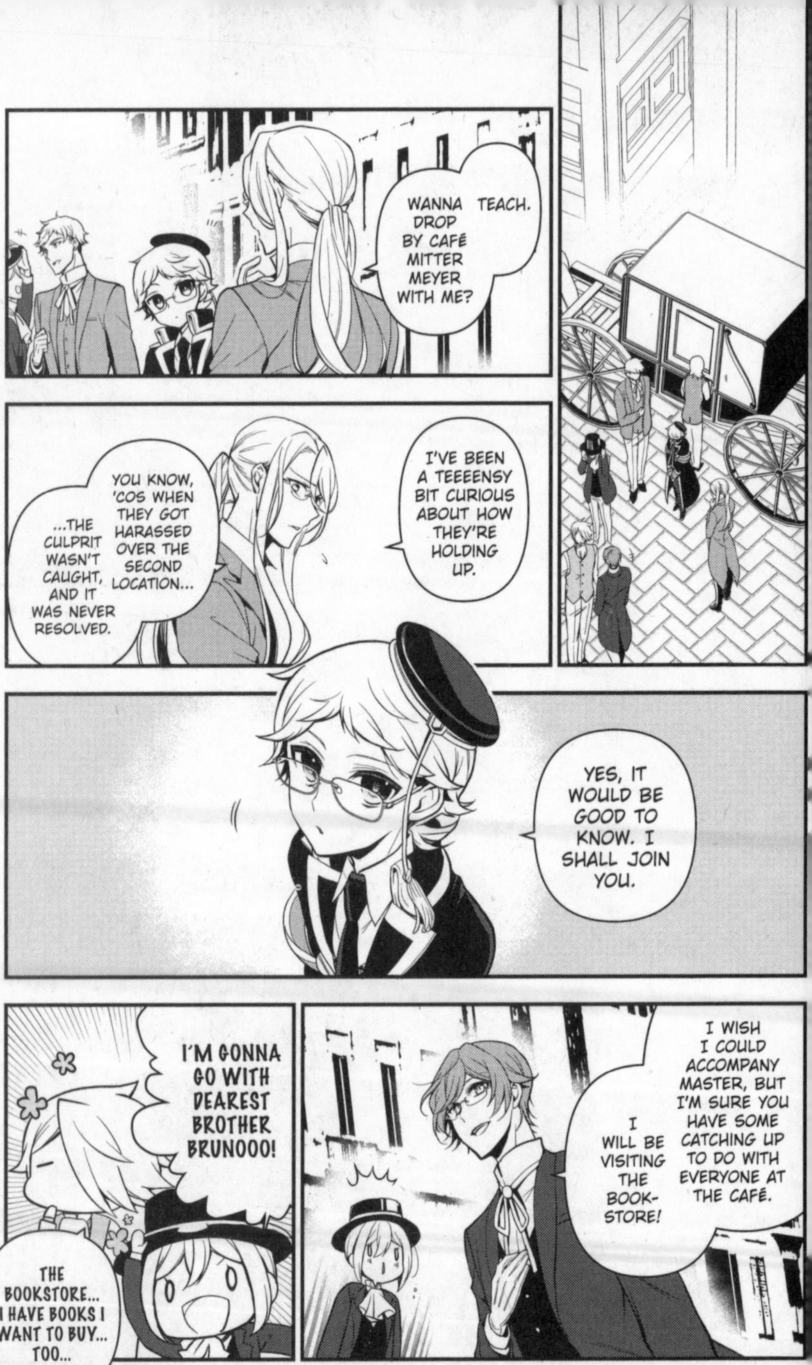
WANNA TEACH. DROP BY CAFÉ MITTER MEYER WITH ME?
I'VE BEEN A TEEEENSY BIT CURIOUS ABOUT HOW THEY'RE HOLDING UP.
YOU KNOW, 'COS WHEN THEY GOT HARASSED OVER THE SECOND LOCATION...
...THE CULPRIT WASN'T CAUGHT, AND IT WAS NEVER RESOLVED.
YES, IT WOULD BE GOOD TO KNOW. I SHALL JOIN YOU.
I WISH I COULD ACCOMPANY MASTER, BUT I'M SURE YOU HAVE SOME CATCHING UP TO DO WITH EVERYONE AT THE CAFÉ.
I WILL BE VISITING THE BOOK-STORE!
I'M GONNA GO WITH DEAREST BROTHER BRUNOOO!
THE BOOKSTORE... I HAVE BOOKS I WANT TO BUY... TOO...

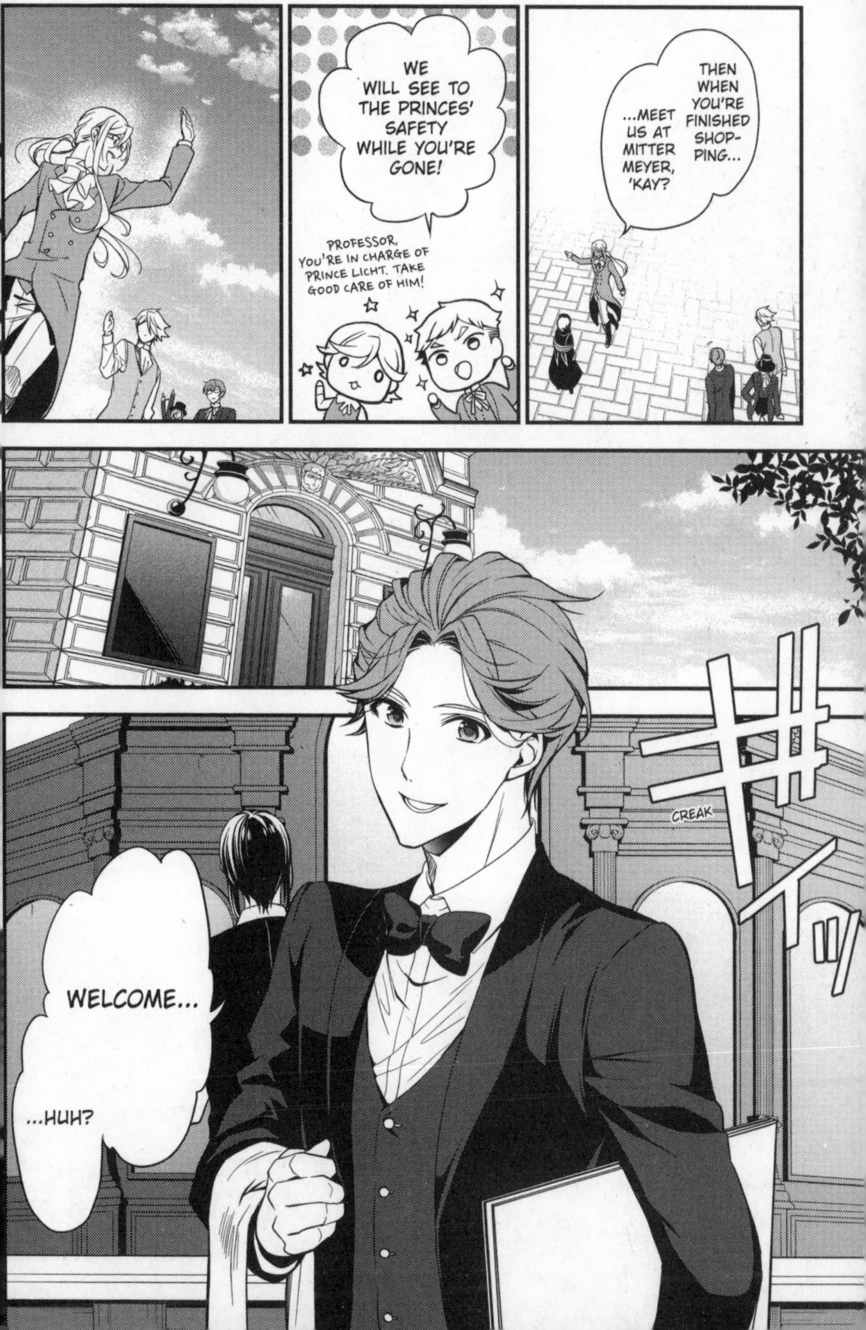
THEN WHEN YOU'RE FINISHED SHOP-PING...
...MEET US AT MITTER MEYER, 'KAY?
WE WILL SEE TO THE PRINCES' SAFETY WHILE YOU'RE GONE!
PROFESSOR, YOU'RE IN CHARGE OF PRINCE LICHT. TAKE GOOD CARE OF HIM!
CREAK
WELCOME...
...HUH?

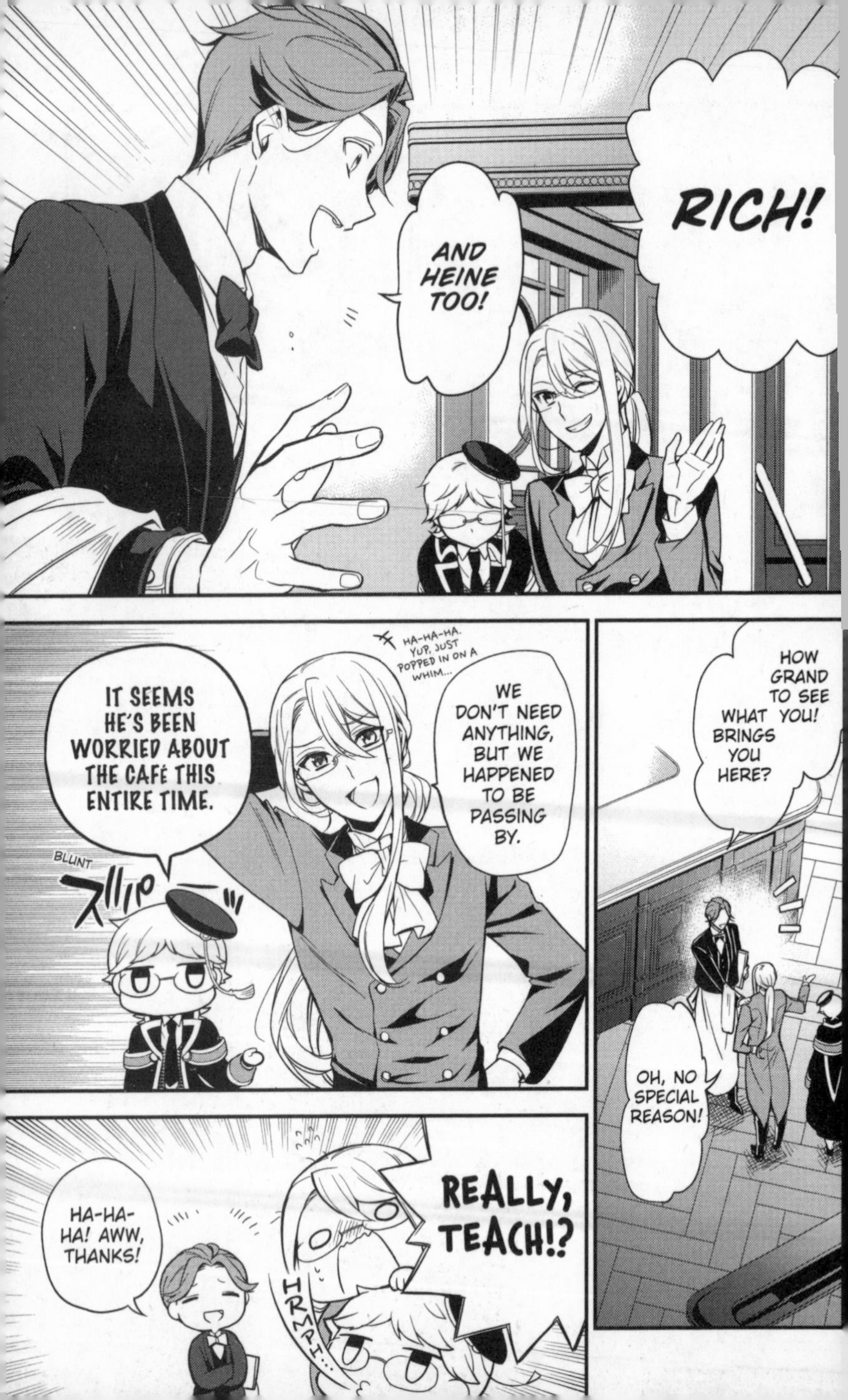
RICH!
AND HEINE TOO!
HOW GRAND TO SEE YOU! WHAT BRINGS YOU HERE?
OH, NO SPECIAL REASON!
HA-HA-HA. YUP, JUST POPPED IN ON A WHIM...
WE DON'T NEED ANYTHING, BUT WE HAPPENED TO BE PASSING BY.
IT SEEMS HE'S BEEN WORRIED ABOUT THE CAFÉ THIS ENTIRE TIME.
BLUNT
REALLY, TEACH!?
HRMPH...
HA-HA-HA! AWW, THANKS!

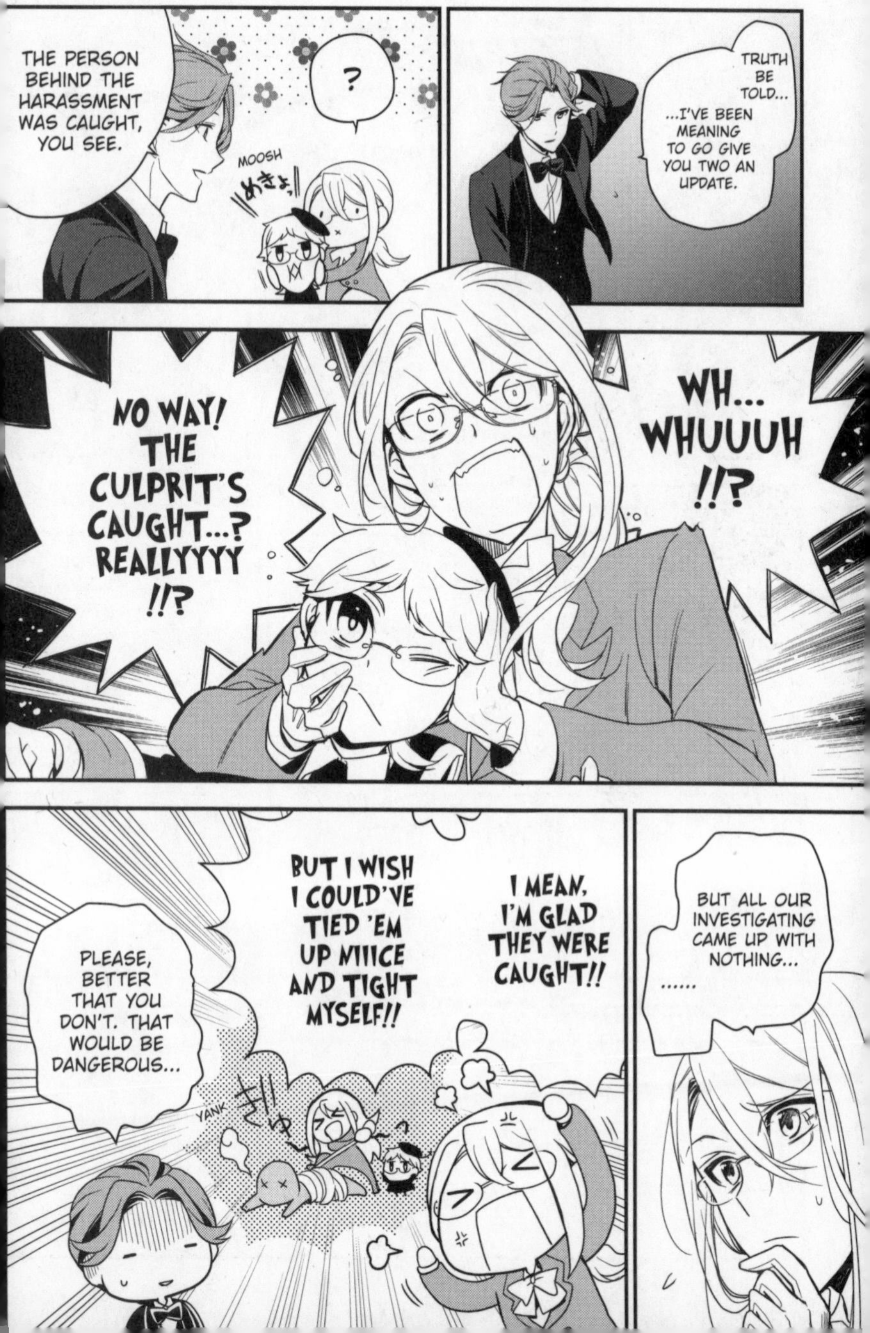
TRUTH BE TOLD...
...I'VE BEEN MEANING TO GO GIVE YOU TWO AN UPDATE.
THE PERSON BEHIND THE HARASSMENT WAS CAUGHT, YOU SEE.
?
MOOSH
めきょ
WH... WHUUUH!!?
NO WAY! THE CULPRIT'S CAUGHT...? REALLYYYY!!?
BUT ALL OUR INVESTIGATING CAME UP WITH NOTHING...
......
I MEAN, I'M GLAD THEY WERE CAUGHT!!
BUT I WISH I COULD'VE TIED 'EM UP NIIICE AND TIGHT MYSELF!!
YANK
ぎゅ
PLEASE, BETTER THAT YOU DON'T. THAT WOULD BE DANGEROUS...

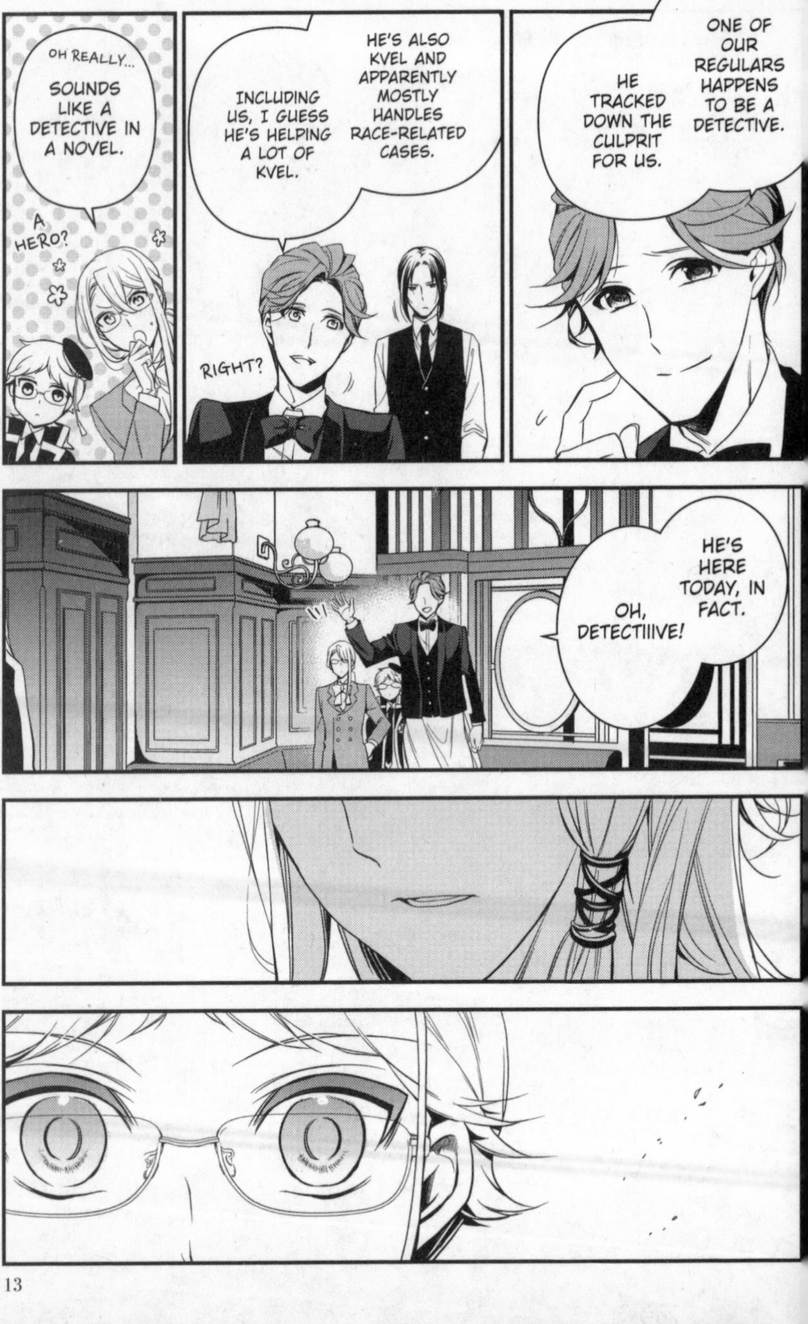
ONE OF OUR REGULARS HAPPENS TO BE A DETECTIVE.
HE TRACKED DOWN THE CULPRIT FOR US.
HE'S ALSO KVEL AND APPARENTLY MOSTLY HANDLES RACE-RELATED CASES.
INCLUDING US, I GUESS HE'S HELPING A LOT OF KVEL.
RIGHT?
OH REALLY...
SOUNDS LIKE A DETECTIVE IN A NOVEL.
A HERO?
HE'S HERE TODAY, IN FACT.
OH, DETECTIIIVE!

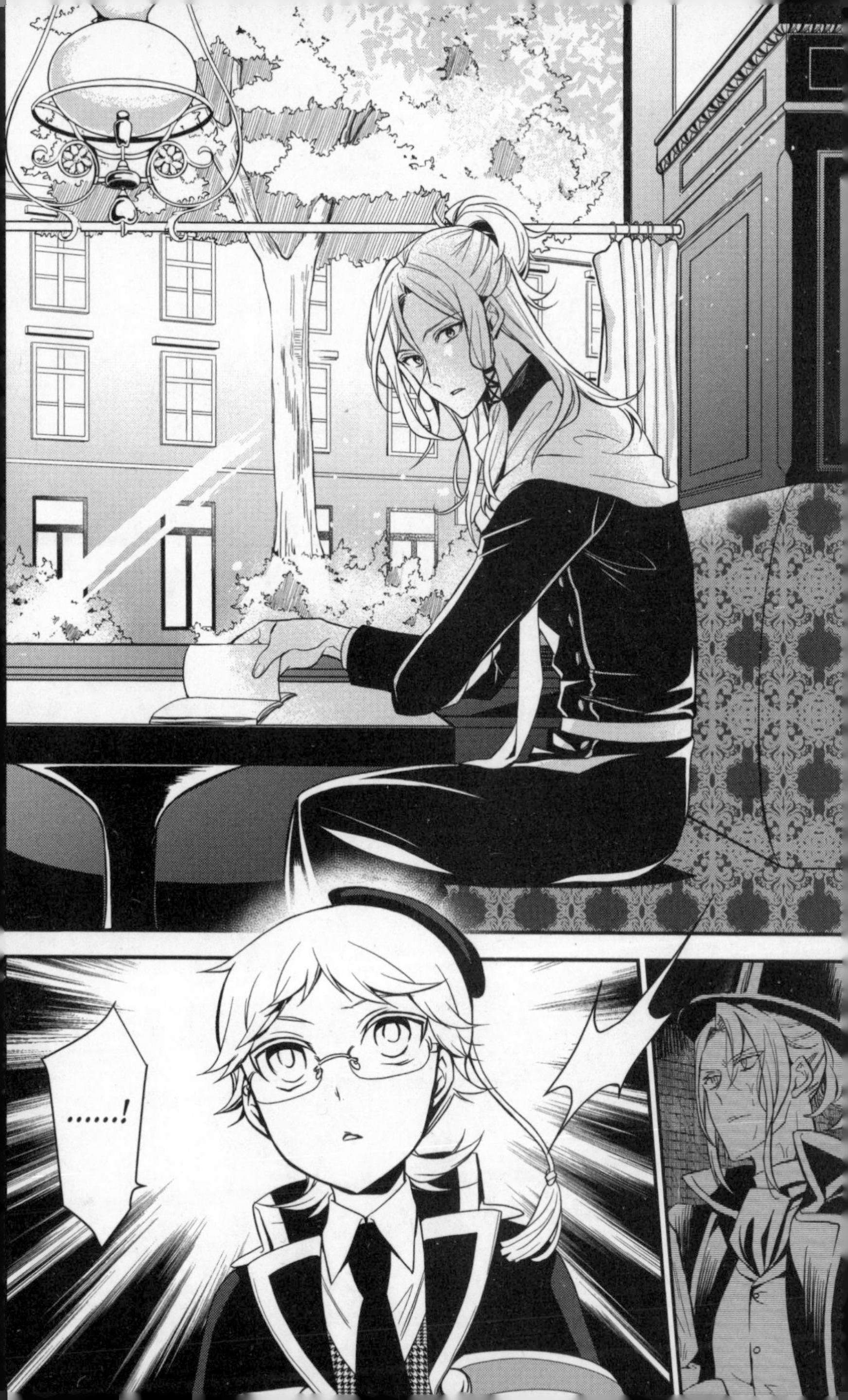
......!

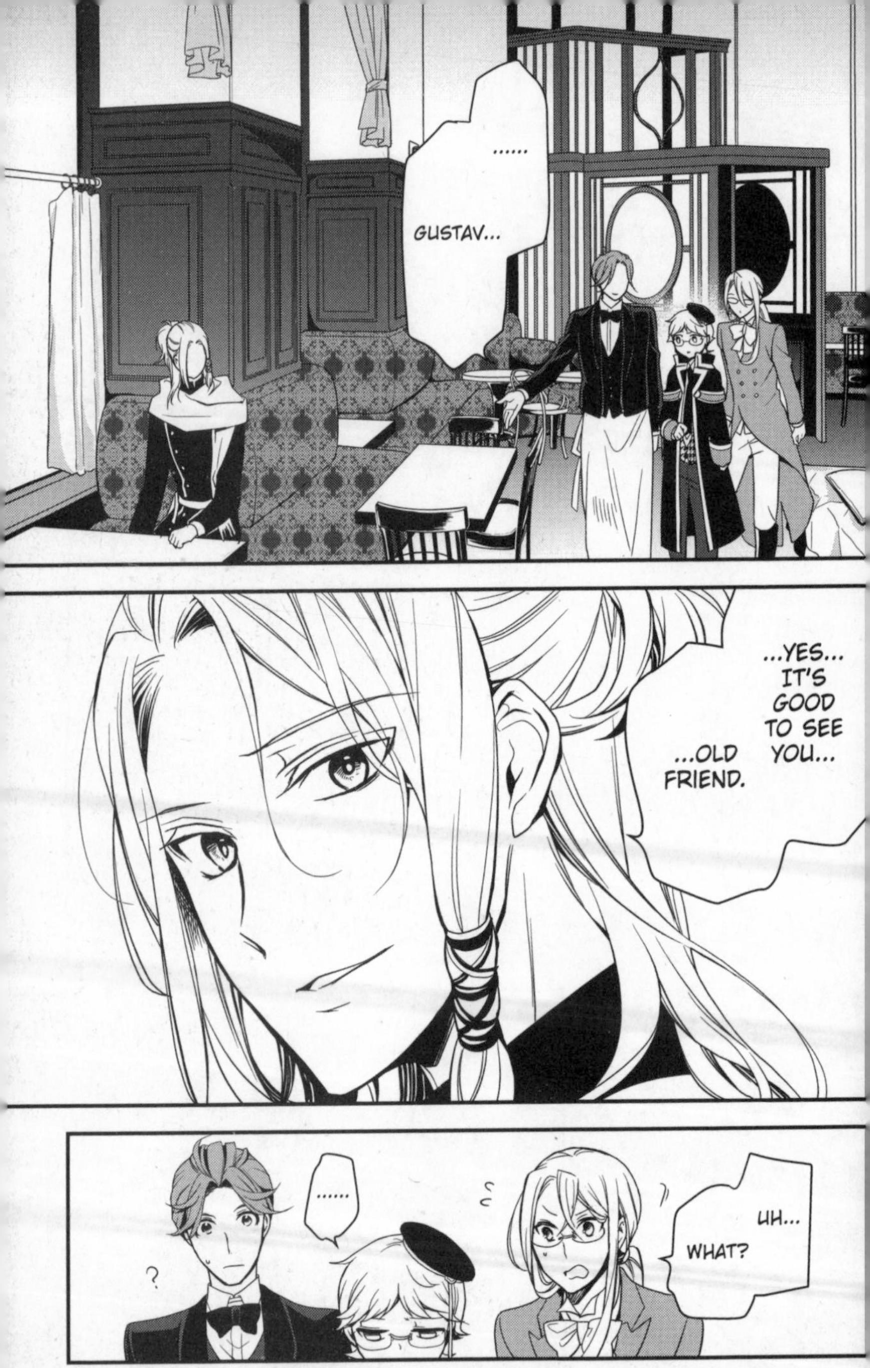
......
GUSTAV...
...YES... IT'S GOOD TO SEE YOU...
...OLD FRIEND.
UH... WHAT?
......

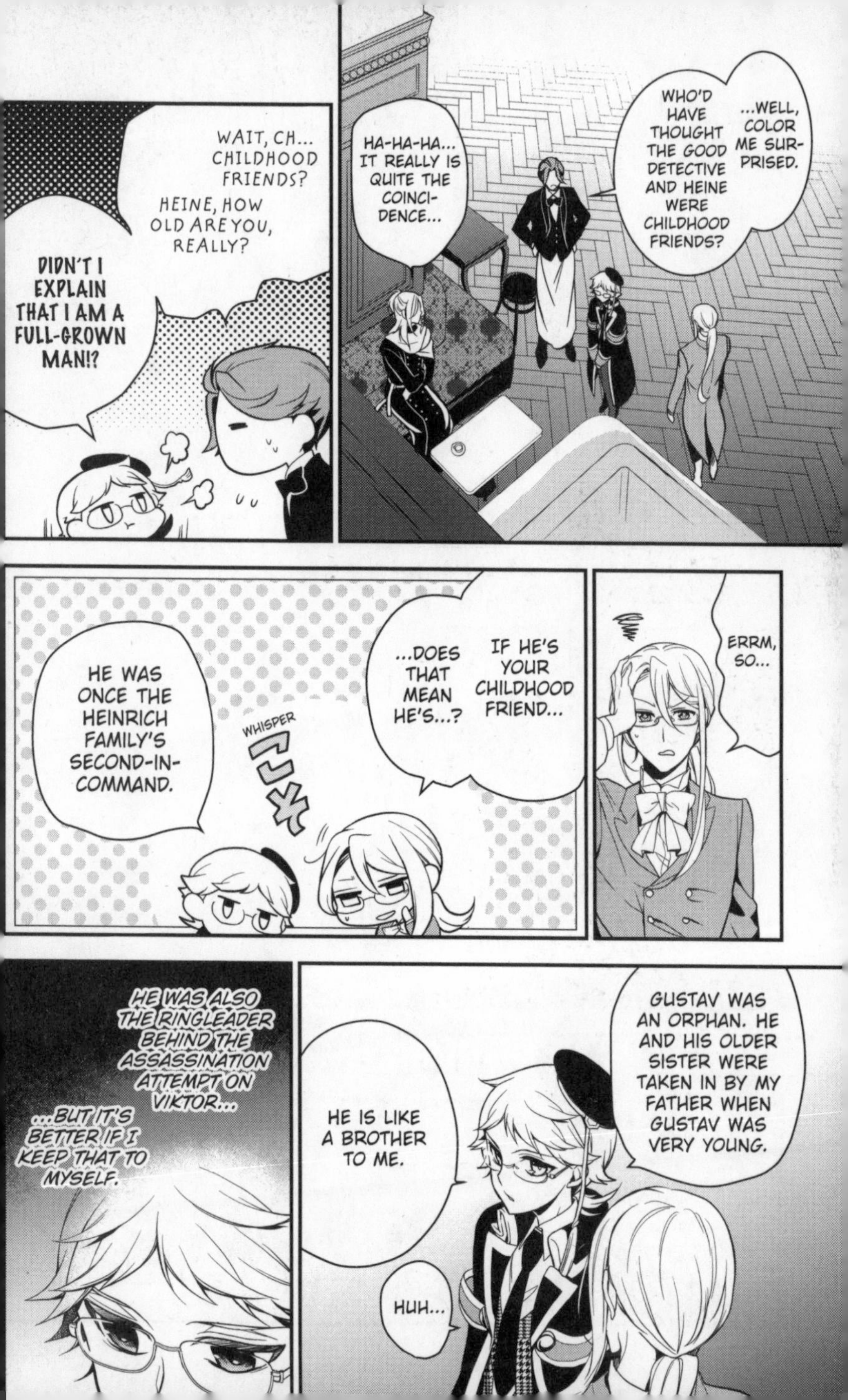
...WELL, COLOR ME SURPRISED.
WHO'D HAVE THOUGHT THE GOOD DETECTIVE AND HEINE WERE CHILDHOOD FRIENDS?
HA-HA-HA... IT REALLY IS QUITE THE COINCIDENCE...
WAIT, CH... CHILDHOOD FRIENDS?
HEINE, HOW OLD ARE YOU, REALLY?
DIDN'T I EXPLAIN THAT I AM A FULL-GROWN MAN!?
ERRM, SO...
IF HE'S YOUR CHILDHOOD FRIEND...
...DOES THAT MEAN HE'S...?
WHISPER
HE WAS ONCE THE HEINRICH FAMILY'S SECOND-IN-COMMAND.
GUSTAV WAS AN ORPHAN. HE AND HIS OLDER SISTER WERE TAKEN IN BY MY FATHER WHEN GUSTAV WAS VERY YOUNG.
HE IS LIKE A BROTHER TO ME.
HUH...
HE WAS ALSO THE RINGLEADER BEHIND THE ASSASSINATION ATTEMPT ON VIKTOR...
...BUT IT'S BETTER IF I KEEP THAT TO MYSELF.

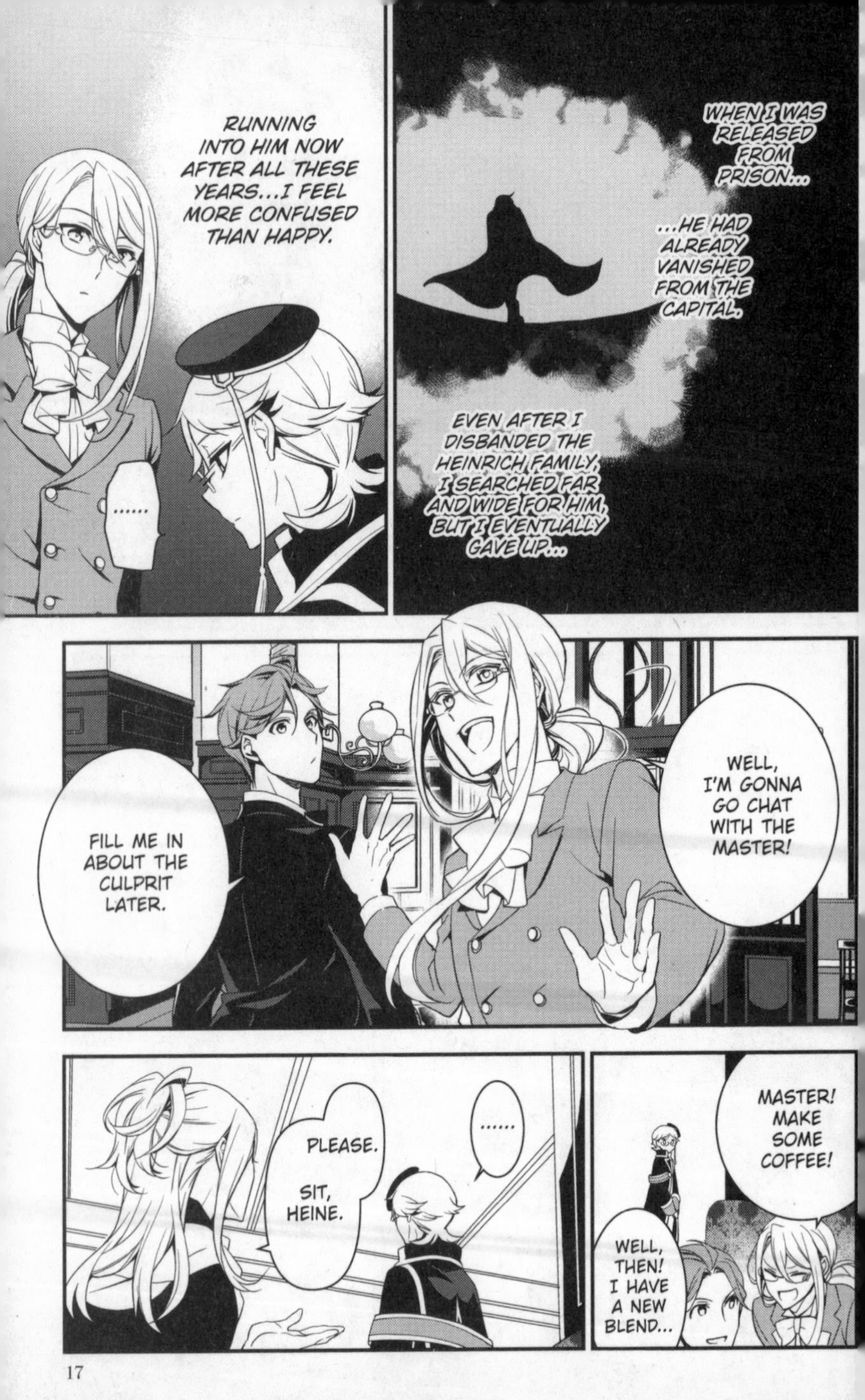
WHEN I WAS RELEASED FROM PRISON...
...HE HAD ALREADY VANISHED FROM THE CAPITAL.
EVEN AFTER I DISBANDED THE HEINRICH FAMILY, I SEARCHED FAR AND WIDE FOR HIM, BUT I EVENTUALLY GAVE UP...
RUNNING INTO HIM NOW AFTER ALL THESE YEARS...I FEEL MORE CONFUSED THAN HAPPY.
......
WELL, I'M GONNA GO CHAT WITH THE MASTER!
FILL ME IN ABOUT THE CULPRIT LATER.
MASTER! MAKE SOME COFFEE!
WELL, THEN! I HAVE A NEW BLEND...
......
PLEASE.
SIT, HEINE.

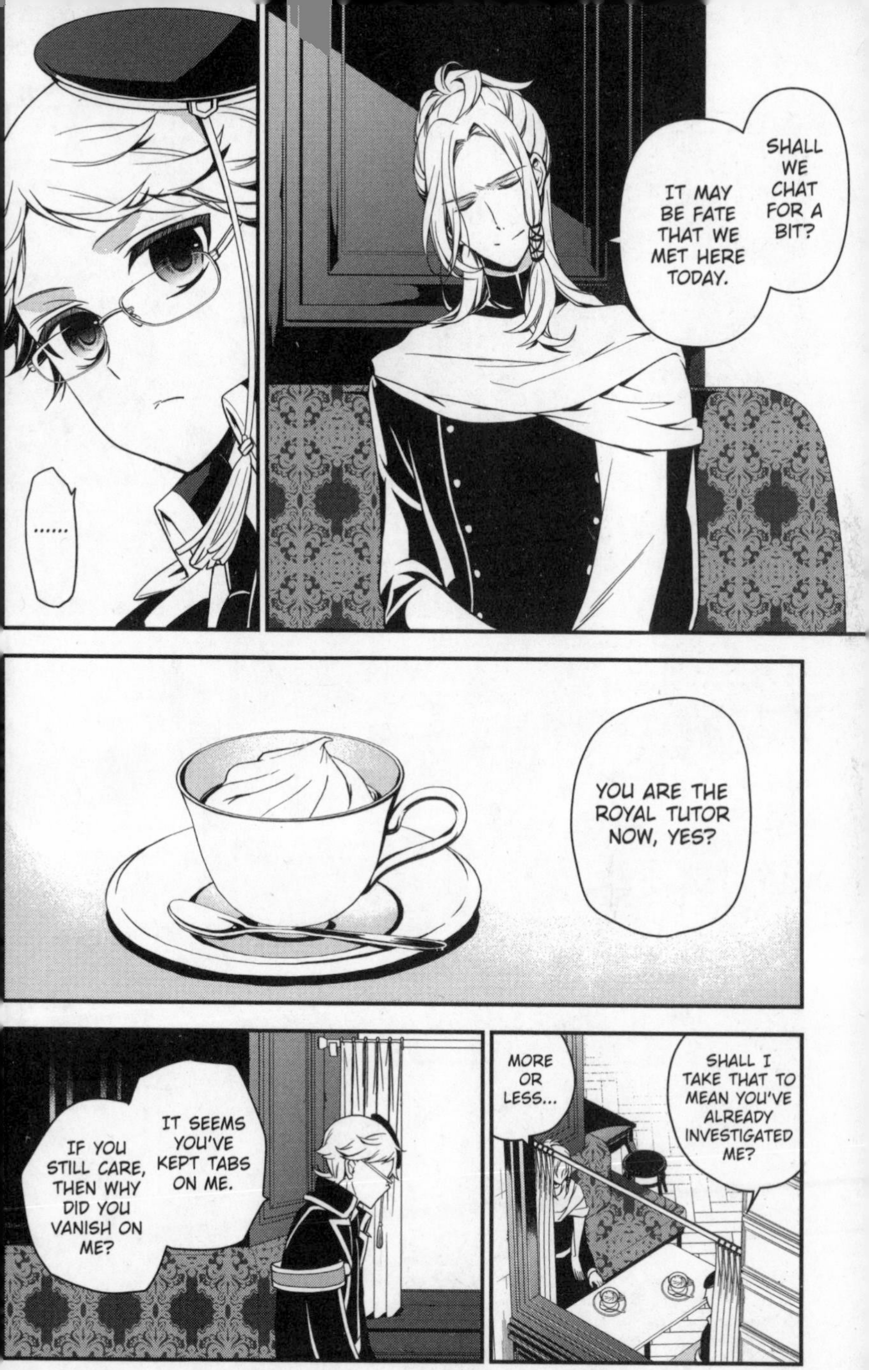
SHALL WE CHAT FOR A BIT?
IT MAY BE FATE THAT WE MET HERE TODAY.
......
YOU ARE THE ROYAL TUTOR NOW, YES?
SHALL I TAKE THAT TO MEAN YOU'VE ALREADY INVESTIGATED ME?
MORE OR LESS...
IT SEEMS YOU'VE KEPT TABS ON ME.
IF YOU STILL CARE, THEN WHY DID YOU VANISH ON ME?

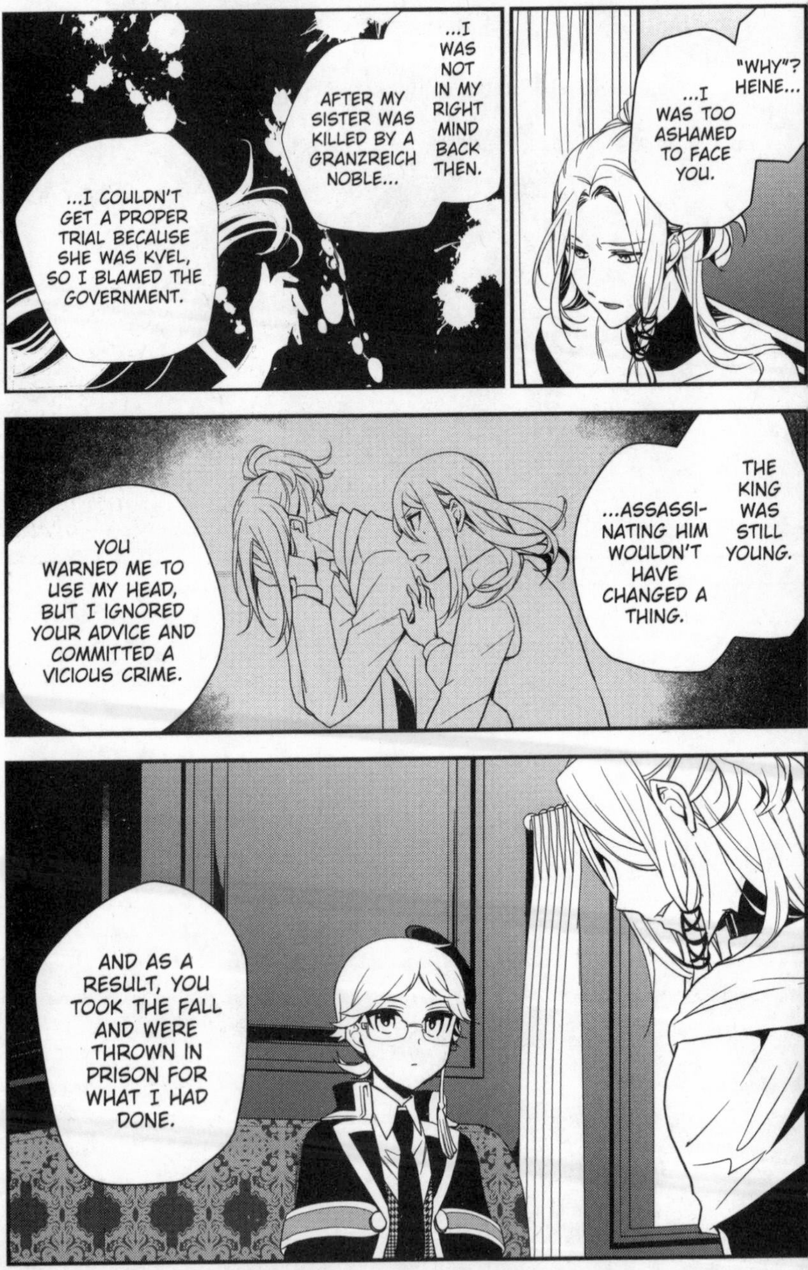
"WHY"? HEINE...
...I WAS TOO ASHAMED TO FACE YOU.
...I WAS NOT IN MY RIGHT MIND BACK THEN.
AFTER MY SISTER WAS KILLED BY A GRANZREICH NOBLE...
...I COULDN'T GET A PROPER TRIAL BECAUSE SHE WAS KVEL, SO I BLAMED THE GOVERNMENT.
THE KING WAS STILL YOUNG.
...ASSASSINATING HIM WOULDN'T HAVE CHANGED A THING.
YOU WARNED ME TO USE MY HEAD, BUT I IGNORED YOUR ADVICE AND COMMITTED A VICIOUS CRIME.
AND AS A RESULT, YOU TOOK THE FALL AND WERE THROWN IN PRISON FOR WHAT I HAD DONE.

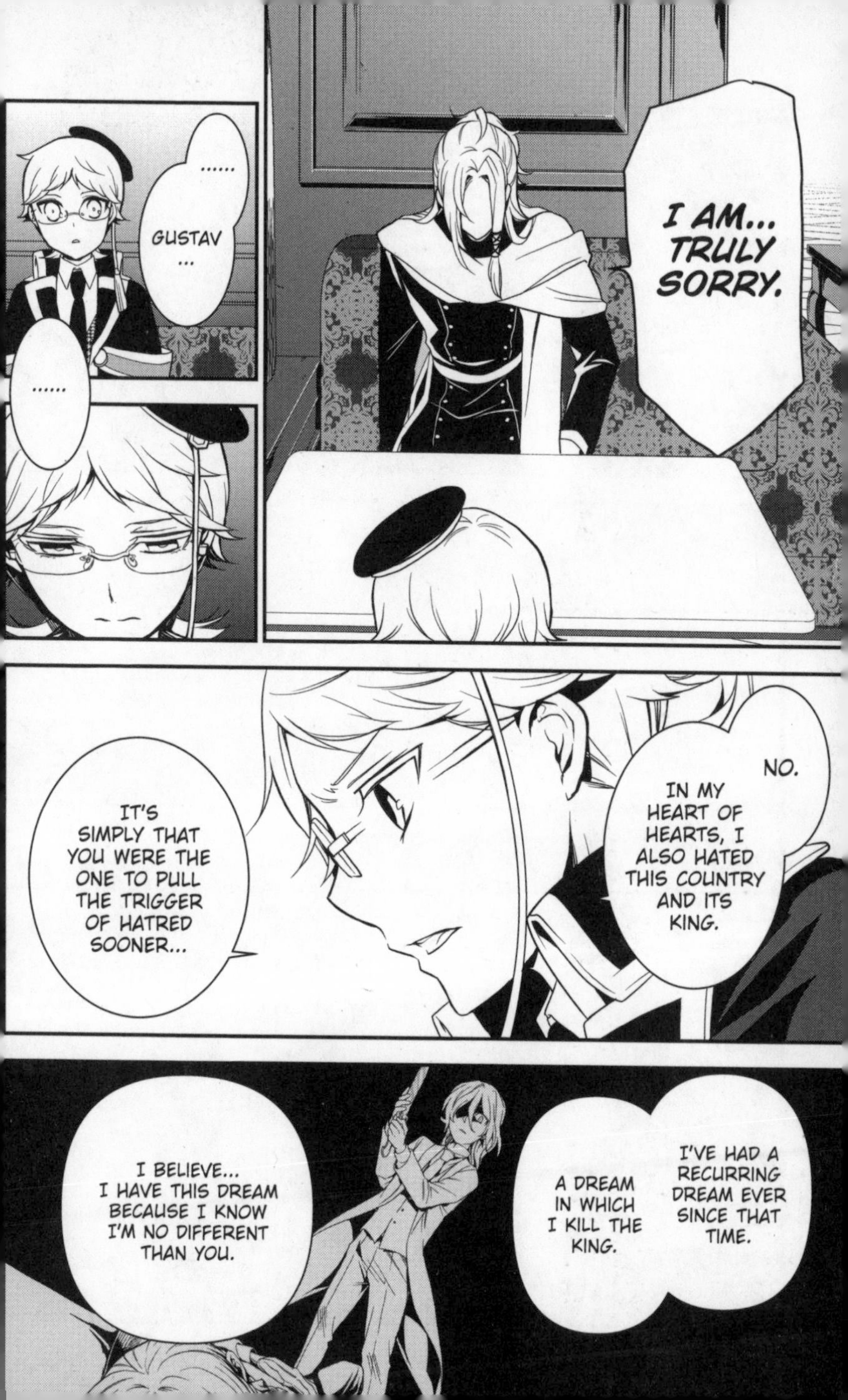
I AM... TRULY SORRY.
......
GUSTAV ...
......
NO.
IN MY HEART OF HEARTS, I ALSO HATED THIS COUNTRY AND ITS KING.
IT'S SIMPLY THAT YOU WERE THE ONE TO PULL THE TRIGGER OF HATRED SOONER...
I'VE HAD A RECURRING DREAM EVER SINCE THAT TIME.
A DREAM IN WHICH I KILL THE KING.
I BELIEVE... I HAVE THIS DREAM BECAUSE I KNOW I'M NO DIFFERENT THAN YOU.

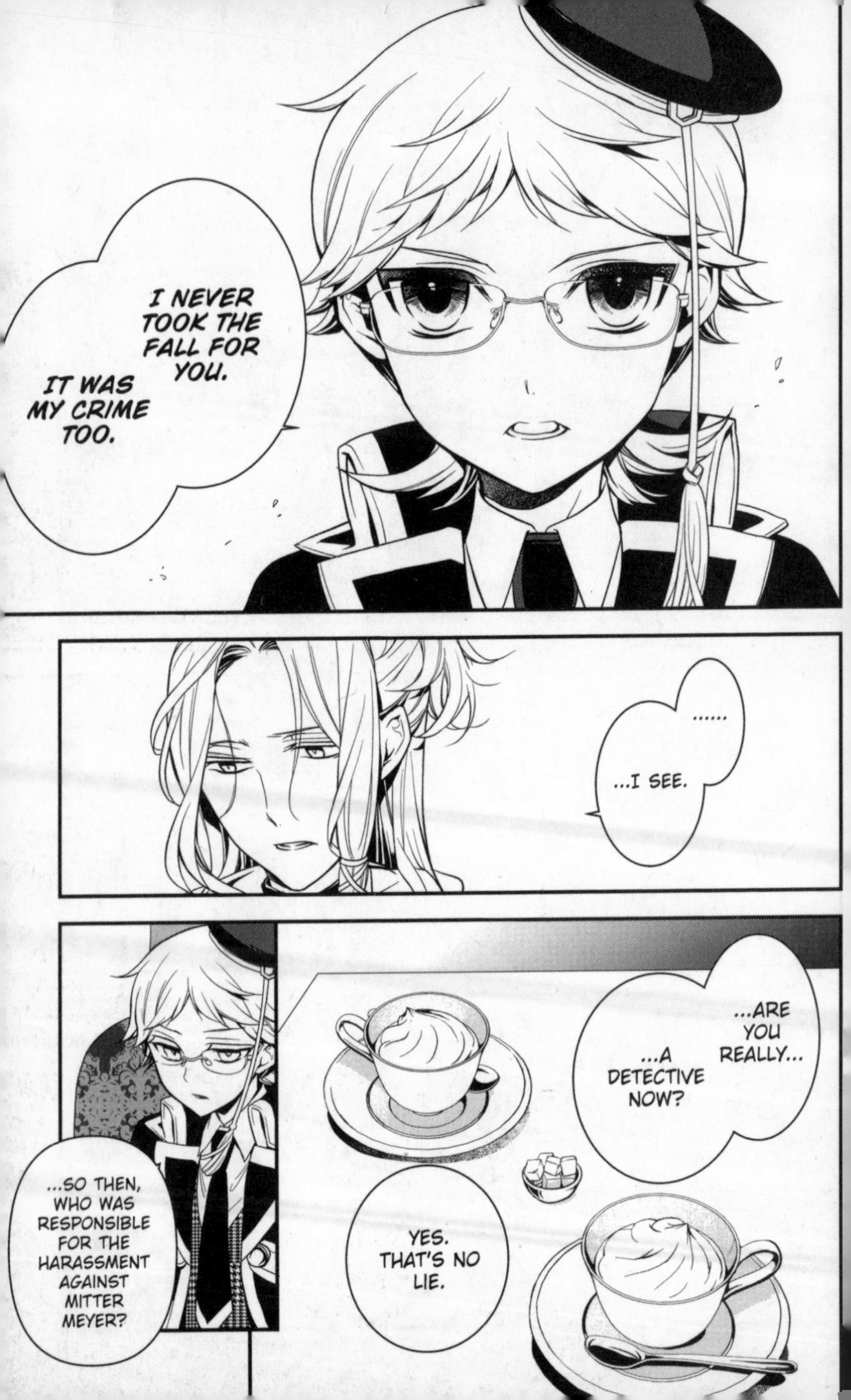
I NEVER TOOK THE FALL FOR YOU.
IT WAS MY CRIME TOO.
......
...I SEE.
...ARE YOU REALLY...
...A DETECTIVE NOW?
YES. THAT'S NO LIE.
...SO THEN, WHO WAS RESPONSIBLE FOR THE HARASSMENT AGAINST MITTER MEYER?

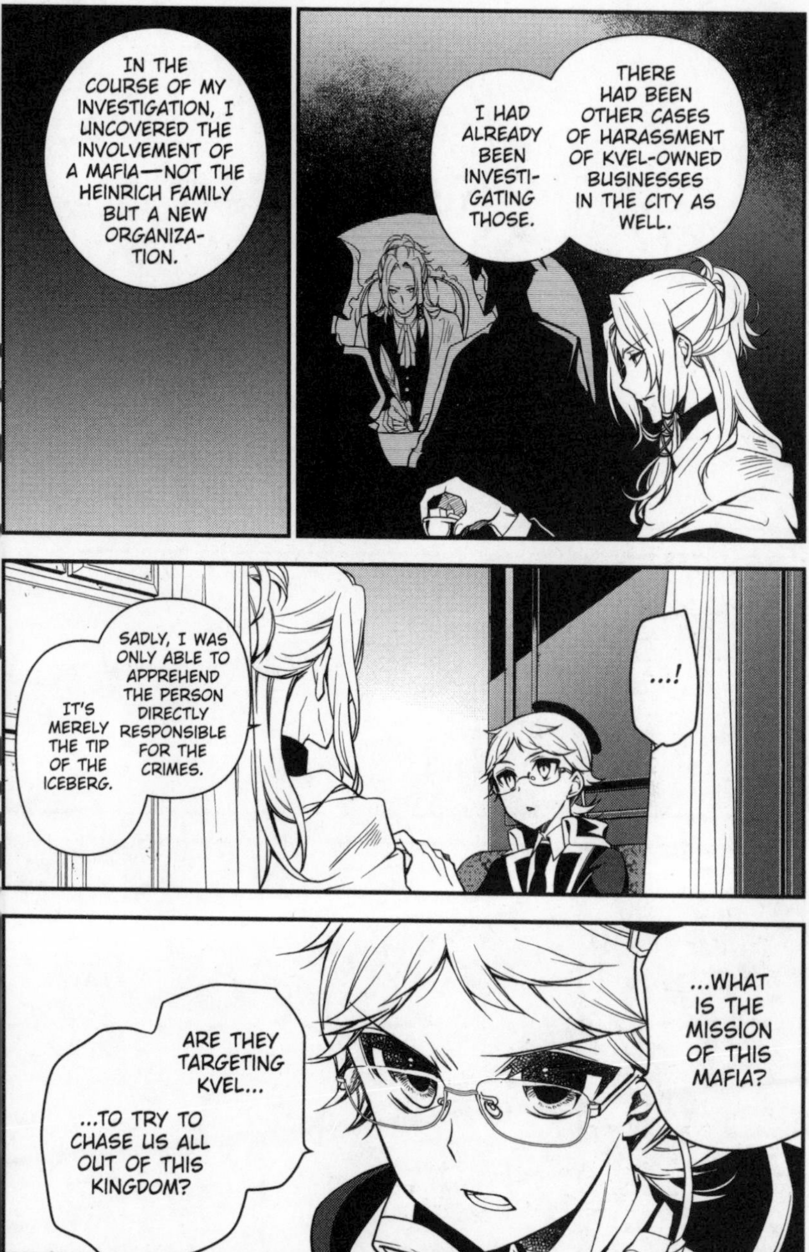
THERE HAD BEEN OTHER CASES OF HARASSMENT OF KVEL-OWNED BUSINESSES IN THE CITY AS WELL.
I HAD ALREADY BEEN INVESTI-GATING THOSE.
IN THE COURSE OF MY INVESTIGATION, I UNCOVERED THE INVOLVEMENT OF A MAFIA—NOT THE HEINRICH FAMILY BUT A NEW ORGANIZA-TION.
...!
SADLY, I WAS ONLY ABLE TO APPREHEND THE PERSON DIRECTLY RESPONSIBLE FOR THE CRIMES.
IT'S MERELY THE TIP OF THE ICEBERG.
...WHAT IS THE MISSION OF THIS MAFIA?
ARE THEY TARGETING KVEL...
...TO TRY TO CHASE US ALL OUT OF THIS KINGDOM?

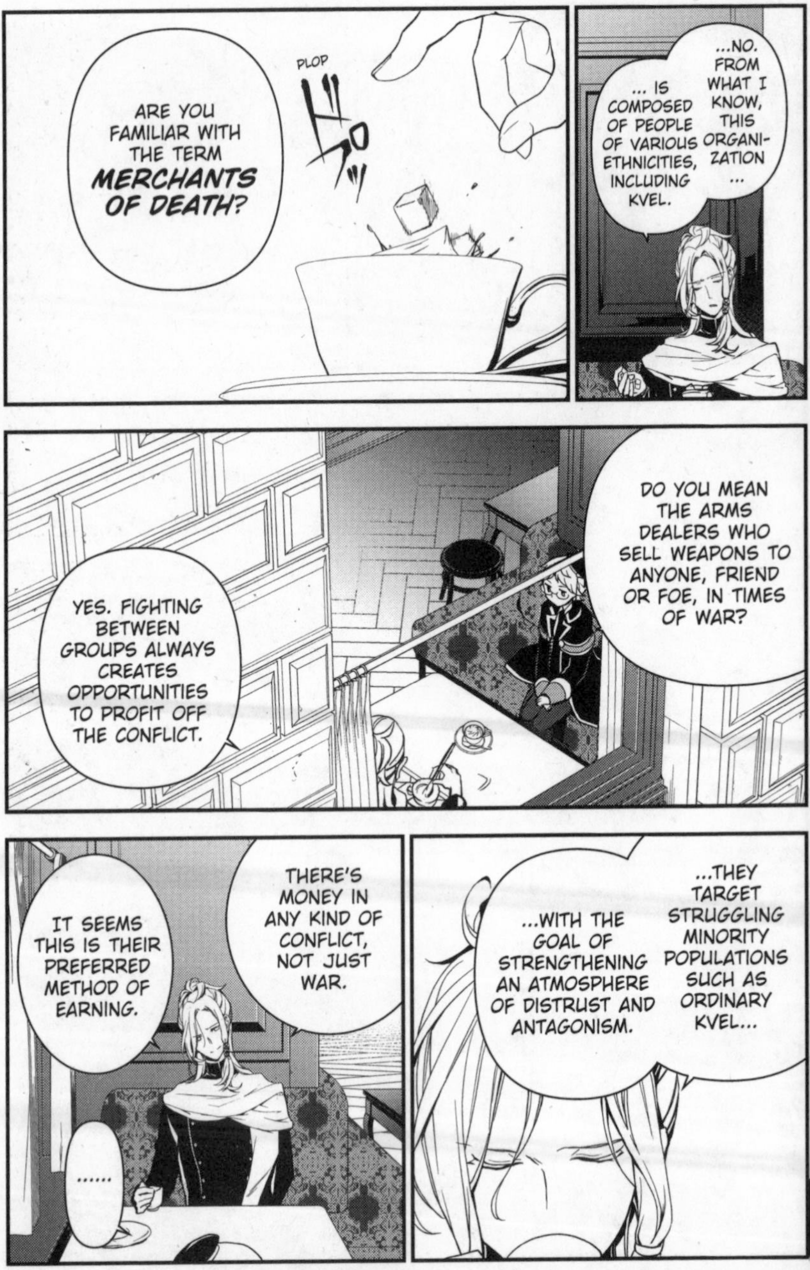
...NO. FROM WHAT I KNOW, THIS ORGANIZATION ...
... IS COMPOSED OF PEOPLE OF VARIOUS ETHNICITIES, INCLUDING KVEL.
PLOP
ARE YOU FAMILIAR WITH THE TERM ***MERCHANTS OF DEATH?***
DO YOU MEAN THE ARMS DEALERS WHO SELL WEAPONS TO ANYONE, FRIEND OR FOE, IN TIMES OF WAR?
YES. FIGHTING BETWEEN GROUPS ALWAYS CREATES OPPORTUNITIES TO PROFIT OFF THE CONFLICT.
...THEY TARGET STRUGGLING MINORITY POPULATIONS SUCH AS ORDINARY KVEL...
...WITH THE GOAL OF STRENGTHENING AN ATMOSPHERE OF DISTRUST AND ANTAGONISM.
THERE'S MONEY IN ANY KIND OF CONFLICT, NOT JUST WAR.
IT SEEMS THIS IS THEIR PREFERRED METHOD OF EARNING.
......

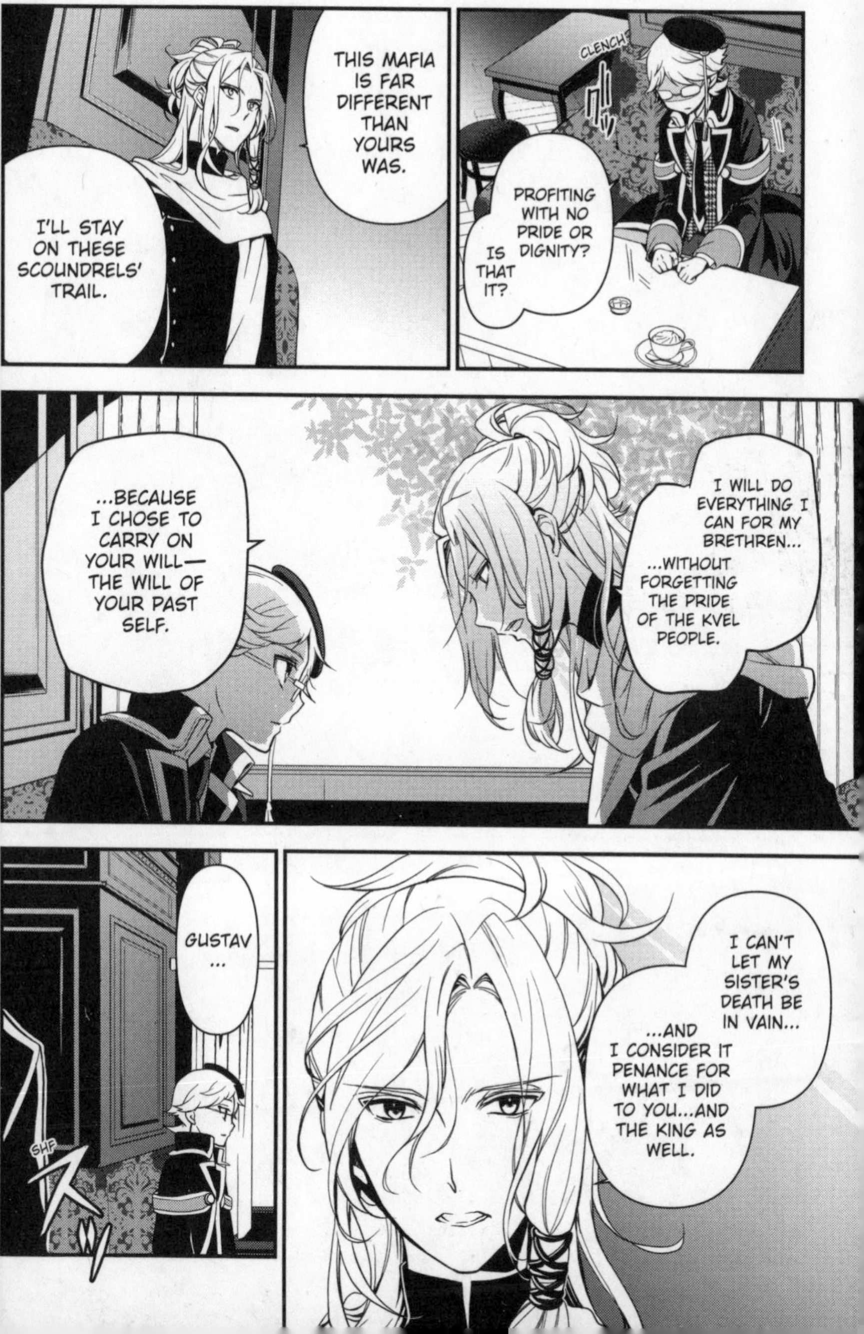
CLENCH
PROFITING WITH NO PRIDE OR DIGNITY?
IS THAT IT?
THIS MAFIA IS FAR DIFFERENT THAN YOURS WAS.
I'LL STAY ON THESE SCOUNDRELS' TRAIL.
I WILL DO EVERYTHING I CAN FOR MY BRETHREN...
...WITHOUT FORGETTING THE PRIDE OF THE KVEL PEOPLE.
...BECAUSE I CHOSE TO CARRY ON YOUR WILL—THE WILL OF YOUR PAST SELF.
I CAN'T LET MY SISTER'S DEATH BE IN VAIN...
...AND I CONSIDER IT PENANCE FOR WHAT I DID TO YOU...AND THE KING AS WELL.
GUSTAV...
SHF

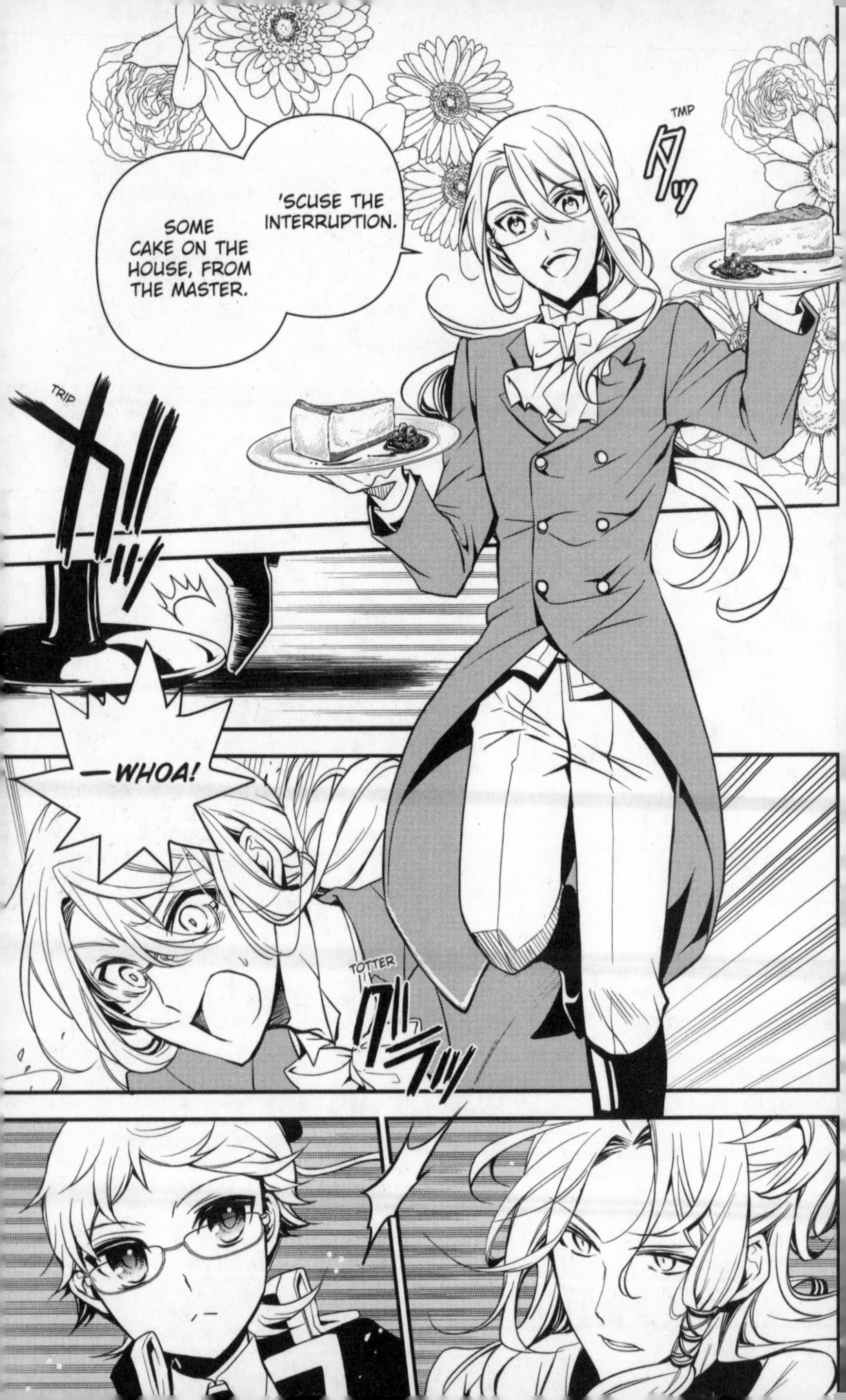
TMP
'SCUSE THE INTERRUPTION.
SOME CAKE ON THE HOUSE, FROM THE MASTER.
TRIP
—WHOA!
TOTTER

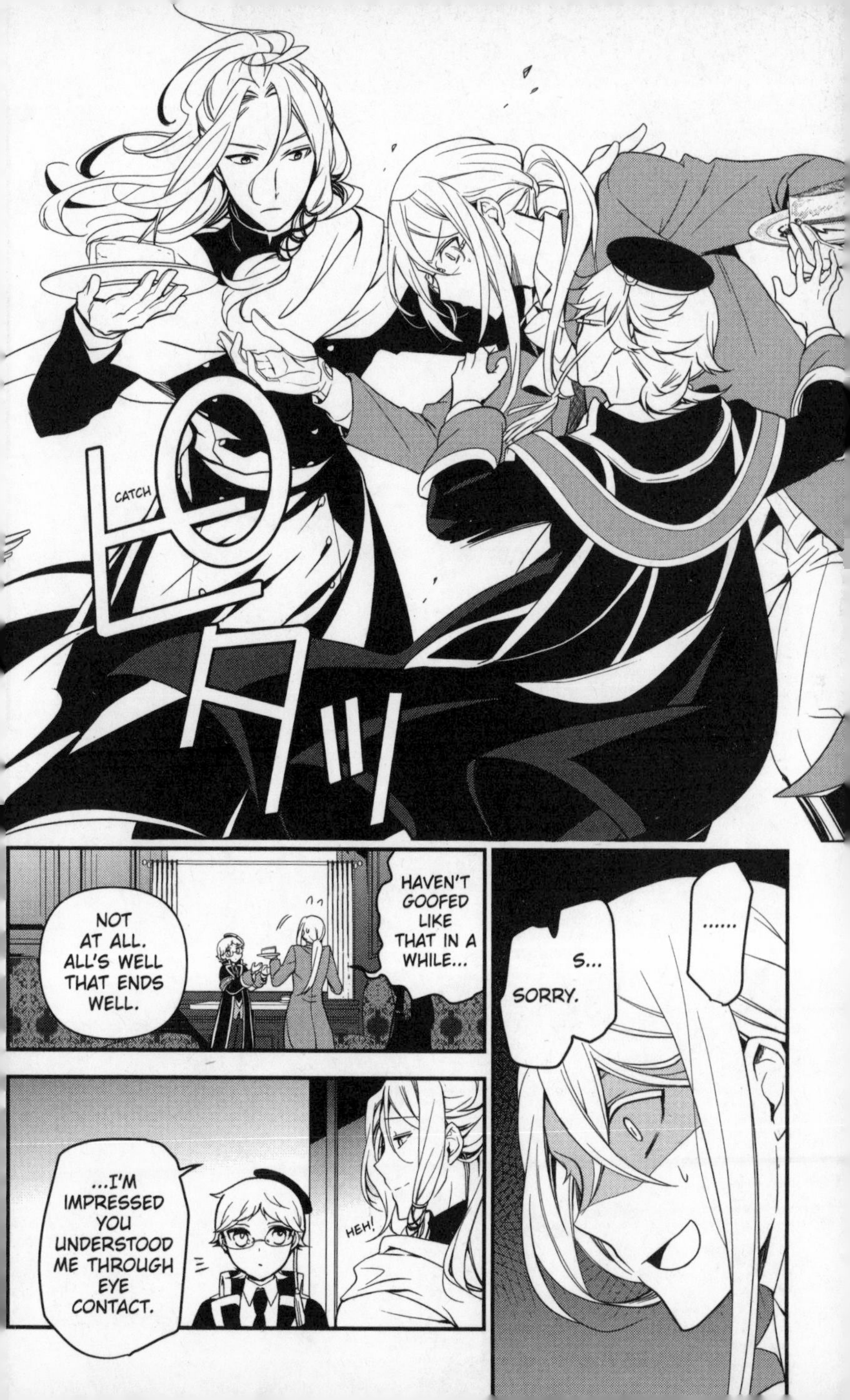
CATCH
......
S... SORRY.
HAVEN'T GOOFED LIKE THAT IN A WHILE...
NOT AT ALL. ALL'S WELL THAT ENDS WELL.
HEH!
...I'M IMPRESSED YOU UNDERSTOOD ME THROUGH EYE CONTACT.

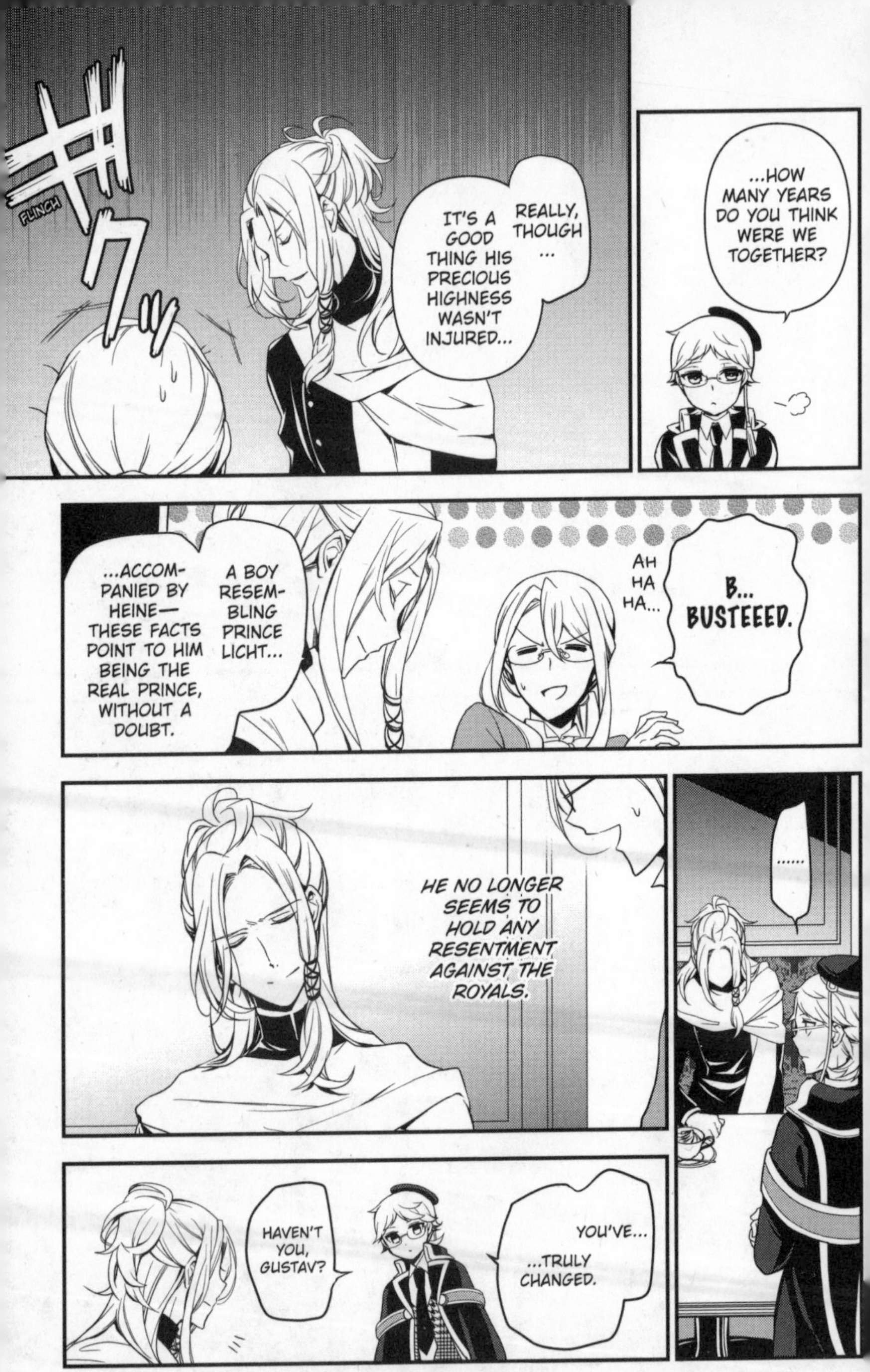
...HOW MANY YEARS DO YOU THINK WERE WE TOGETHER?
REALLY, THOUGH...
IT'S A GOOD THING HIS PRECIOUS HIGHNESS WASN'T INJURED...
FLINCH
B... BUSTEEED.
AH HA HA...
A BOY RESEMBLING PRINCE LICHT...
...ACCOMPANIED BY HEINE—THESE FACTS POINT TO HIM BEING THE REAL PRINCE, WITHOUT A DOUBT.
......
HE NO LONGER SEEMS TO HOLD ANY RESENTMENT AGAINST THE ROYALS.
YOU'VE... ...TRULY CHANGED.
HAVEN'T YOU, GUSTAV?

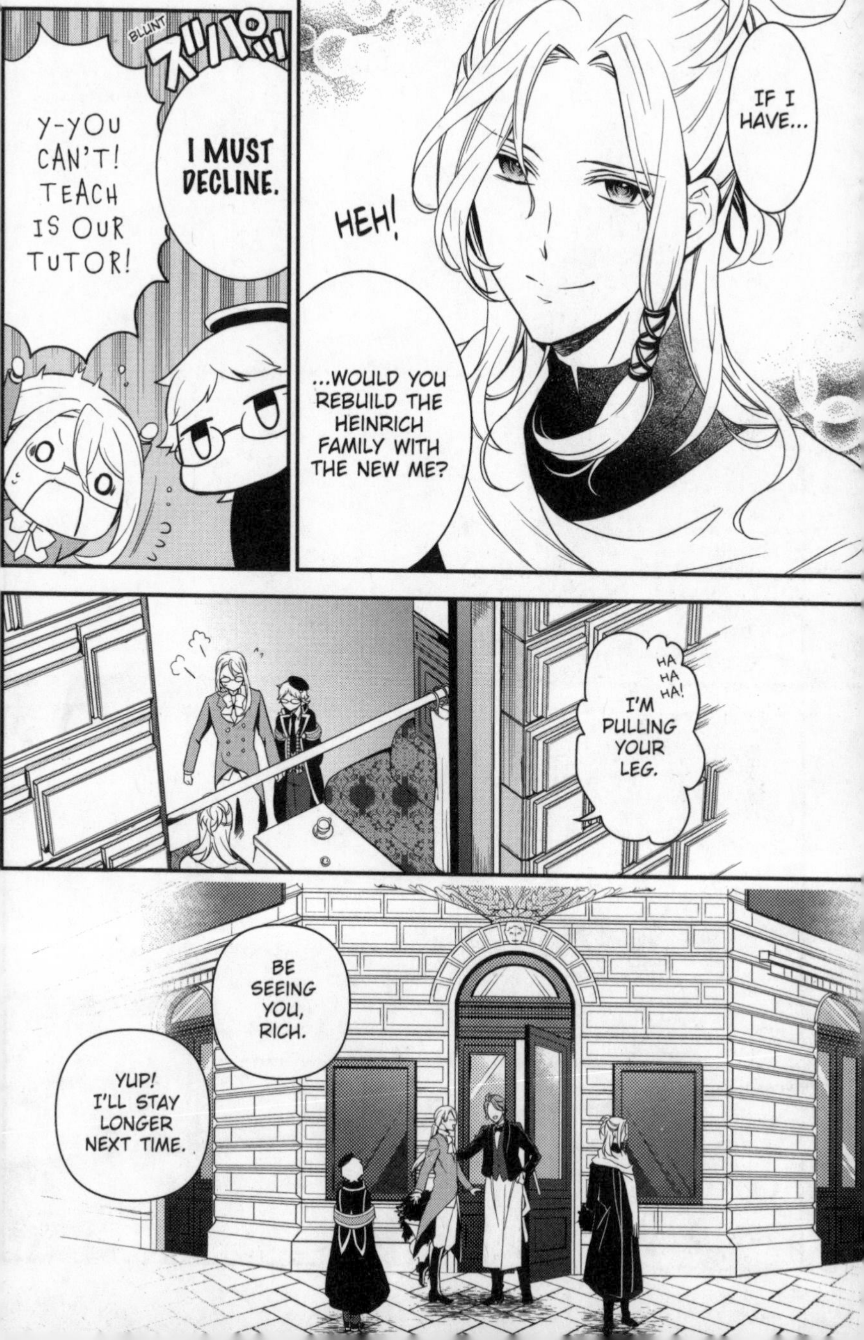
IF I HAVE...
HEH!
...WOULD YOU REBUILD THE HEINRICH FAMILY WITH THE NEW ME?
BLUNT
I MUST DECLINE.
Y-YOU CAN'T! TEACH IS OUR TUTOR!
HA HA HA!
I'M PULLING YOUR LEG.
BE SEEING YOU, RICH.
YUP! I'LL STAY LONGER NEXT TIME.

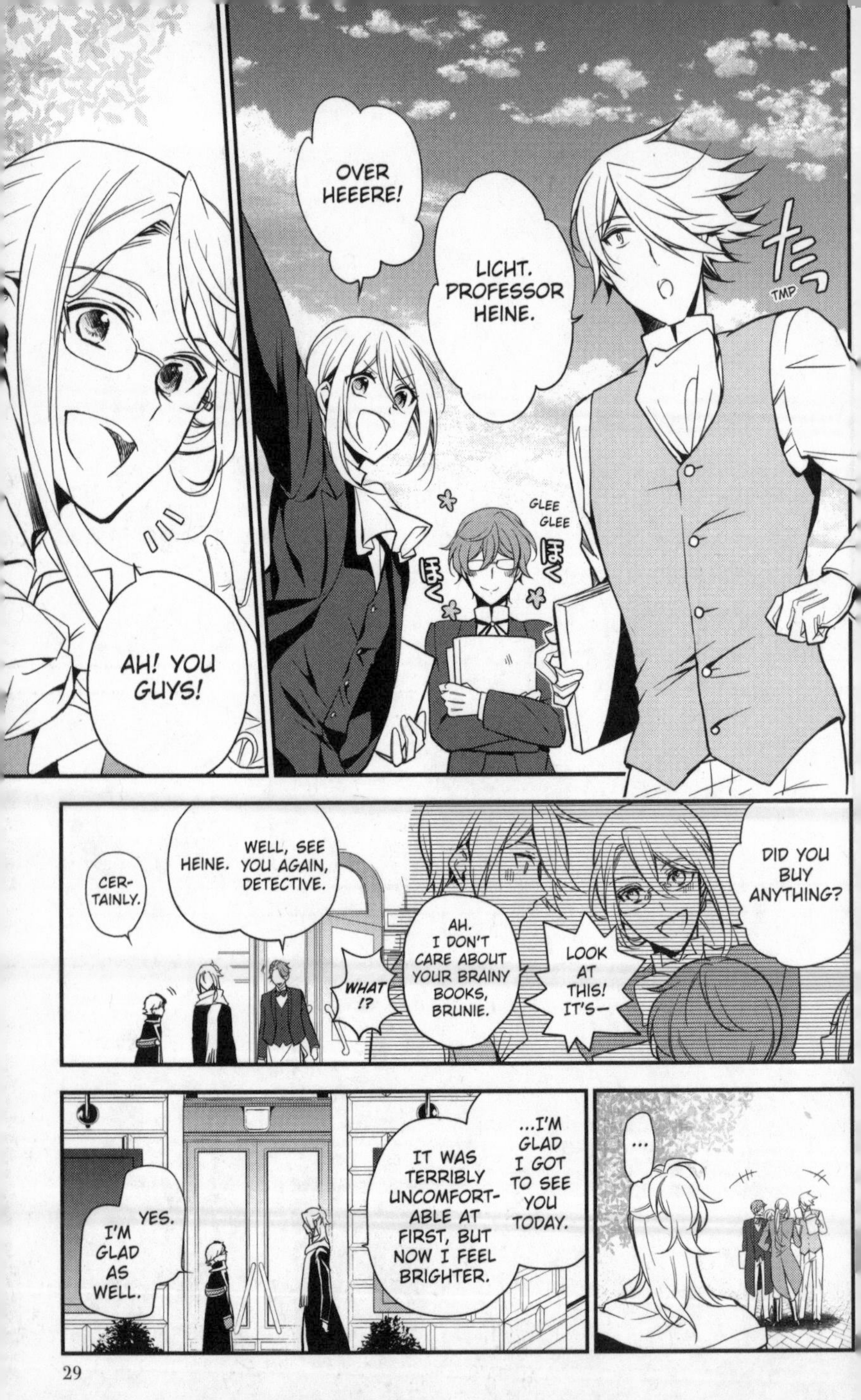
OVER HEEERE!
LICHT. PROFESSOR HEINE.
TMP
GLEE GLEE
AH! YOU GUYS!
DID YOU BUY ANYTHING?
LOOK AT THIS! IT'S—
AH. I DON'T CARE ABOUT YOUR BRAINY BOOKS, BRUNIE.
WHAT!?
WELL, SEE YOU AGAIN, DETECTIVE.
HEINE.
CER-TAINLY.
...
...I'M GLAD I GOT TO SEE YOU TODAY.
IT WAS TERRIBLY UNCOMFORT-ABLE AT FIRST, BUT NOW I FEEL BRIGHTER.
YES. I'M GLAD AS WELL.

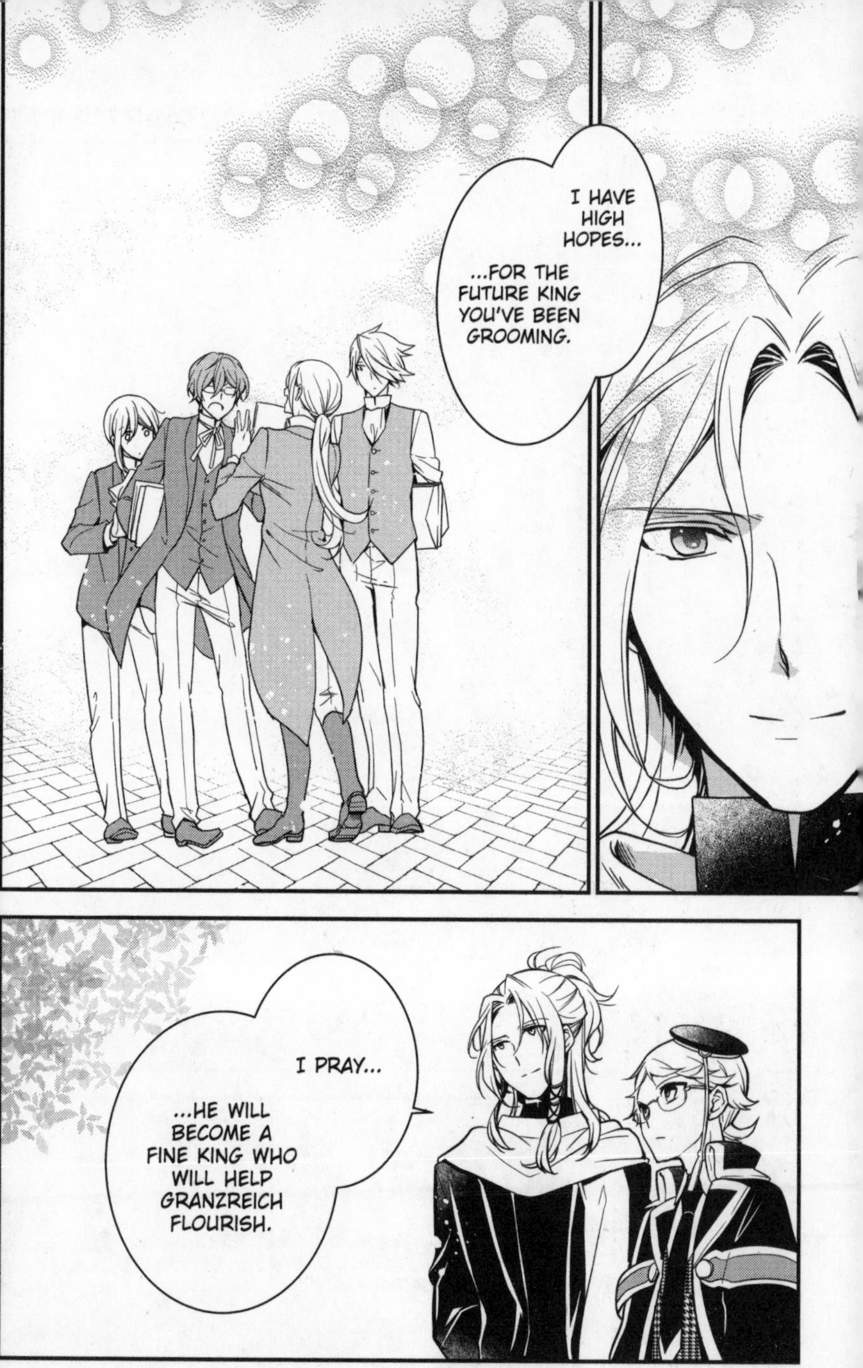
I HAVE HIGH HOPES...
...FOR THE FUTURE KING YOU'VE BEEN GROOMING.
I PRAY...
...HE WILL BECOME A FINE KING WHO WILL HELP GRANZREICH FLOURISH.

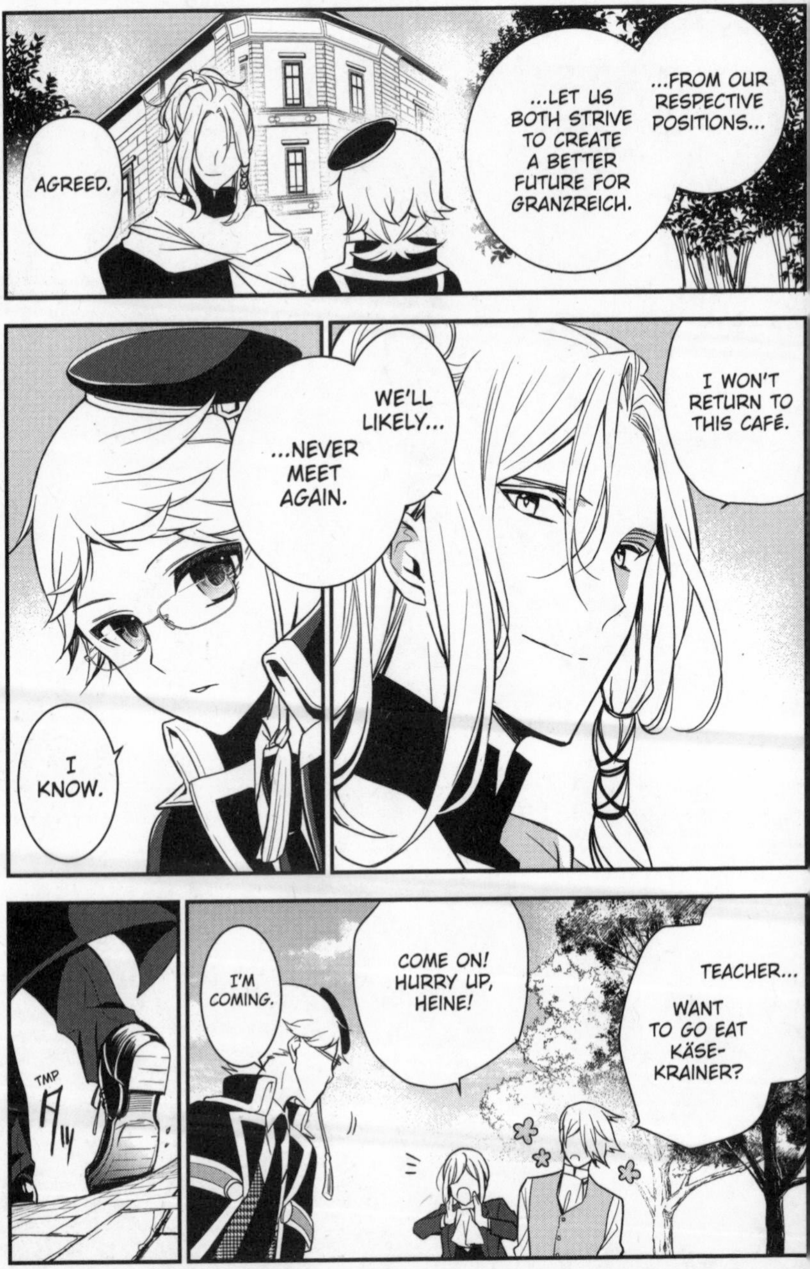
...FROM OUR RESPECTIVE POSITIONS...
...LET US BOTH STRIVE TO CREATE A BETTER FUTURE FOR GRANZREICH.
AGREED.
I WON'T RETURN TO THIS CAFÉ.
WE'LL LIKELY...
...NEVER MEET AGAIN.
I KNOW.
TEACHER...
WANT TO GO EAT KÄSE-KRAINER?
COME ON! HURRY UP, HEINE!
I'M COMING.
TMP

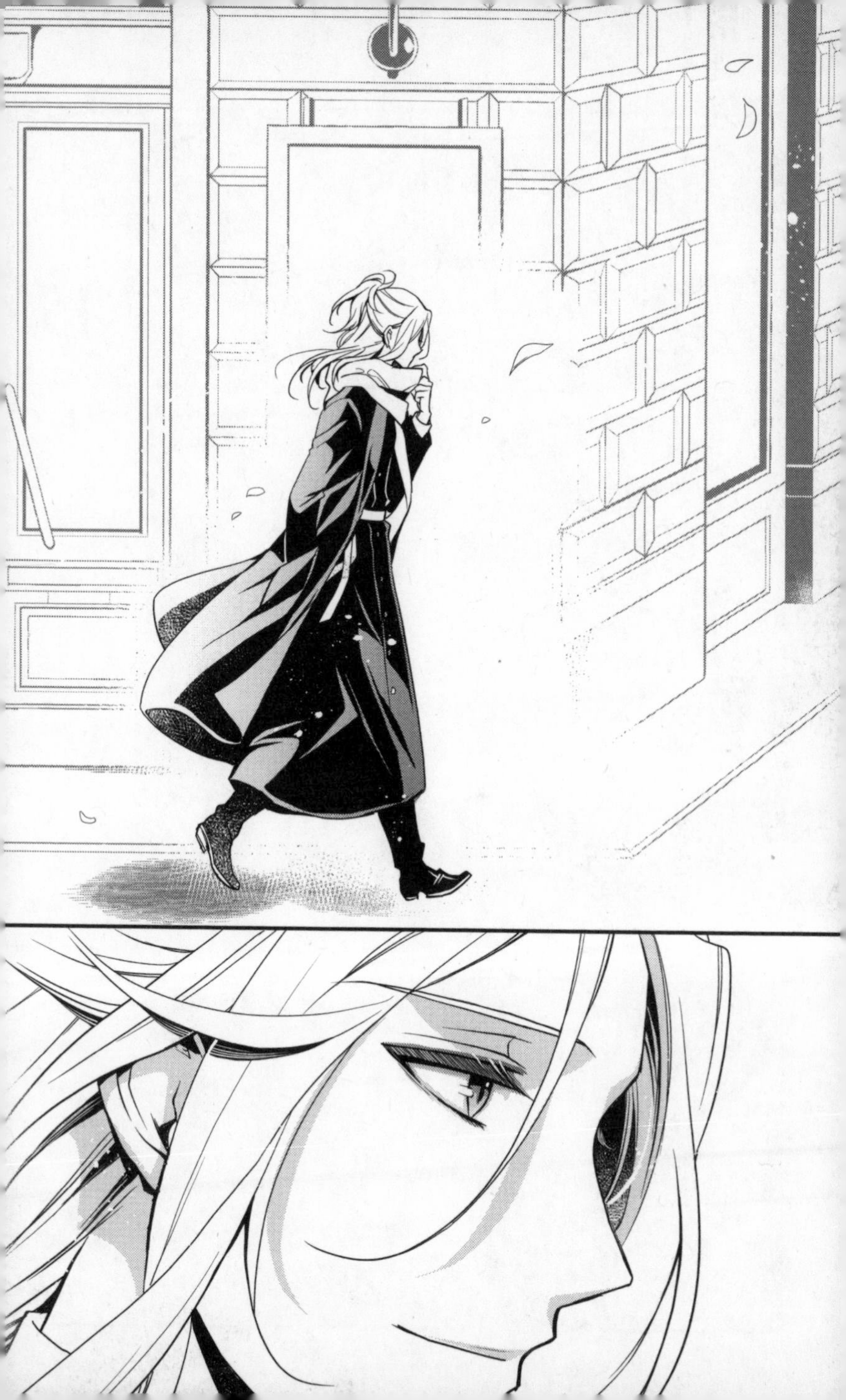

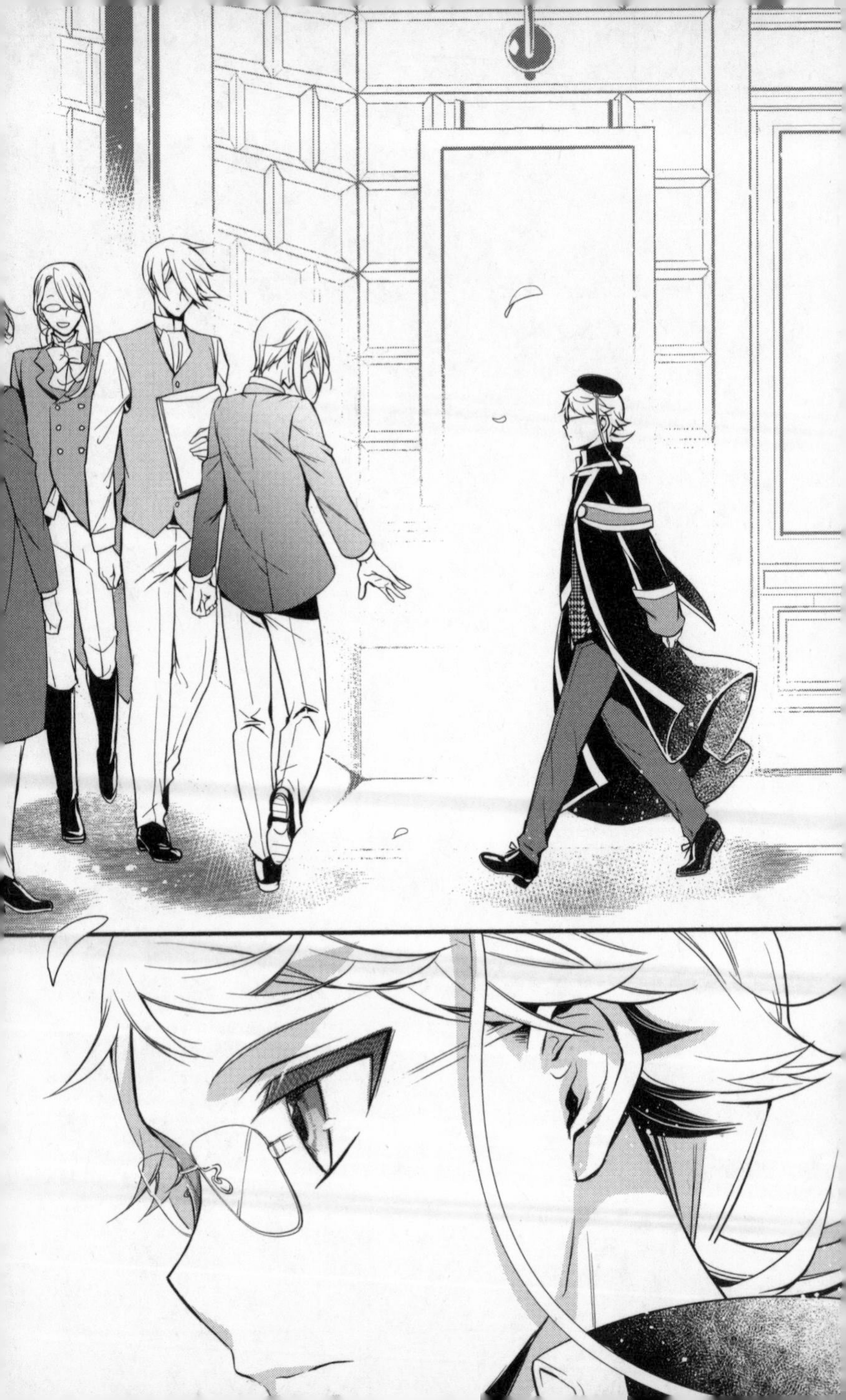

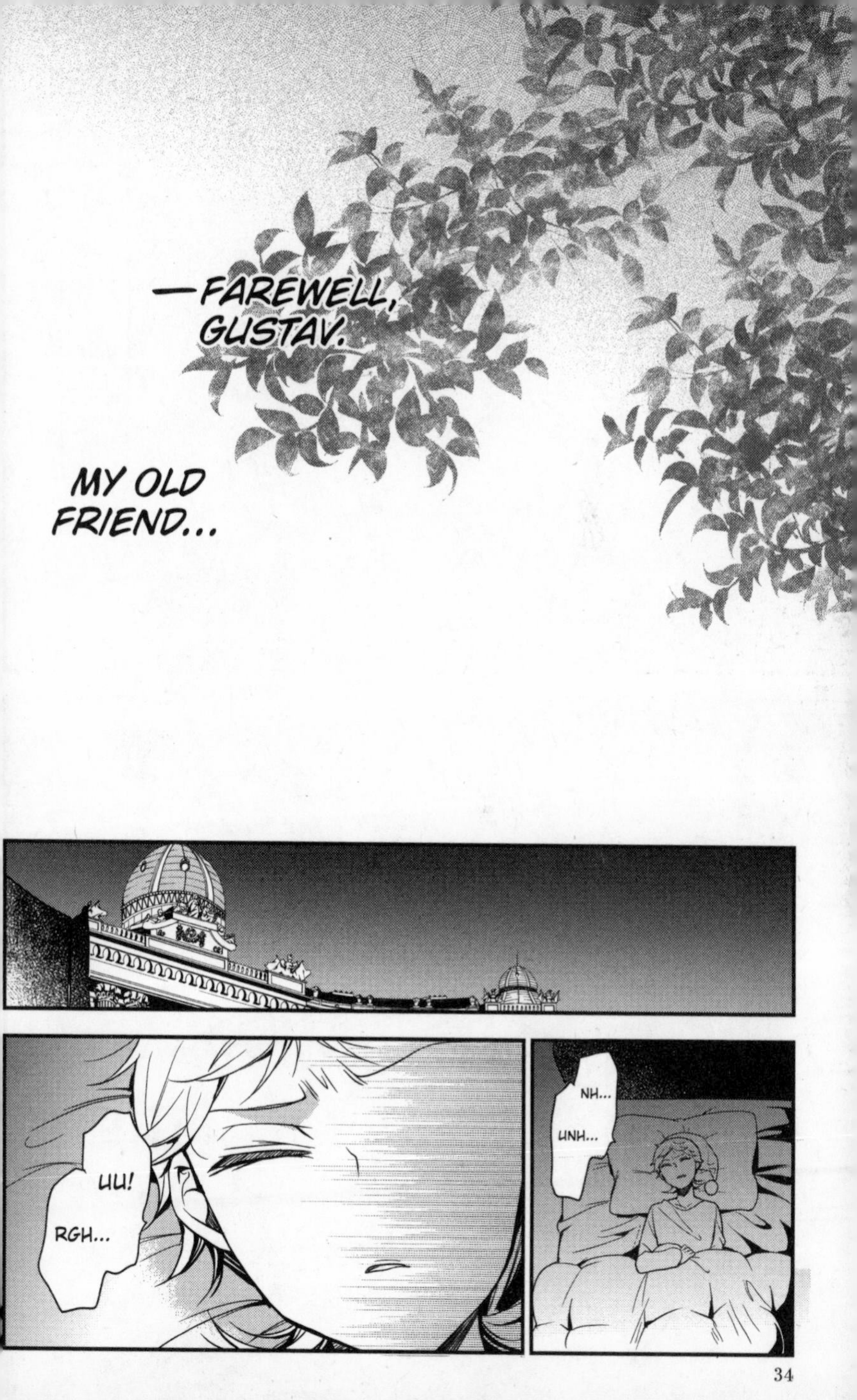
—FAREWELL, GUSTAV.
MY OLD FRIEND...
NH...
UNH...
UU!
RGH...

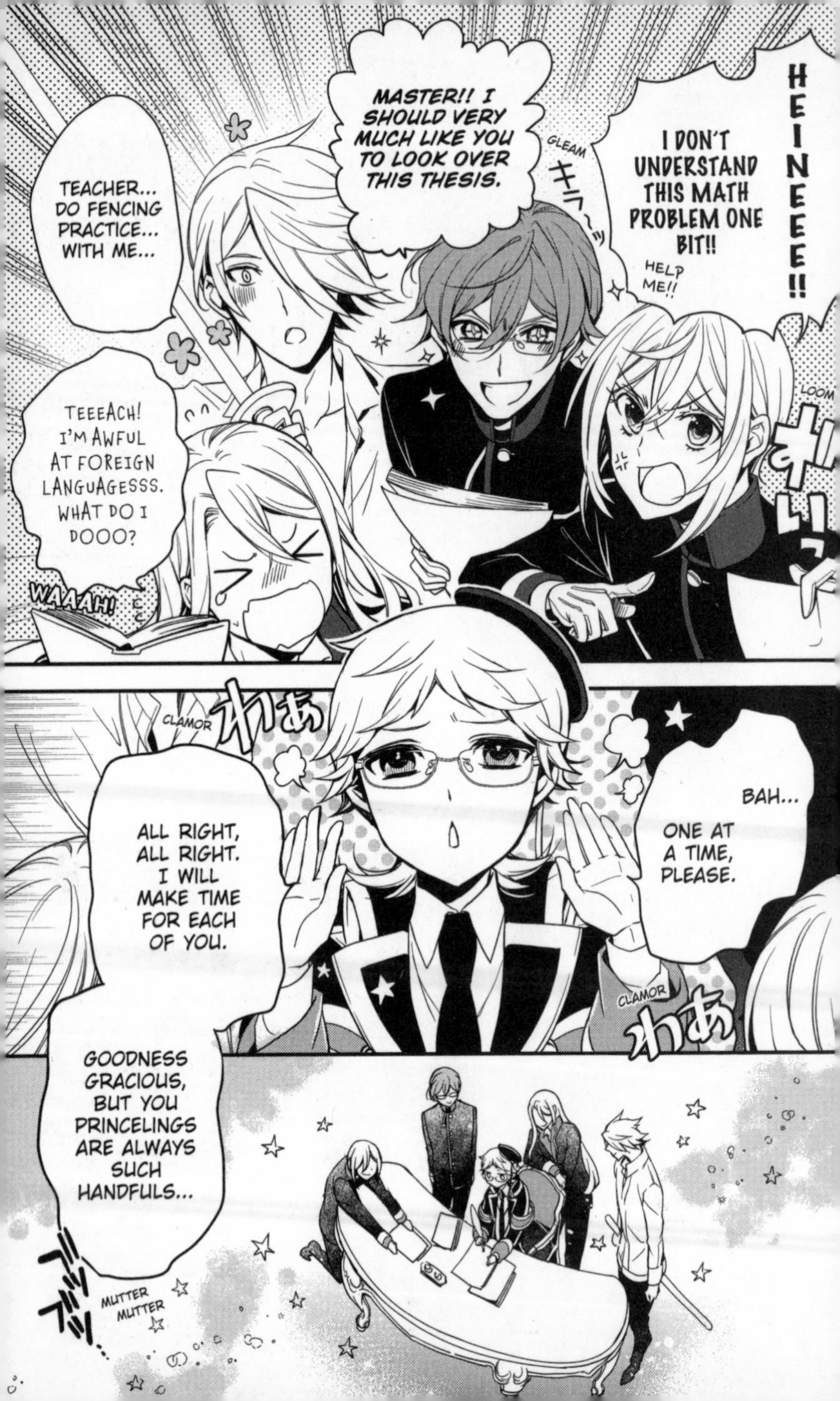
HEINEEE!!
I DON'T UNDERSTAND THIS MATH PROBLEM ONE BIT!!
HELP ME!!
LOOM
GLEAM
MASTER!! I SHOULD VERY MUCH LIKE YOU TO LOOK OVER THIS THESIS.
TEACHER... DO FENCING PRACTICE... WITH ME...
TEEEACH! I'M AWFUL AT FOREIGN LANGUAGESSS. WHAT DO I DOOO?
WAAAH!
BAH... ONE AT A TIME, PLEASE.
CLAMOR
わあ
ALL RIGHT, ALL RIGHT. I WILL MAKE TIME FOR EACH OF YOU.
CLAMOR
わあ
GOODNESS GRACIOUS, BUT YOU PRINCELINGS ARE ALWAYS SUCH HANDFULS...
MUTTER MUTTER

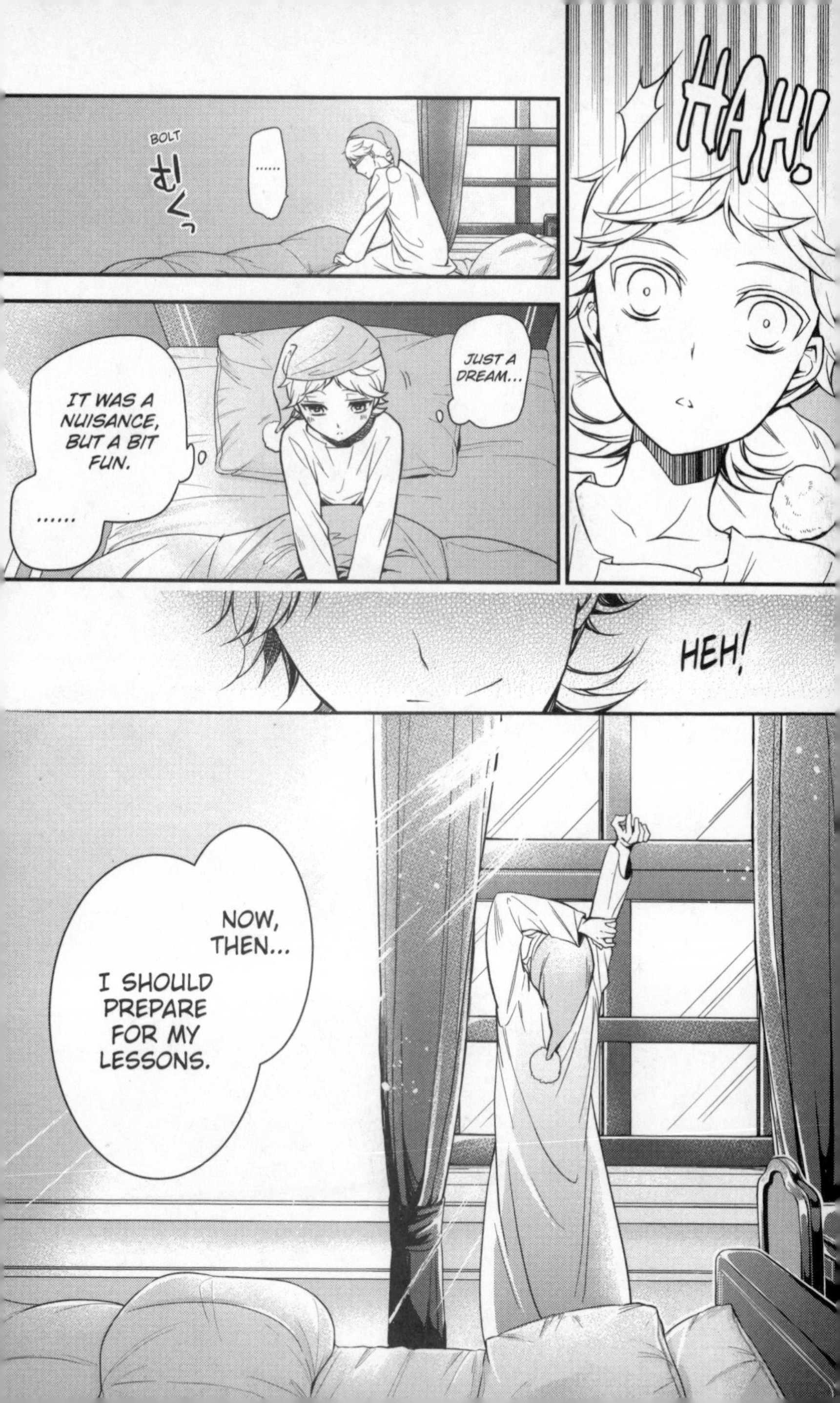
HAH!
BOLT
むくっ
......
JUST A DREAM...
IT WAS A NUISANCE, BUT A BIT FUN.
......
HEH!
NOW, THEN... I SHOULD PREPARE FOR MY LESSONS.

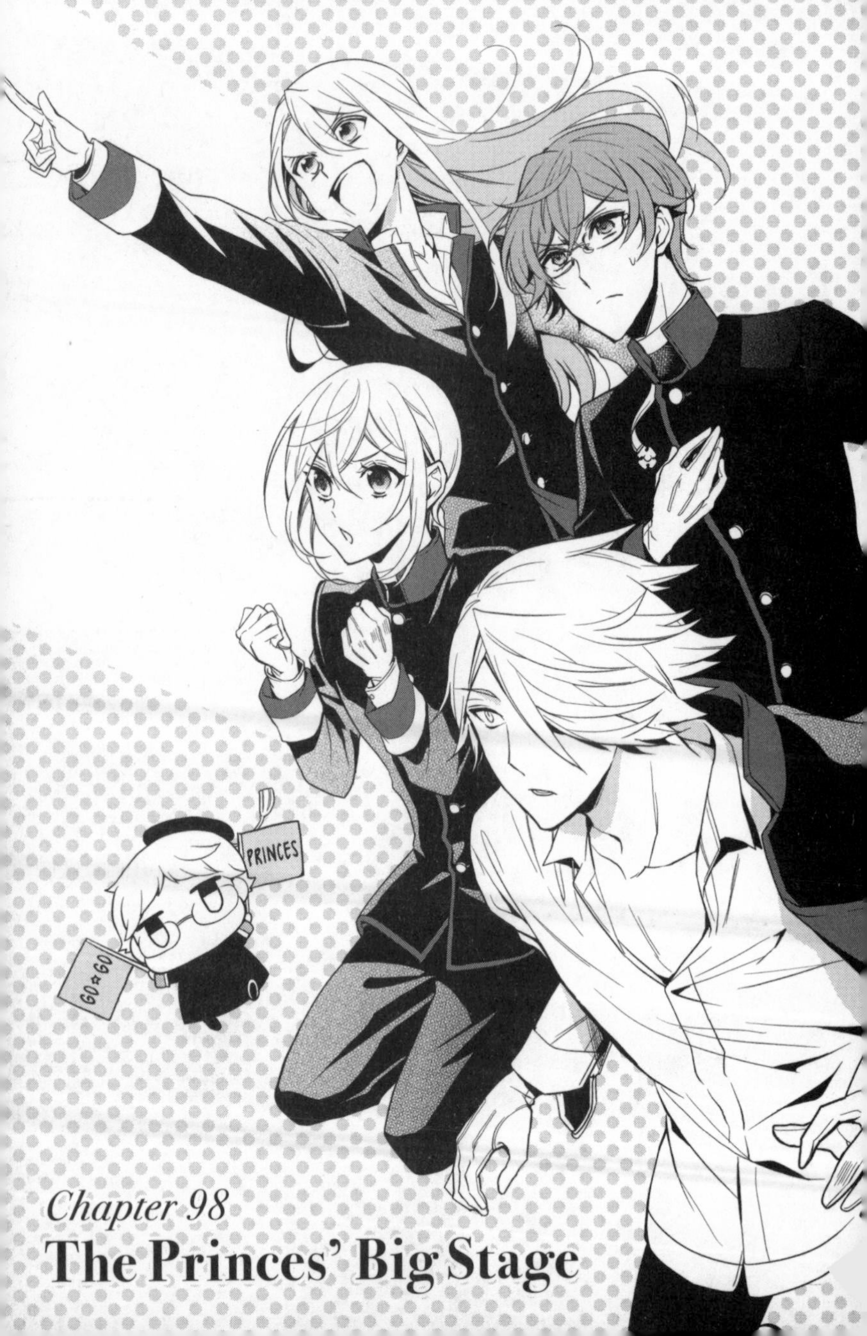
PRINCES
GO☆GO

Chapter 98

The Princes' Big Stage

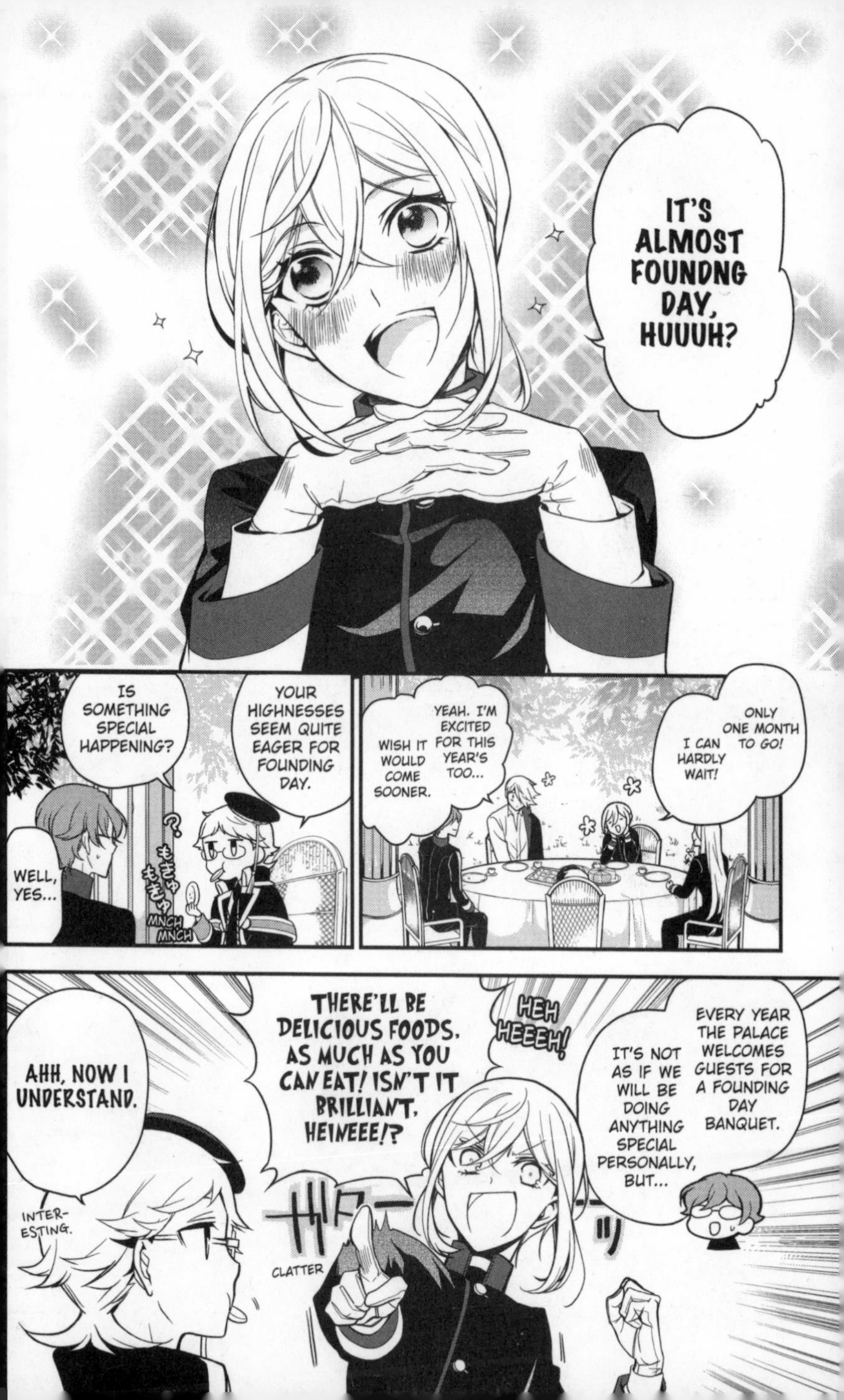
IT'S ALMOST FOUNDNG DAY, HUUUH?
ONLY ONE MONTH TO GO!
I CAN HARDLY WAIT!
YEAH. I'M EXCITED FOR THIS YEAR'S TOO...
WISH IT WOULD COME SOONER.
YOUR HIGHNESSES SEEM QUITE EAGER FOR FOUNDING DAY.
もきゅもきゅ
MNCH MNCH
IS SOMETHING SPECIAL HAPPENING?
WELL, YES...
EVERY YEAR THE PALACE WELCOMES GUESTS FOR A FOUNDING DAY BANQUET.
IT'S NOT AS IF WE WILL BE DOING ANYTHING SPECIAL PERSONALLY, BUT...
HEH HEEEH!
THERE'LL BE DELICIOUS FOODS, AS MUCH AS YOU CAN EAT! ISN'T IT BRILLIANT, HEINEEE!?
CLATTER
AHH, NOW I UNDERSTAND.
INTER-ESTING.

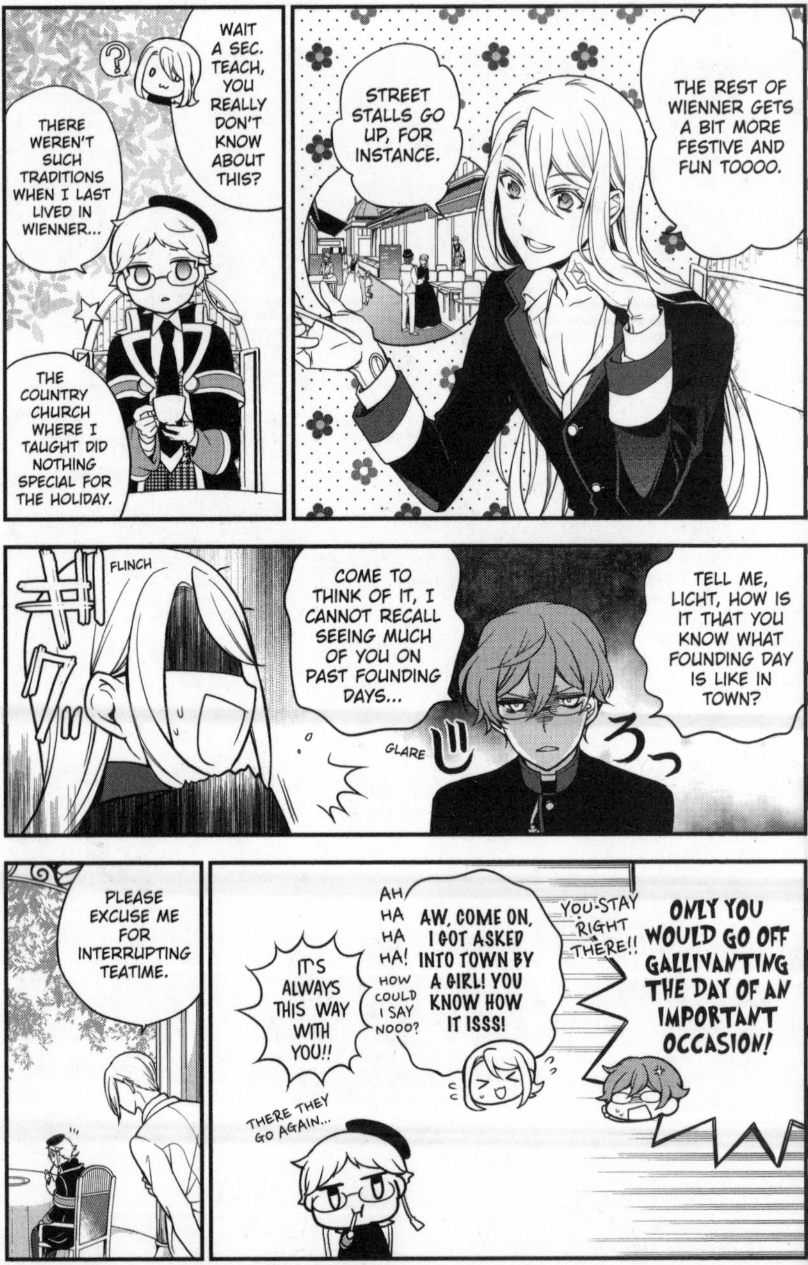
THE REST OF WIENNER GETS A BIT MORE FESTIVE AND FUN TOOOO.
STREET STALLS GO UP, FOR INSTANCE.
WAIT A SEC. TEACH, YOU REALLY DON'T KNOW ABOUT THIS?
THERE WEREN'T SUCH TRADITIONS WHEN I LAST LIVED IN WIENNER...
THE COUNTRY CHURCH WHERE I TAUGHT DID NOTHING SPECIAL FOR THE HOLIDAY.
TELL ME, LICHT, HOW IS IT THAT YOU KNOW WHAT FOUNDING DAY IS LIKE IN TOWN?
GLARE
COME TO THINK OF IT, I CANNOT RECALL SEEING MUCH OF YOU ON PAST FOUNDING DAYS...
FLINCH
ONLY YOU WOULD GO OFF GALLIVANTING THE DAY OF AN IMPORTANT OCCASION!
YOU STAY RIGHT THERE!!
AW, COME ON, I GOT ASKED INTO TOWN BY A GIRL! YOU KNOW HOW IT ISSS!
AH HA HA HA! HOW COULD I SAY NOOO?
IT'S ALWAYS THIS WAY WITH YOU!!
THERE THEY GO AGAIN...
PLEASE EXCUSE ME FOR INTERRUPTING TEATIME.

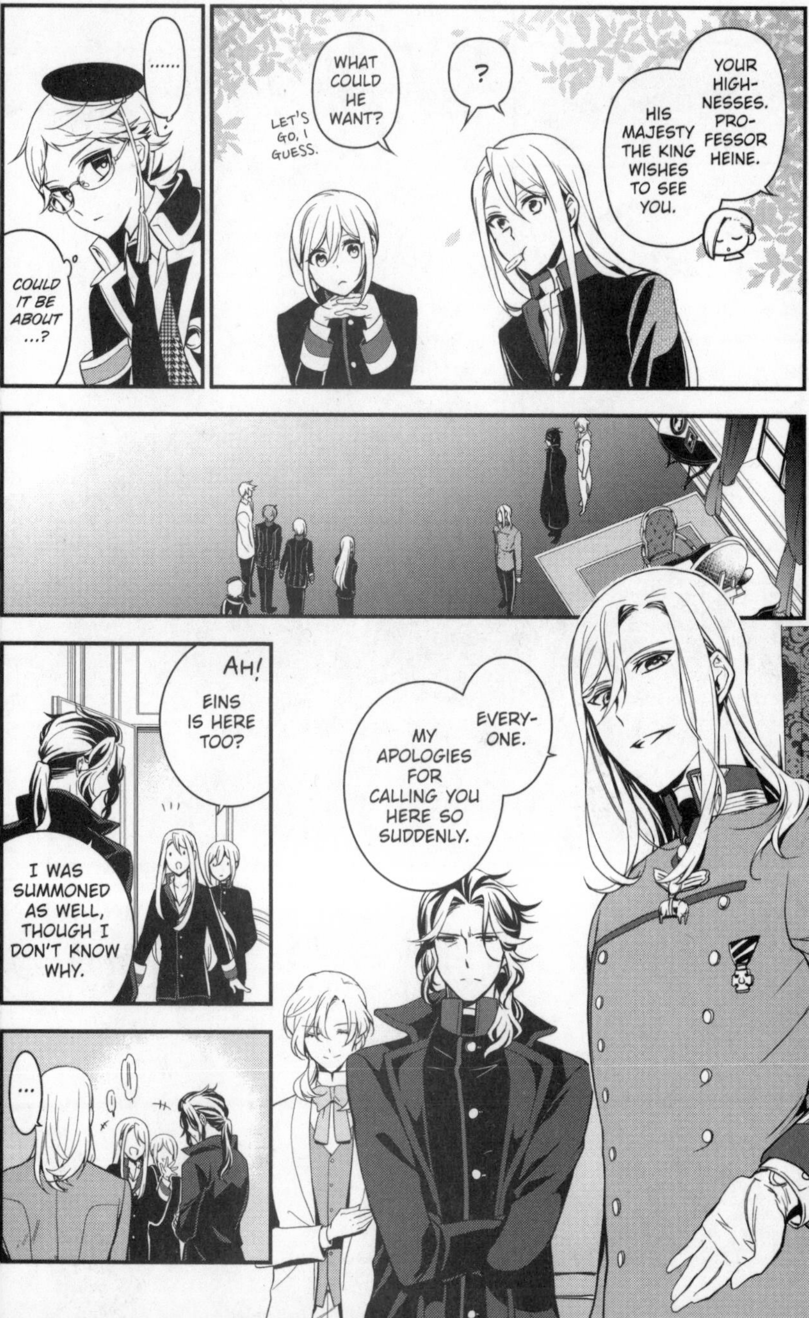
YOUR HIGHNESSES. PROFESSOR HEINE.
HIS MAJESTY THE KING WISHES TO SEE YOU.
?
WHAT COULD HE WANT?
LET'S GO, I GUESS.
......
COULD IT BE ABOUT ...?
EVERYONE.
MY APOLOGIES FOR CALLING YOU HERE SO SUDDENLY.
AH! EINS IS HERE TOO?
I WAS SUMMONED AS WELL, THOUGH I DON'T KNOW WHY.
...

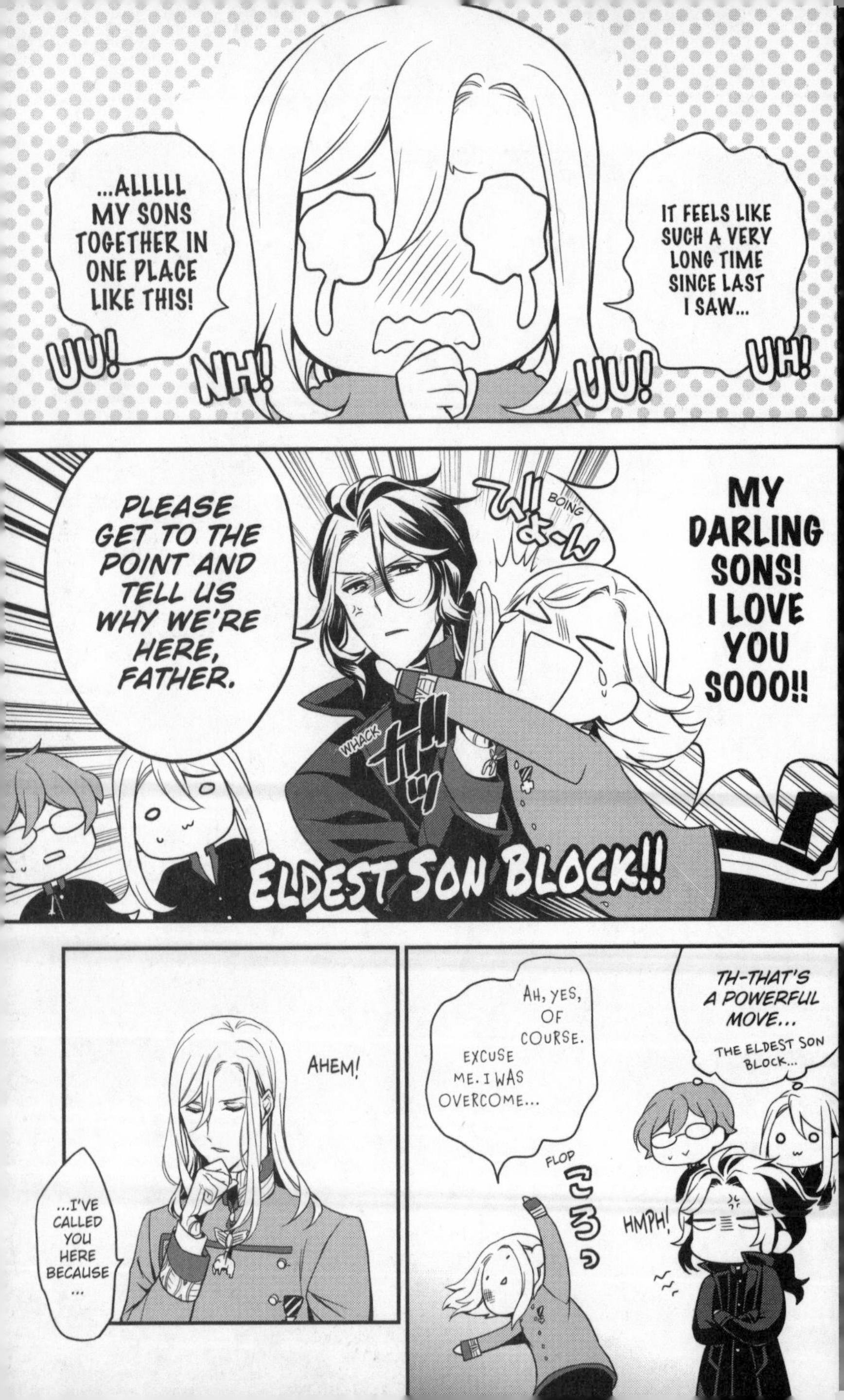
UH!
IT FEELS LIKE SUCH A VERY LONG TIME SINCE LAST I SAW...
UU!
NH!
...ALLLLL MY SONS TOGETHER IN ONE PLACE LIKE THIS!
UU!
MY DARLING SONS! I LOVE YOU SOOO!!
BOING
PLEASE GET TO THE POINT AND TELL US WHY WE'RE HERE, FATHER.
WHACK
ELDEST SON BLOCK!!
TH-THAT'S A POWERFUL MOVE...
THE ELDEST SON BLOCK...
AH, YES, OF COURSE.
EXCUSE ME. I WAS OVERCOME...
HMPH!
FLOP
AHEM!
...I'VE CALLED YOU HERE BECAUSE ...

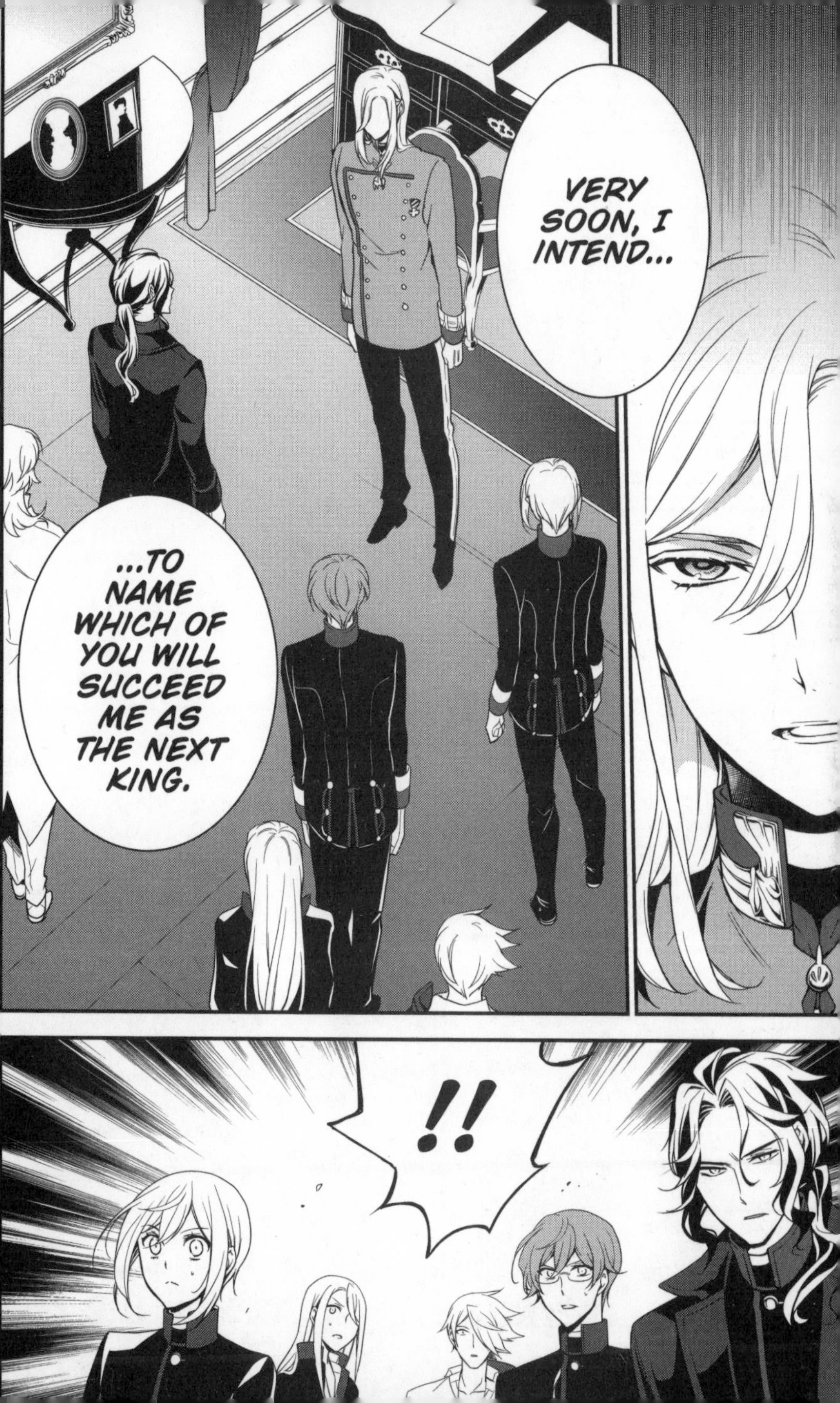
VERY SOON, I INTEND...
...TO NAME WHICH OF YOU WILL SUCCEED ME AS THE NEXT KING.
!!

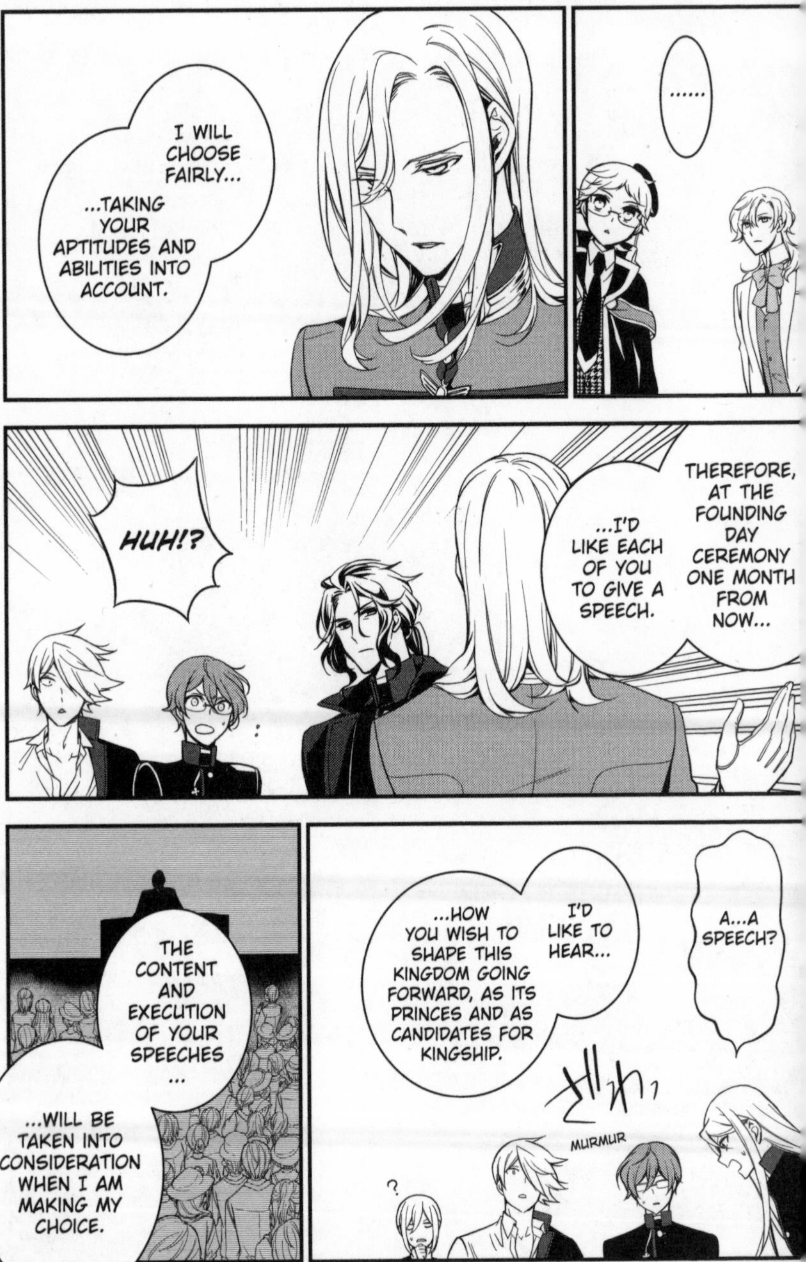
......
I WILL CHOOSE FAIRLY...
...TAKING YOUR APTITUDES AND ABILITIES INTO ACCOUNT.
THEREFORE, AT THE FOUNDING DAY CEREMONY ONE MONTH FROM NOW...
...I'D LIKE EACH OF YOU TO GIVE A SPEECH.
HUH!?
A...A SPEECH?
I'D LIKE TO HEAR...
...HOW YOU WISH TO SHAPE THIS KINGDOM GOING FORWARD, AS ITS PRINCES AND AS CANDIDATES FOR KINGSHIP.
MURMUR
?
THE CONTENT AND EXECUTION OF YOUR SPEECHES...
...WILL BE TAKEN INTO CONSIDERATION WHEN I AM MAKING MY CHOICE.

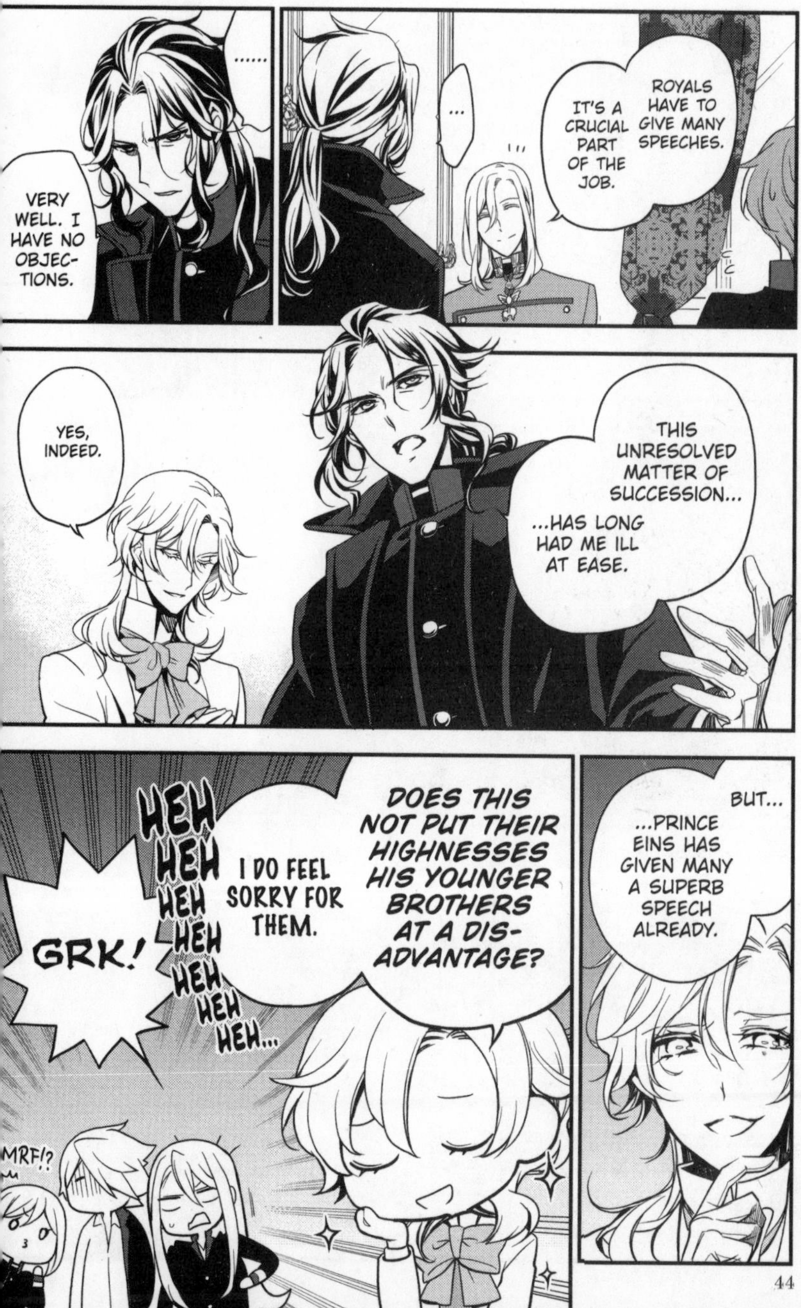
ROYALS HAVE TO GIVE MANY SPEECHES.
IT'S A CRUCIAL PART OF THE JOB.
...
......
VERY WELL. I HAVE NO OBJECTIONS.
THIS UNRESOLVED MATTER OF SUCCESSION...
...HAS LONG HAD ME ILL AT EASE.
YES, INDEED.
BUT...
...PRINCE EINS HAS GIVEN MANY A SUPERB SPEECH ALREADY.
DOES THIS NOT PUT THEIR HIGHNESSES HIS YOUNGER BROTHERS AT A DIS-ADVANTAGE?
I DO FEEL SORRY FOR THEM.
HEH HEH HEH HEH HEH HEH HEH...
GRK!
MRF!?

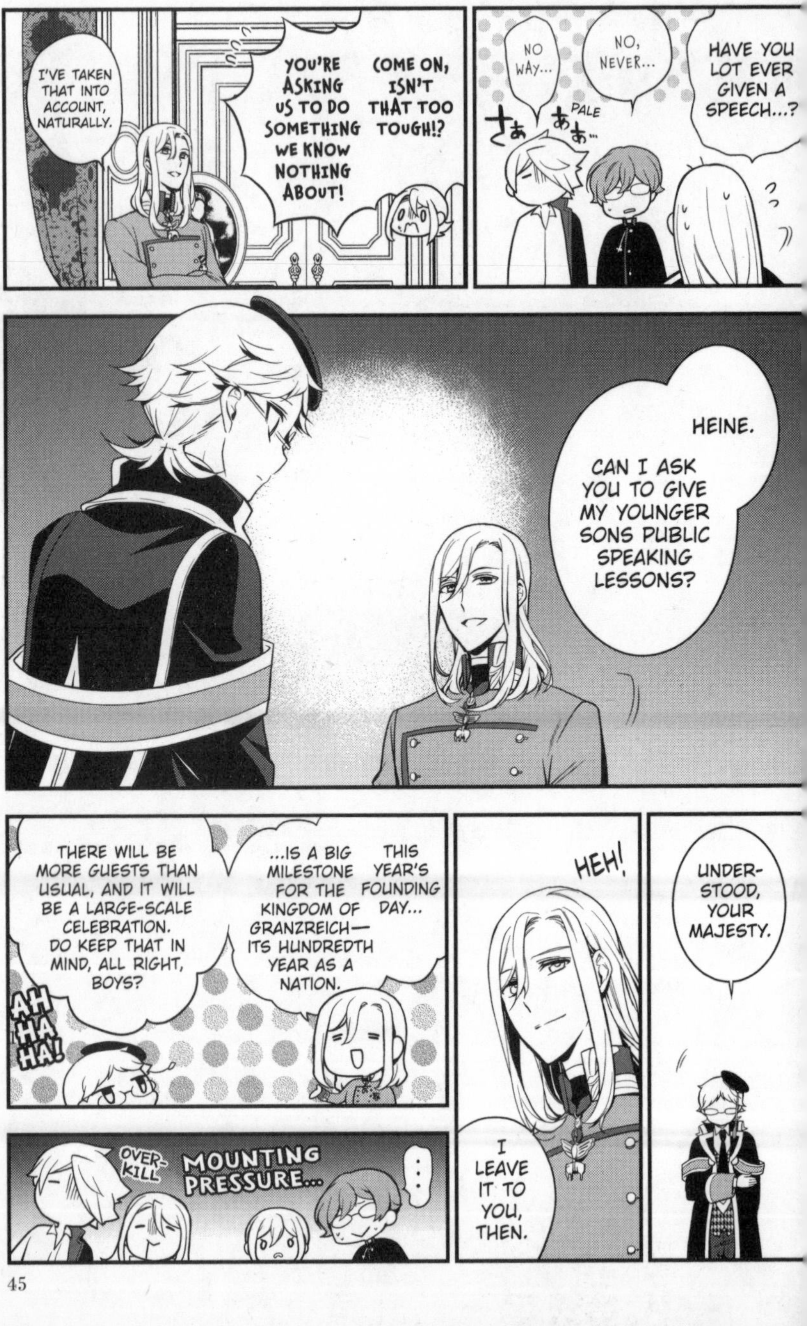
HAVE YOU LOT EVER GIVEN A SPEECH...?
NO, NEVER...
NO WAY...
PALE
さぁ あぁ…
COME ON, ISN'T THAT TOO TOUGH!?
YOU'RE ASKING US TO DO SOMETHING WE KNOW NOTHING ABOUT!
I'VE TAKEN THAT INTO ACCOUNT, NATURALLY.
HEINE.
CAN I ASK YOU TO GIVE MY YOUNGER SONS PUBLIC SPEAKING LESSONS?
UNDER-STOOD, YOUR MAJESTY.
HEH!
I LEAVE IT TO YOU, THEN.
THIS YEAR'S FOUNDING DAY...
...IS A BIG MILESTONE FOR THE KINGDOM OF GRANZREICH—ITS HUNDREDTH YEAR AS A NATION.
THERE WILL BE MORE GUESTS THAN USUAL, AND IT WILL BE A LARGE-SCALE CELEBRATION. DO KEEP THAT IN MIND, ALL RIGHT, BOYS?
AH HA HA!
...
MOUNTING PRESSURE...
OVER-KILL

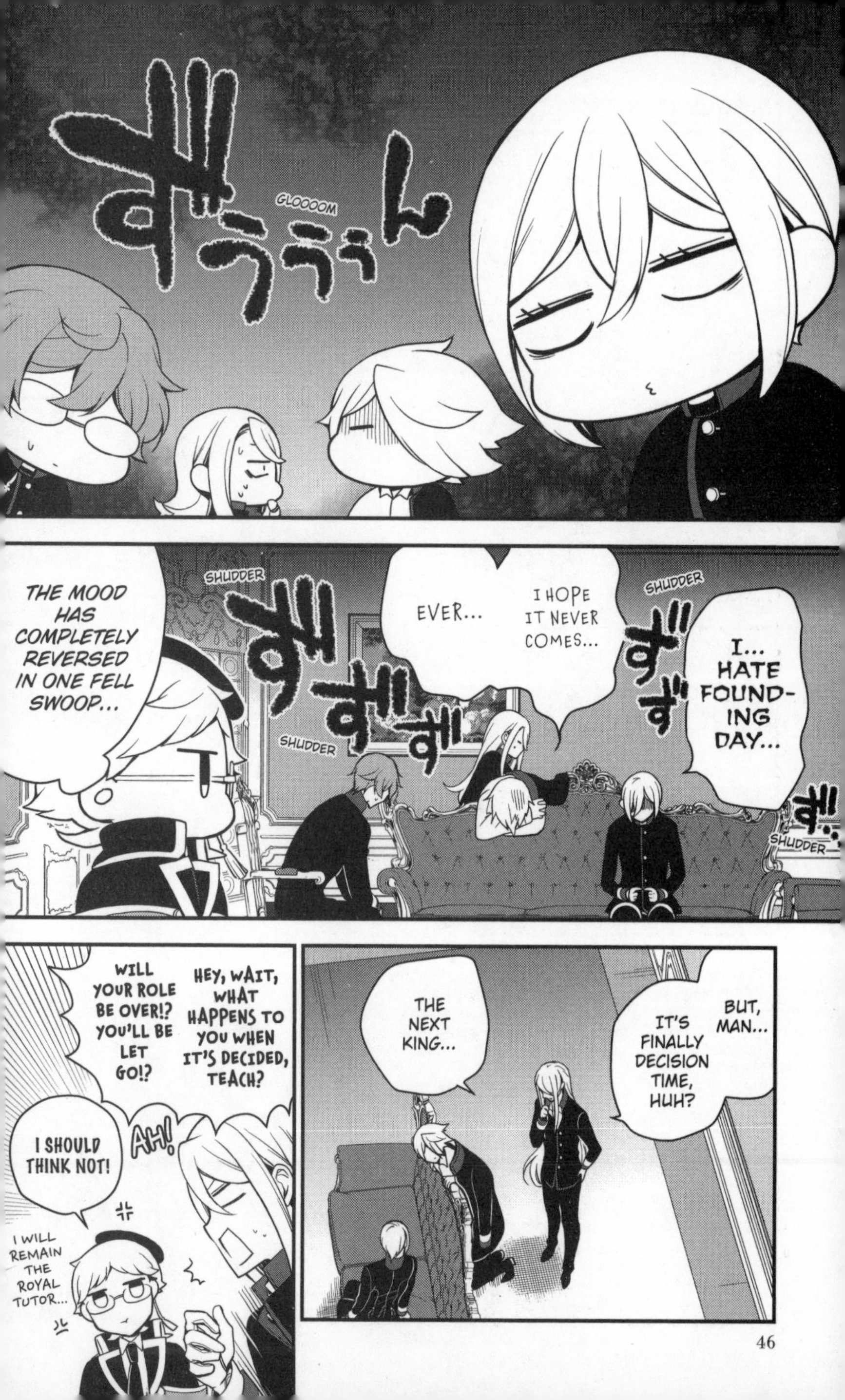
GLOOOOM
I... HATE FOUNDING-DAY...
SHUDDER
I HOPE IT NEVER COMES...
EVER...
SHUDDER
SHUDDER
THE MOOD HAS COMPLETELY REVERSED IN ONE FELL SWOOP...
SHUDDER
BUT, MAN...
IT'S FINALLY DECISION TIME, HUH?
THE NEXT KING...
HEY, WAIT, WHAT HAPPENS TO YOU WHEN IT'S DECIDED, TEACH?
WILL YOUR ROLE BE OVER!? YOU'LL BE LET GO!?
AH!
I SHOULD THINK NOT!
I WILL REMAIN THE ROYAL TUTOR...

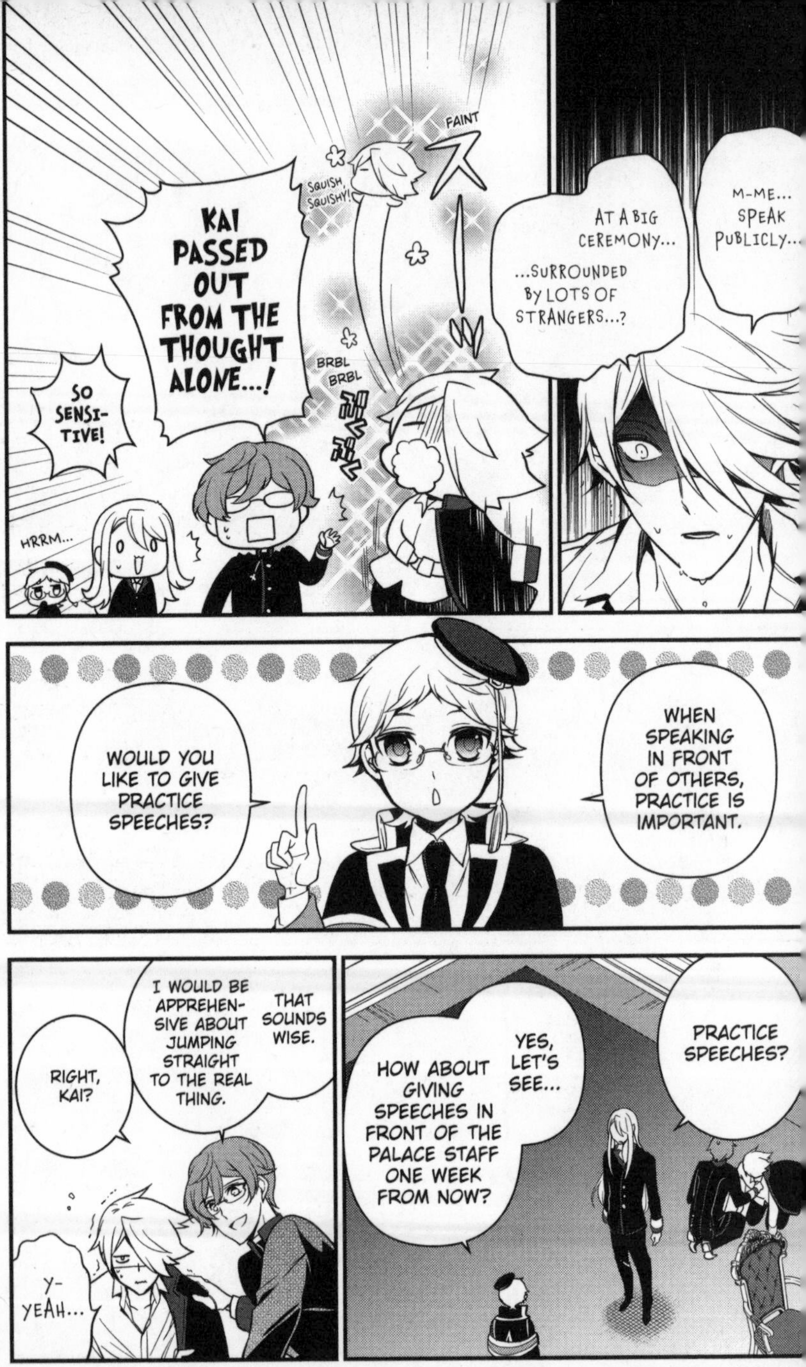
M-ME... SPEAK PUBLICLY...
AT A BIG CEREMONY...
...SURROUNDED BY LOTS OF STRANGERS...?
FAINT
SQUISH, SQUISHY!
KAI PASSED OUT FROM THE THOUGHT ALONE...!
BRBL BRBL
SO SENSI-TIVE!
HRRM...
WHEN SPEAKING IN FRONT OF OTHERS, PRACTICE IS IMPORTANT.
WOULD YOU LIKE TO GIVE PRACTICE SPEECHES?
PRACTICE SPEECHES?
YES, LET'S SEE...
HOW ABOUT GIVING SPEECHES IN FRONT OF THE PALACE STAFF ONE WEEK FROM NOW?
THAT SOUNDS WISE.
I WOULD BE APPREHEN-SIVE ABOUT JUMPING STRAIGHT TO THE REAL THING.
RIGHT, KAI?
Y-YEAH...

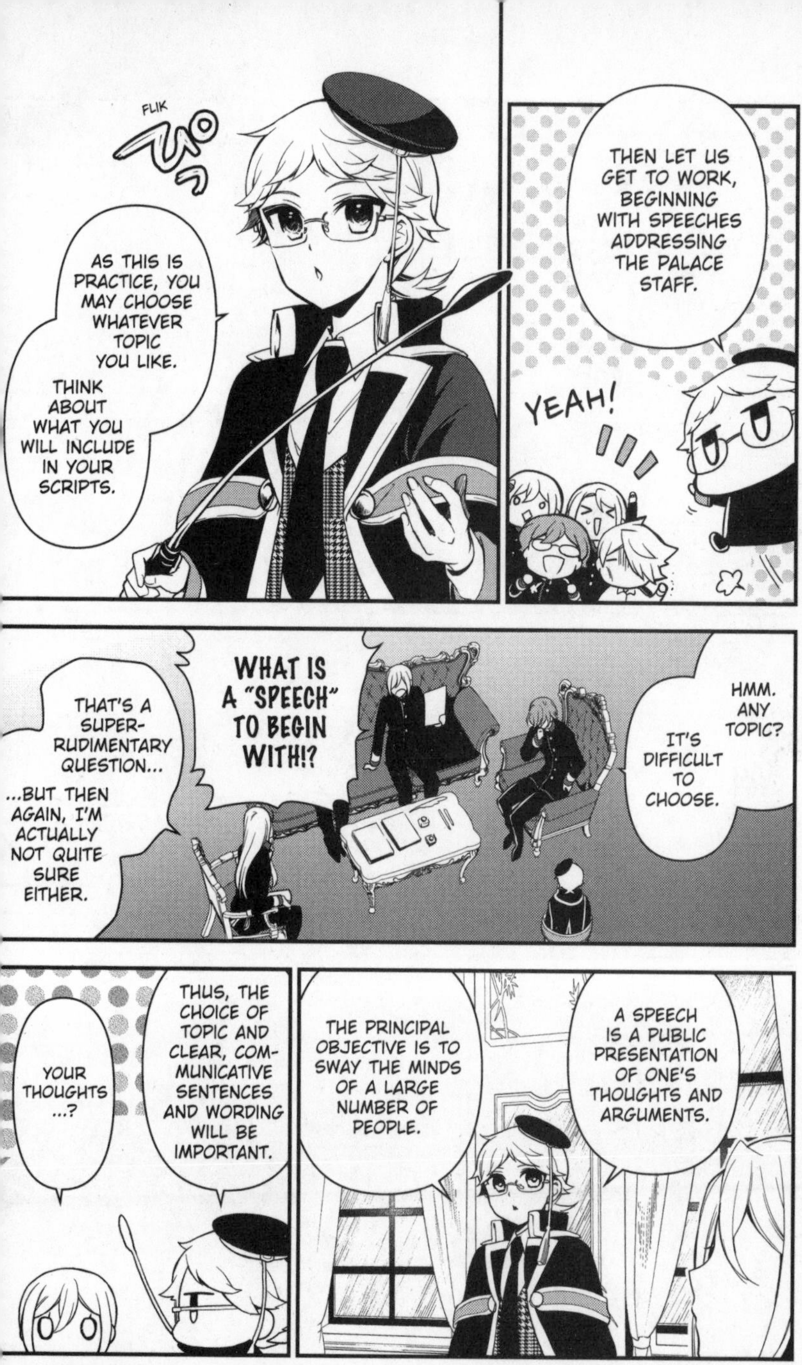
THEN LET US GET TO WORK, BEGINNING WITH SPEECHES ADDRESSING THE PALACE STAFF.
YEAH!
FLIK
AS THIS IS PRACTICE, YOU MAY CHOOSE WHATEVER TOPIC YOU LIKE.
THINK ABOUT WHAT YOU WILL INCLUDE IN YOUR SCRIPTS.
HMM. ANY TOPIC?
IT'S DIFFICULT TO CHOOSE.
WHAT IS A "SPEECH" TO BEGIN WITH!?
THAT'S A SUPER-RUDIMENTARY QUESTION...
...BUT THEN AGAIN, I'M ACTUALLY NOT QUITE SURE EITHER.
A SPEECH IS A PUBLIC PRESENTATION OF ONE'S THOUGHTS AND ARGUMENTS.
THE PRINCIPAL OBJECTIVE IS TO SWAY THE MINDS OF A LARGE NUMBER OF PEOPLE.
THUS, THE CHOICE OF TOPIC AND CLEAR, COM-MUNICATIVE SENTENCES AND WORDING WILL BE IMPORTANT.
YOUR THOUGHTS ...?

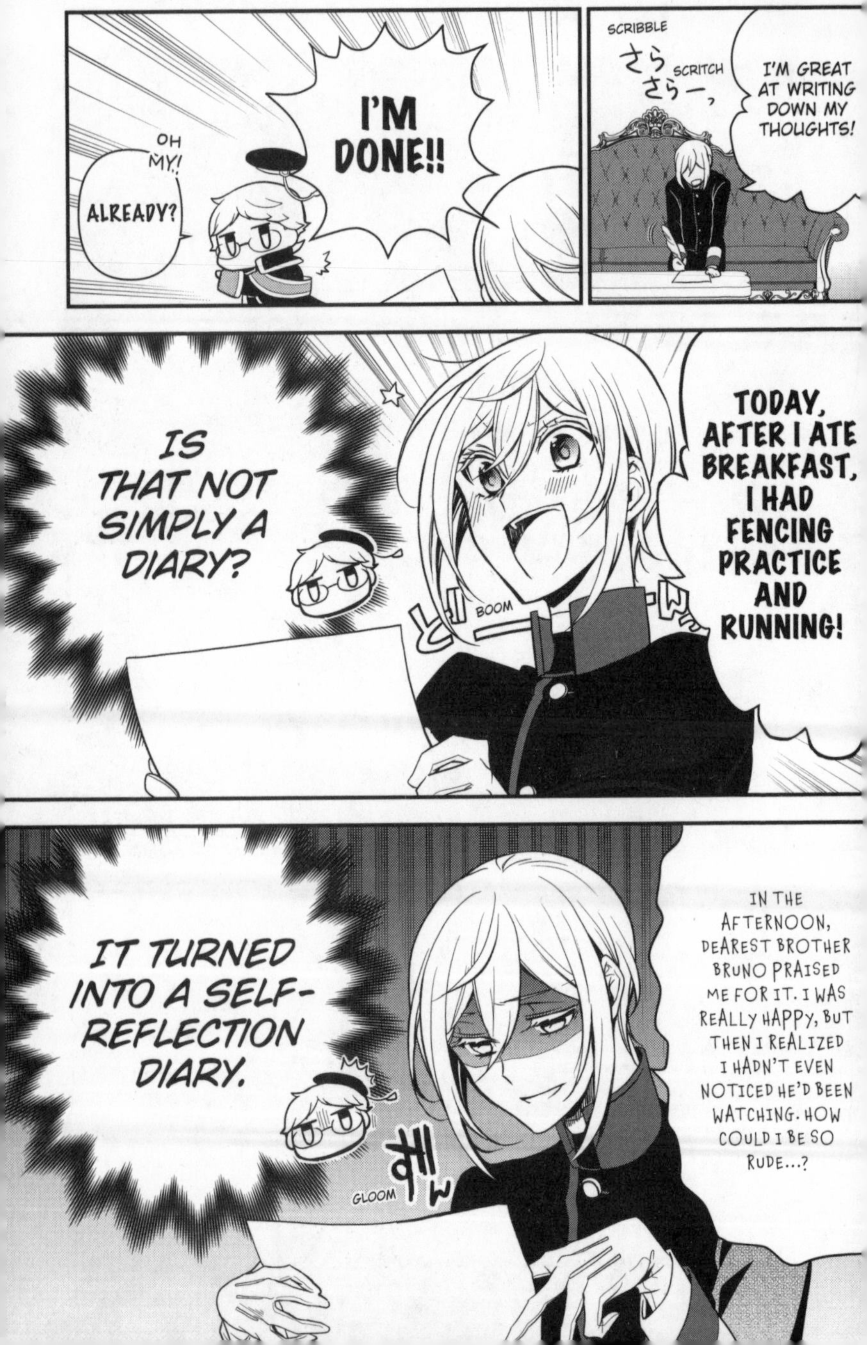
I'M GREAT AT WRITING DOWN MY THOUGHTS!
SCRIBBLE
さらさらー
SCRITCH
I'M DONE!!
OH MY!
ALREADY?
TODAY, AFTER I ATE BREAKFAST, I HAD FENCING PRACTICE AND RUNNING!
BOOM
IS THAT NOT SIMPLY A DIARY?
IN THE AFTERNOON, DEAREST BROTHER BRUNO PRAISED ME FOR IT. I WAS REALLY HAPPY, BUT THEN I REALIZED I HADN'T EVEN NOTICED HE'D BEEN WATCHING. HOW COULD I BE SO RUDE...?
GLOOM
IT TURNED INTO A SELF-REFLECTION DIARY.

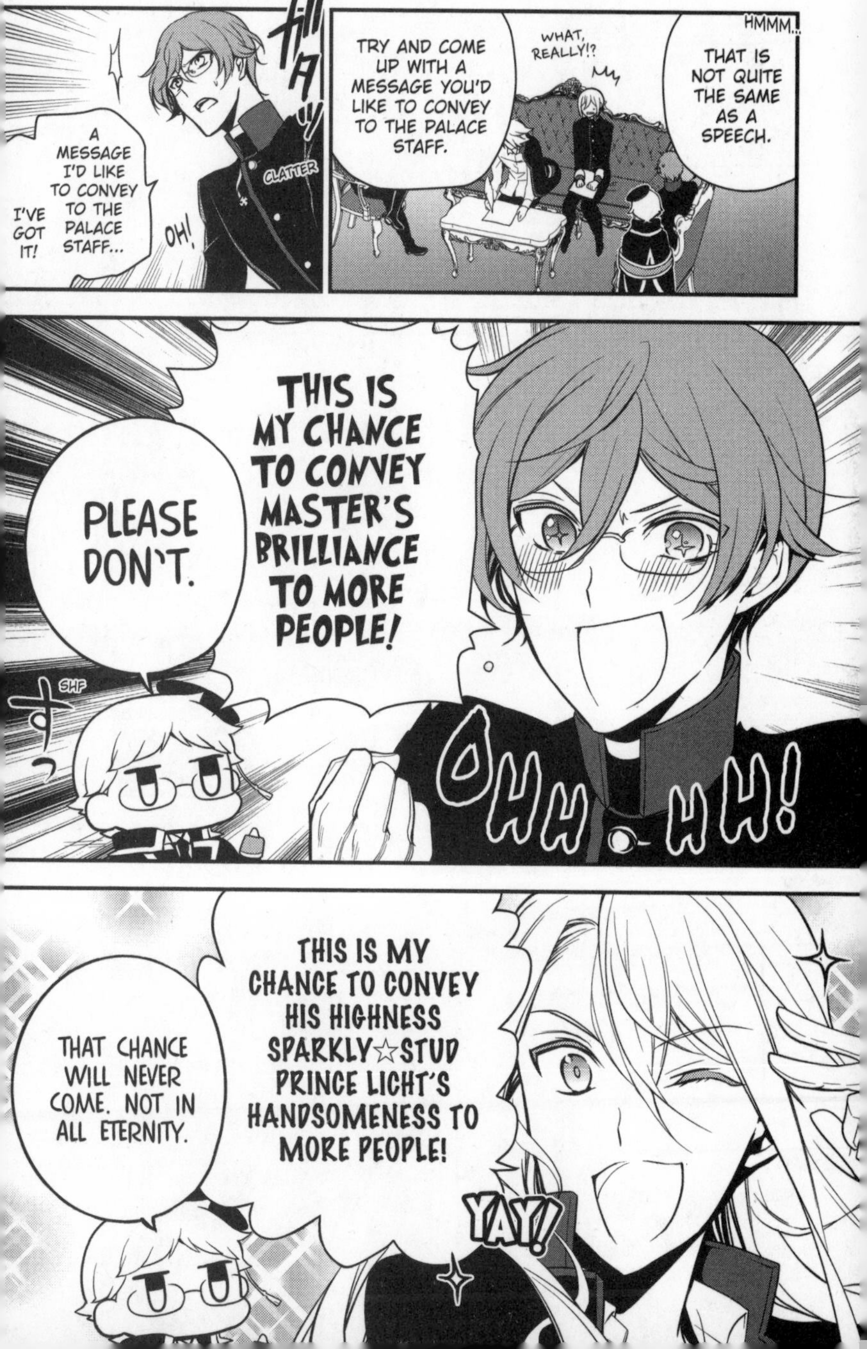
HMMM...
THAT IS NOT QUITE THE SAME AS A SPEECH.
WHAT, REALLY!?
TRY AND COME UP WITH A MESSAGE YOU'D LIKE TO CONVEY TO THE PALACE STAFF.
CLATTER
OH!
A MESSAGE I'D LIKE TO CONVEY TO THE PALACE STAFF...
I'VE GOT IT!
THIS IS MY CHANCE TO CONVEY MASTER'S BRILLIANCE TO MORE PEOPLE!
OHH...HH!
PLEASE DON'T.
SHF
THIS IS MY CHANCE TO CONVEY HIS HIGHNESS SPARKLY☆STUD PRINCE LICHT'S HANDSOMENESS TO MORE PEOPLE!
YAY!
THAT CHANCE WILL NEVER COME. NOT IN ALL ETERNITY.

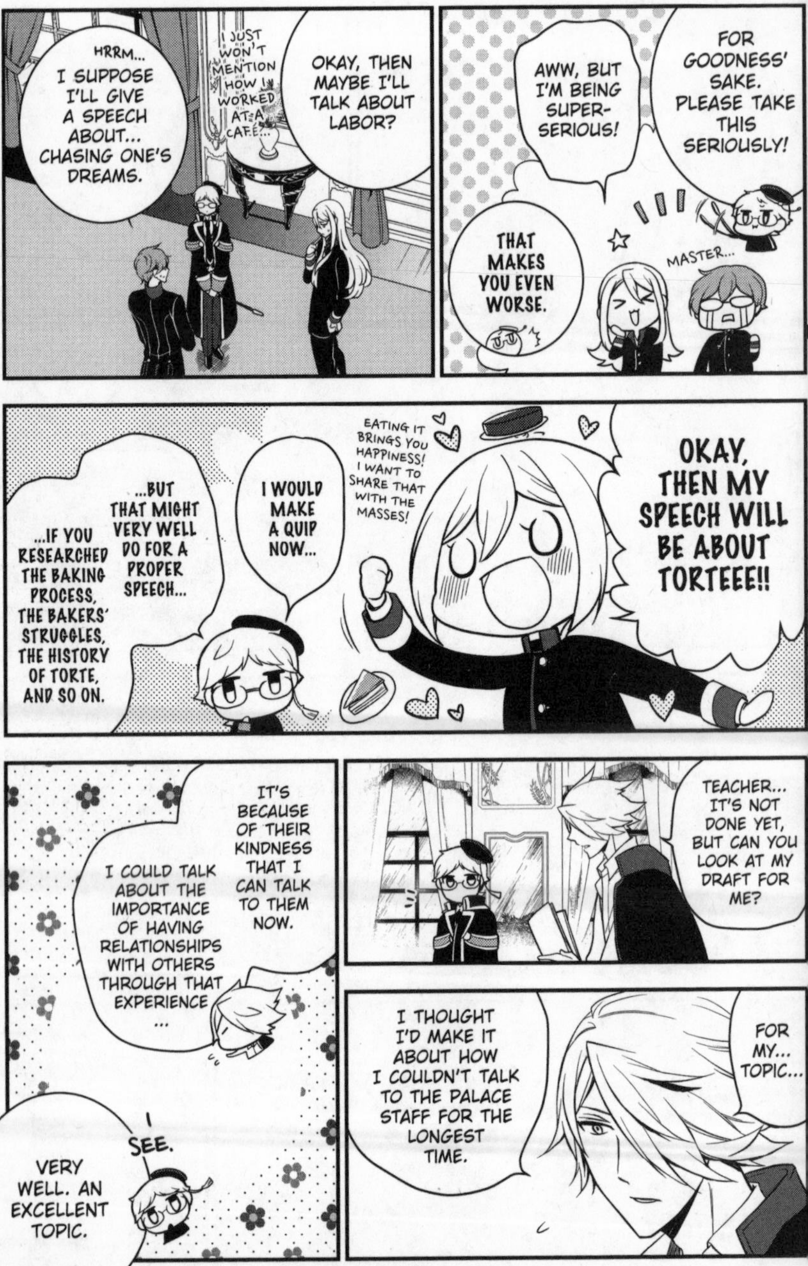
FOR GOODNESS' SAKE. PLEASE TAKE THIS SERIOUSLY!
AWW, BUT I'M BEING SUPER-SERIOUS!
MASTER...
THAT MAKES YOU EVEN WORSE.
OKAY, THEN MAYBE I'LL TALK ABOUT LABOR?
I JUST WON'T MENTION HOW I WORKED AT A CAFÉ...
HRRM... I SUPPOSE I'LL GIVE A SPEECH ABOUT... CHASING ONE'S DREAMS.
OKAY, THEN MY SPEECH WILL BE ABOUT TORTEEE!!
EATING IT BRINGS YOU HAPPINESS! I WANT TO SHARE THAT WITH THE MASSES!
I WOULD MAKE A QUIP NOW...
...BUT THAT MIGHT VERY WELL DO FOR A PROPER SPEECH...
...IF YOU RESEARCHED THE BAKING PROCESS, THE BAKERS' STRUGGLES, THE HISTORY OF TORTE, AND SO ON.
TEACHER... IT'S NOT DONE YET, BUT CAN YOU LOOK AT MY DRAFT FOR ME?
FOR MY... TOPIC...
I THOUGHT I'D MAKE IT ABOUT HOW I COULDN'T TALK TO THE PALACE STAFF FOR THE LONGEST TIME.
IT'S BECAUSE OF THEIR KINDNESS THAT I CAN TALK TO THEM NOW.
I COULD TALK ABOUT THE IMPORTANCE OF HAVING RELATIONSHIPS WITH OTHERS THROUGH THAT EXPERIENCE ...
I SEE.
VERY WELL. AN EXCELLENT TOPIC.

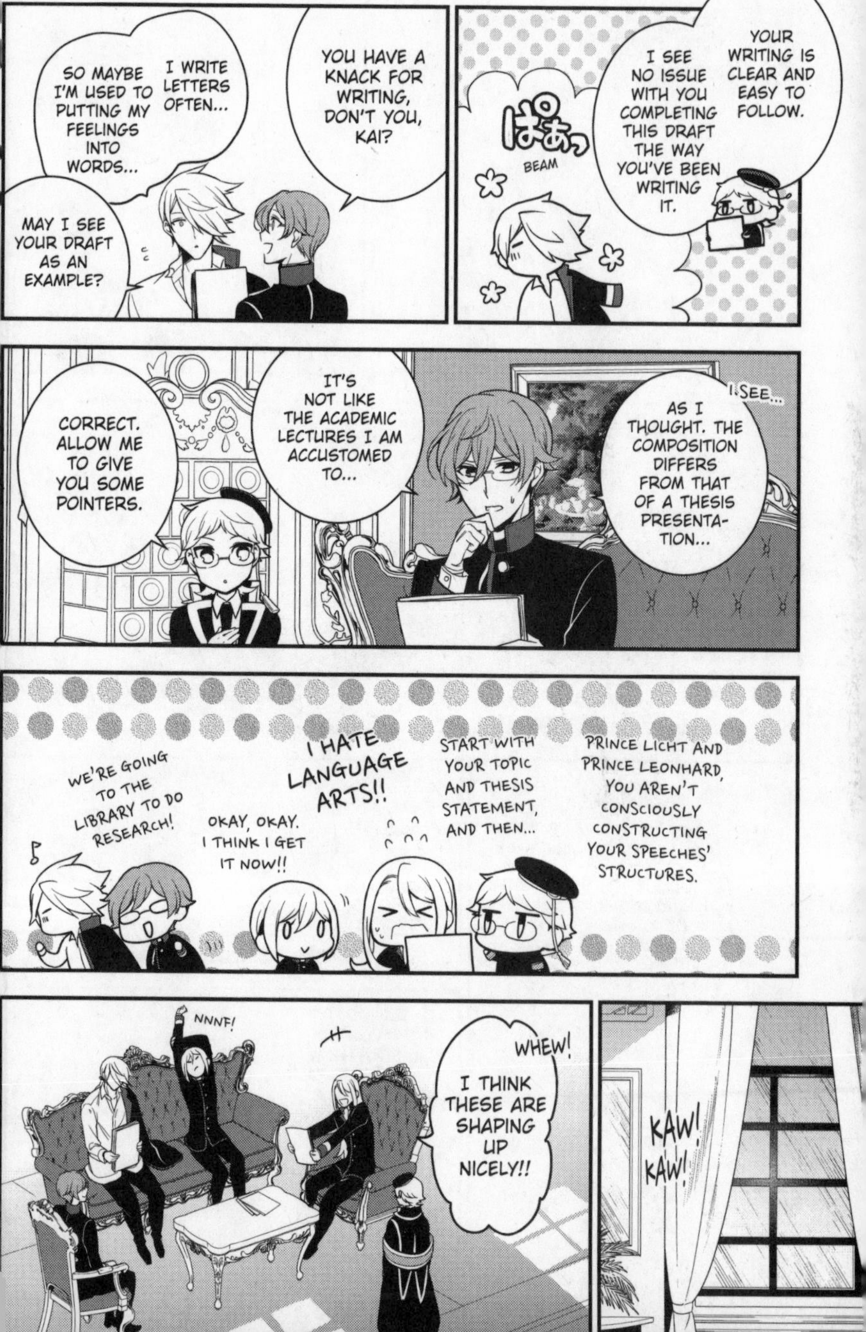
YOUR WRITING IS CLEAR AND EASY TO FOLLOW.
I SEE NO ISSUE WITH YOU COMPLETING THIS DRAFT THE WAY YOU'VE BEEN WRITING IT.
ぱあっ
BEAM
YOU HAVE A KNACK FOR WRITING, DON'T YOU, KAI?
I WRITE LETTERS OFTEN...
SO MAYBE I'M USED TO PUTTING MY FEELINGS INTO WORDS...
MAY I SEE YOUR DRAFT AS AN EXAMPLE?
I SEE...
AS I THOUGHT. THE COMPOSITION DIFFERS FROM THAT OF A THESIS PRESENTATION...
IT'S NOT LIKE THE ACADEMIC LECTURES I AM ACCUSTOMED TO...
CORRECT. ALLOW ME TO GIVE YOU SOME POINTERS.
PRINCE LICHT AND PRINCE LEONHARD, YOU AREN'T CONSCIOUSLY CONSTRUCTING YOUR SPEECHES' STRUCTURES.
START WITH YOUR TOPIC AND THESIS STATEMENT, AND THEN...
I HATE LANGUAGE ARTS!!
OKAY, OKAY. I THINK I GET IT NOW!!
WE'RE GOING TO THE LIBRARY TO DO RESEARCH!
KAW! KAW!
WHEW!
I THINK THESE ARE SHAPING UP NICELY!!
NNNF!

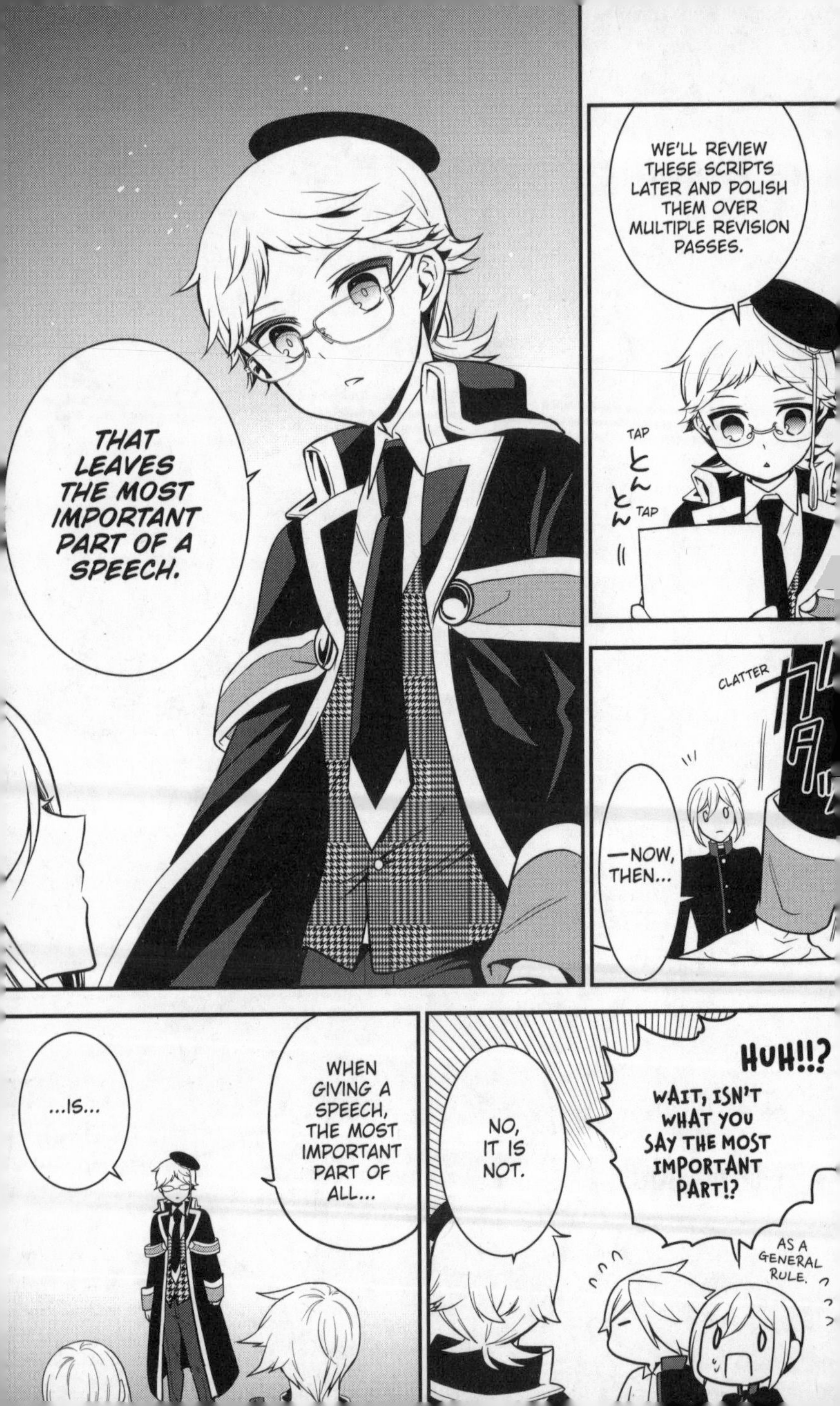
WE'LL REVIEW THESE SCRIPTS LATER AND POLISH THEM OVER MULTIPLE REVISION PASSES.
TAP
とん
とん
TAP
CLATTER
ガタッ
—NOW, THEN...
THAT LEAVES THE MOST IMPORTANT PART OF A SPEECH.
HUH!!?
WAIT, ISN'T WHAT YOU SAY THE MOST IMPORTANT PART!?
NO, IT IS NOT.
AS A GENERAL RULE.
WHEN GIVING A SPEECH, THE MOST IMPORTANT PART OF ALL...
...IS...

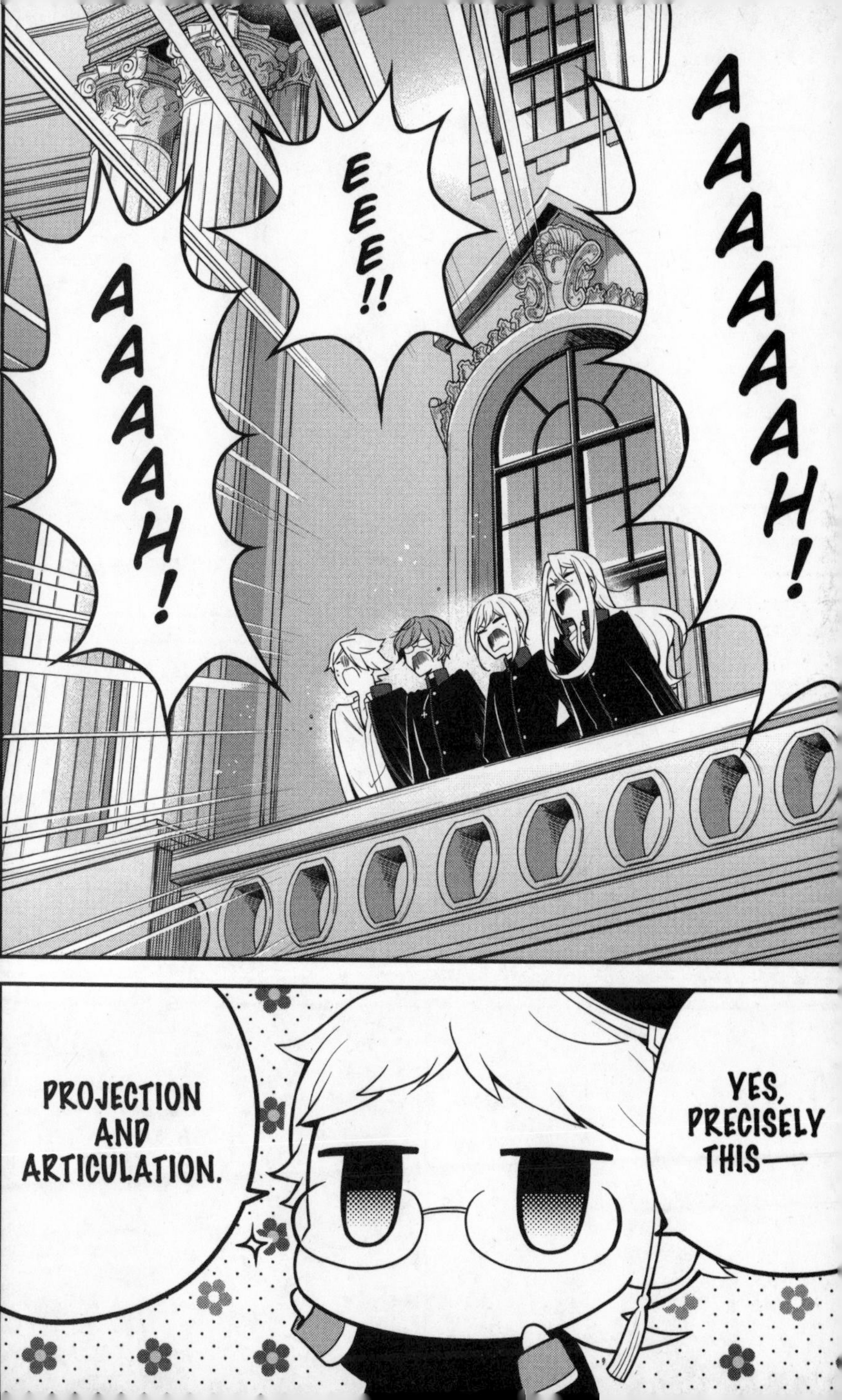
AAAAAAH!
EEE!!
AAAAH!
YES, PRECISELY THIS—
PROJECTION AND ARTICULATION.

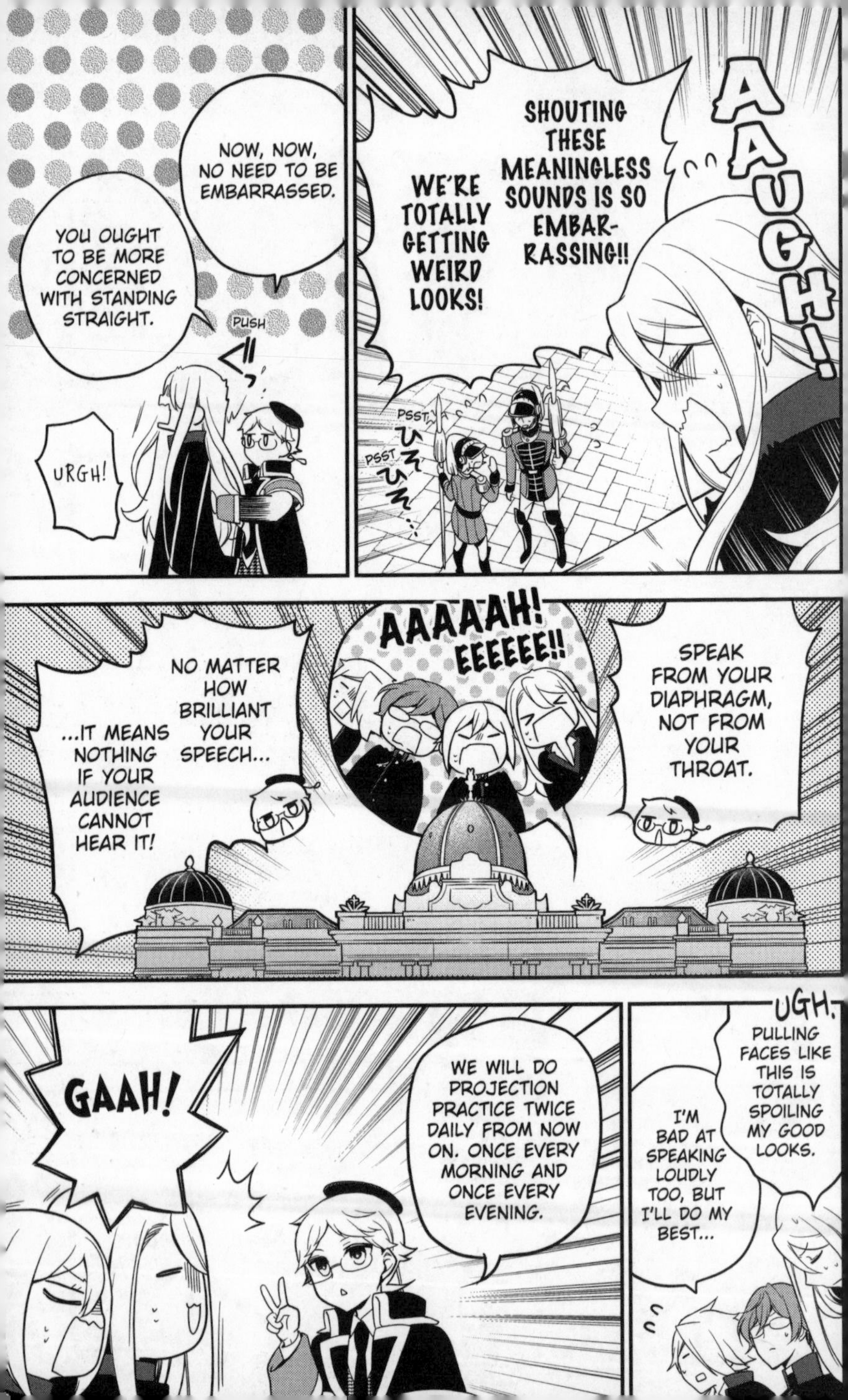
AAUGH!!
SHOUTING THESE MEANINGLESS SOUNDS IS SO EMBAR-RASSING!!
WE'RE TOTALLY GETTING WEIRD LOOKS!
PSST
PSST
NOW, NOW, NO NEED TO BE EMBARRASSED.
YOU OUGHT TO BE MORE CONCERNED WITH STANDING STRAIGHT.
PUSH
URGH!
SPEAK FROM YOUR DIAPHRAGM, NOT FROM YOUR THROAT.
AAAAAH! EEEEEE!!
NO MATTER HOW BRILLIANT YOUR SPEECH...
...IT MEANS NOTHING IF YOUR AUDIENCE CANNOT HEAR IT!
UGH.
PULLING FACES LIKE THIS IS TOTALLY SPOILING MY GOOD LOOKS.
I'M BAD AT SPEAKING LOUDLY TOO, BUT I'LL DO MY BEST...
WE WILL DO PROJECTION PRACTICE TWICE DAILY FROM NOW ON. ONCE EVERY MORNING AND ONCE EVERY EVENING.
GAAH!

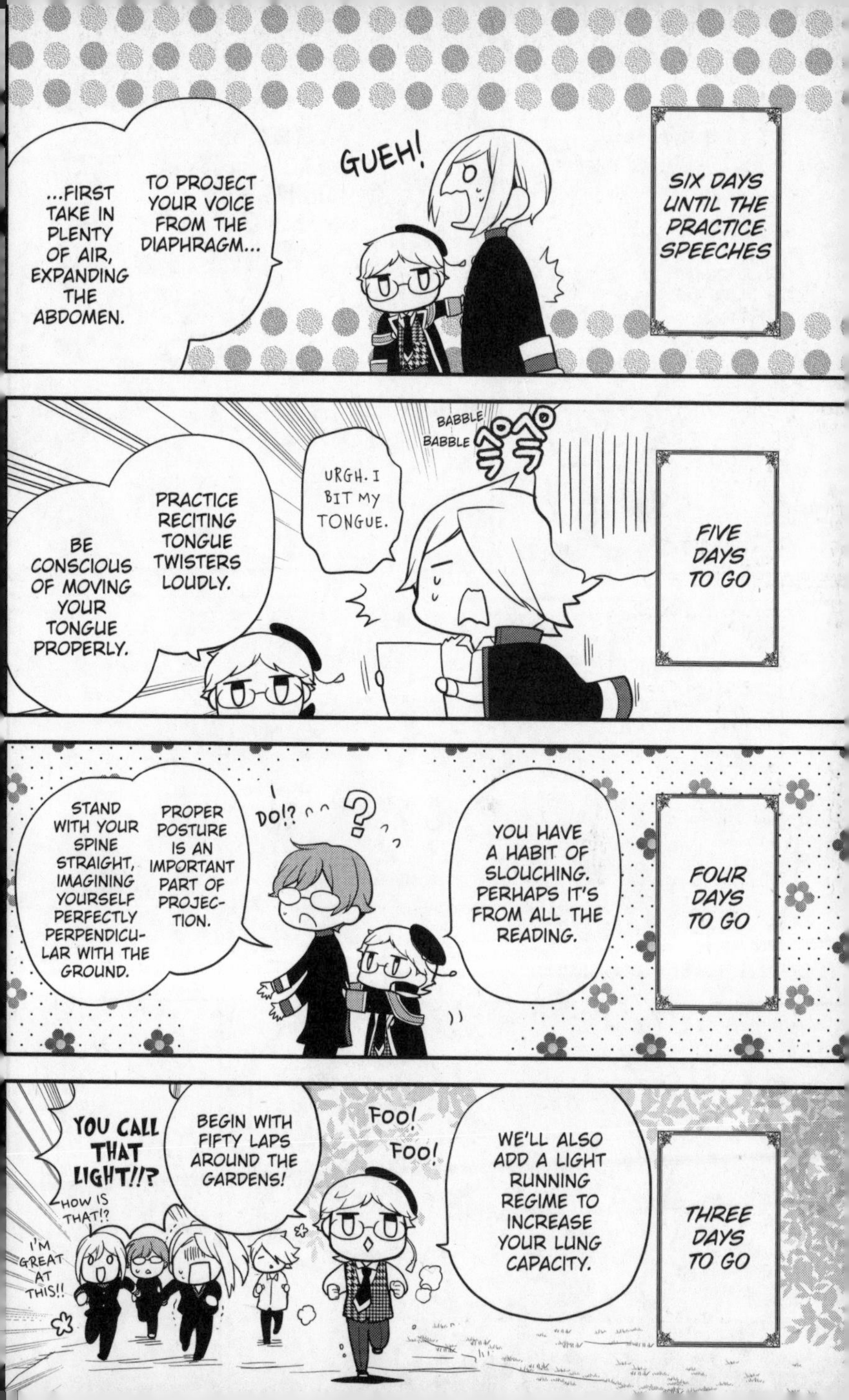
SIX DAYS UNTIL THE PRACTICE SPEECHES
GUEH!
TO PROJECT YOUR VOICE FROM THE DIAPHRAGM...
...FIRST TAKE IN PLENTY OF AIR, EXPANDING THE ABDOMEN.
FIVE DAYS TO GO
BABBLE BABBLE
URGH. I BIT MY TONGUE.
PRACTICE RECITING TONGUE TWISTERS LOUDLY.
BE CONSCIOUS OF MOVING YOUR TONGUE PROPERLY.
FOUR DAYS TO GO
YOU HAVE A HABIT OF SLOUCHING. PERHAPS IT'S FROM ALL THE READING.
DO!?
PROPER POSTURE IS AN IMPORTANT PART OF PROJEC-TION.
STAND WITH YOUR SPINE STRAIGHT, IMAGINING YOURSELF PERFECTLY PERPENDICU-LAR WITH THE GROUND.
THREE DAYS TO GO
WE'LL ALSO ADD A LIGHT RUNNING REGIME TO INCREASE YOUR LUNG CAPACITY.
FOO!
FOO!
BEGIN WITH FIFTY LAPS AROUND THE GARDENS!
YOU CALL THAT LIGHT!!?
HOW IS THAT!?
I'M GREAT AT THIS!!

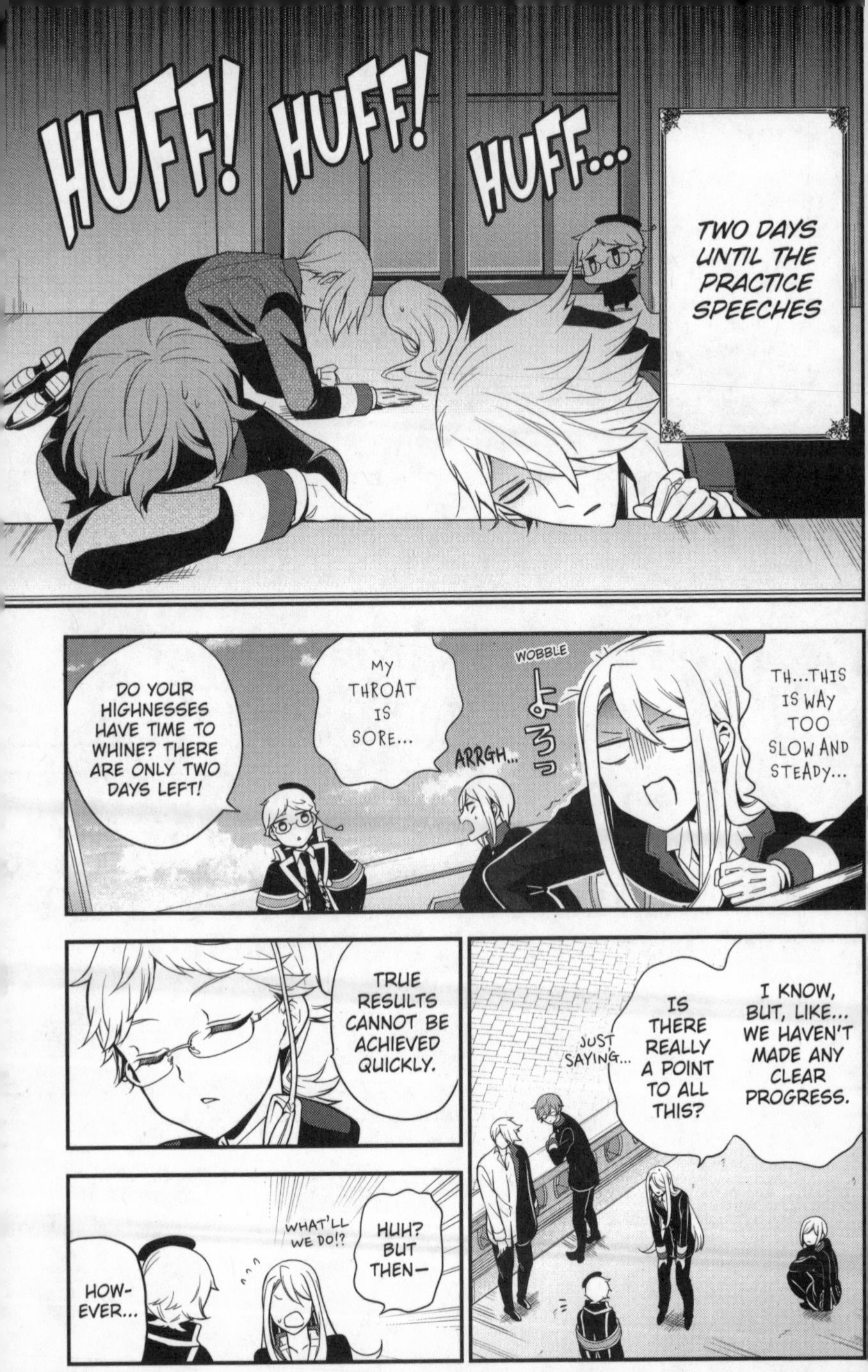
TWO DAYS UNTIL THE PRACTICE SPEECHES
HUFF! HUFF! HUFF...
TH...THIS IS WAY TOO SLOW AND STEADY...
WOBBLE
よろっ
ARRGH...
MY THROAT IS SORE...
DO YOUR HIGHNESSES HAVE TIME TO WHINE? THERE ARE ONLY TWO DAYS LEFT!
I KNOW, BUT, LIKE... WE HAVEN'T MADE ANY CLEAR PROGRESS.
IS THERE REALLY A POINT TO ALL THIS?
JUST SAYING...
TRUE RESULTS CANNOT BE ACHIEVED QUICKLY.
HUH? BUT THEN—
WHAT'LL WE DO!?
HOW-EVER...

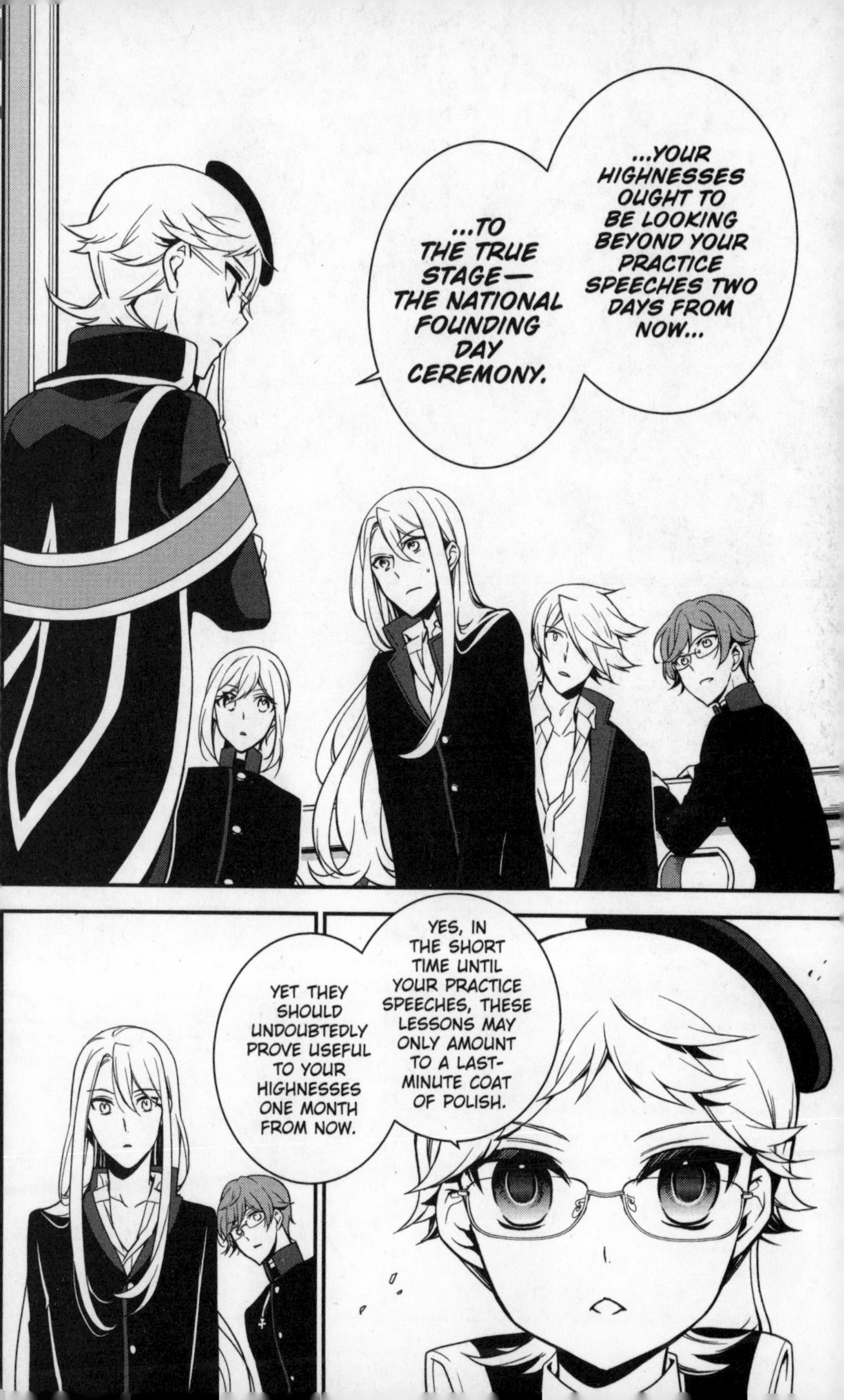
...YOUR HIGHNESSES OUGHT TO BE LOOKING BEYOND YOUR PRACTICE SPEECHES TWO DAYS FROM NOW...
...TO THE TRUE STAGE— THE NATIONAL FOUNDING DAY CEREMONY.
YES, IN THE SHORT TIME UNTIL YOUR PRACTICE SPEECHES, THESE LESSONS MAY ONLY AMOUNT TO A LAST-MINUTE COAT OF POLISH.
YET THEY SHOULD UNDOUBTEDLY PROVE USEFUL TO YOUR HIGHNESSES ONE MONTH FROM NOW.

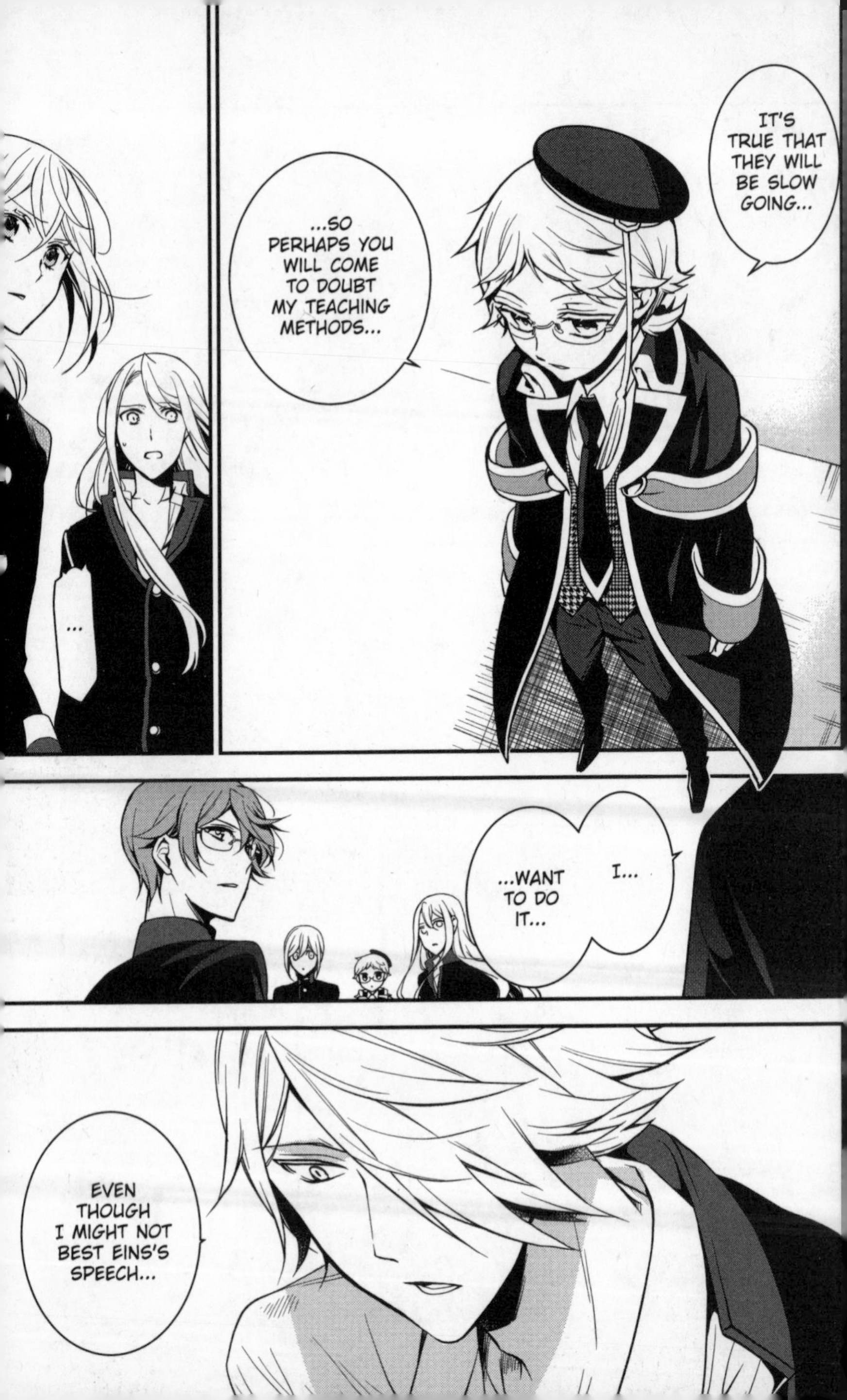
IT'S TRUE THAT THEY WILL BE SLOW GOING...
...SO PERHAPS YOU WILL COME TO DOUBT MY TEACHING METHODS...
...
I...
...WANT TO DO IT...
EVEN THOUGH I MIGHT NOT BEST EINS'S SPEECH...

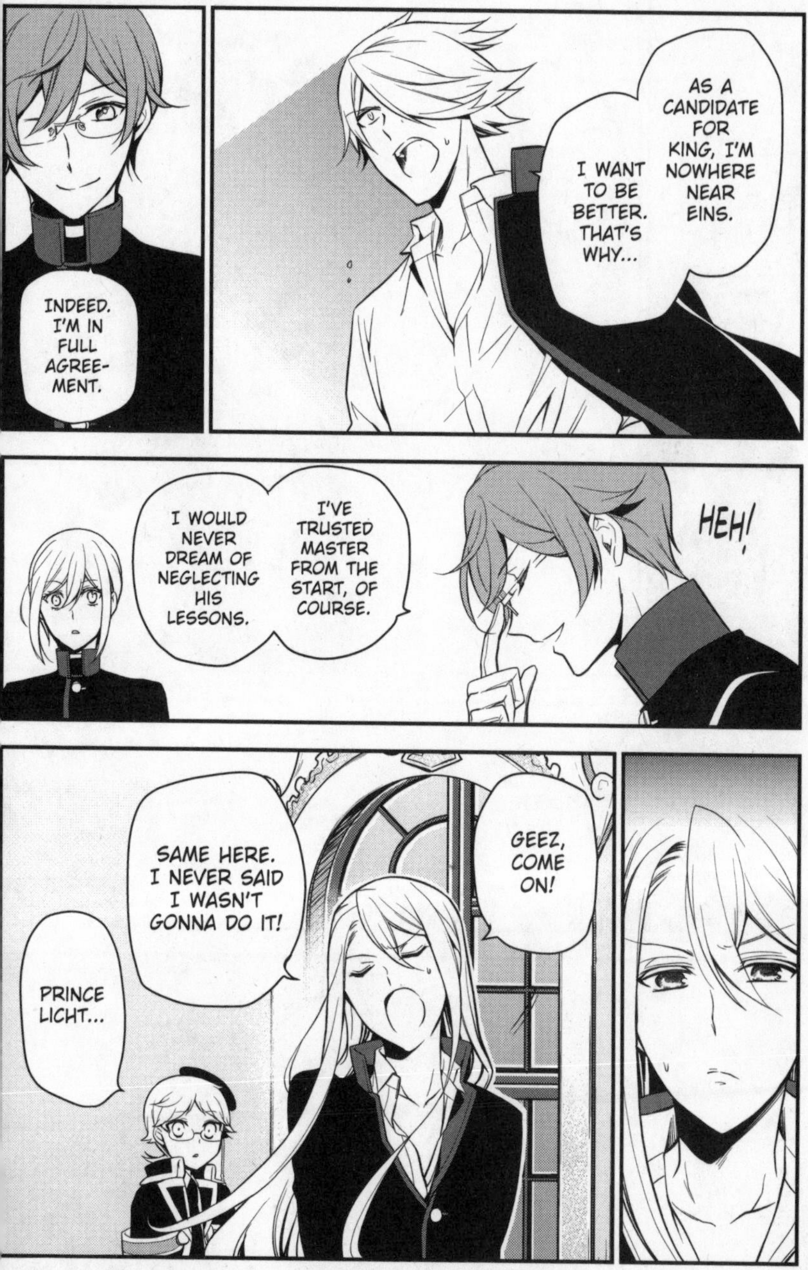
AS A CANDIDATE FOR KING, I'M NOWHERE NEAR EINS.
I WANT TO BE BETTER. THAT'S WHY...
INDEED. I'M IN FULL AGREE-MENT.
HEH!
I'VE TRUSTED MASTER FROM THE START, OF COURSE.
I WOULD NEVER DREAM OF NEGLECTING HIS LESSONS.
GEEZ, COME ON!
SAME HERE. I NEVER SAID I WASN'T GONNA DO IT!
PRINCE LICHT...

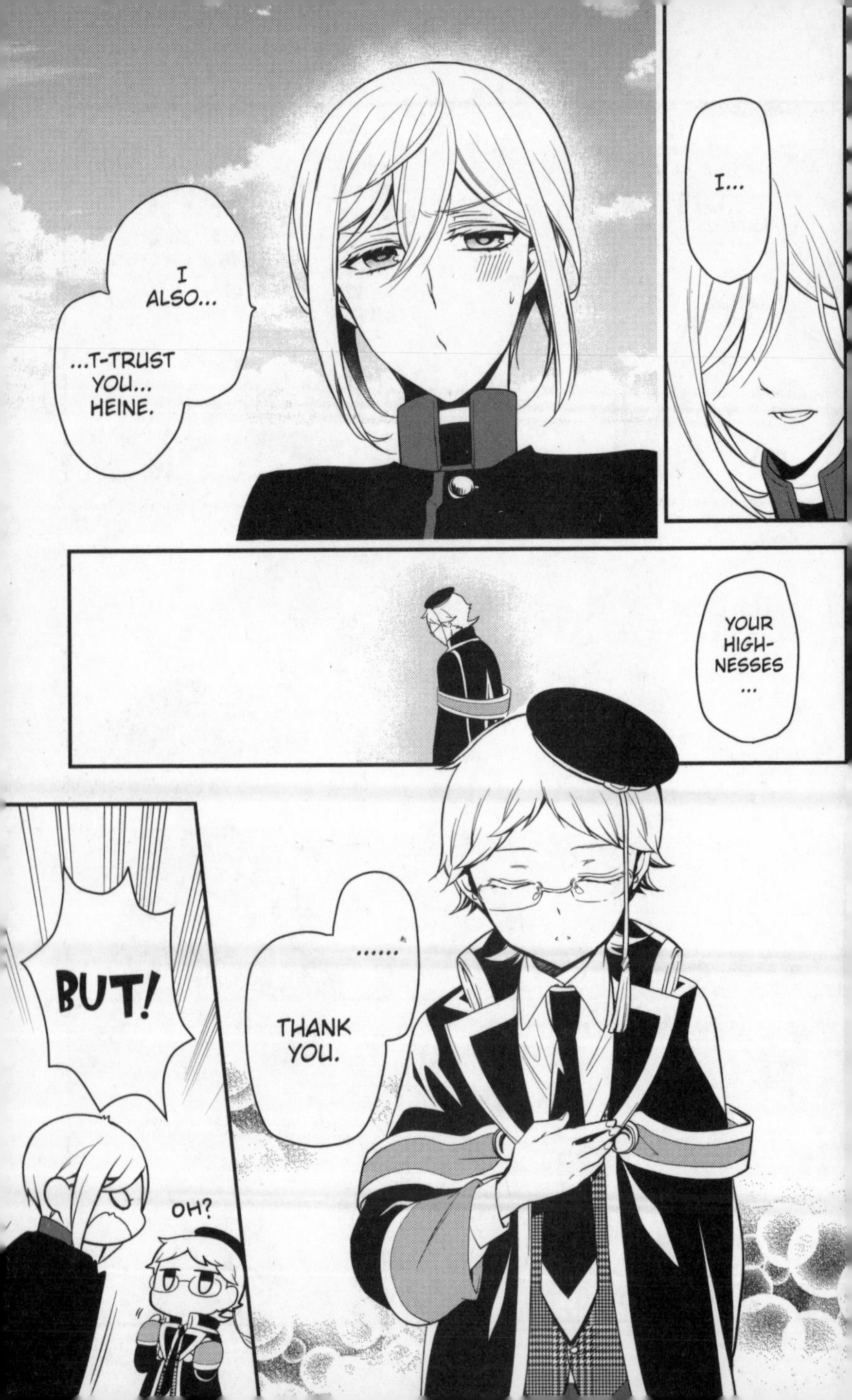
I...
I ALSO...
...T-TRUST YOU... HEINE.
YOUR HIGH-NESSES...
......
THANK YOU.
BUT!
OH?

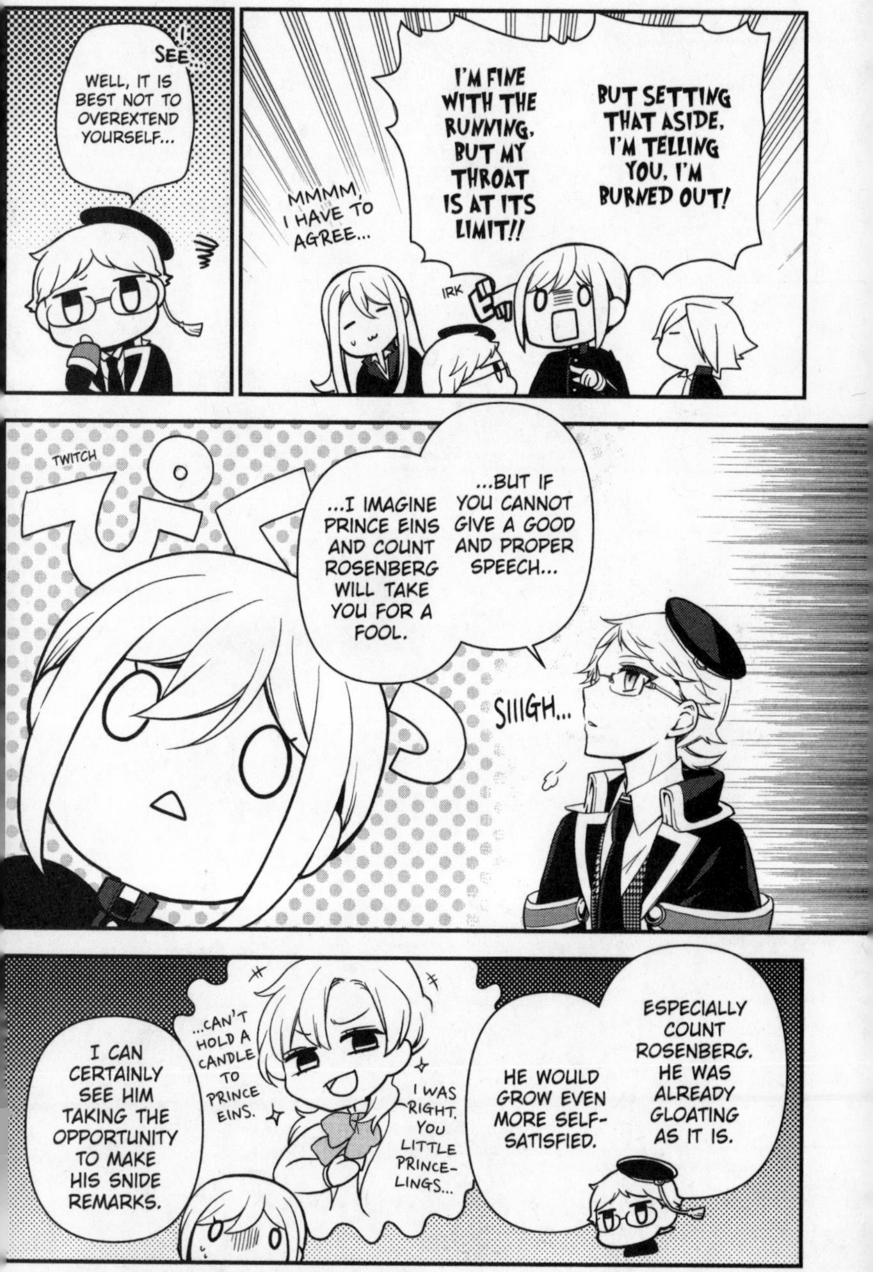
BUT SETTING THAT ASIDE, I'M TELLING YOU, I'M BURNED OUT!
I'M FINE WITH THE RUNNING, BUT MY THROAT IS AT ITS LIMIT!!
MMMM, I HAVE TO AGREE...
IRK
I SEE...
WELL, IT IS BEST NOT TO OVEREXTEND YOURSELF...
...BUT IF YOU CANNOT GIVE A GOOD AND PROPER SPEECH...
...I IMAGINE PRINCE EINS AND COUNT ROSENBERG WILL TAKE YOU FOR A FOOL.
SIIIGH...
TWITCH
ESPECIALLY COUNT ROSENBERG. HE WAS ALREADY GLOATING AS IT IS.
HE WOULD GROW EVEN MORE SELF-SATISFIED.
I WAS RIGHT. YOU LITTLE PRINCE-LINGS...
...CAN'T HOLD A CANDLE TO PRINCE EINS.
I CAN CERTAINLY SEE HIM TAKING THE OPPORTUNITY TO MAKE HIS SNIDE REMARKS.

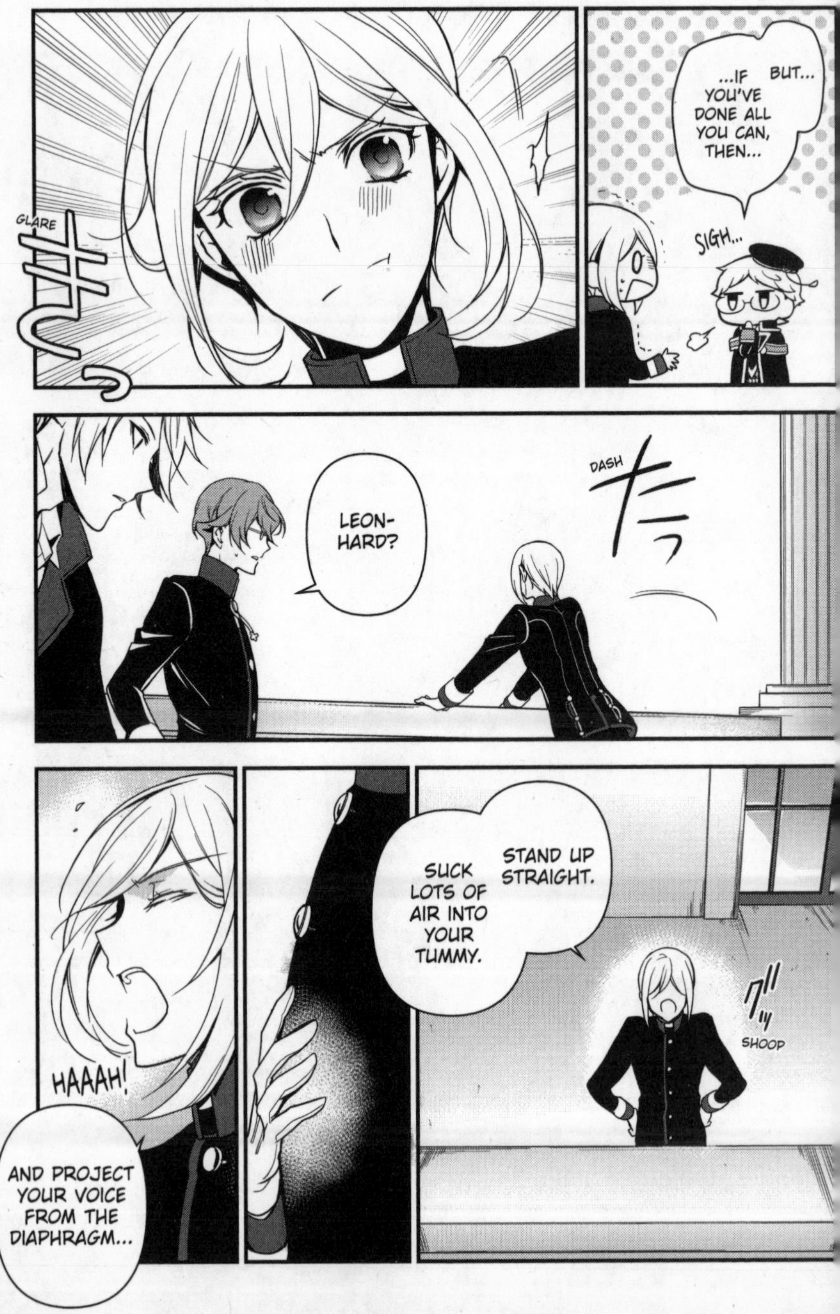
BUT...
...IF YOU'VE DONE ALL YOU CAN, THEN...
SIGH...
GLARE
DASH
LEON-HARD?
STAND UP STRAIGHT.
SUCK LOTS OF AIR INTO YOUR TUMMY.
SHOOP
HAAAH!
AND PROJECT YOUR VOICE FROM THE DIAPHRAGM...

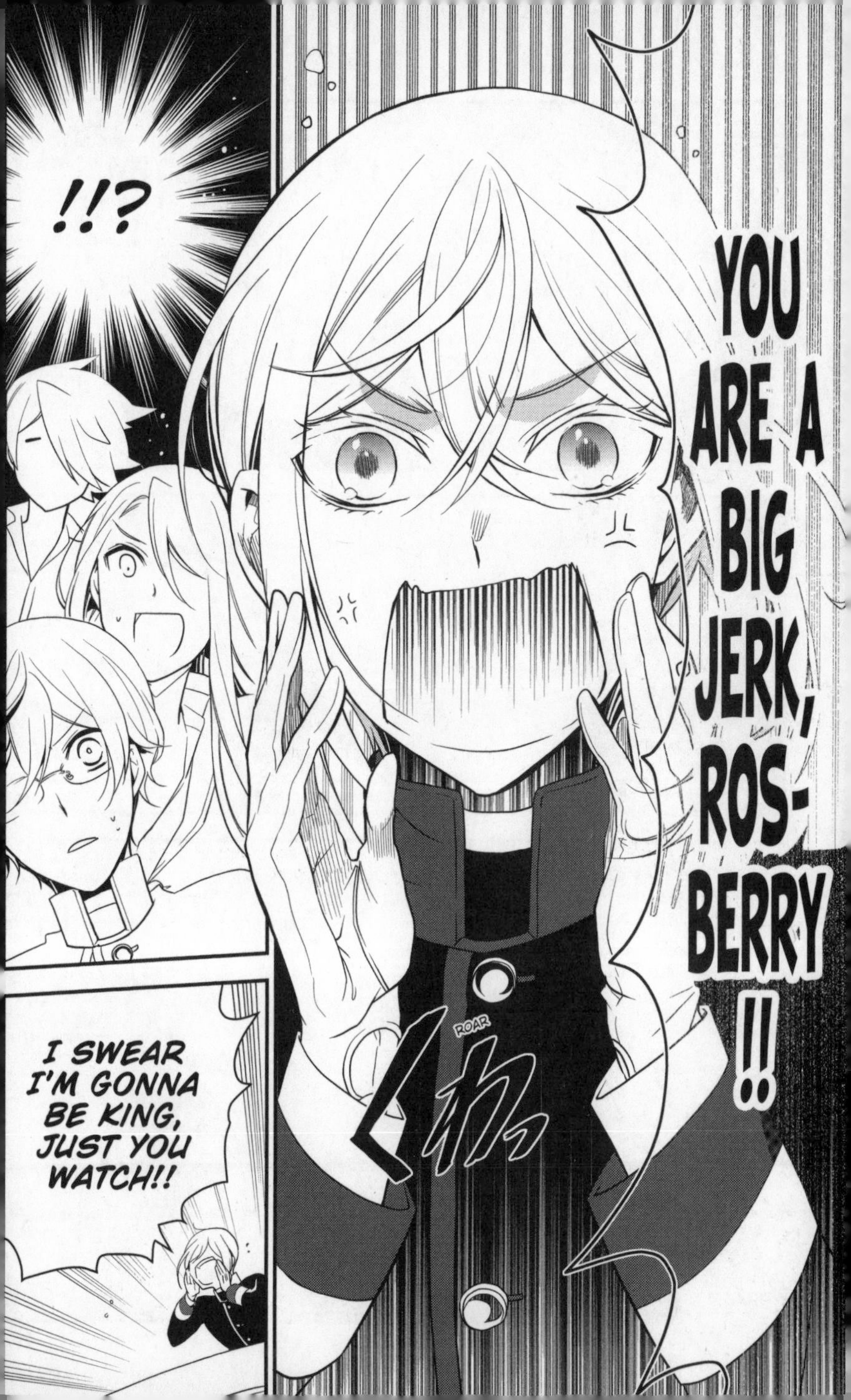
YOU ARE A BIG JERK, ROS-BERRY!!
ROAR
!!?
I SWEAR I'M GONNA BE KING, JUST YOU WATCH!!

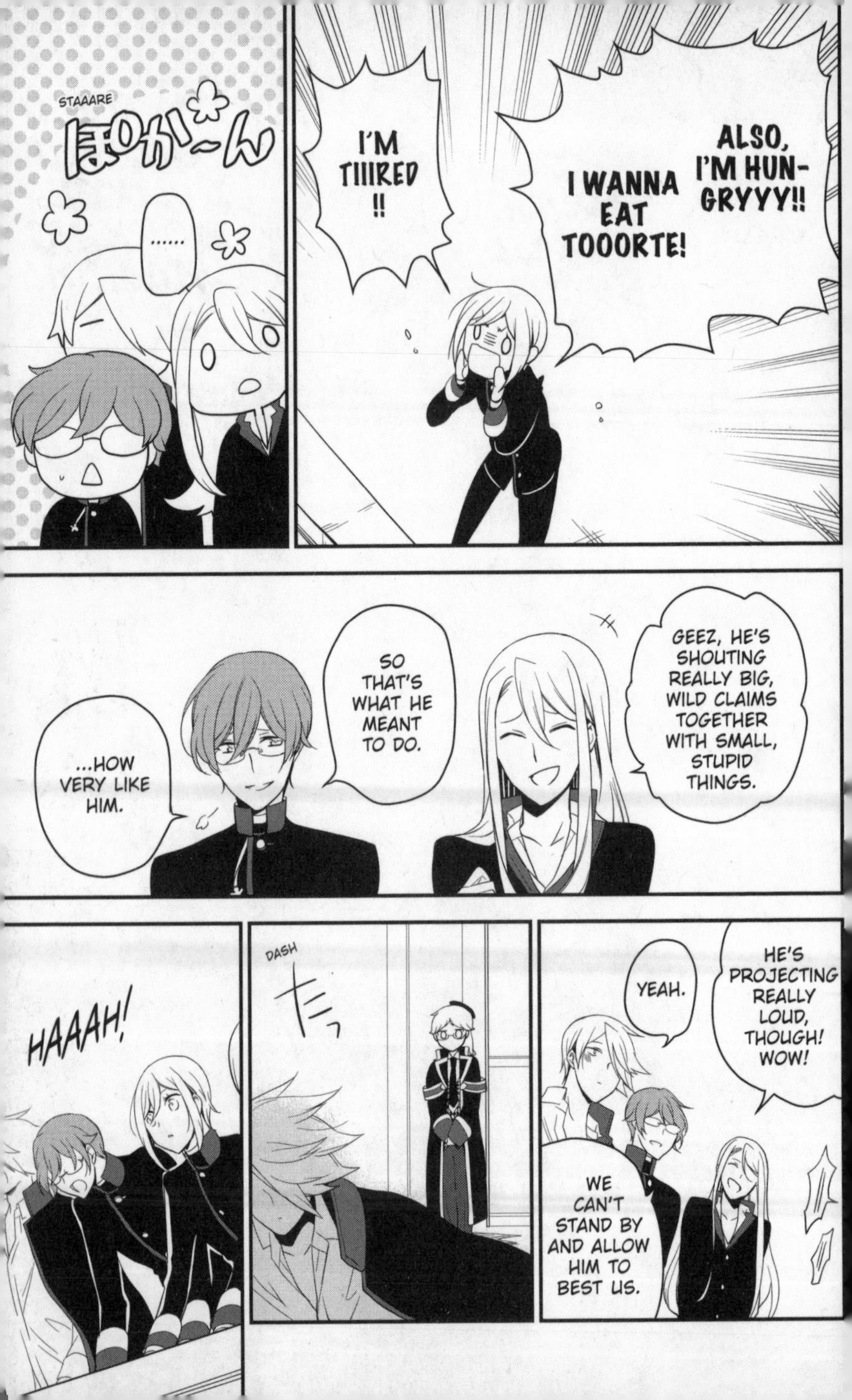
ALSO, I'M HUN-GRYYY!!
I WANNA EAT TOOORTE!
I'M TIIIRED !!
STAAARE
......
GEEZ, HE'S SHOUTING REALLY BIG, WILD CLAIMS TOGETHER WITH SMALL, STUPID THINGS.
SO THAT'S WHAT HE MEANT TO DO.
...HOW VERY LIKE HIM.
HE'S PROJECTING REALLY LOUD, THOUGH! WOW!
YEAH.
WE CAN'T STAND BY AND ALLOW HIM TO BEST US.
DASH
HAAAH!

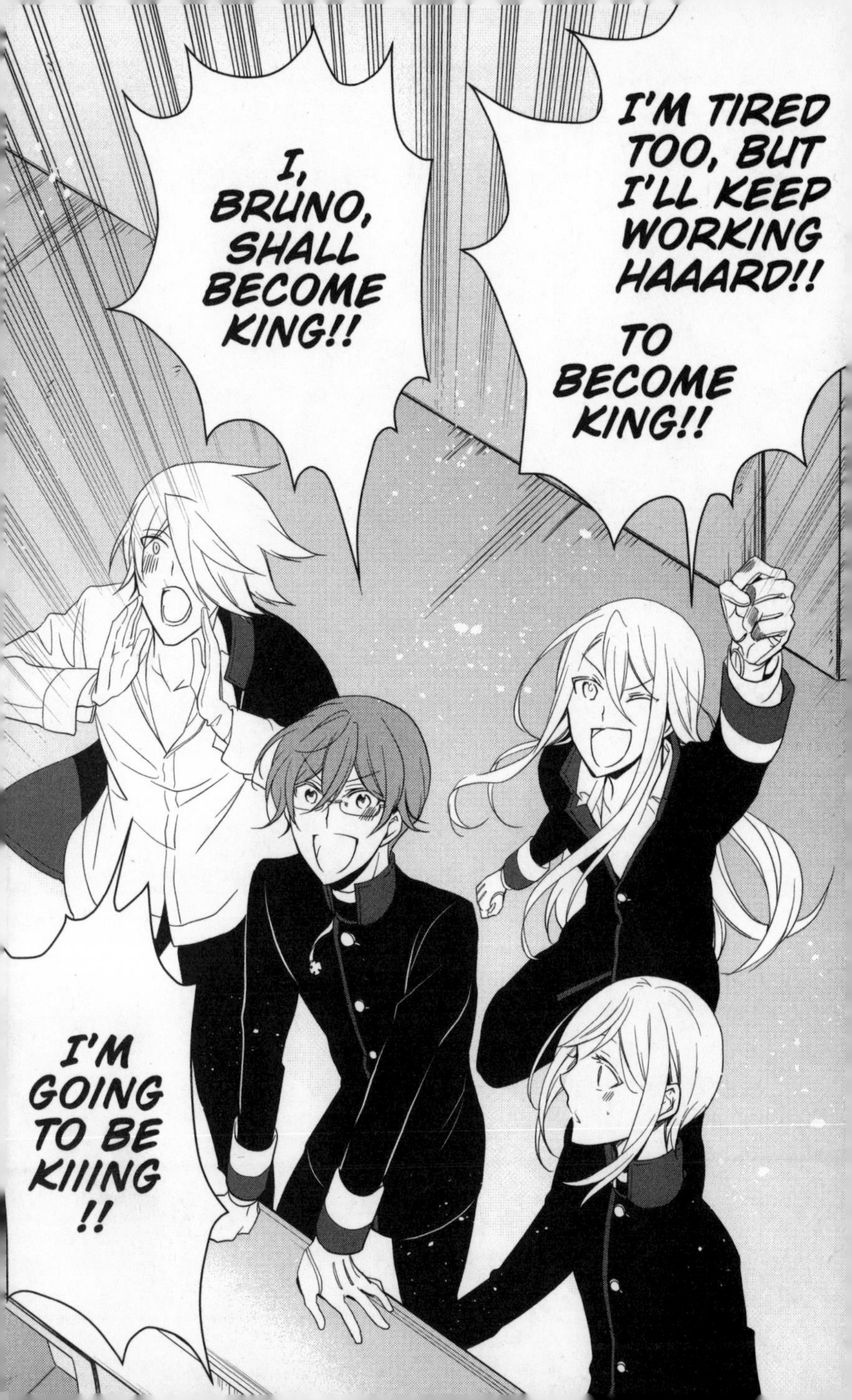
I'M TIRED TOO, BUT I'LL KEEP WORKING HAAARD!!
TO BECOME KING!!
I, BRUNO, SHALL BECOME KING!!
I'M GOING TO BE KIIING!!

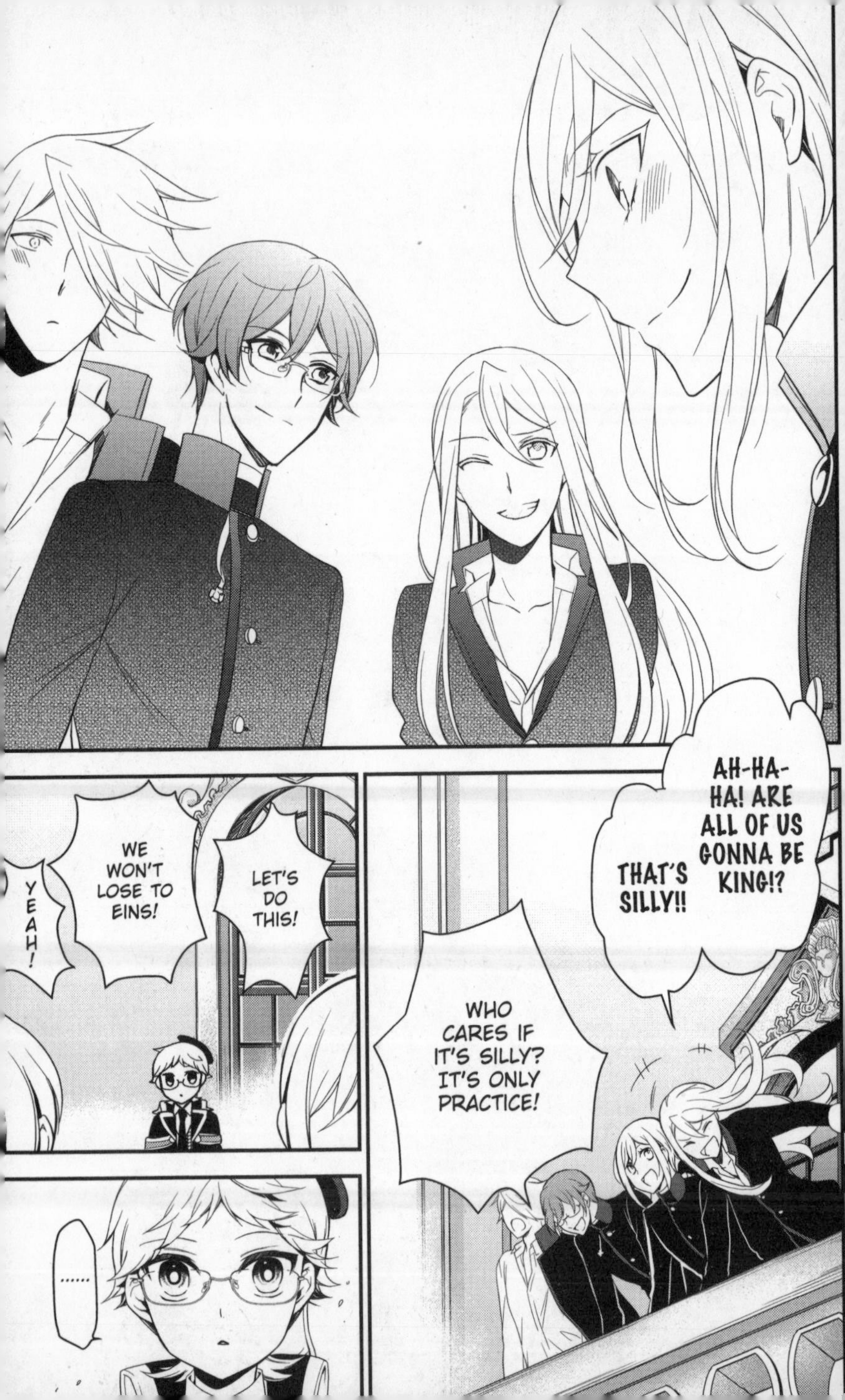

AH-HA-HA! ARE ALL OF US GONNA BE KING!?
THAT'S SILLY!!
WHO CARES IF IT'S SILLY? IT'S ONLY PRACTICE!
LET'S DO THIS!
WE WON'T LOSE TO EINS!
YEAH!
......

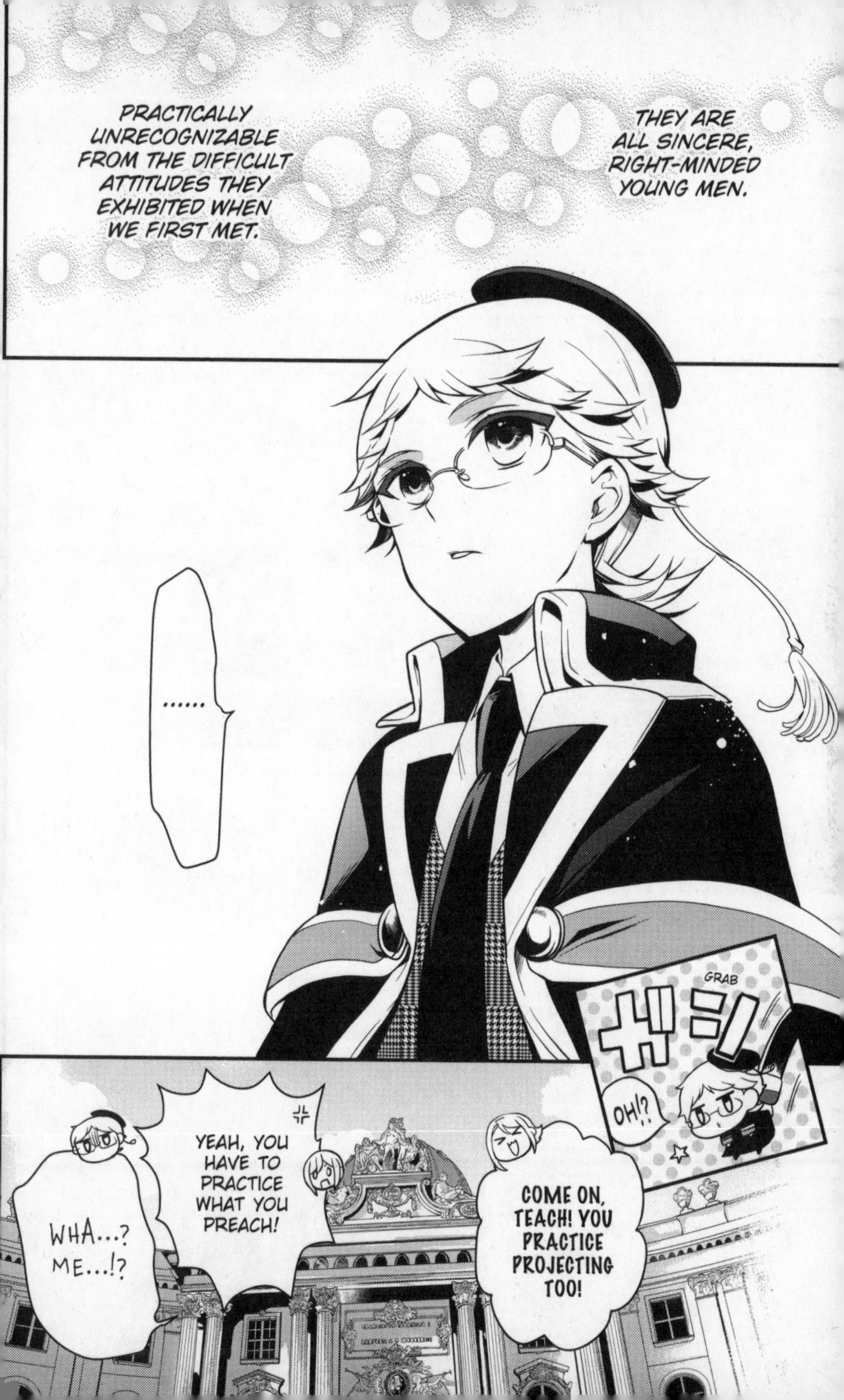
THEY ARE ALL SINCERE, RIGHT-MINDED YOUNG MEN.
PRACTICALLY UNRECOGNIZABLE FROM THE DIFFICULT ATTITUDES THEY EXHIBITED WHEN WE FIRST MET.
......
GRAB
OH!?
COME ON, TEACH! YOU PRACTICE PROJECTING TOO!
YEAH, YOU HAVE TO PRACTICE WHAT YOU PREACH!
WHA...? ME...!?

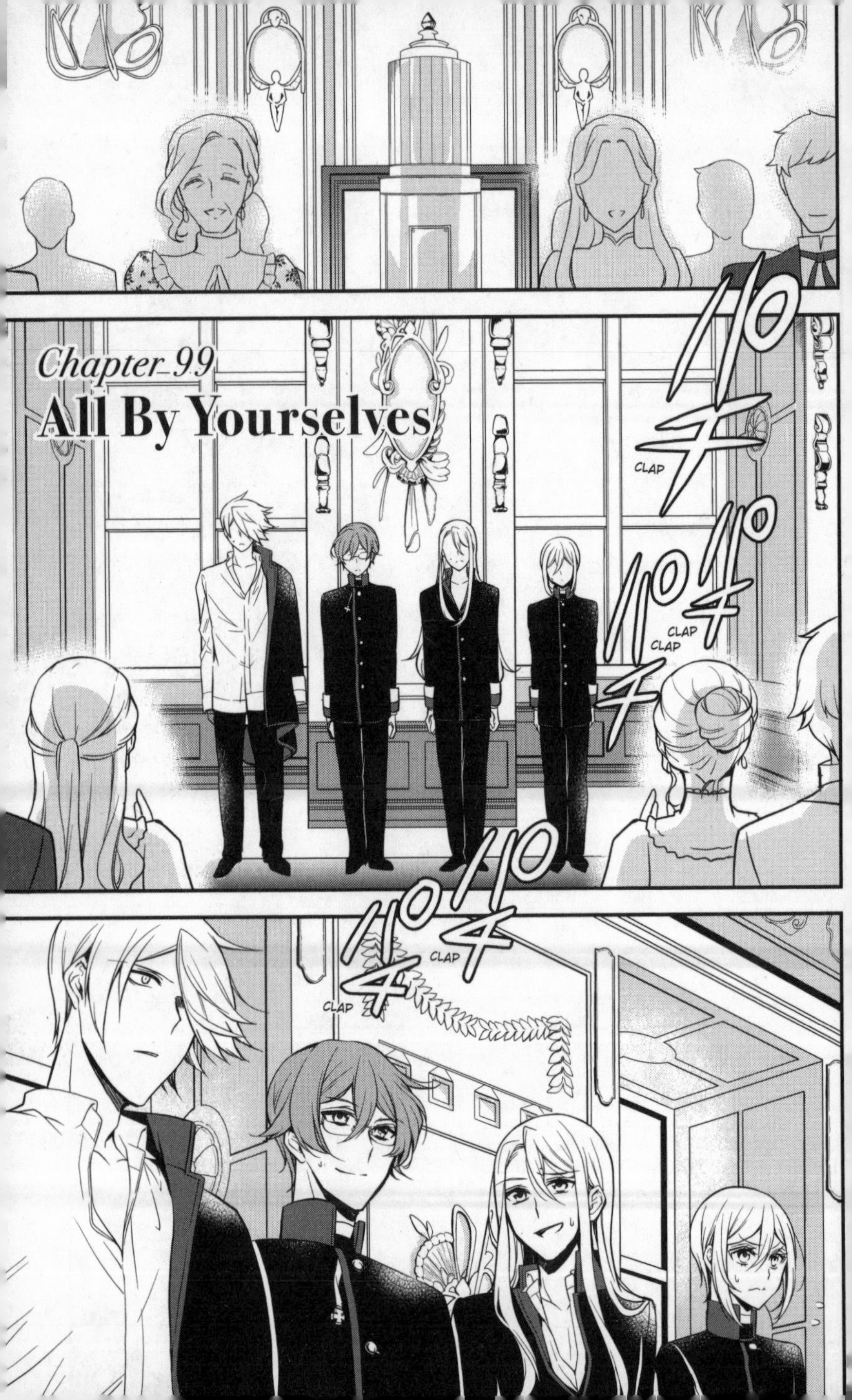

Chapter_99
All By Yourselves
パチ
CLAP
パチパチ
CLAP
CLAP
パチ
パチ
CLAP
CLAP

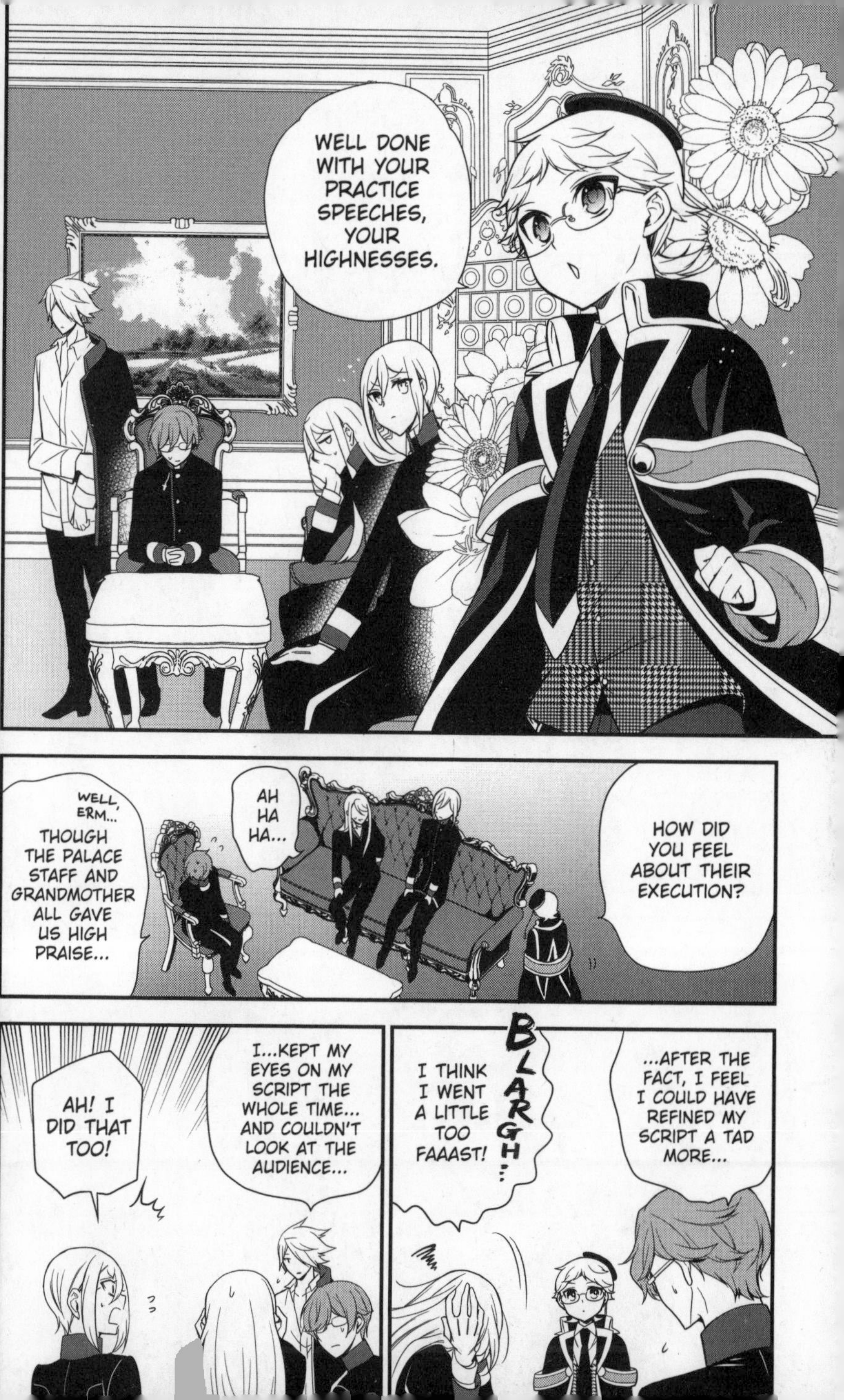
WELL DONE WITH YOUR PRACTICE SPEECHES, YOUR HIGHNESSES.
HOW DID YOU FEEL ABOUT THEIR EXECUTION?
AH HA HA...
WELL, ERM...
THOUGH THE PALACE STAFF AND GRANDMOTHER ALL GAVE US HIGH PRAISE...
...AFTER THE FACT, I FEEL I COULD HAVE REFINED MY SCRIPT A TAD MORE...
BLARGH...
I THINK I WENT A LITTLE TOO FAAAST!
I...KEPT MY EYES ON MY SCRIPT THE WHOLE TIME... AND COULDN'T LOOK AT THE AUDIENCE...
AH! I DID THAT TOO!

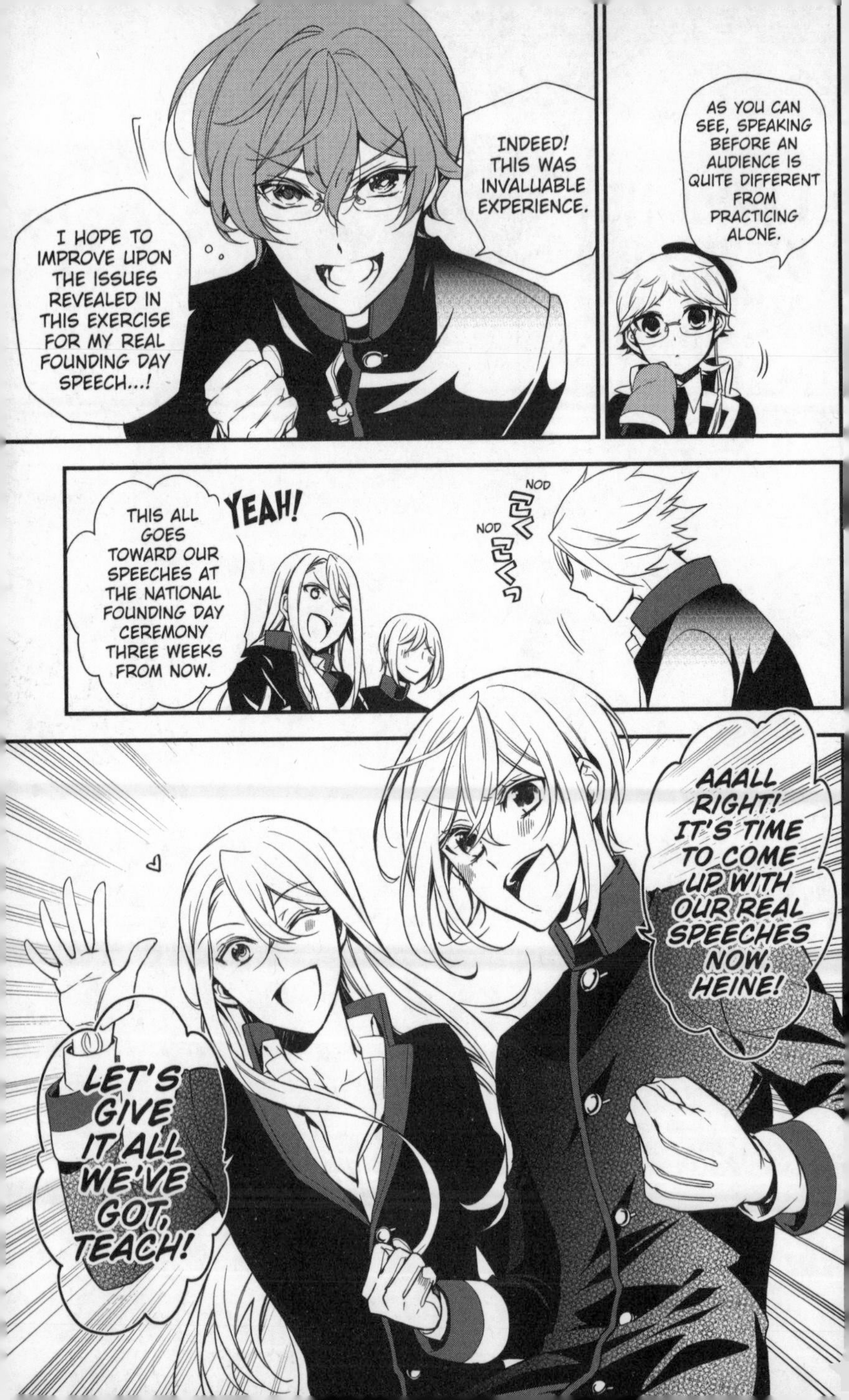
AS YOU CAN SEE, SPEAKING BEFORE AN AUDIENCE IS QUITE DIFFERENT FROM PRACTICING ALONE.
INDEED! THIS WAS INVALUABLE EXPERIENCE.
I HOPE TO IMPROVE UPON THE ISSUES REVEALED IN THIS EXERCISE FOR MY REAL FOUNDING DAY SPEECH...!
NOD
NOD
YEAH!
THIS ALL GOES TOWARD OUR SPEECHES AT THE NATIONAL FOUNDING DAY CEREMONY THREE WEEKS FROM NOW.
AAALL RIGHT! IT'S TIME TO COME UP WITH OUR REAL SPEECHES NOW, HEINE!
LET'S GIVE IT ALL WE'VE GOT, TEACH!

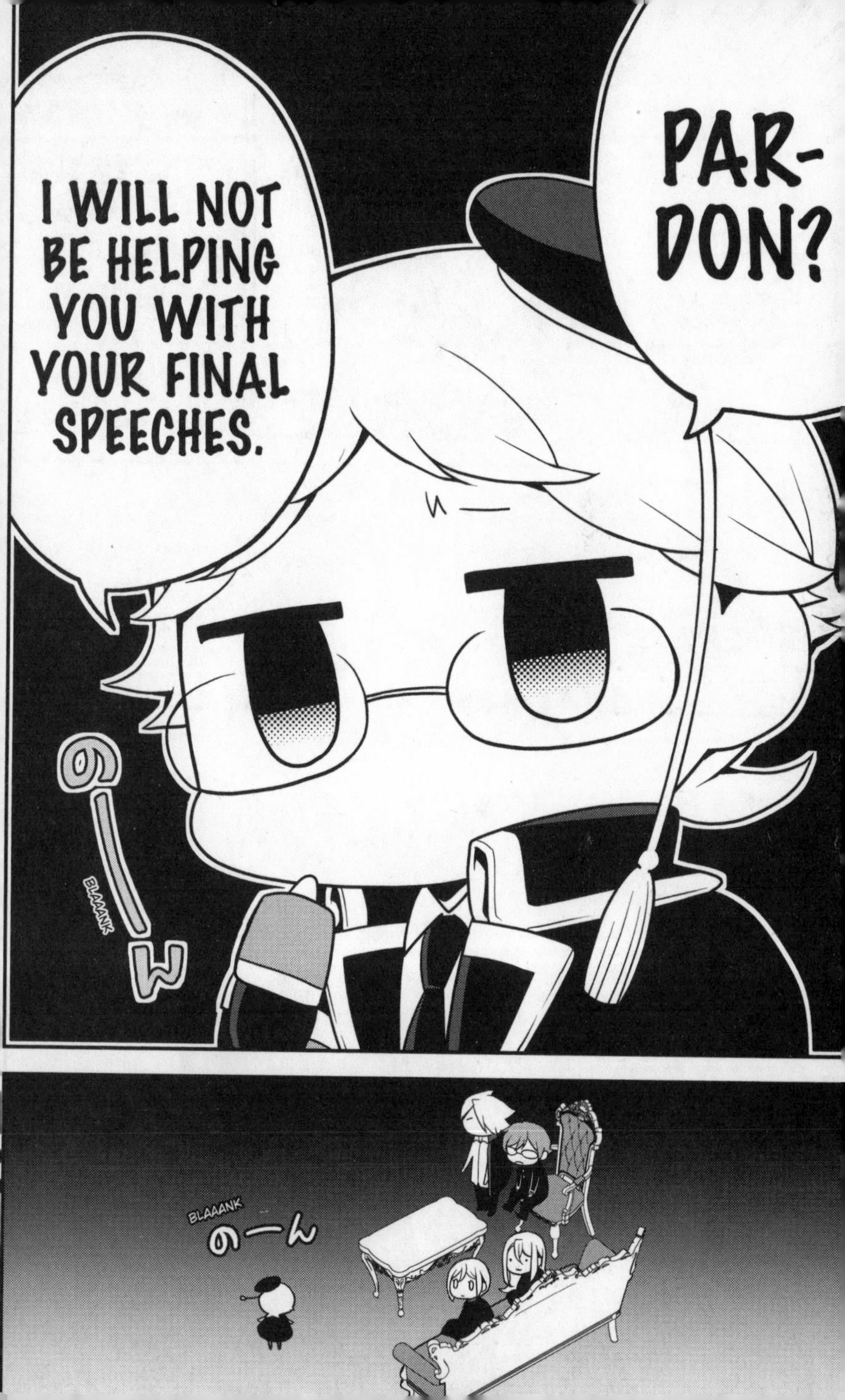
PAR-DON?
I WILL NOT BE HELPING YOU WITH YOUR FINAL SPEECHES.
のーん
BLAAANK
のーん
BLAAANK

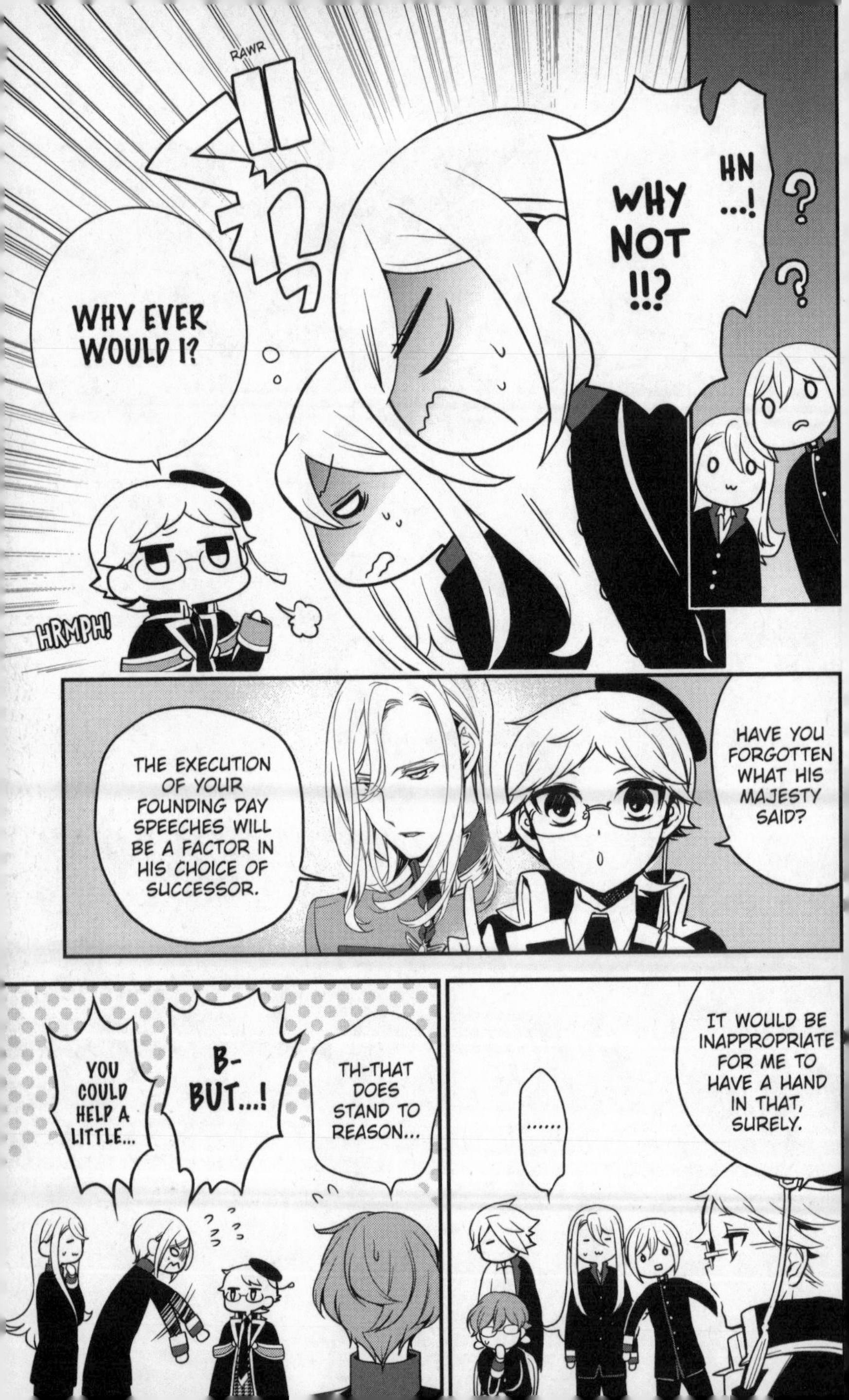
HN ...!
WHY NOT !!?
RAWR
WHY EVER WOULD I?
HRMPH!
HAVE YOU FORGOTTEN WHAT HIS MAJESTY SAID?
THE EXECUTION OF YOUR FOUNDING DAY SPEECHES WILL BE A FACTOR IN HIS CHOICE OF SUCCESSOR.
IT WOULD BE INAPPROPRIATE FOR ME TO HAVE A HAND IN THAT, SURELY.
......
TH-THAT DOES STAND TO REASON...
B-BUT...!
YOU COULD HELP A LITTLE...

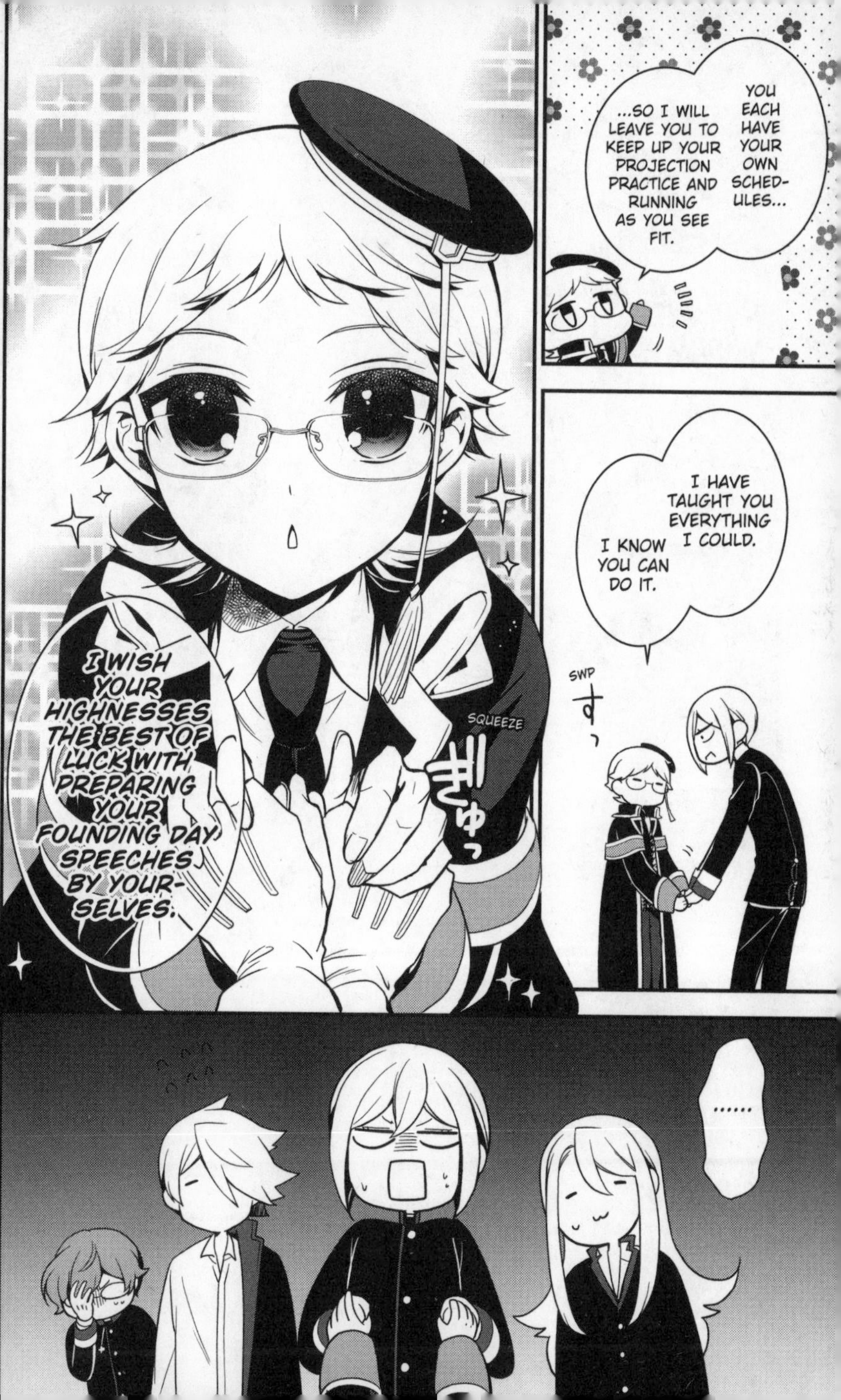
YOU EACH HAVE YOUR OWN SCHEDULES...
...SO I WILL LEAVE YOU TO KEEP UP YOUR PROJECTION PRACTICE AND RUNNING AS YOU SEE FIT.
I HAVE TAUGHT YOU EVERYTHING I COULD.
I KNOW YOU CAN DO IT.
SWP
すっ
SQUEEZE
ぎゅっ
I WISH YOUR HIGHNESSES THE BEST OF LUCK WITH PREPARING YOUR FOUNDING DAY SPEECHES BY YOURSELVES.
......

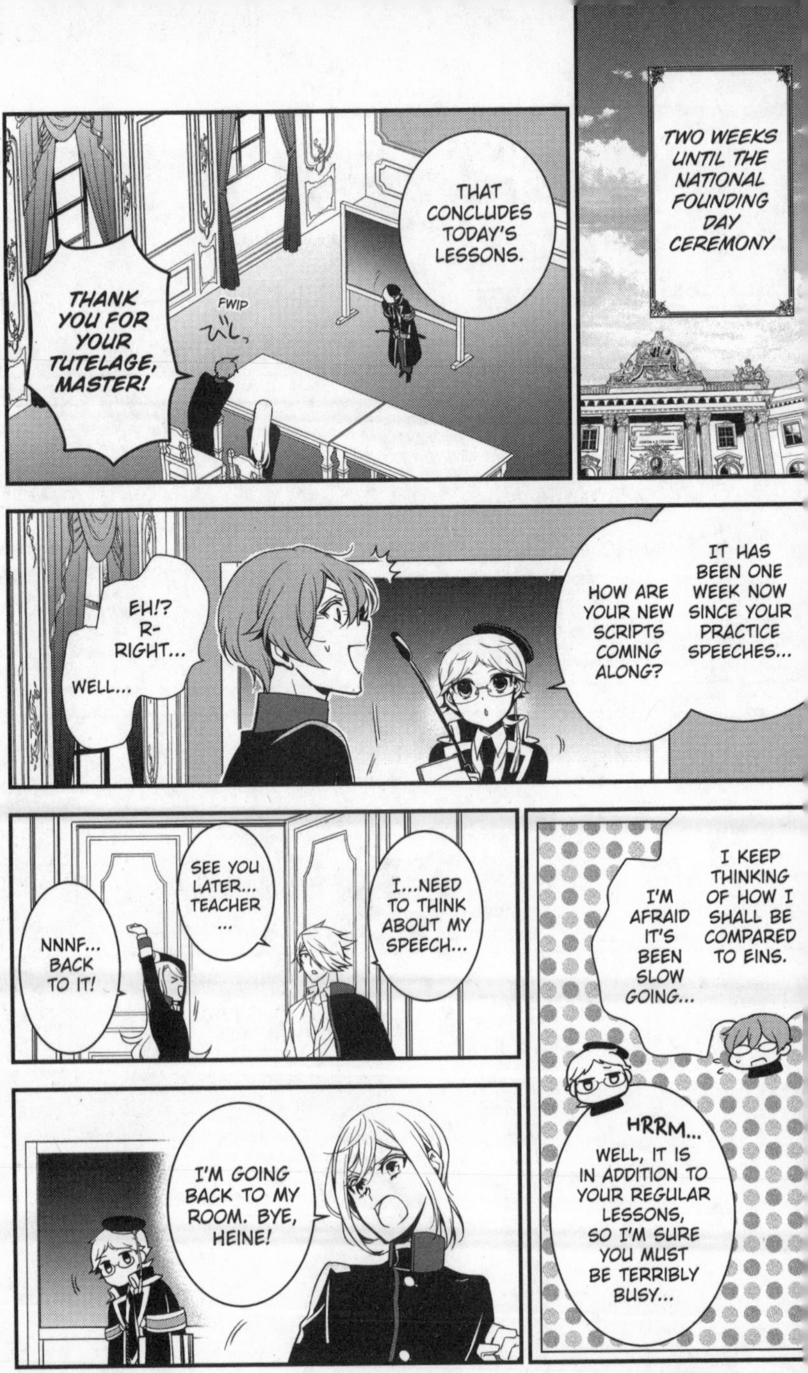
TWO WEEKS UNTIL THE NATIONAL FOUNDING DAY CEREMONY
THAT CONCLUDES TODAY'S LESSONS.
THANK YOU FOR YOUR TUTELAGE, MASTER!
FWIP
IT HAS BEEN ONE WEEK NOW SINCE YOUR PRACTICE SPEECHES...
HOW ARE YOUR NEW SCRIPTS COMING ALONG?
EH!? R-RIGHT...
WELL...
I KEEP THINKING OF HOW I SHALL BE COMPARED TO EINS.
I'M AFRAID IT'S BEEN SLOW GOING...
HRRM...
WELL, IT IS IN ADDITION TO YOUR REGULAR LESSONS, SO I'M SURE YOU MUST BE TERRIBLY BUSY...
I...NEED TO THINK ABOUT MY SPEECH...
SEE YOU LATER... TEACHER...
NNNF... BACK TO IT!
I'M GOING BACK TO MY ROOM. BYE, HEINE!

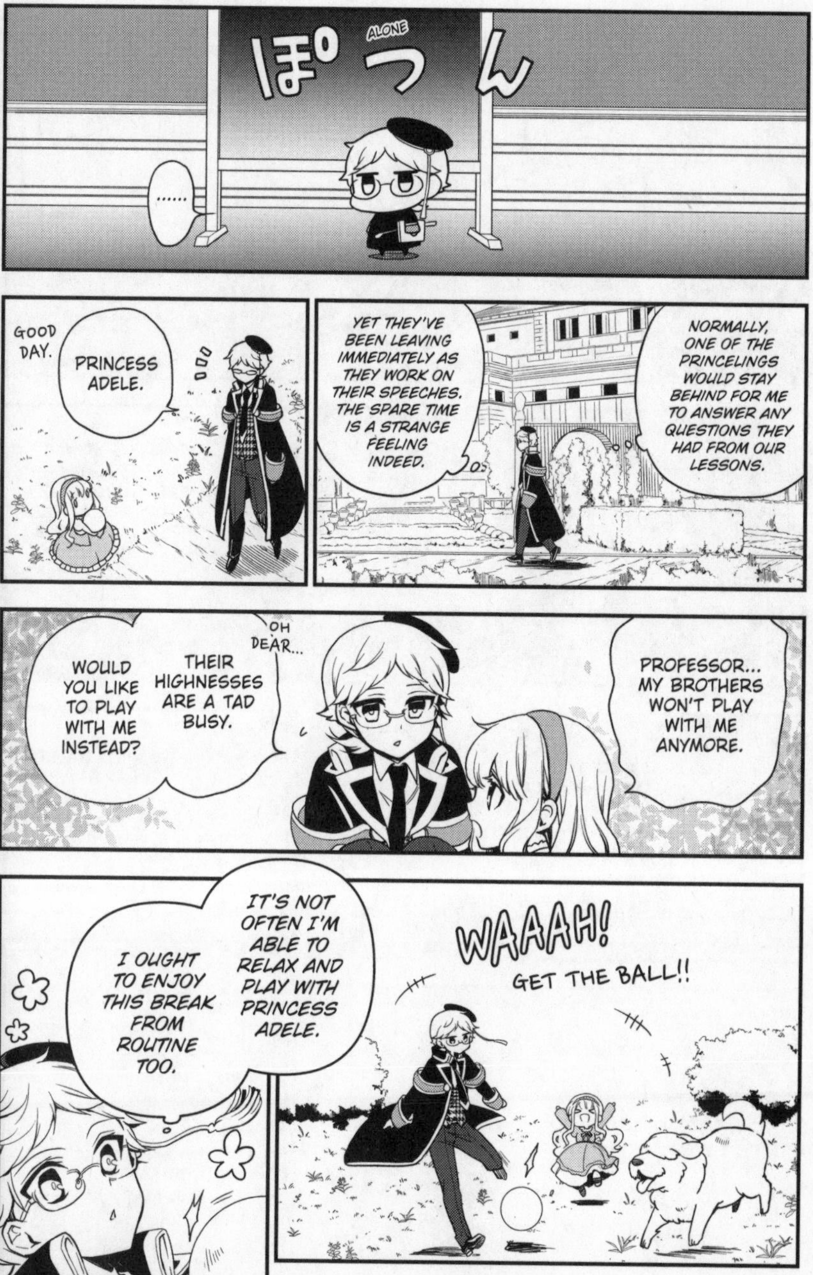
ぽつん
ALONE
......
NORMALLY, ONE OF THE PRINCELINGS WOULD STAY BEHIND FOR ME TO ANSWER ANY QUESTIONS THEY HAD FROM OUR LESSONS.
YET THEY'VE BEEN LEAVING IMMEDIATELY AS THEY WORK ON THEIR SPEECHES. THE SPARE TIME IS A STRANGE FEELING INDEED.
PRINCESS ADELE.
GOOD DAY.
PROFESSOR... MY BROTHERS WON'T PLAY WITH ME ANYMORE.
OH DEAR...
THEIR HIGHNESSES ARE A TAD BUSY.
WOULD YOU LIKE TO PLAY WITH ME INSTEAD?
WAAAH!
GET THE BALL!!
IT'S NOT OFTEN I'M ABLE TO RELAX AND PLAY WITH PRINCESS ADELE.
I OUGHT TO ENJOY THIS BREAK FROM ROUTINE TOO.

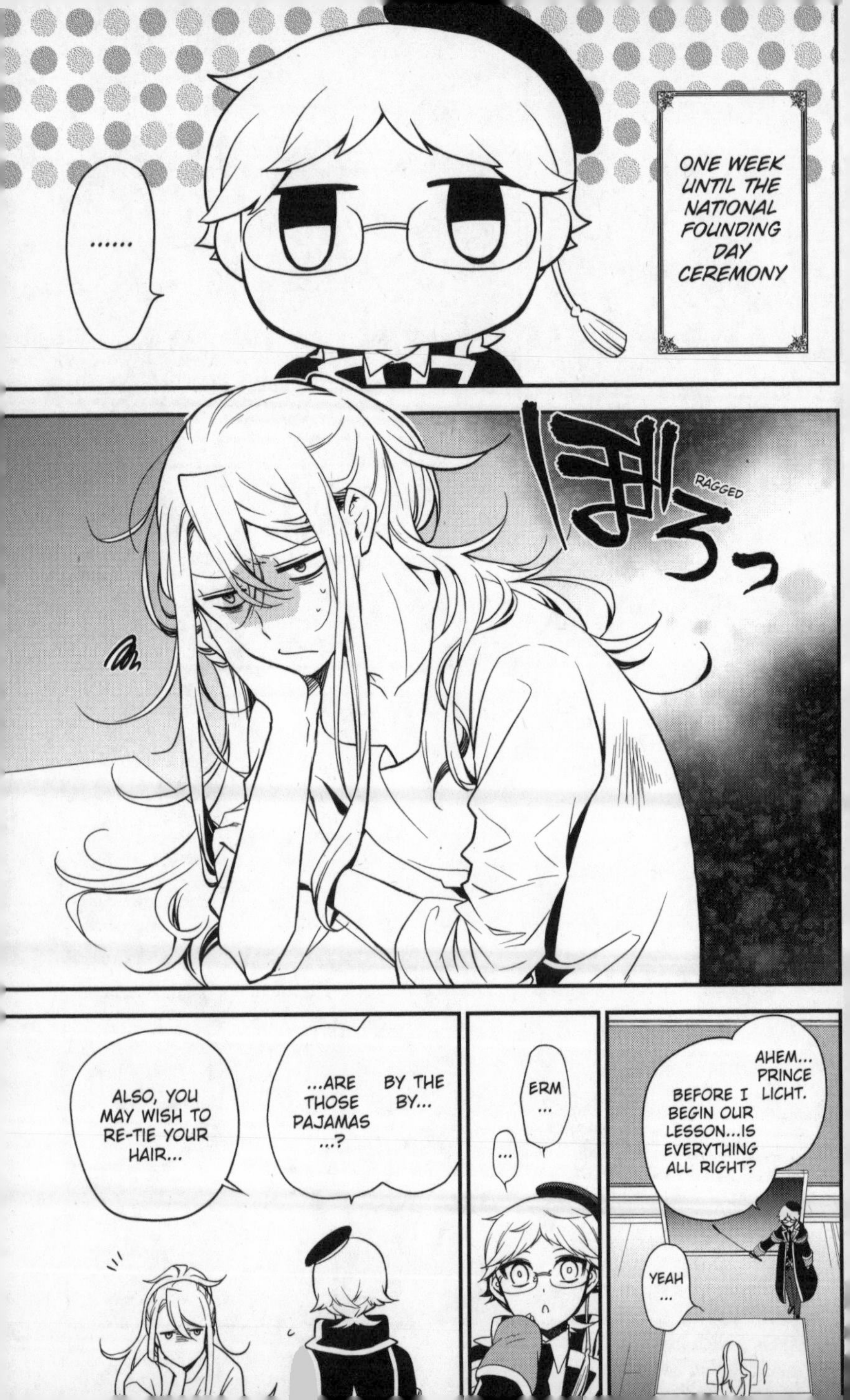
ONE WEEK UNTIL THE NATIONAL FOUNDING DAY CEREMONY
......
ぼろっ
RAGGED
AHEM... PRINCE LICHT.
BEFORE I BEGIN OUR LESSON...IS EVERYTHING ALL RIGHT?
YEAH ...
ERM ...
...
BY THE BY...
...ARE THOSE PAJAMAS ...?
ALSO, YOU MAY WISH TO RE-TIE YOUR HAIR...

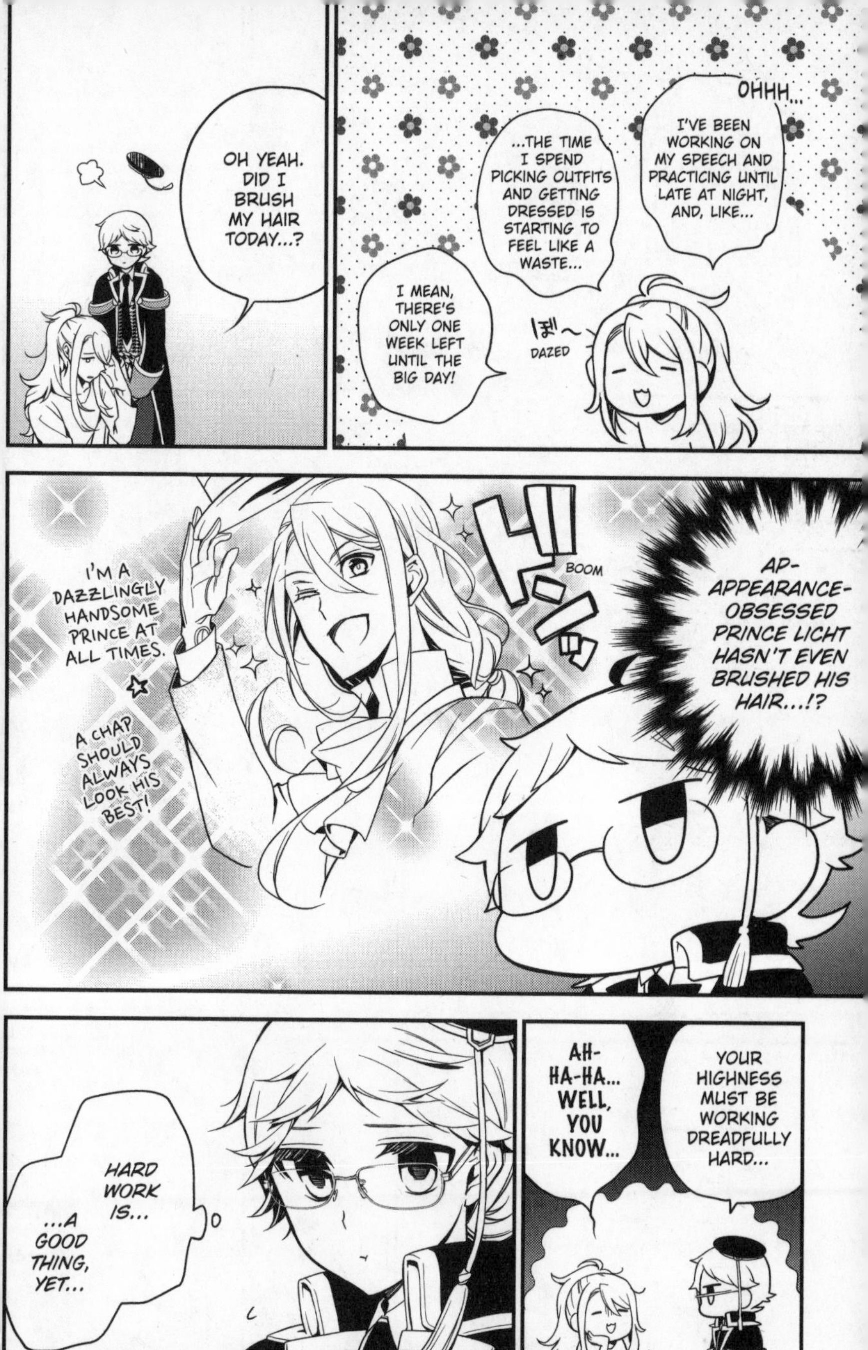
OHHH...
I'VE BEEN WORKING ON MY SPEECH AND PRACTICING UNTIL LATE AT NIGHT, AND, LIKE...
...THE TIME I SPEND PICKING OUTFITS AND GETTING DRESSED IS STARTING TO FEEL LIKE A WASTE...
ぼ~ DAZED
I MEAN, THERE'S ONLY ONE WEEK LEFT UNTIL THE BIG DAY!
OH YEAH. DID I BRUSH MY HAIR TODAY...?
AP-APPEARANCE-OBSESSED PRINCE LICHT HASN'T EVEN BRUSHED HIS HAIR...!?
ドーン BOOM
I'M A DAZZLINGLY HANDSOME PRINCE AT ALL TIMES. ☆
A CHAP SHOULD ALWAYS LOOK HIS BEST!
YOUR HIGHNESS MUST BE WORKING DREADFULLY HARD...
AH-HA-HA... WELL, YOU KNOW...
HARD WORK IS...
...A GOOD THING, YET...

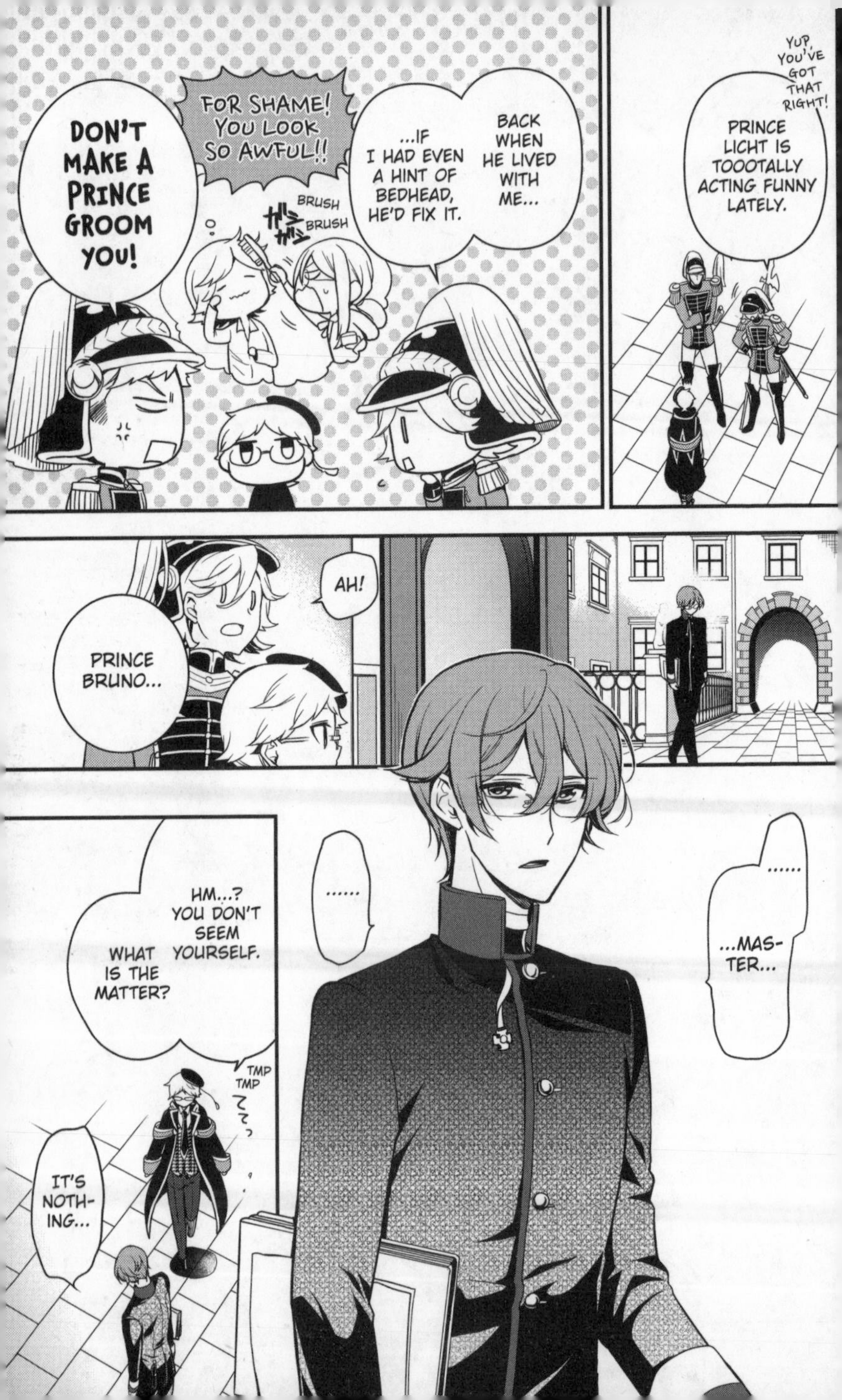
PRINCE LICHT IS TOOOTALLY ACTING FUNNY LATELY.
YUP, YOU'VE GOT THAT RIGHT!
BACK WHEN HE LIVED WITH ME...
...IF I HAD EVEN A HINT OF BEDHEAD, HE'D FIX IT.
FOR SHAME! YOU LOOK SO AWFUL!!
BRUSH BRUSH
DON'T MAKE A PRINCE GROOM YOU!
AH!
PRINCE BRUNO...
......
...MAS- TER...
......
HM...? YOU DON'T SEEM YOURSELF. WHAT IS THE MATTER?
TMP TMP
IT'S NOTH- ING...

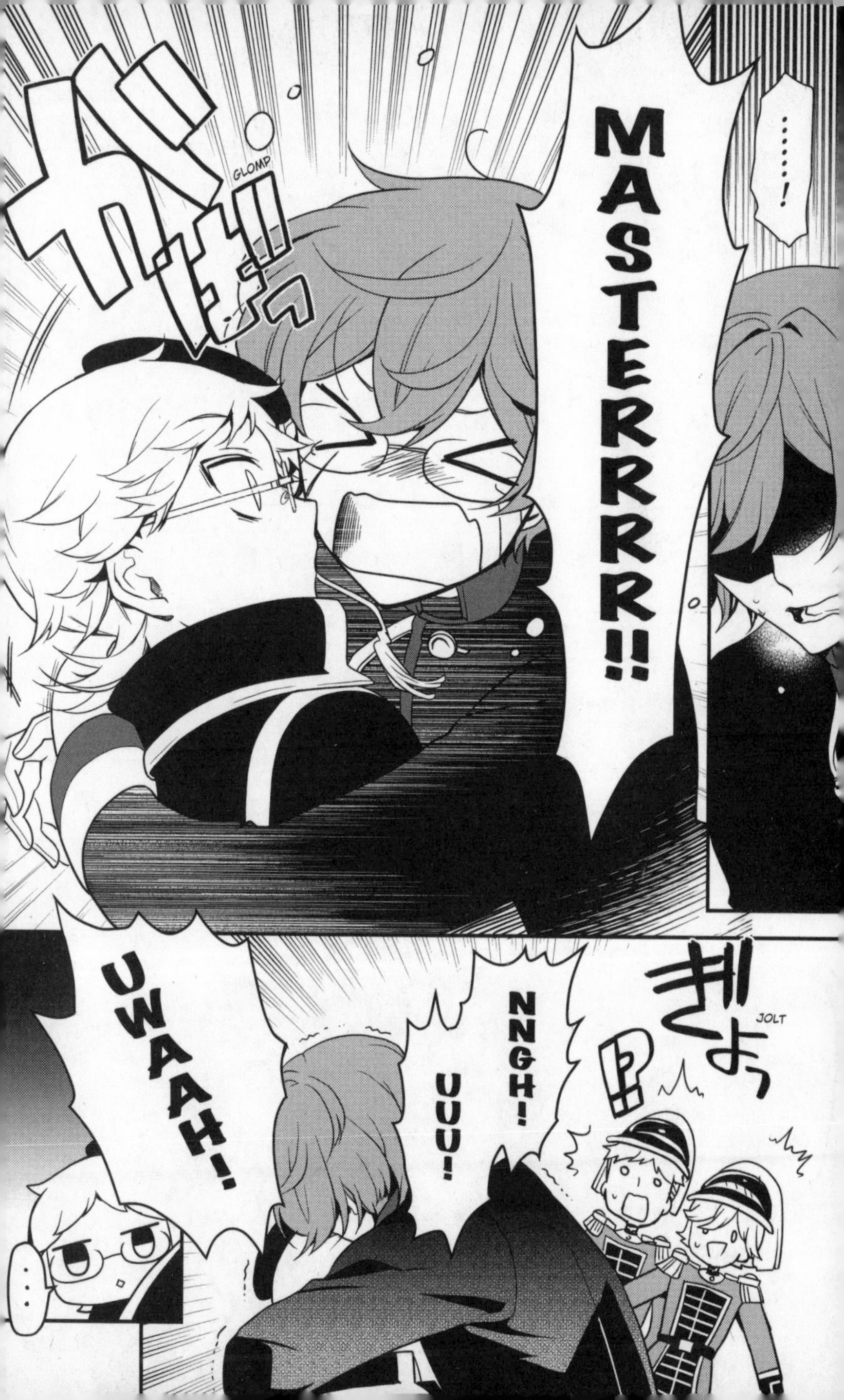
......!
MASTERRRR!!
GLOMP
ぎょっ
JOLT
?!
NNGH!
UUU!
UWAAH!
...

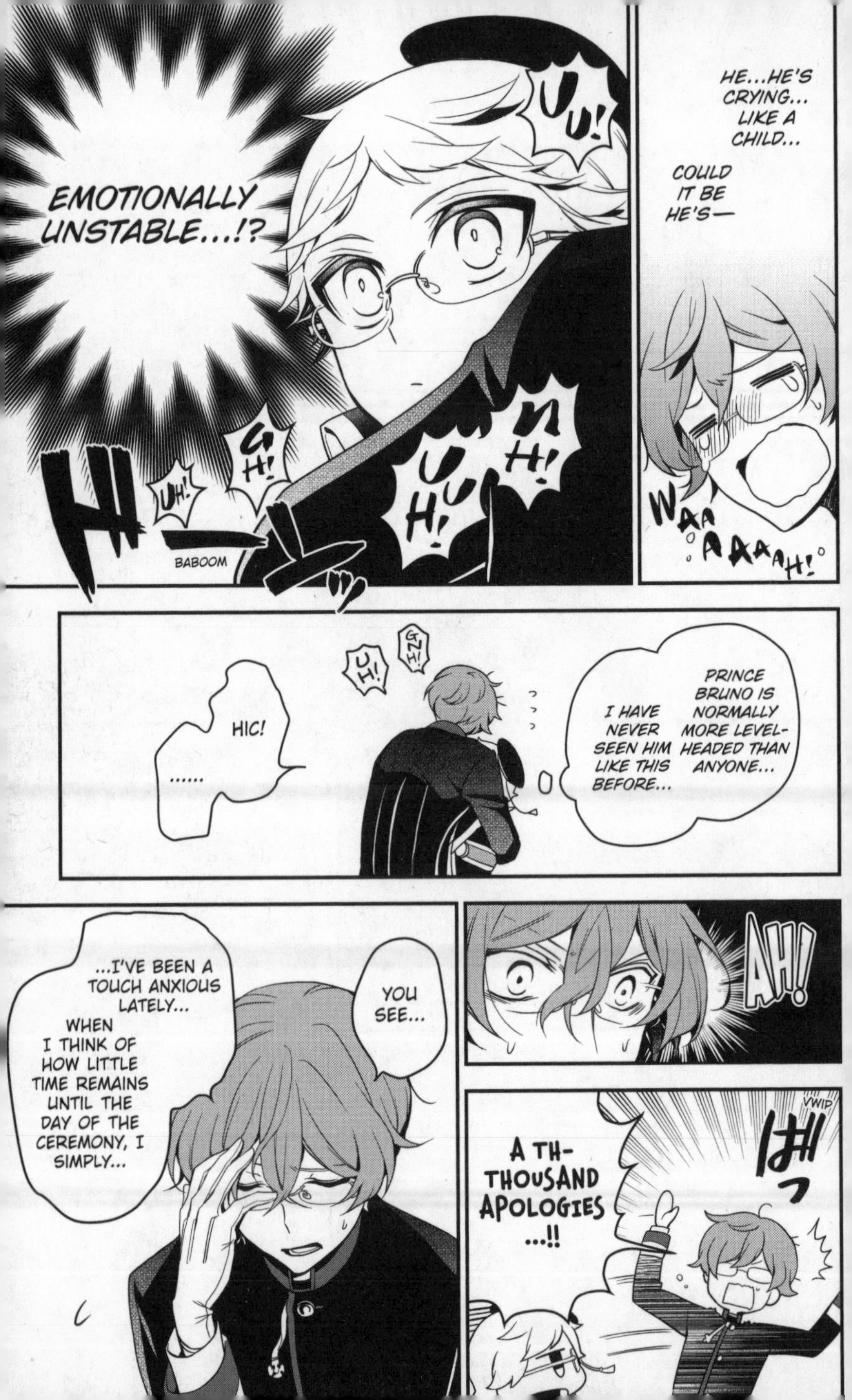
HE...HE'S CRYING... LIKE A CHILD...
COULD IT BE HE'S—
WAAAAAAAH!
UU!
EMOTIONALLY UNSTABLE...!?
NH!
UUH!
GH!
UH!
H—
BABOOM
PRINCE BRUNO IS NORMALLY MORE LEVEL-HEADED THAN ANYONE...
I HAVE NEVER SEEN HIM LIKE THIS BEFORE...
GNH!
UH!
HIC!
......
AH!
VWIP
はっ
A TH-THOUSAND APOLOGIES...!!
YOU SEE...
...I'VE BEEN A TOUCH ANXIOUS LATELY...
WHEN I THINK OF HOW LITTLE TIME REMAINS UNTIL THE DAY OF THE CEREMONY, I SIMPLY...

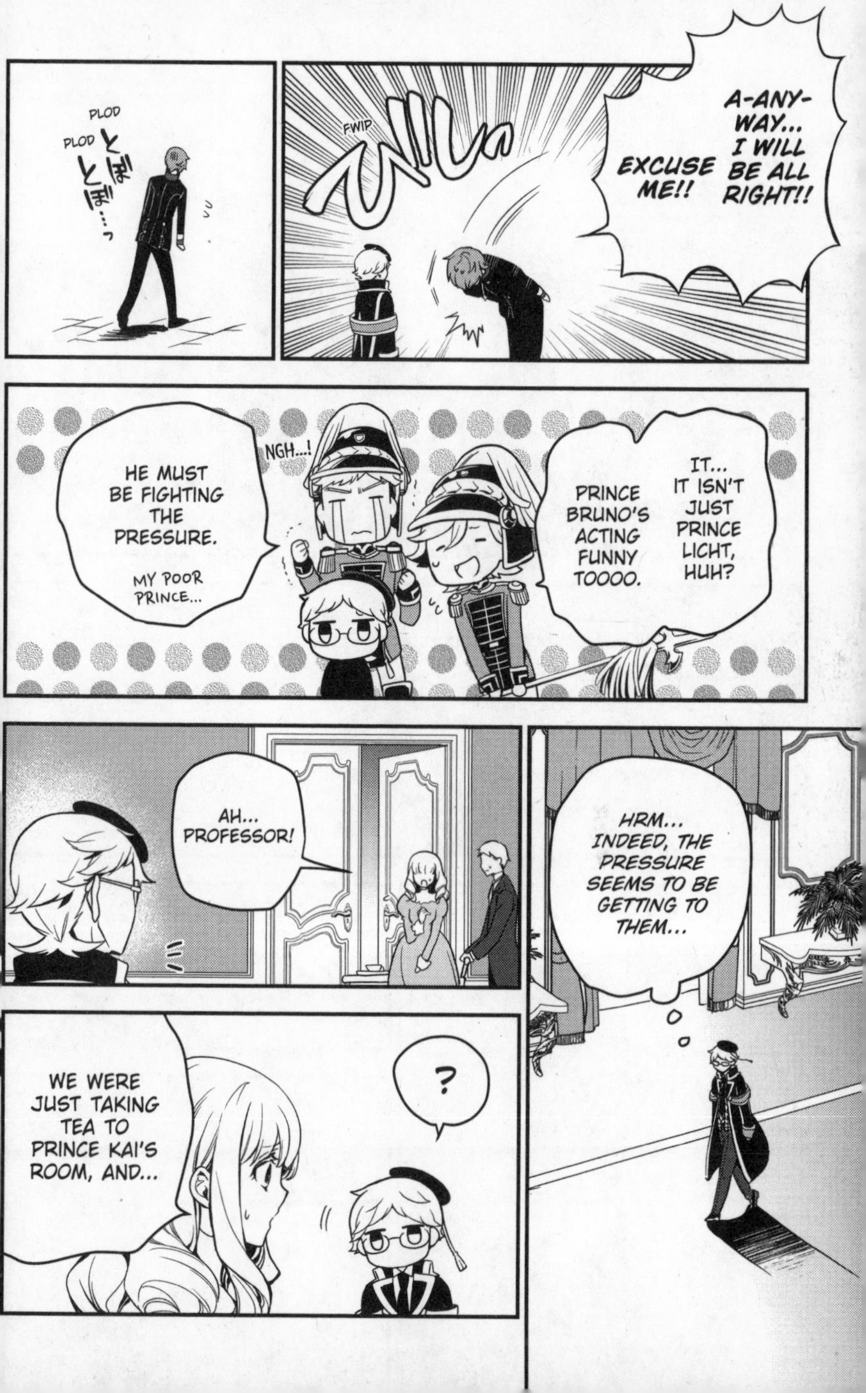
A-ANYWAY... I WILL BE ALL RIGHT!!
EXCUSE ME!!
FWIP
PLOD
PLOD
IT... IT ISN'T JUST PRINCE LICHT, HUH?
PRINCE BRUNO'S ACTING FUNNY TOOOO.
NGH...!
HE MUST BE FIGHTING THE PRESSURE.
MY POOR PRINCE...
HRM... INDEED, THE PRESSURE SEEMS TO BE GETTING TO THEM...
AH... PROFESSOR!
?
WE WERE JUST TAKING TEA TO PRINCE KAI'S ROOM, AND...

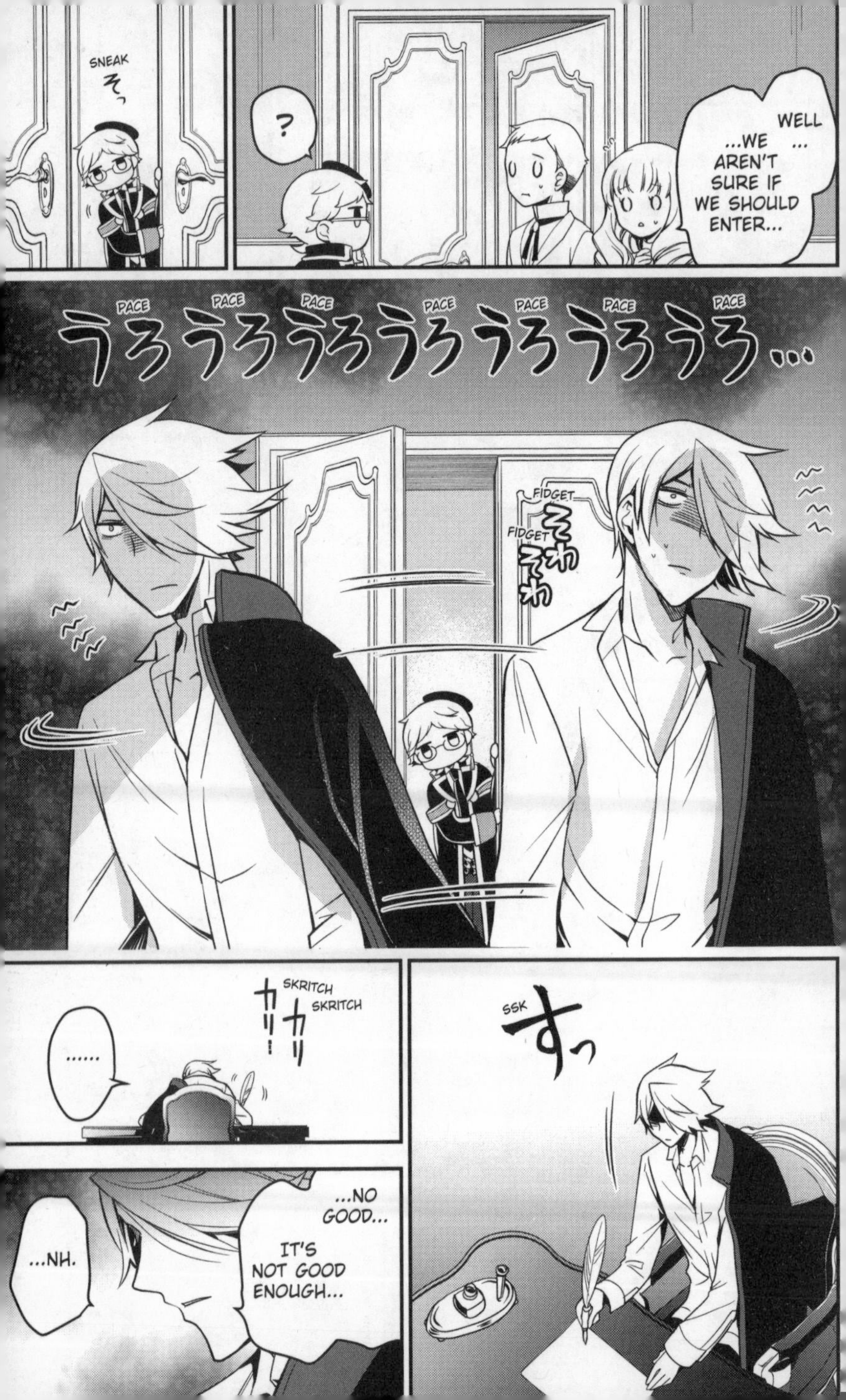
WELL... ...WE AREN'T SURE IF WE SHOULD ENTER...
?
SNEAK
そっ
PACE PACE PACE PACE PACE PACE PACE
うろうろうろうろうろうろうろうろ...
FIDGET FIDGET
そわそわ
SSK
すっ
SKRITCH SKRITCH
カリカリ
......
...NO GOOD...
IT'S NOT GOOD ENOUGH...
...NH.

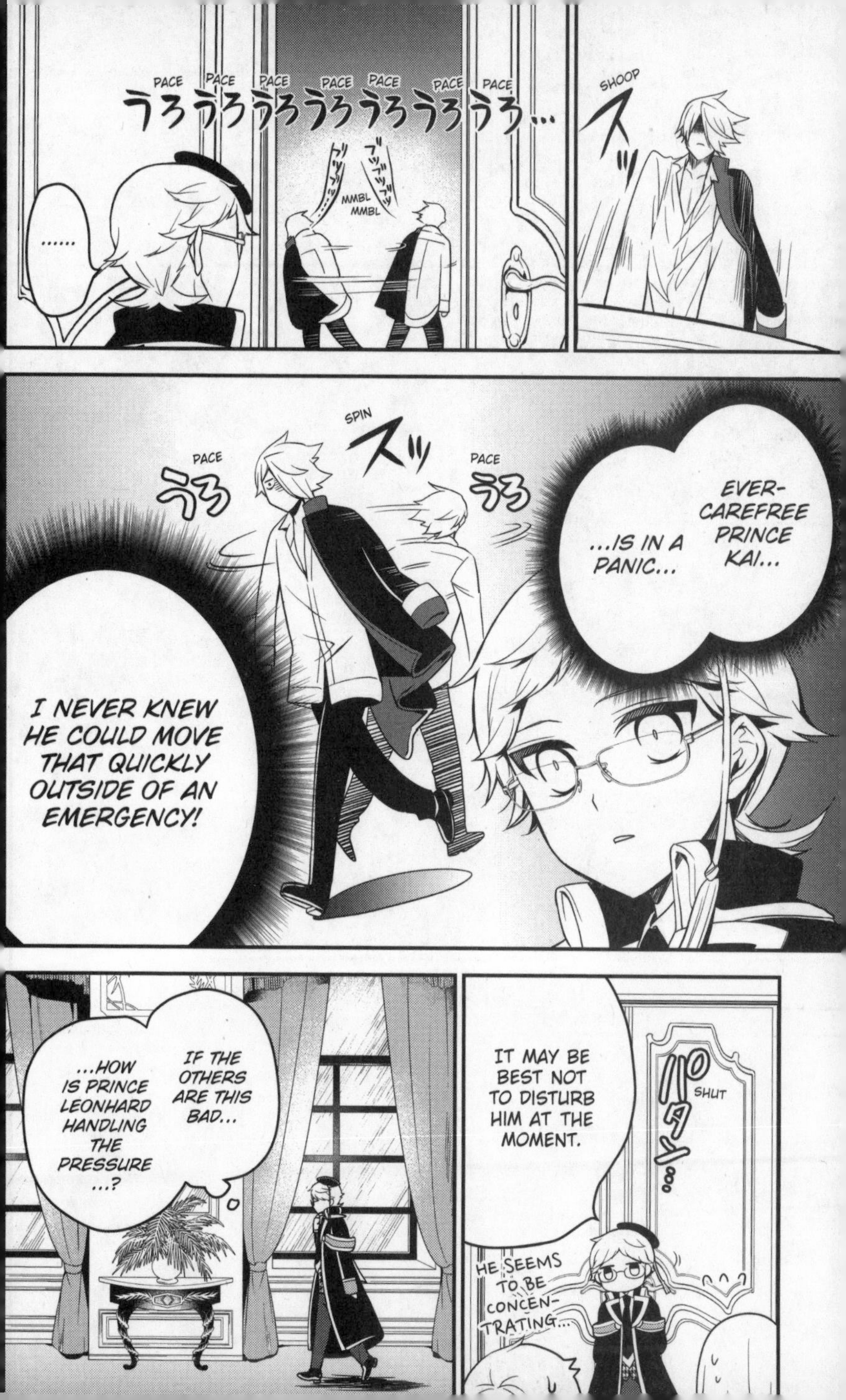
SHOOP
ズッ
PACE PACE PACE PACE PACE PACE PACE
うろうろうろうろうろうろうろ…
MMBL MMBL
ブツブツ
……
EVER-CAREFREE PRINCE KAI…
…IS IN A PANIC…
PACE
うろ
SPIN
スッ
PACE
うろ
I NEVER KNEW HE COULD MOVE THAT QUICKLY OUTSIDE OF AN EMERGENCY!
IT MAY BE BEST NOT TO DISTURB HIM AT THE MOMENT.
SHUT
パタン…
HE SEEMS TO BE CONCENTRATING…
IF THE OTHERS ARE THIS BAD…
…HOW IS PRINCE LEONHARD HANDLING THE PRESSURE…?

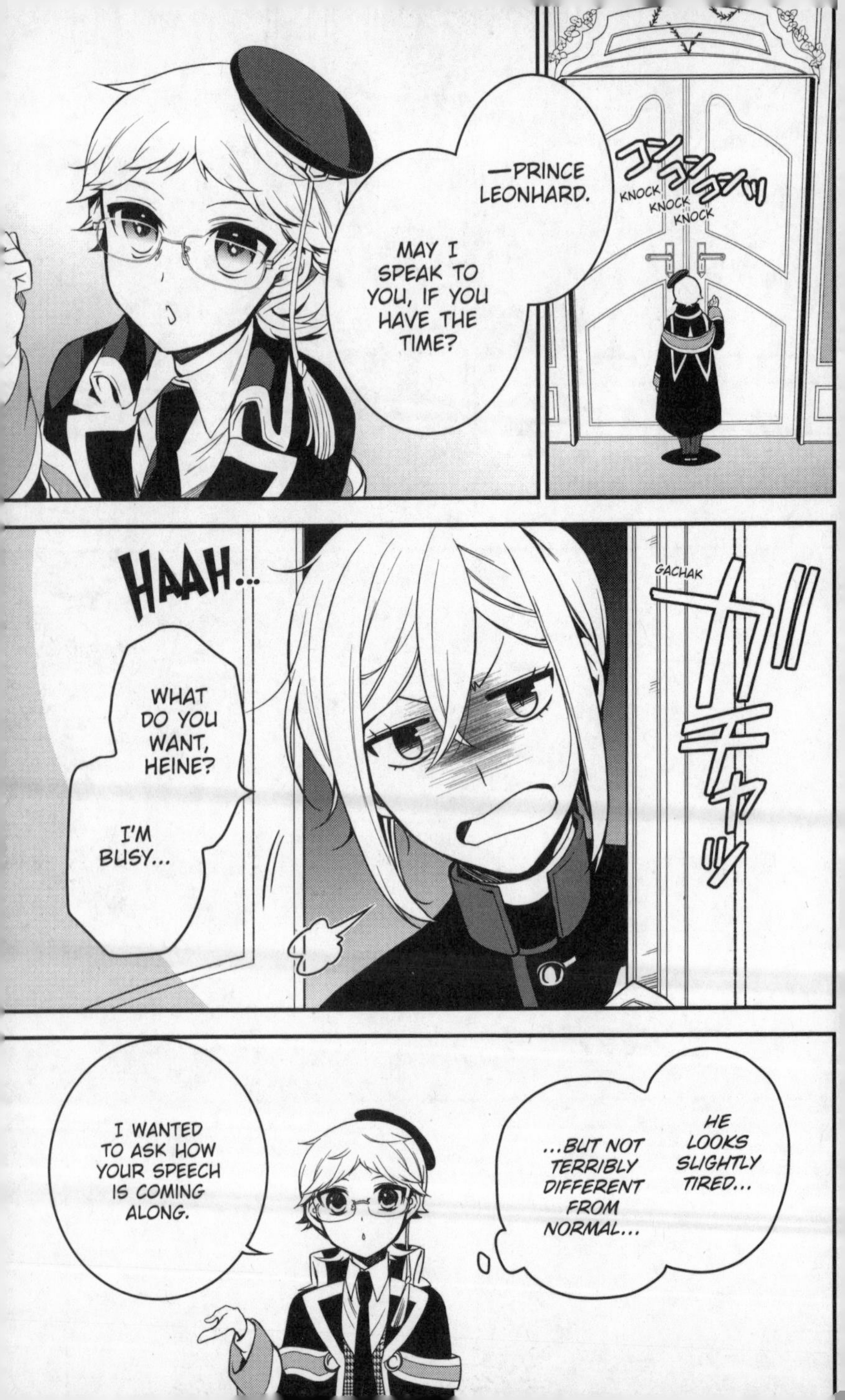
KNOCK KNOCK KNOCK
—PRINCE LEONHARD.
MAY I SPEAK TO YOU, IF YOU HAVE THE TIME?
GACHAK
HAAH...
WHAT DO YOU WANT, HEINE?
I'M BUSY...
HE LOOKS SLIGHTLY TIRED...
...BUT NOT TERRIBLY DIFFERENT FROM NORMAL...
I WANTED TO ASK HOW YOUR SPEECH IS COMING ALONG.

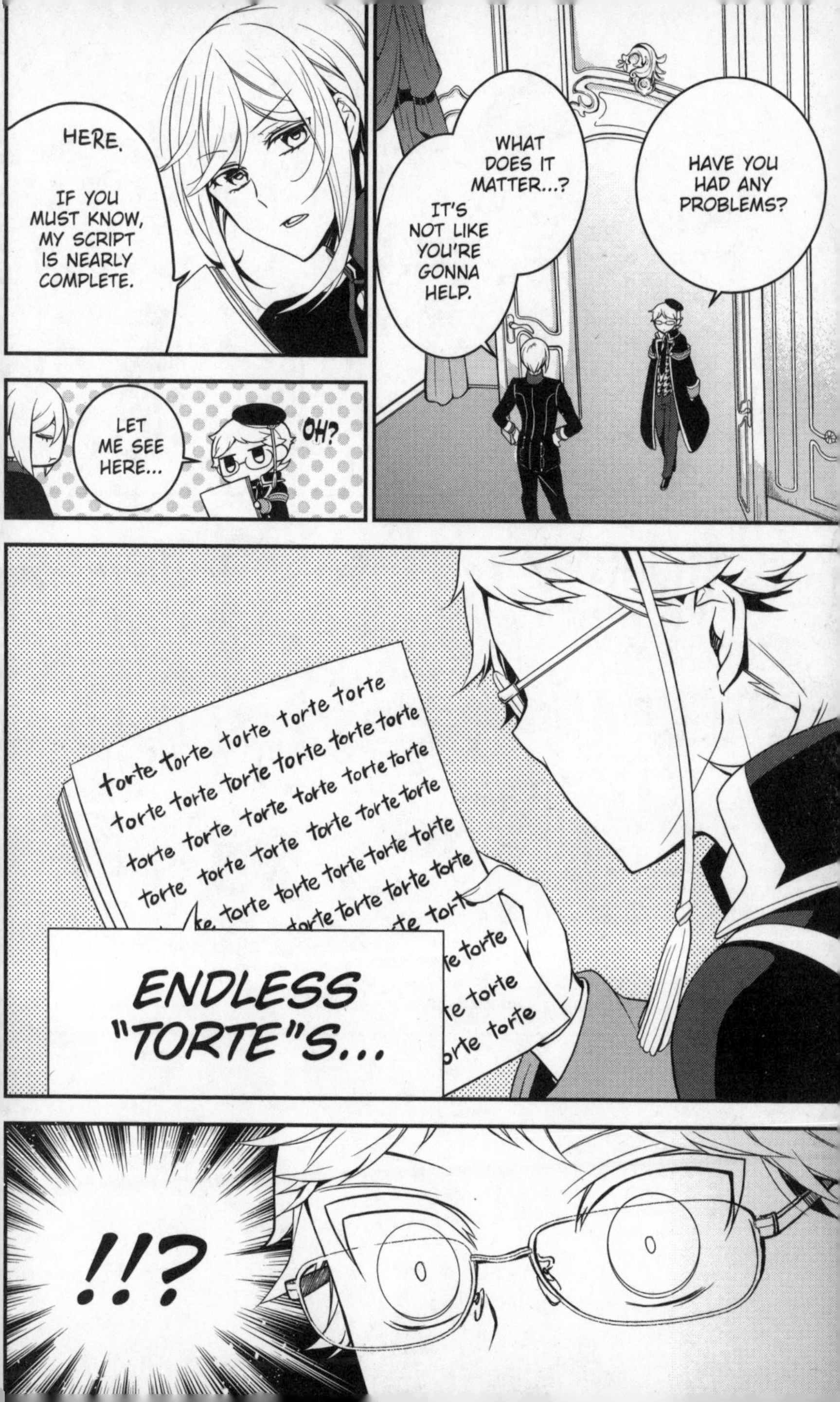
HAVE YOU HAD ANY PROBLEMS?
WHAT DOES IT MATTER...?
IT'S NOT LIKE YOU'RE GONNA HELP.
HERE.
IF YOU MUST KNOW, MY SCRIPT IS NEARLY COMPLETE.
OH?
LET ME SEE HERE...
torte torte torte torte torte
torte torte torte torte torte torte
torte torte torte torte torte torte
torte torte torte torte torte torte
torte torte torte torte torte torte
ENDLESS "TORTE"S...
!!?

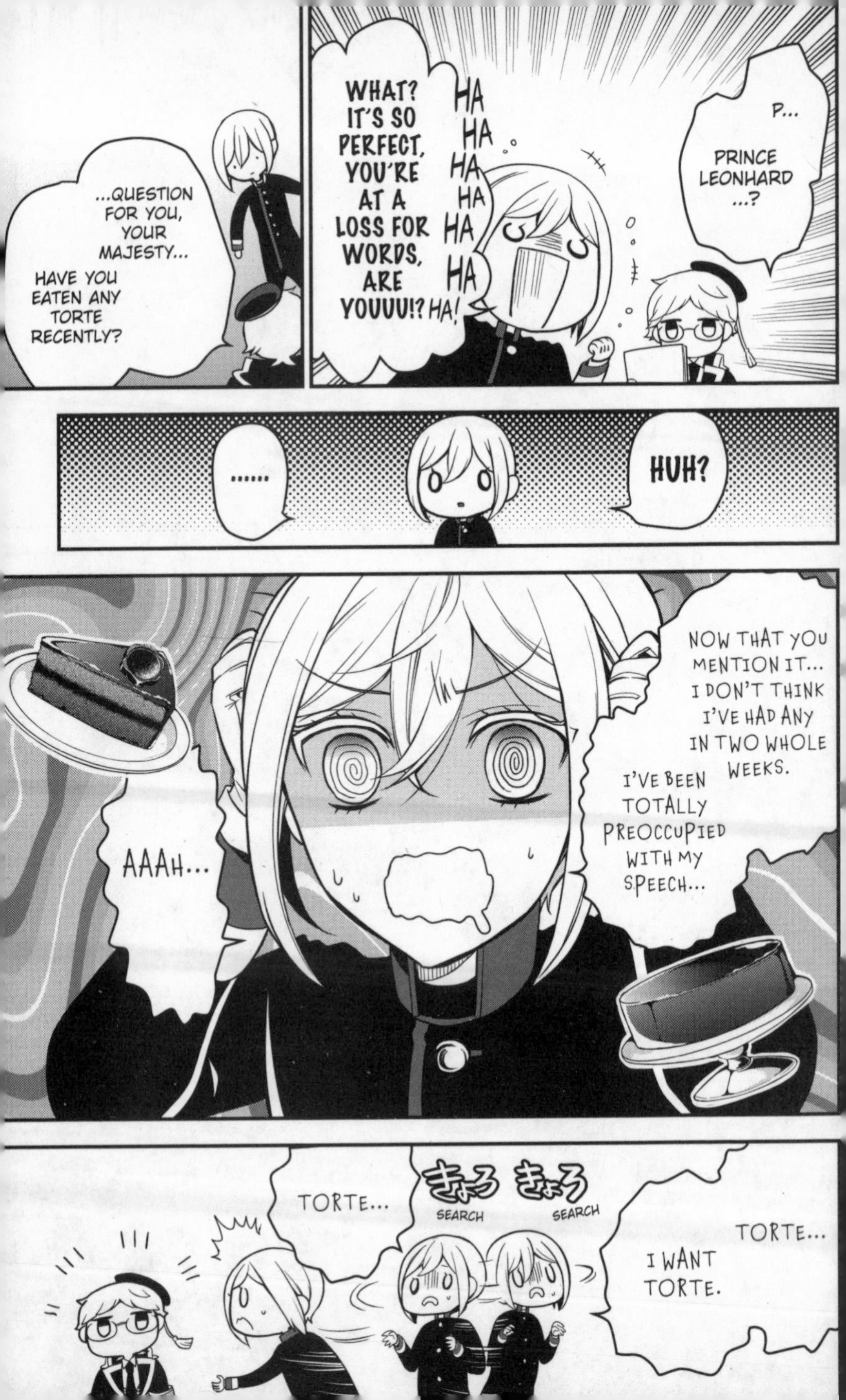
P...
PRINCE LEONHARD...?
WHAT? IT'S SO PERFECT, YOU'RE AT A LOSS FOR WORDS, ARE YOUUU!?
HA HA HA HA HA HA HA!
...QUESTION FOR YOU, YOUR MAJESTY...
HAVE YOU EATEN ANY TORTE RECENTLY?
HUH?
......
NOW THAT YOU MENTION IT... I DON'T THINK I'VE HAD ANY IN TWO WHOLE WEEKS.
I'VE BEEN TOTALLY PREOCCUPIED WITH MY SPEECH...
AAAH...
TORTE...
I WANT TORTE.
きょろ きょろ
SEARCH
SEARCH
TORTE...

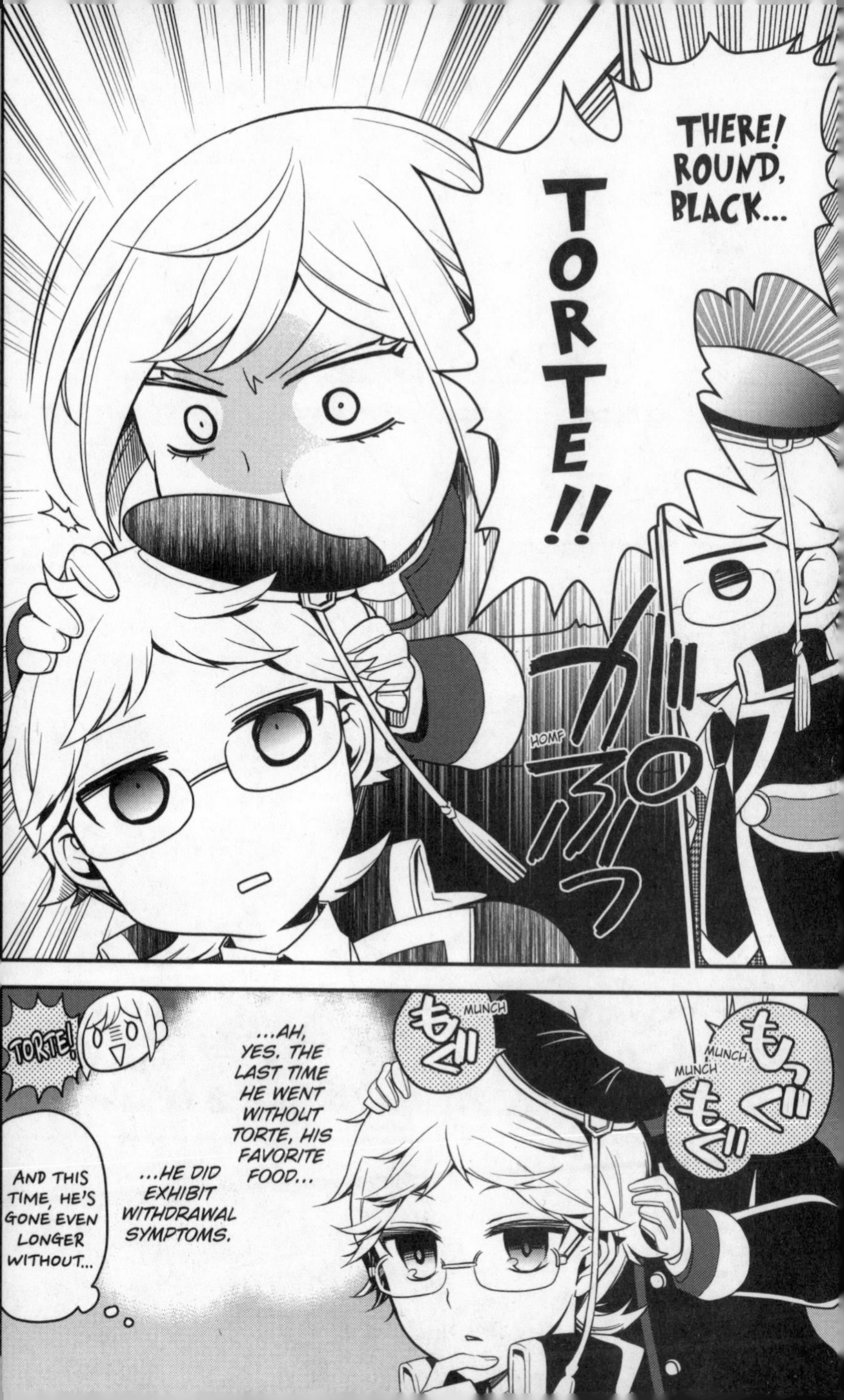
THERE! ROUND, BLACK...
TORTE!!
HOMF
...AH, YES. THE LAST TIME HE WENT WITHOUT TORTE, HIS FAVORITE FOOD...
...HE DID EXHIBIT WITHDRAWAL SYMPTOMS.
MUNCH
MUNCH
MUNCH
TORTE!
AND THIS TIME, HE'S GONE EVEN LONGER WITHOUT...

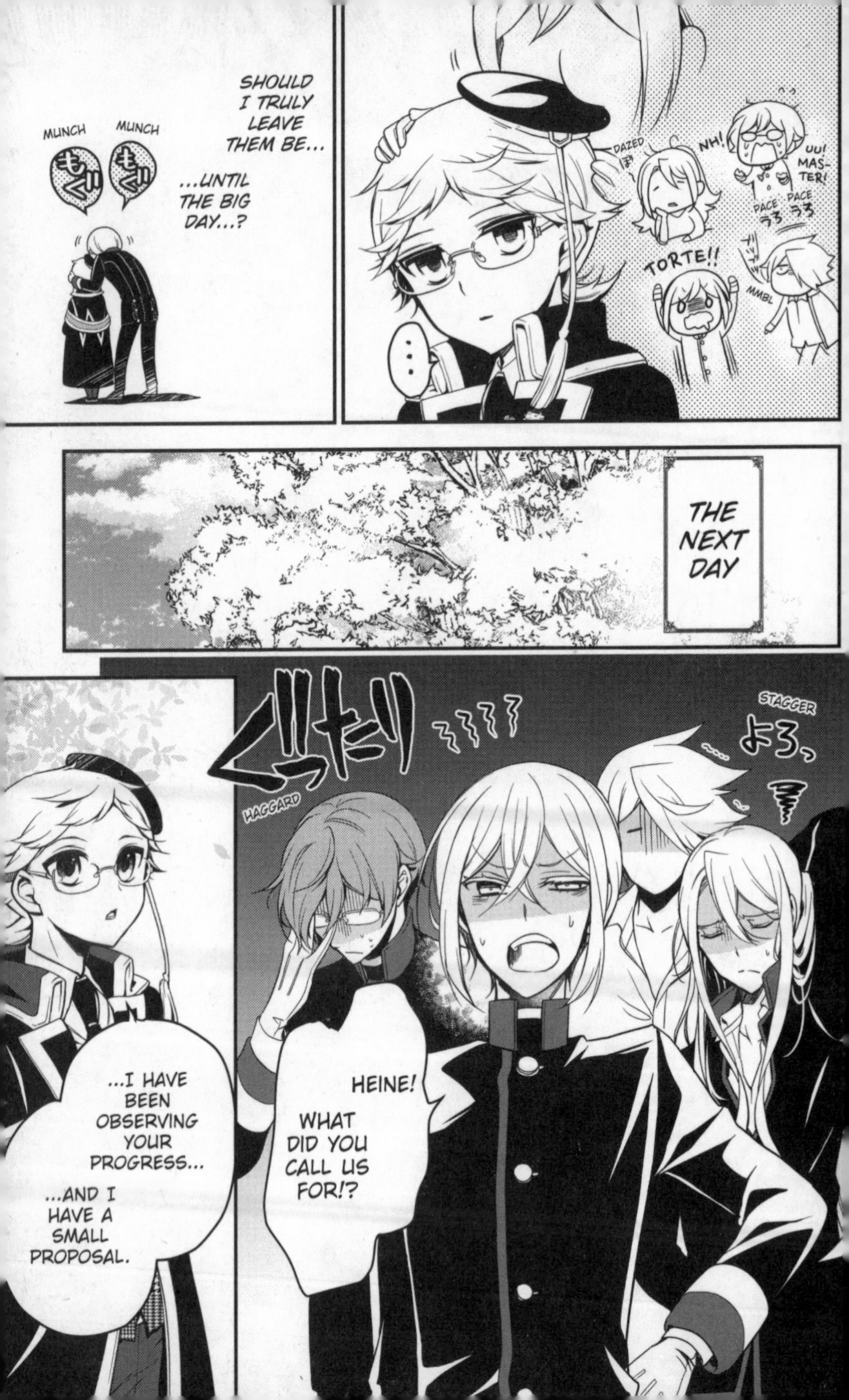
...
DAZED
NH!
UU! MASTER!
PACE うろ PACE うろ
TORTE!!
MMBL
SHOULD I TRULY LEAVE THEM BE...
...UNTIL THE BIG DAY...?
MUNCH もぐ
MUNCH もぐ
THE NEXT DAY
ぐったり
HAGGARD
STAGGER よろっ
HEINE!
WHAT DID YOU CALL US FOR!?
...I HAVE BEEN OBSERVING YOUR PROGRESS...
...AND I HAVE A SMALL PROPOSAL.

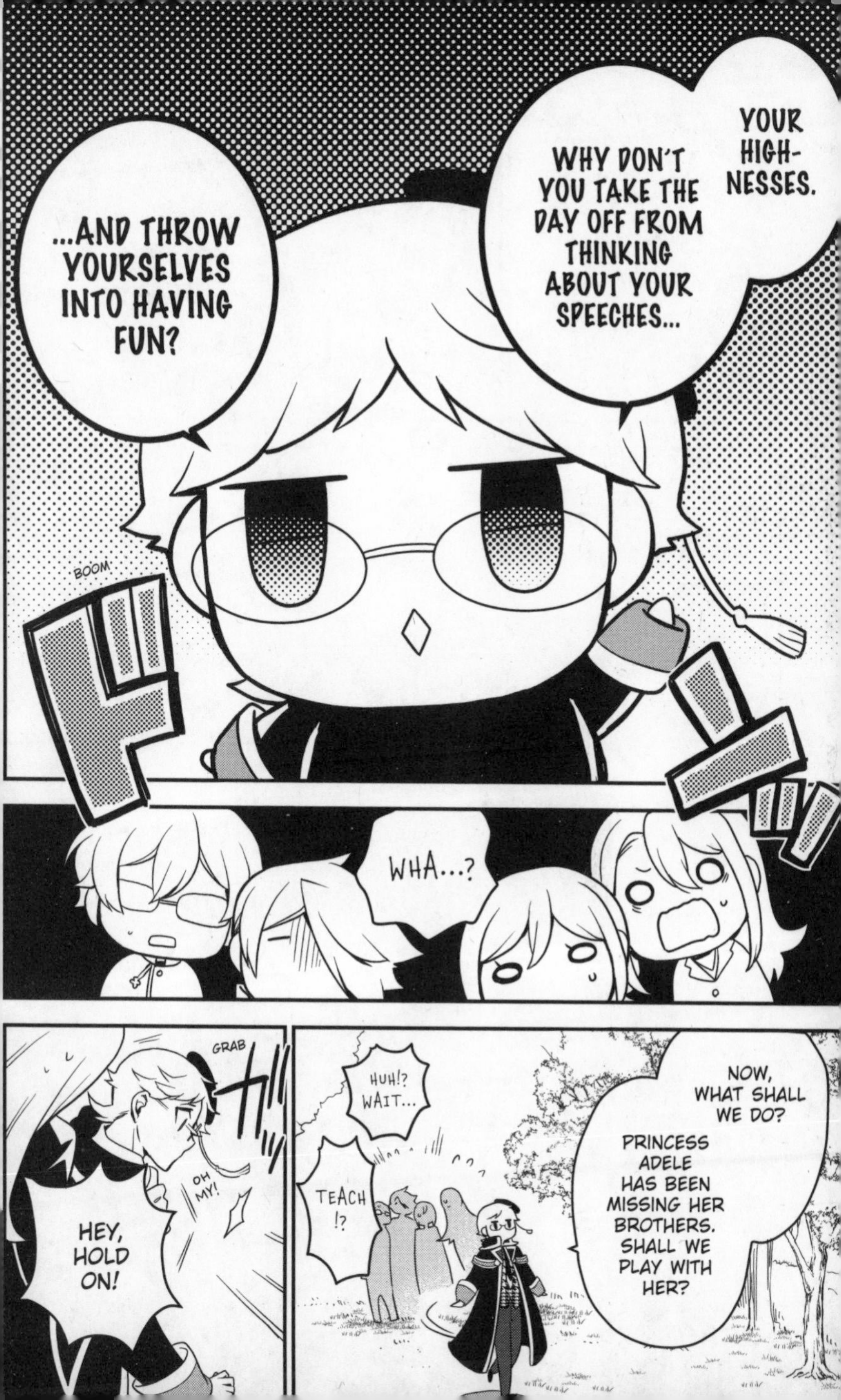
YOUR HIGHNESSES.
WHY DON'T YOU TAKE THE DAY OFF FROM THINKING ABOUT YOUR SPEECHES...
...AND THROW YOURSELVES INTO HAVING FUN?
BOOM
WHA...?
NOW, WHAT SHALL WE DO?
PRINCESS ADELE HAS BEEN MISSING HER BROTHERS. SHALL WE PLAY WITH HER?
HUH!? WAIT...
TEACH !?
GRAB
OH MY!
HEY, HOLD ON!

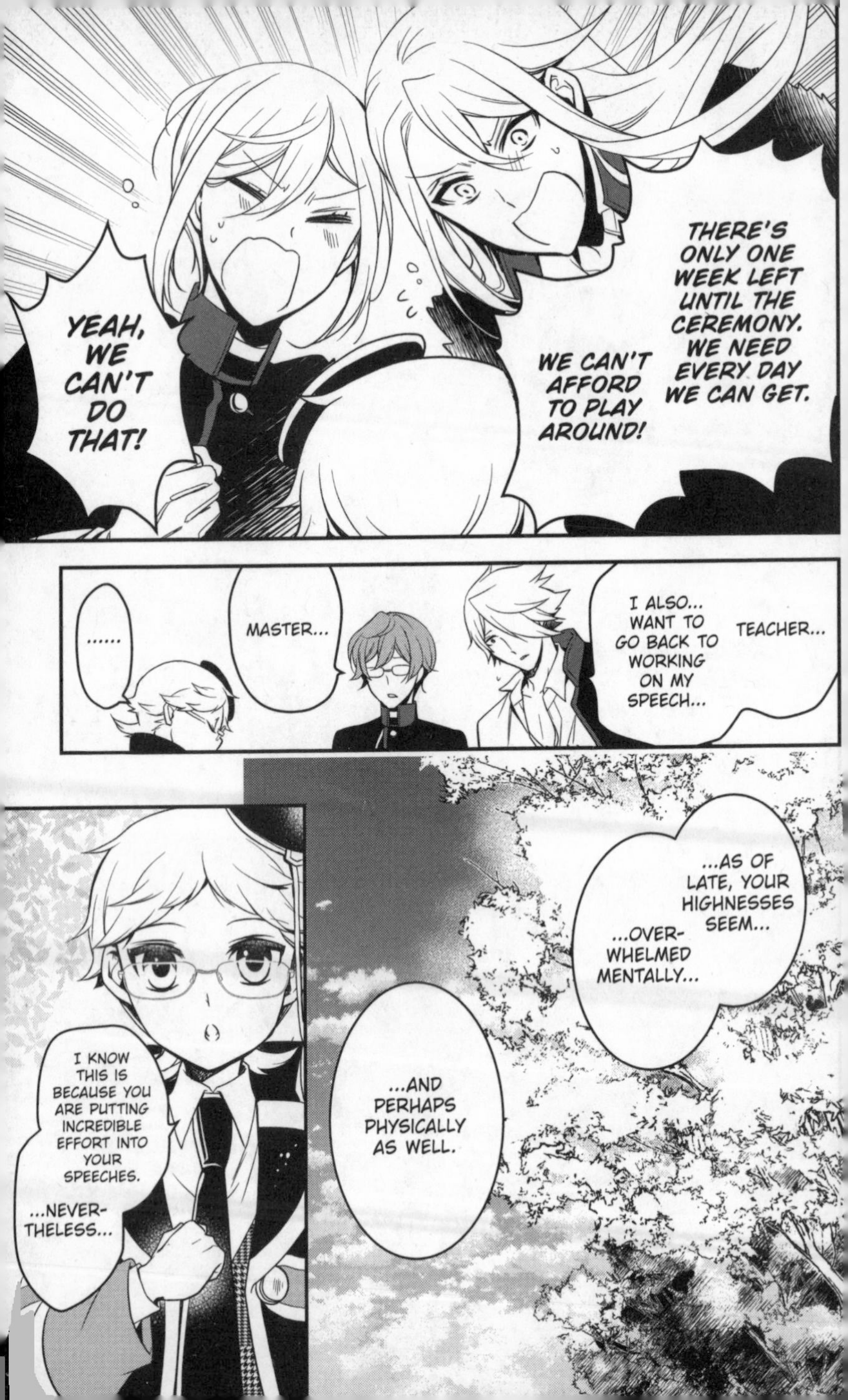
THERE'S ONLY ONE WEEK LEFT UNTIL THE CEREMONY. WE NEED EVERY DAY WE CAN GET.
WE CAN'T AFFORD TO PLAY AROUND!
YEAH, WE CAN'T DO THAT!
TEACHER...
I ALSO... WANT TO GO BACK TO WORKING ON MY SPEECH...
MASTER...
......
...AS OF LATE, YOUR HIGHNESSES SEEM...
...OVER-WHELMED MENTALLY...
...AND PERHAPS PHYSICALLY AS WELL.
I KNOW THIS IS BECAUSE YOU ARE PUTTING INCREDIBLE EFFORT INTO YOUR SPEECHES.
...NEVER-THELESS...

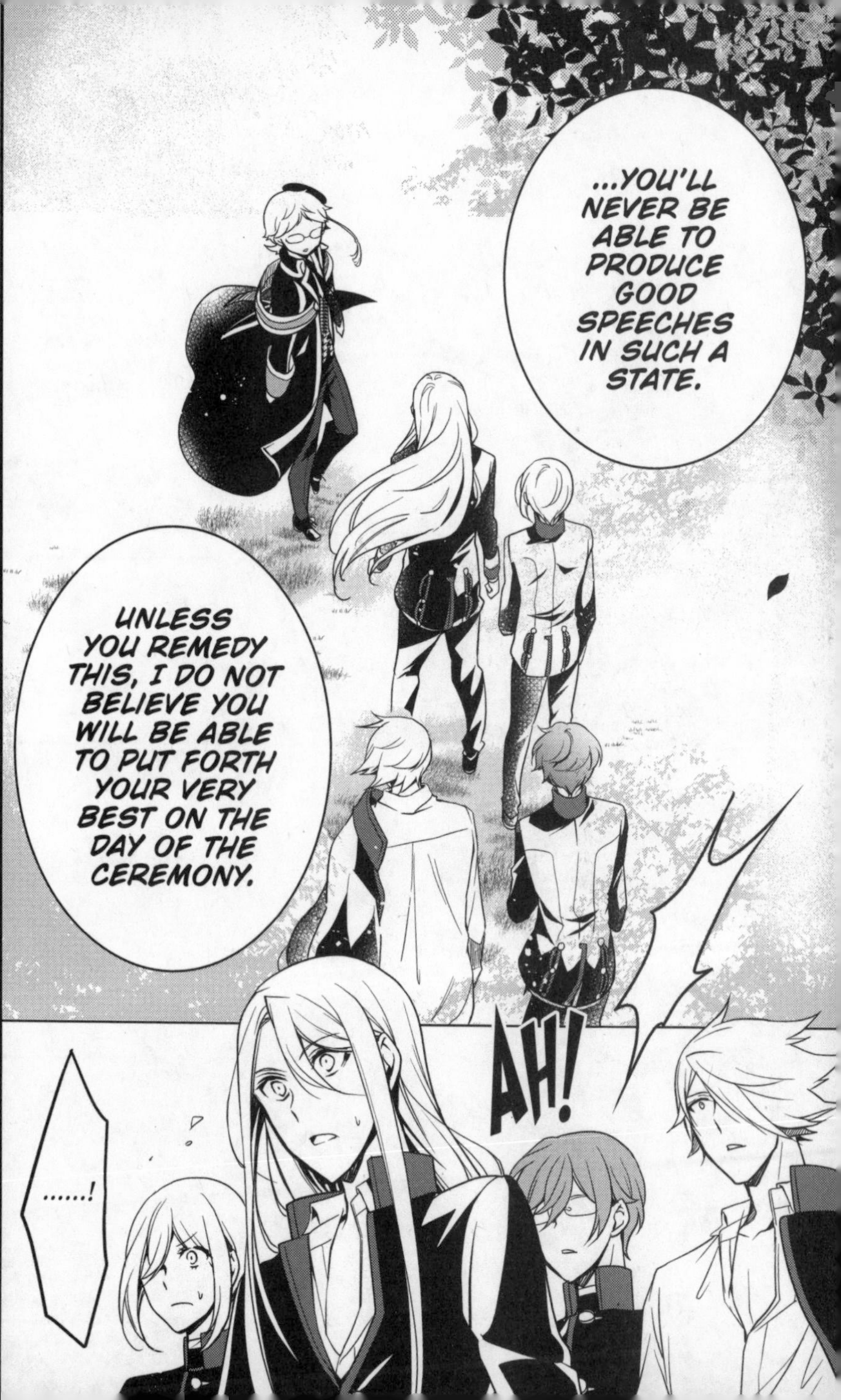
...YOU'LL NEVER BE ABLE TO PRODUCE GOOD SPEECHES IN SUCH A STATE.
UNLESS YOU REMEDY THIS, I DO NOT BELIEVE YOU WILL BE ABLE TO PUT FORTH YOUR VERY BEST ON THE DAY OF THE CEREMONY.
AH!
......!

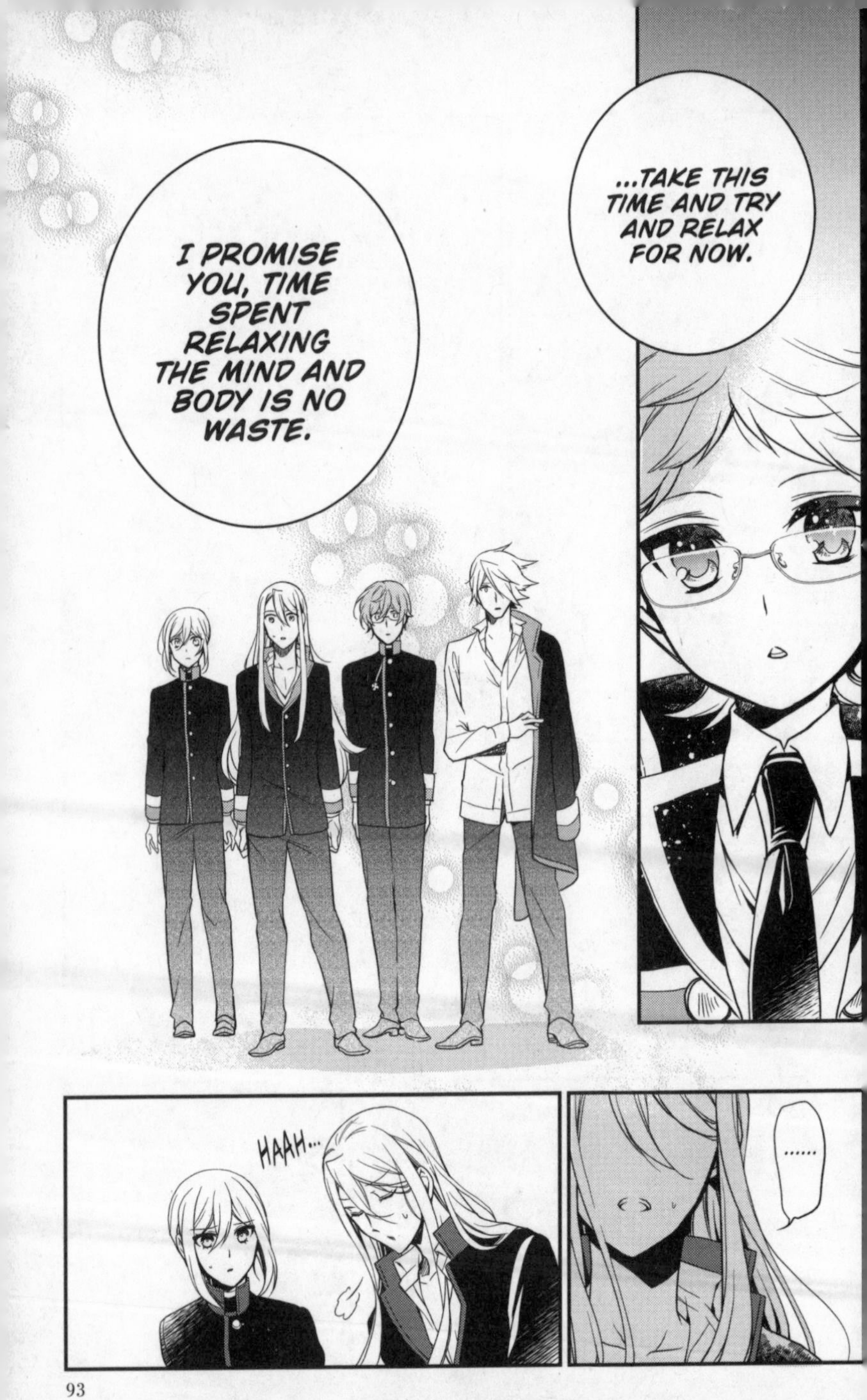

...TAKE THIS TIME AND TRY AND RELAX FOR NOW.
I PROMISE YOU, TIME SPENT RELAXING THE MIND AND BODY IS NO WASTE.
......
HAAH...

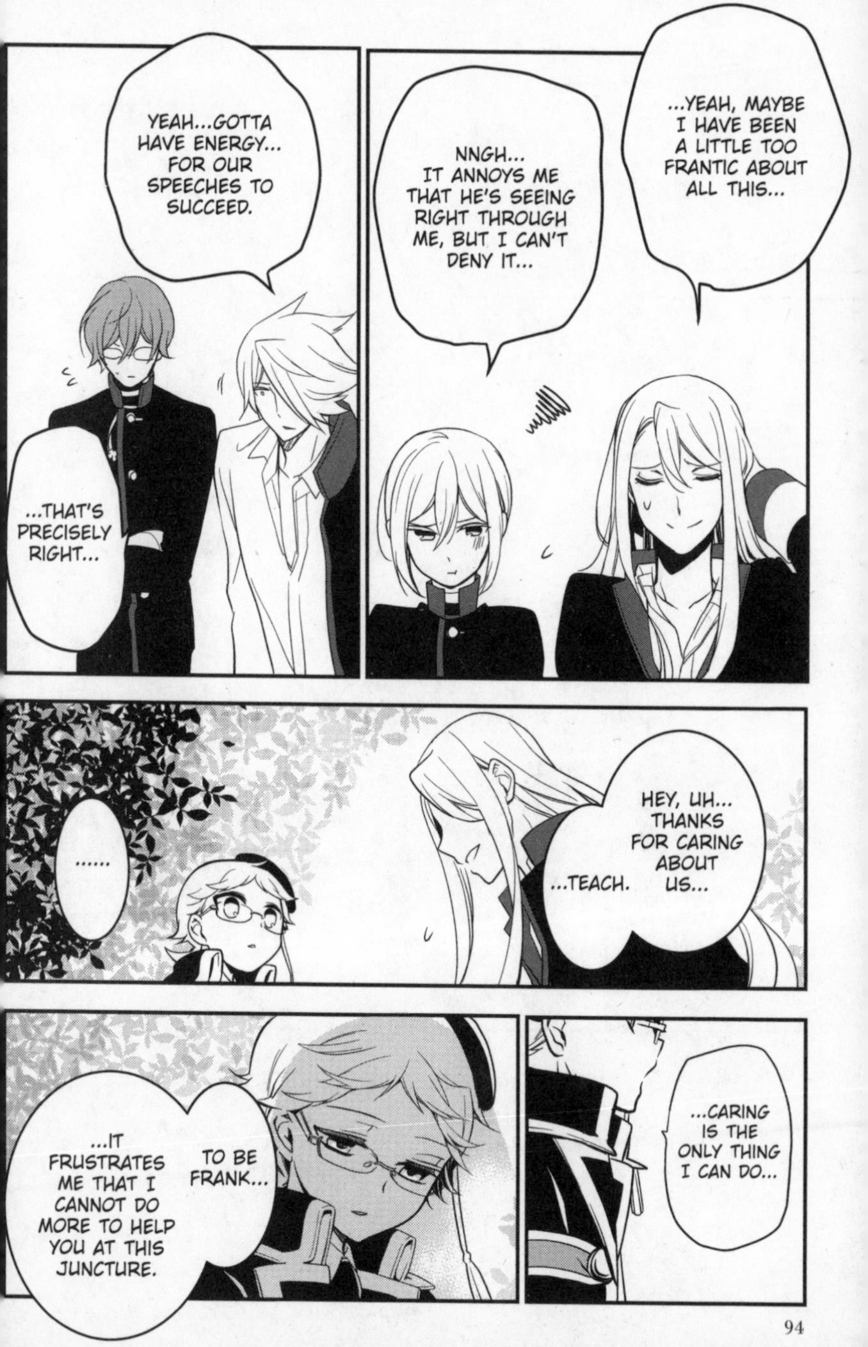
...YEAH, MAYBE I HAVE BEEN A LITTLE TOO FRANTIC ABOUT ALL THIS...
NNGH... IT ANNOYS ME THAT HE'S SEEING RIGHT THROUGH ME, BUT I CAN'T DENY IT...
YEAH...GOTTA HAVE ENERGY... FOR OUR SPEECHES TO SUCCEED.
...THAT'S PRECISELY RIGHT...
HEY, UH... THANKS FOR CARING ABOUT US...
...TEACH.
......
...CARING IS THE ONLY THING I CAN DO...
TO BE FRANK...
...IT FRUSTRATES ME THAT I CANNOT DO MORE TO HELP YOU AT THIS JUNCTURE.

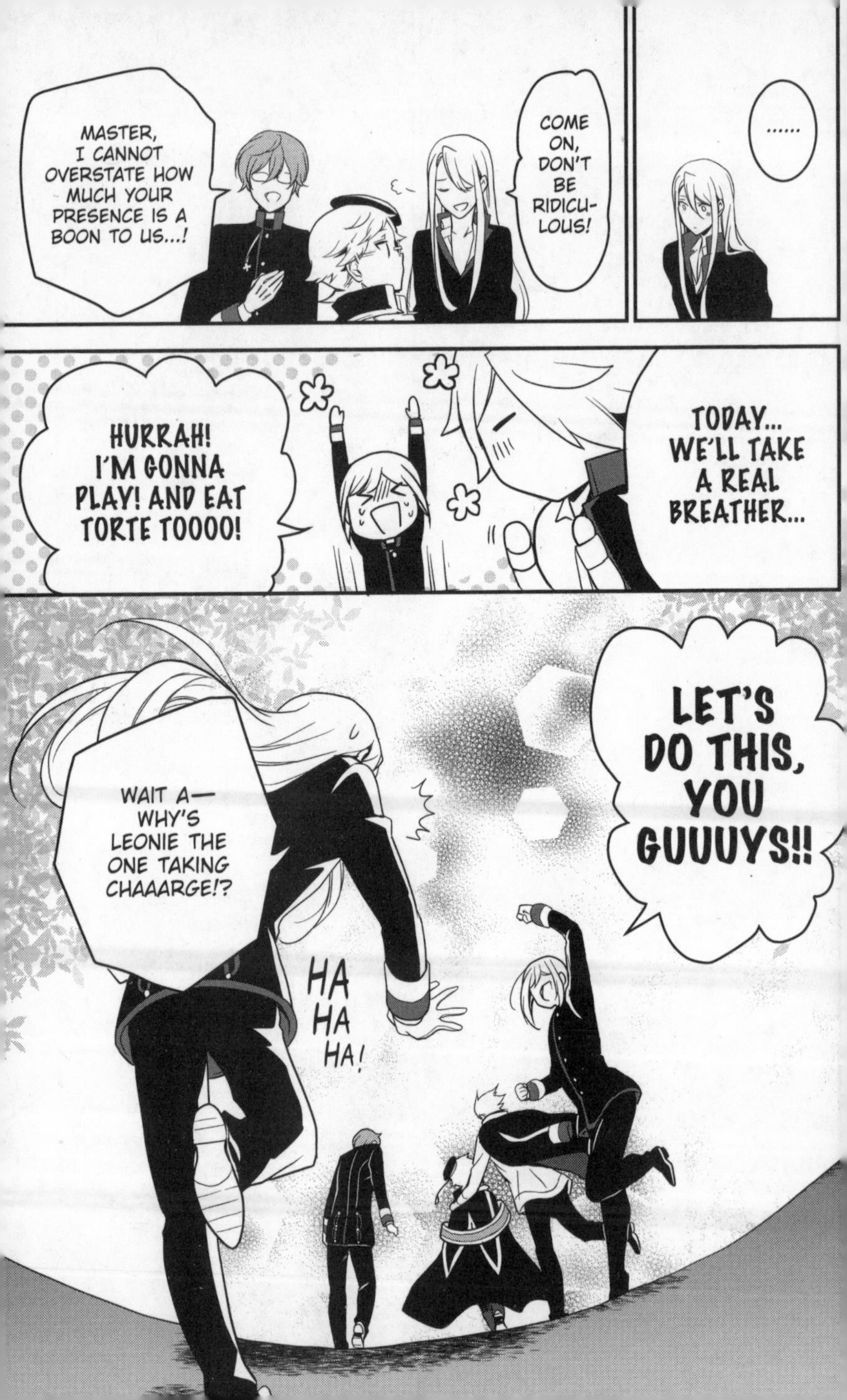
......
COME ON, DON'T BE RIDICU-LOUS!
MASTER, I CANNOT OVERSTATE HOW MUCH YOUR PRESENCE IS A BOON TO US...!
TODAY... WE'LL TAKE A REAL BREATHER...
HURRAH! I'M GONNA PLAY! AND EAT TORTE TOOOO!
LET'S DO THIS, YOU GUUUYS!!
WAIT A— WHY'S LEONIE THE ONE TAKING CHAAARGE!?
HA HA HA!

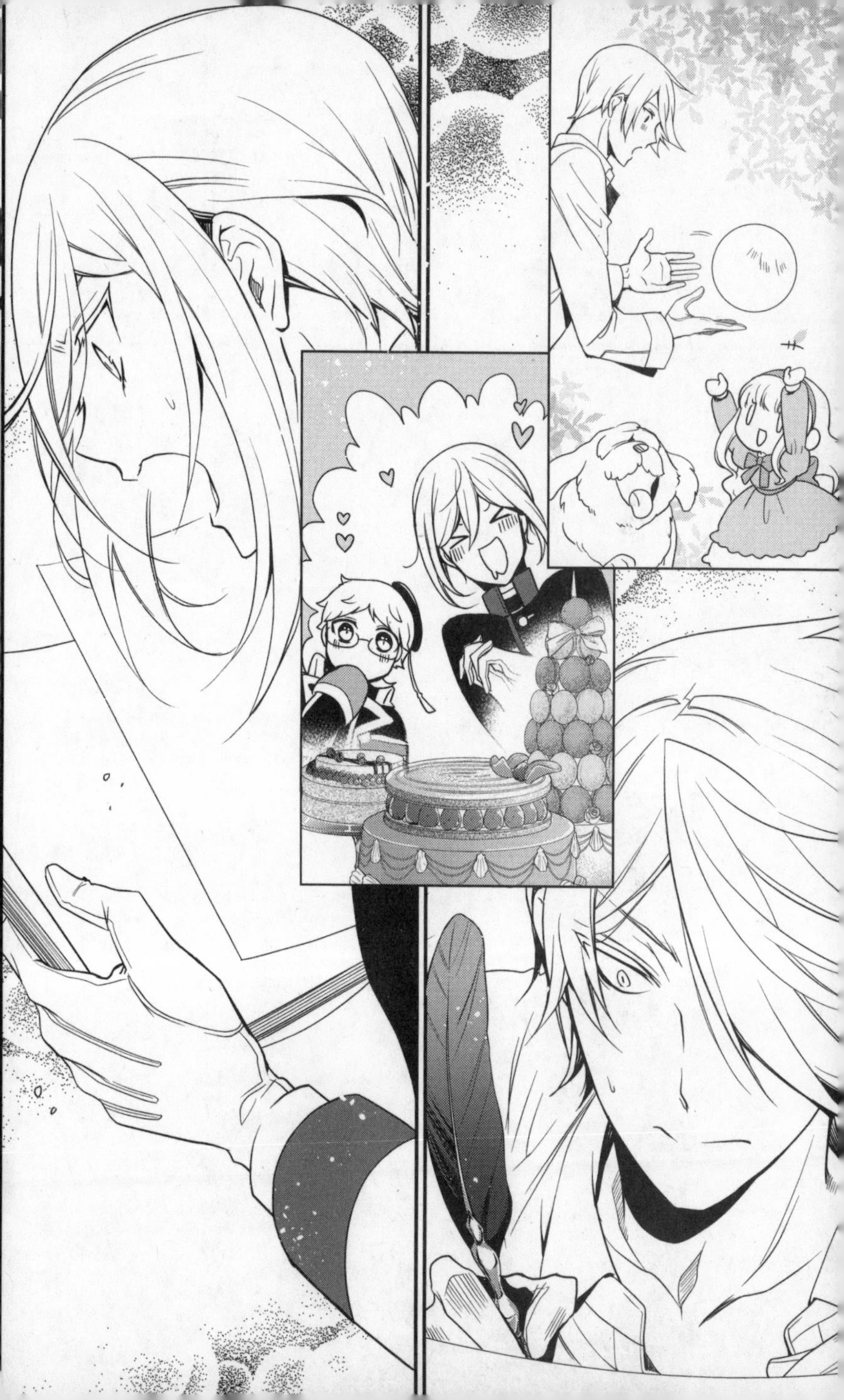

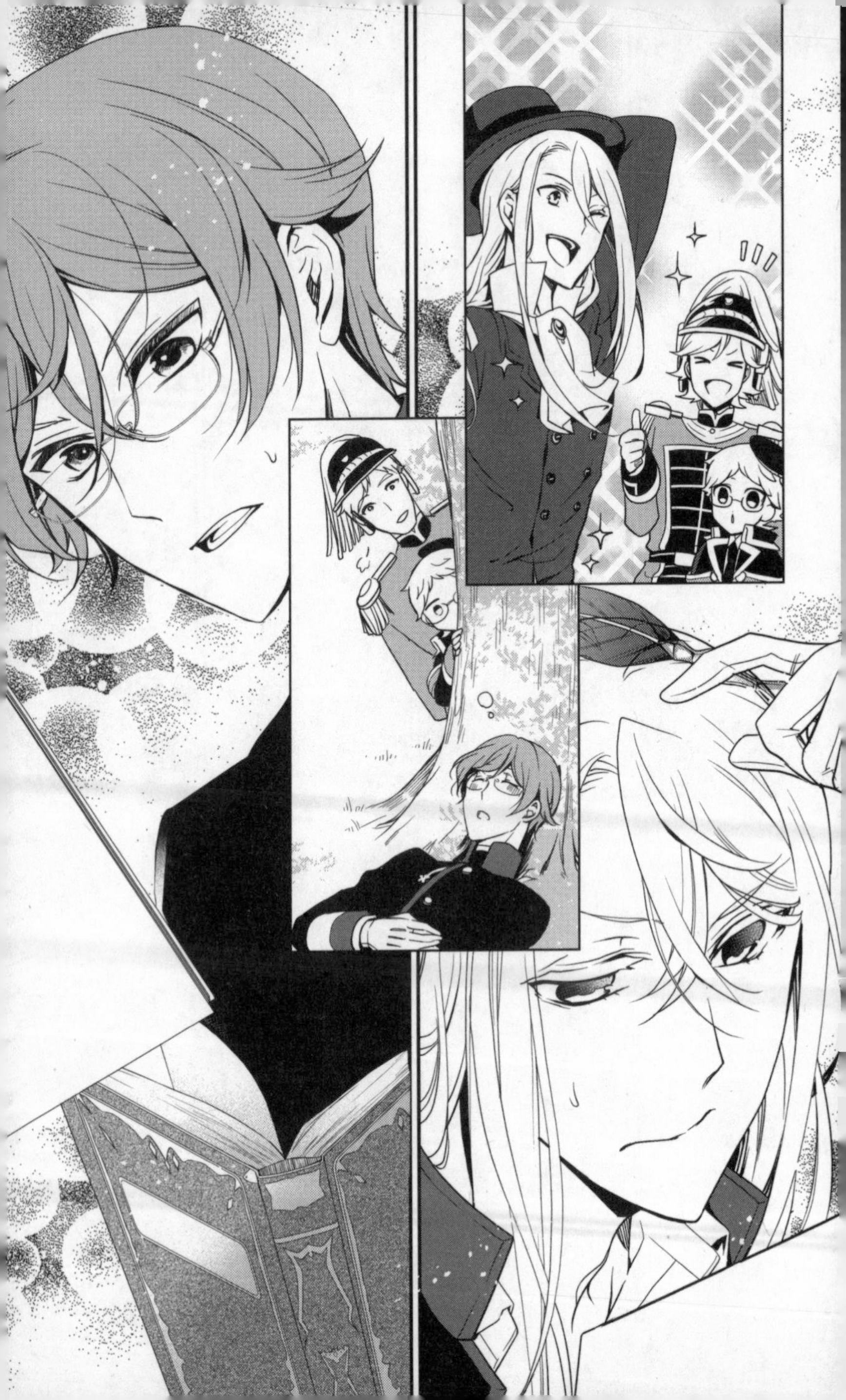

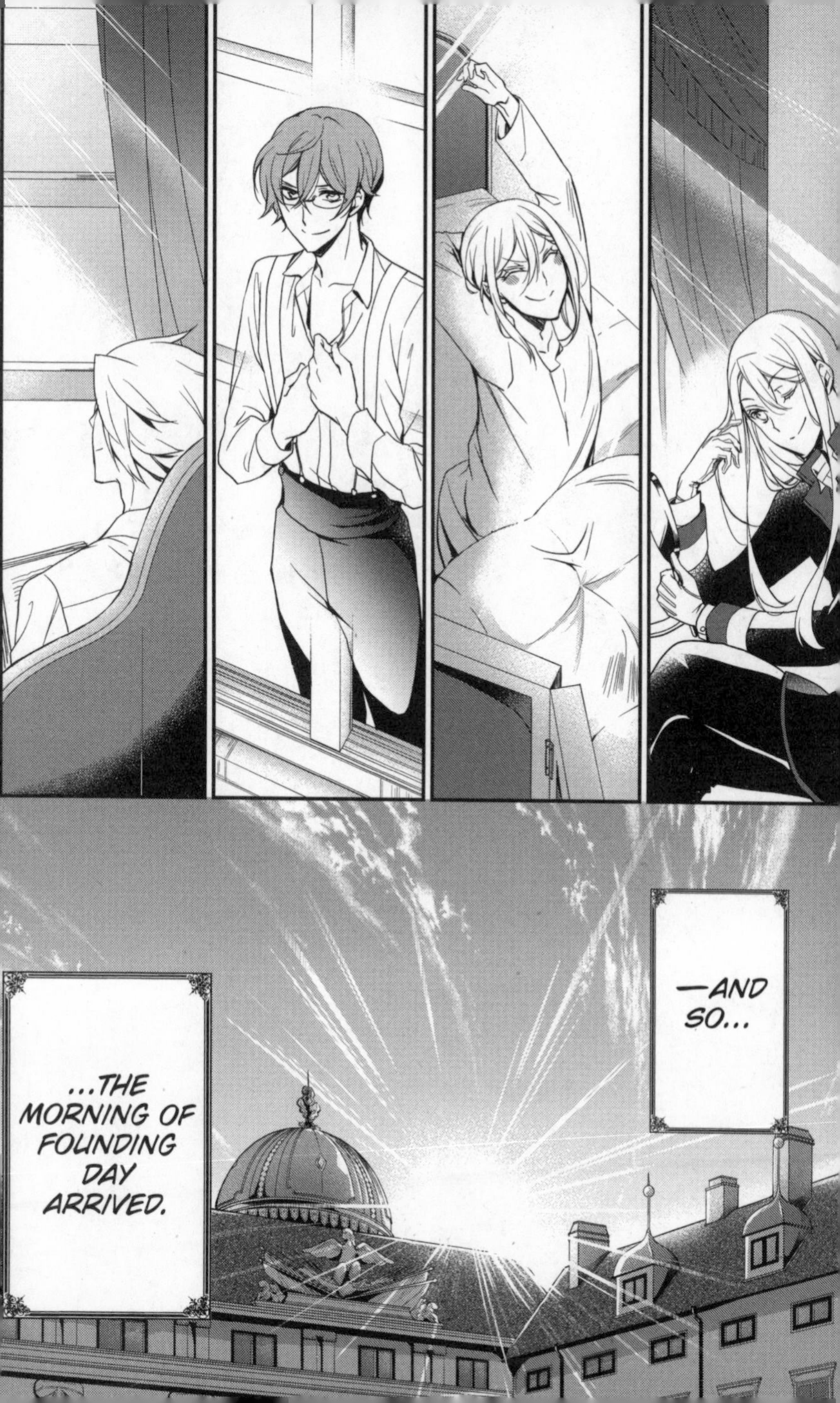
—AND SO...
...THE MORNING OF FOUNDING DAY ARRIVED.

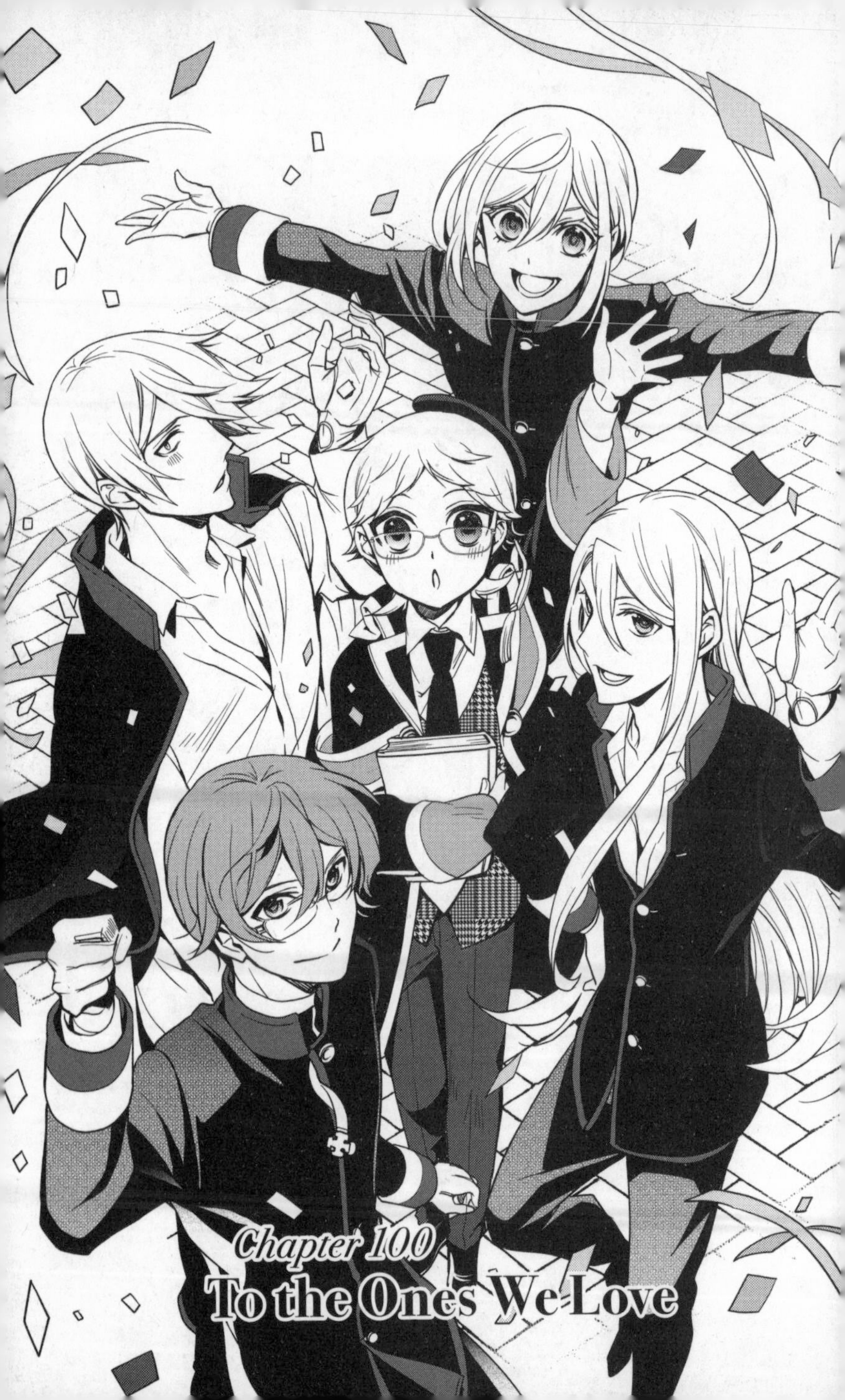
Chapter 100
To the Ones We Love

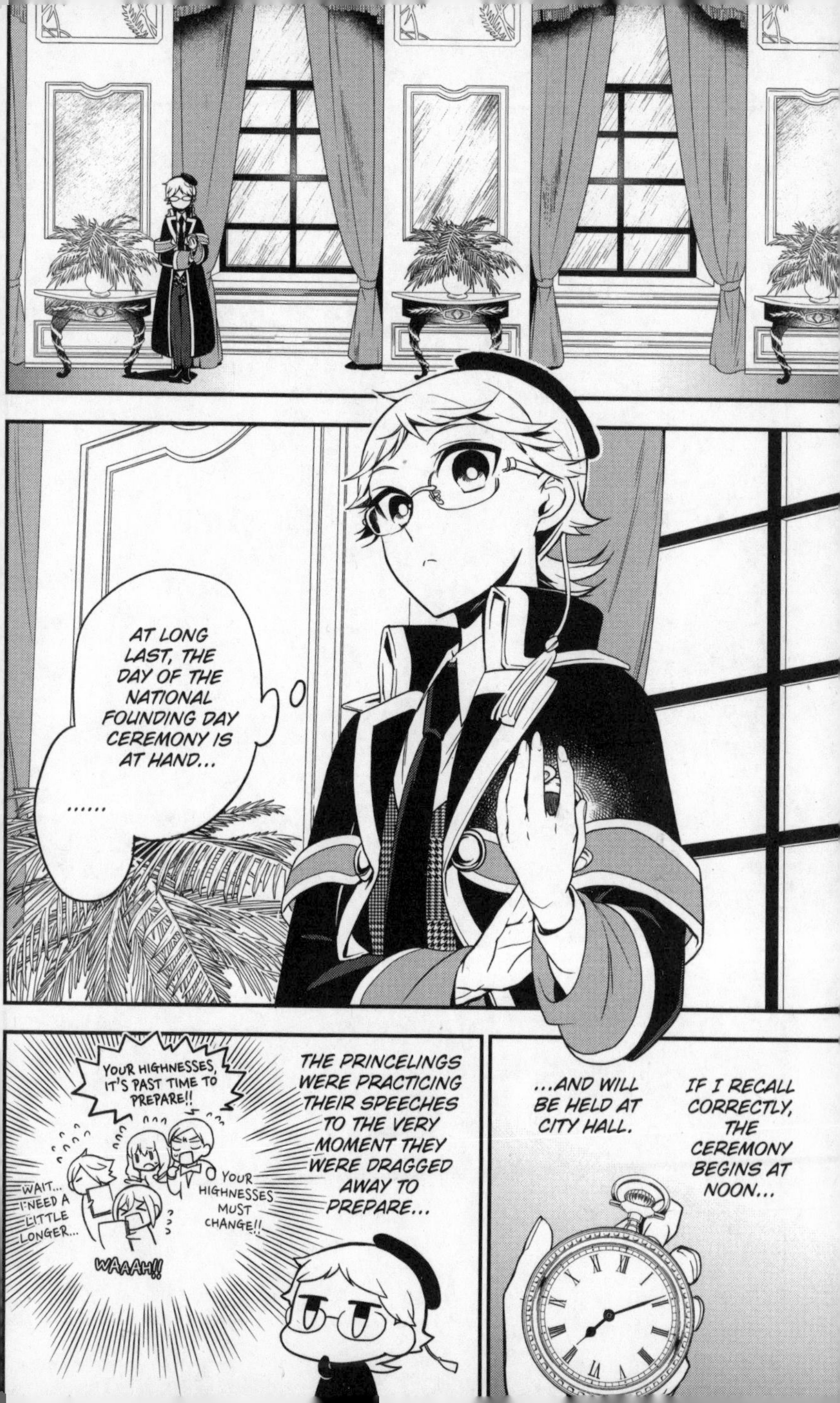
AT LONG LAST, THE DAY OF THE NATIONAL FOUNDING DAY CEREMONY IS AT HAND...
......
IF I RECALL CORRECTLY, THE CEREMONY BEGINS AT NOON...
...AND WILL BE HELD AT CITY HALL.
THE PRINCELINGS WERE PRACTICING THEIR SPEECHES TO THE VERY MOMENT THEY WERE DRAGGED AWAY TO PREPARE...
YOUR HIGHNESSES, IT'S PAST TIME TO PREPARE!!
YOUR HIGHNESSES MUST CHANGE!!
WAIT... I NEED A LITTLE LONGER...
WAAAH!!

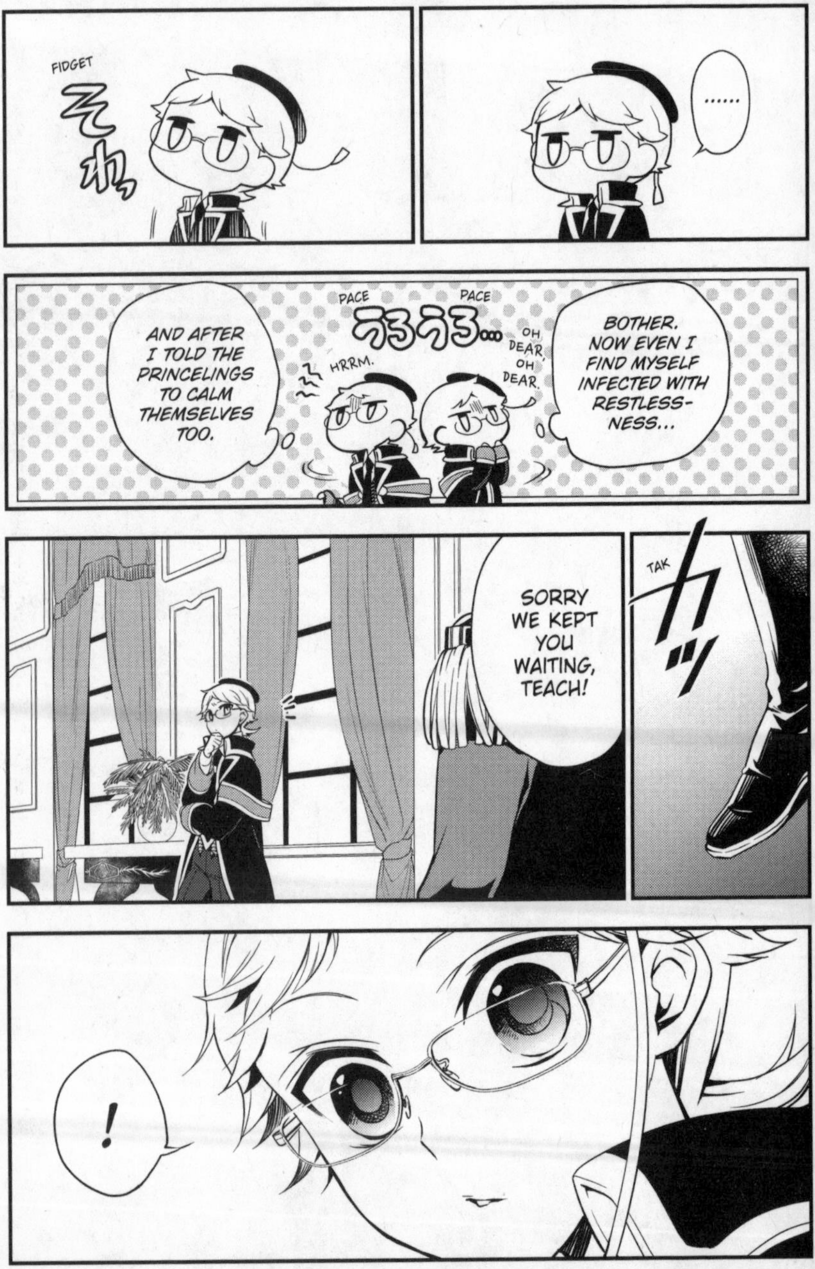
......
FIDGET
そわっ
BOTHER. NOW EVEN I FIND MYSELF INFECTED WITH RESTLESS-NESS...
PACE PACE
うろうろ…
OH DEAR, OH DEAR.
HRRM.
AND AFTER I TOLD THE PRINCELINGS TO CALM THEMSELVES TOO.
TAK
SORRY WE KEPT YOU WAITING, TEACH!
!

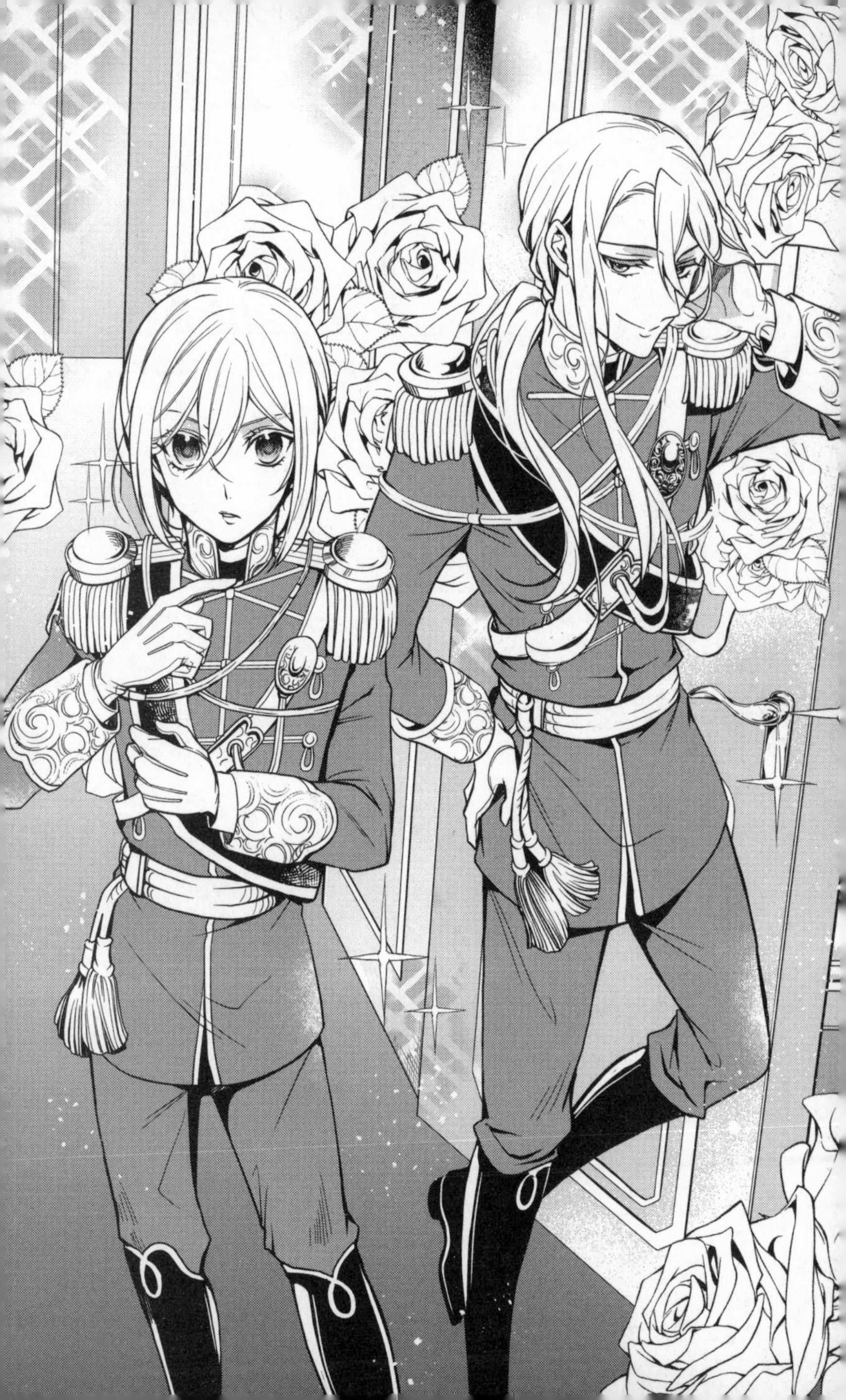

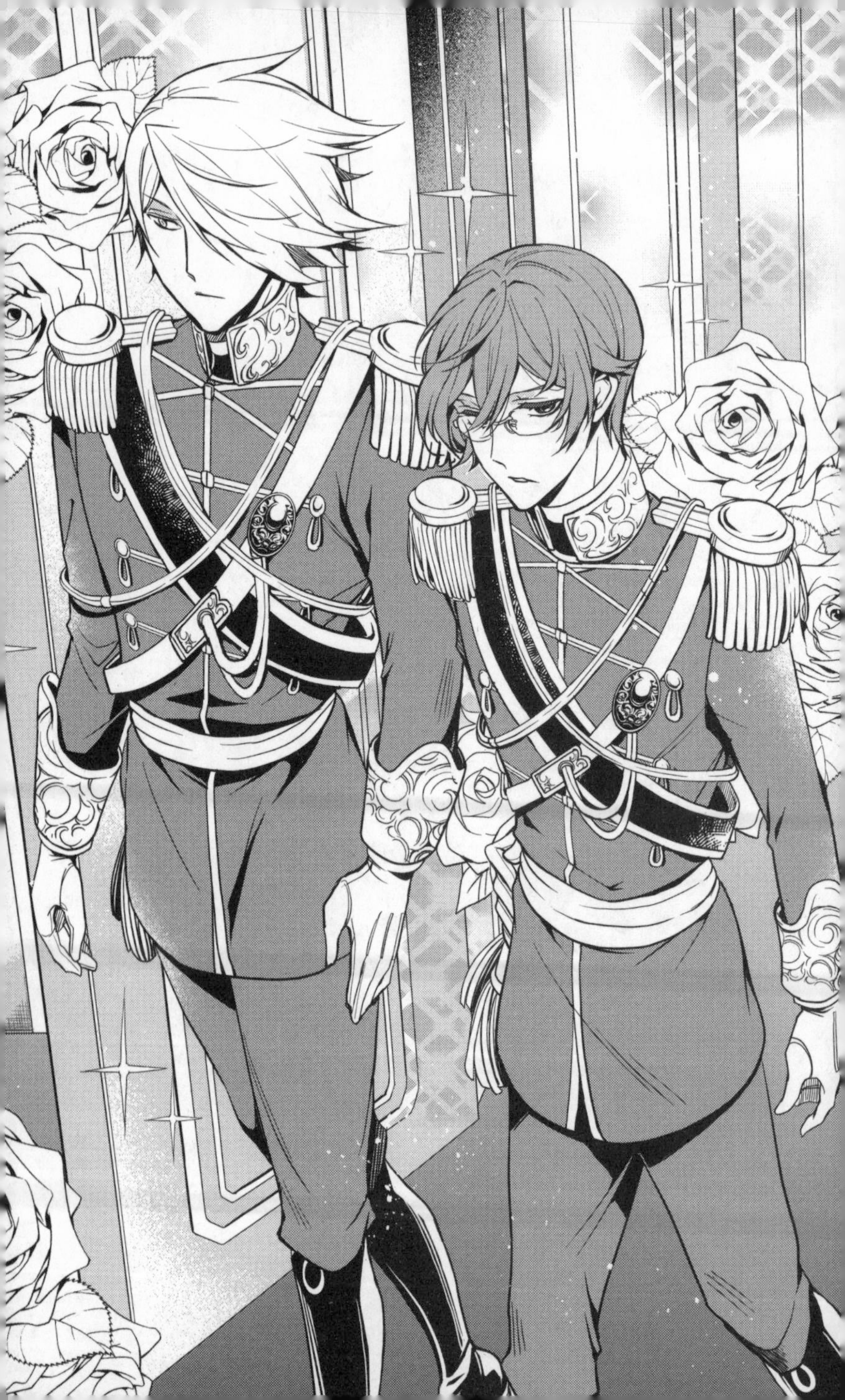

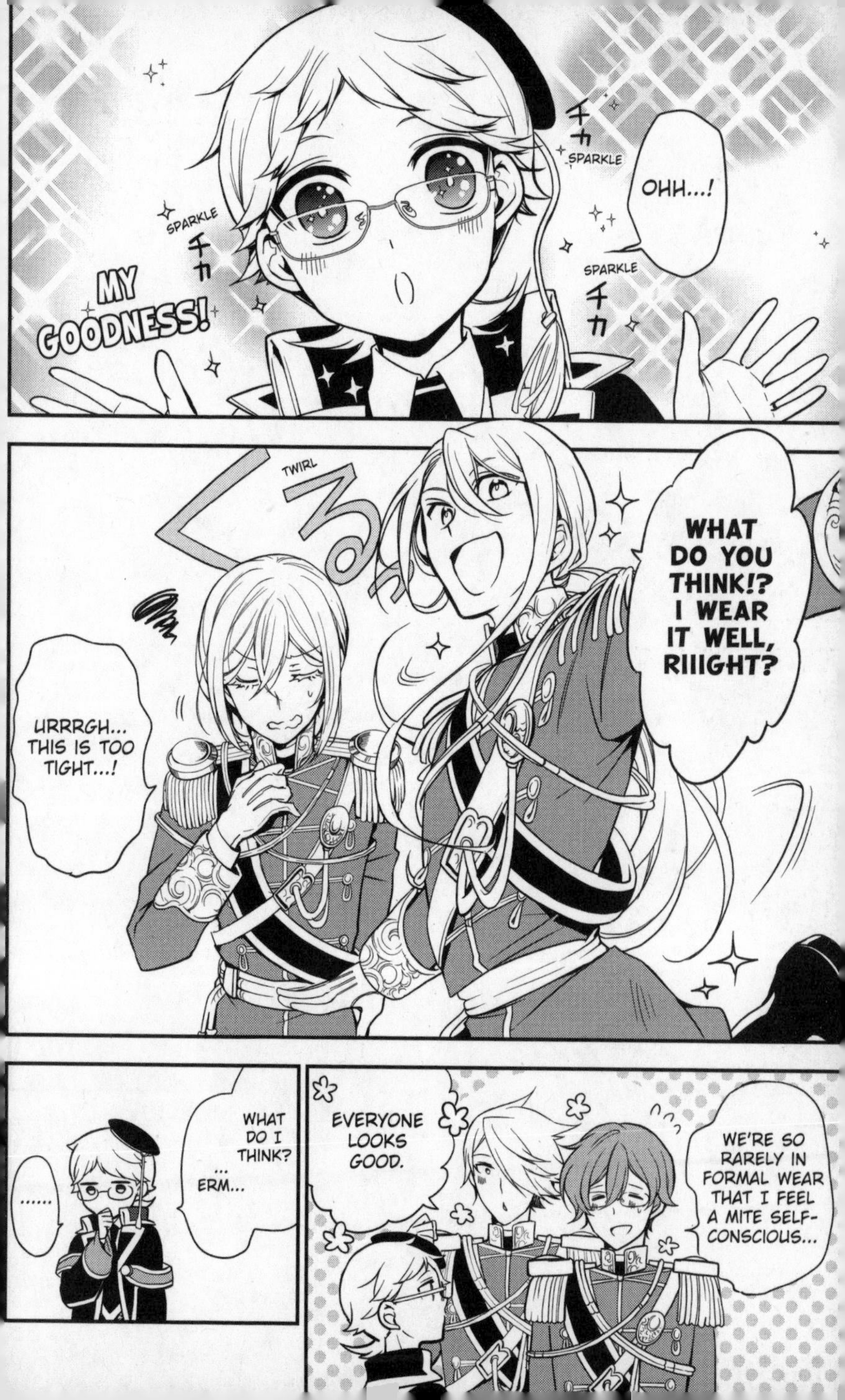
OHH...!
チカ SPARKLE
チカ SPARKLE
チカ SPARKLE
MY GOODNESS!
WHAT DO YOU THINK!? I WEAR IT WELL, RIIIGHT?
TWIRL
URRRGH... THIS IS TOO TIGHT...!
WE'RE SO RARELY IN FORMAL WEAR THAT I FEEL A MITE SELF-CONSCIOUS...
EVERYONE LOOKS GOOD.
WHAT DO I THINK? ... ERM...
......

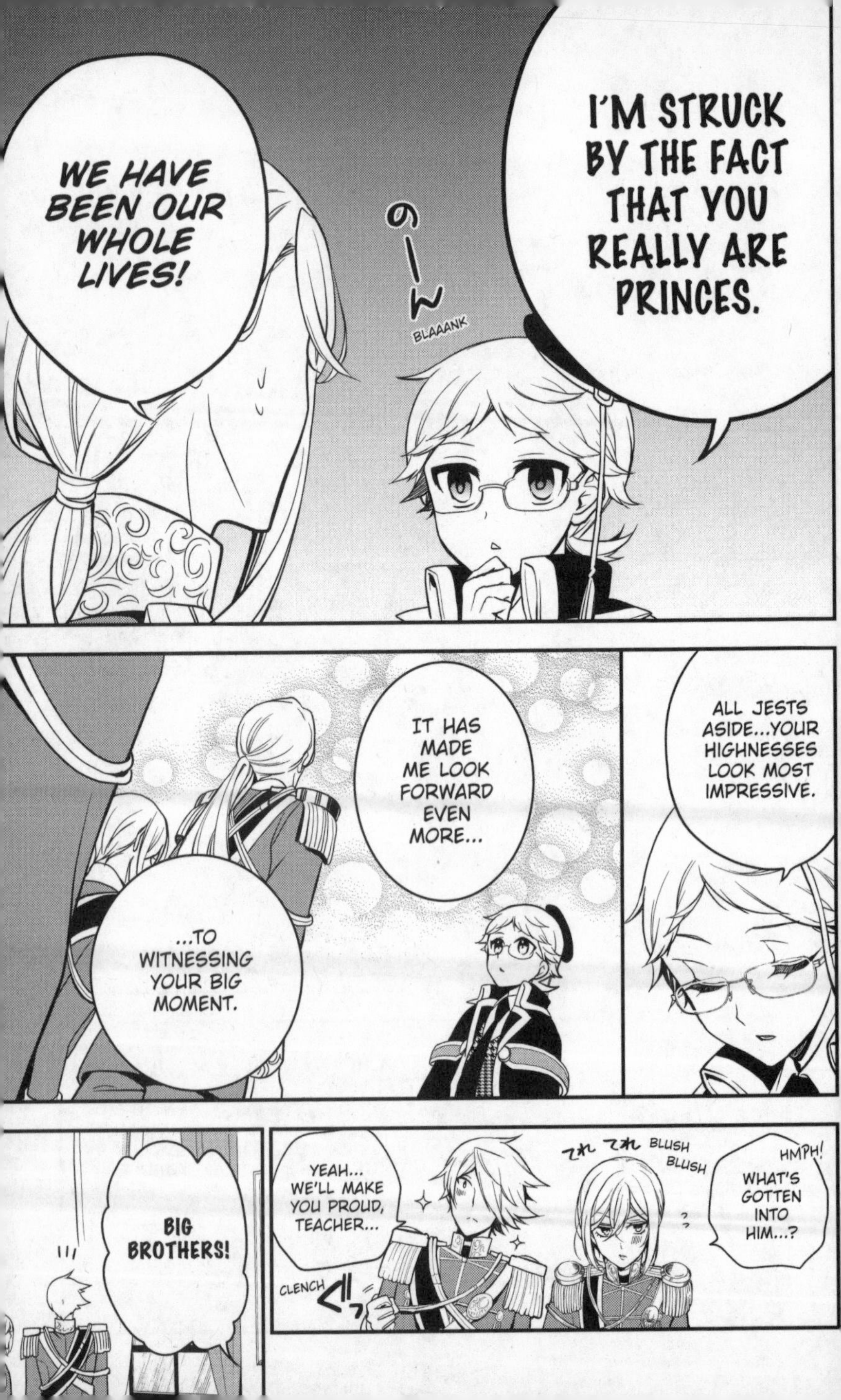
I'M STRUCK BY THE FACT THAT YOU REALLY ARE PRINCES.
のーん
BLAAANK
WE HAVE BEEN OUR WHOLE LIVES!
ALL JESTS ASIDE...YOUR HIGHNESSES LOOK MOST IMPRESSIVE.
IT HAS MADE ME LOOK FORWARD EVEN MORE...
...TO WITNESSING YOUR BIG MOMENT.
HMPH!
WHAT'S GOTTEN INTO HIM...?
てれ てれ
BLUSH BLUSH
YEAH... WE'LL MAKE YOU PROUD, TEACHER...
CLENCH
ぐッ
BIG BROTHERS!

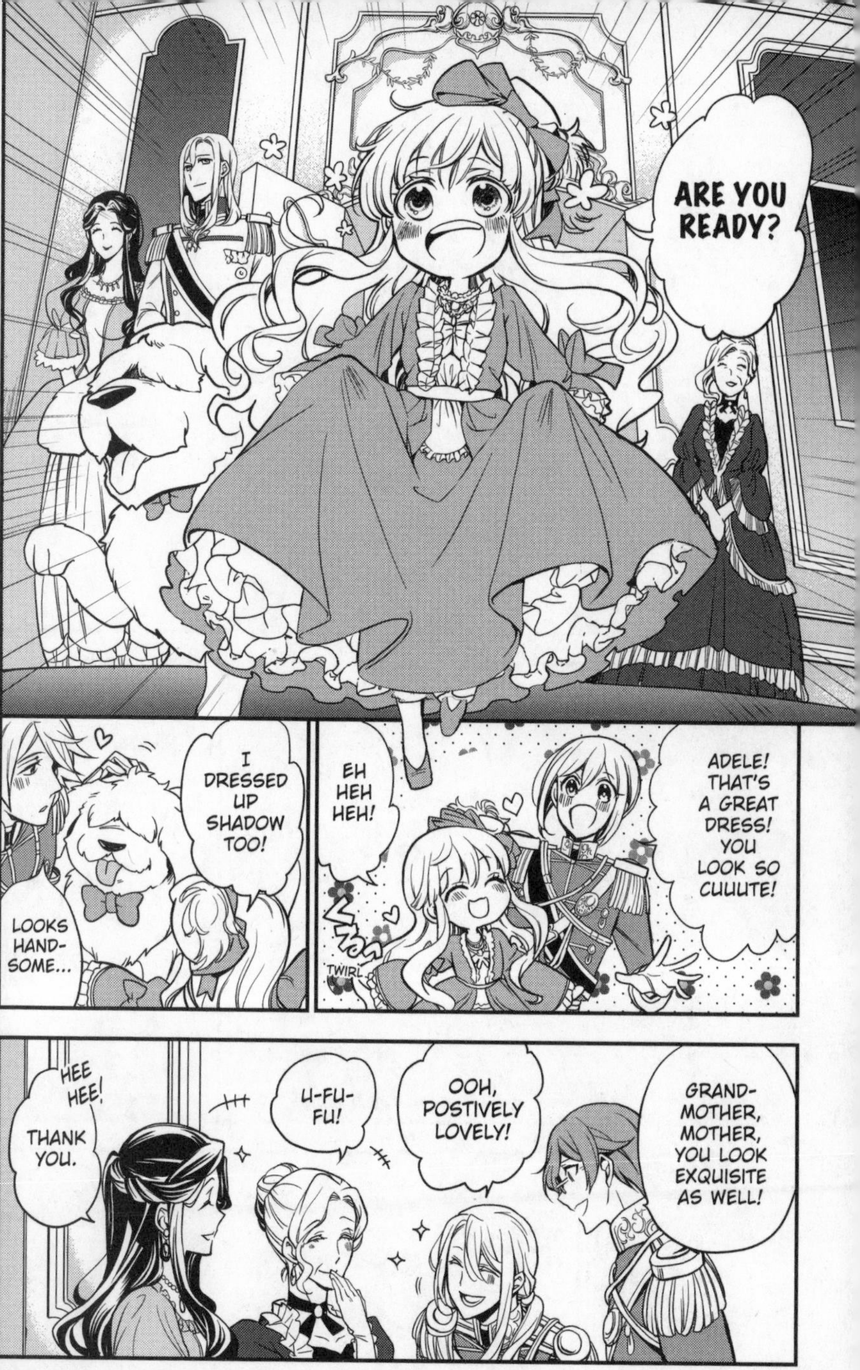
ARE YOU READY?
ADELE! THAT'S A GREAT DRESS! YOU LOOK SO CUUUTE!
EH HEH HEH!
くるっ
TWIRL
I DRESSED UP SHADOW TOO!
LOOKS HANDSOME...
GRAND-MOTHER, MOTHER, YOU LOOK EXQUISITE AS WELL!
OOH, POSTIVELY LOVELY!
U-FU-FU!
HEE HEE!
THANK YOU.

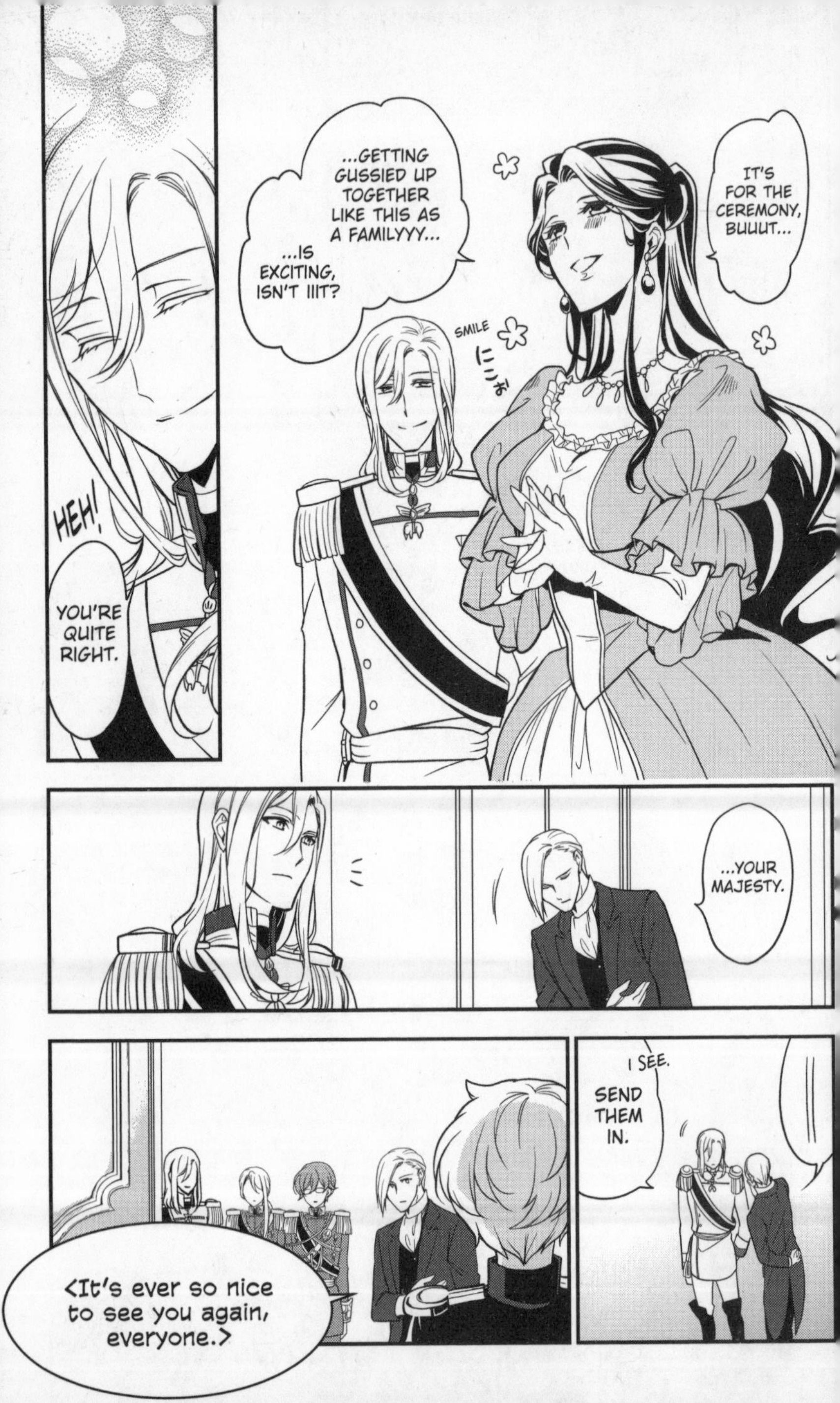
IT'S FOR THE CEREMONY, BUUUT...
...GETTING GUSSIED UP TOGETHER LIKE THIS AS A FAMILYYY...
...IS EXCITING, ISN'T IIIT?
SMILE
にこぉ
HEH!
YOU'RE QUITE RIGHT.
...YOUR MAJESTY.
I SEE.
SEND THEM IN.
<It's ever so nice to see you again, everyone.>

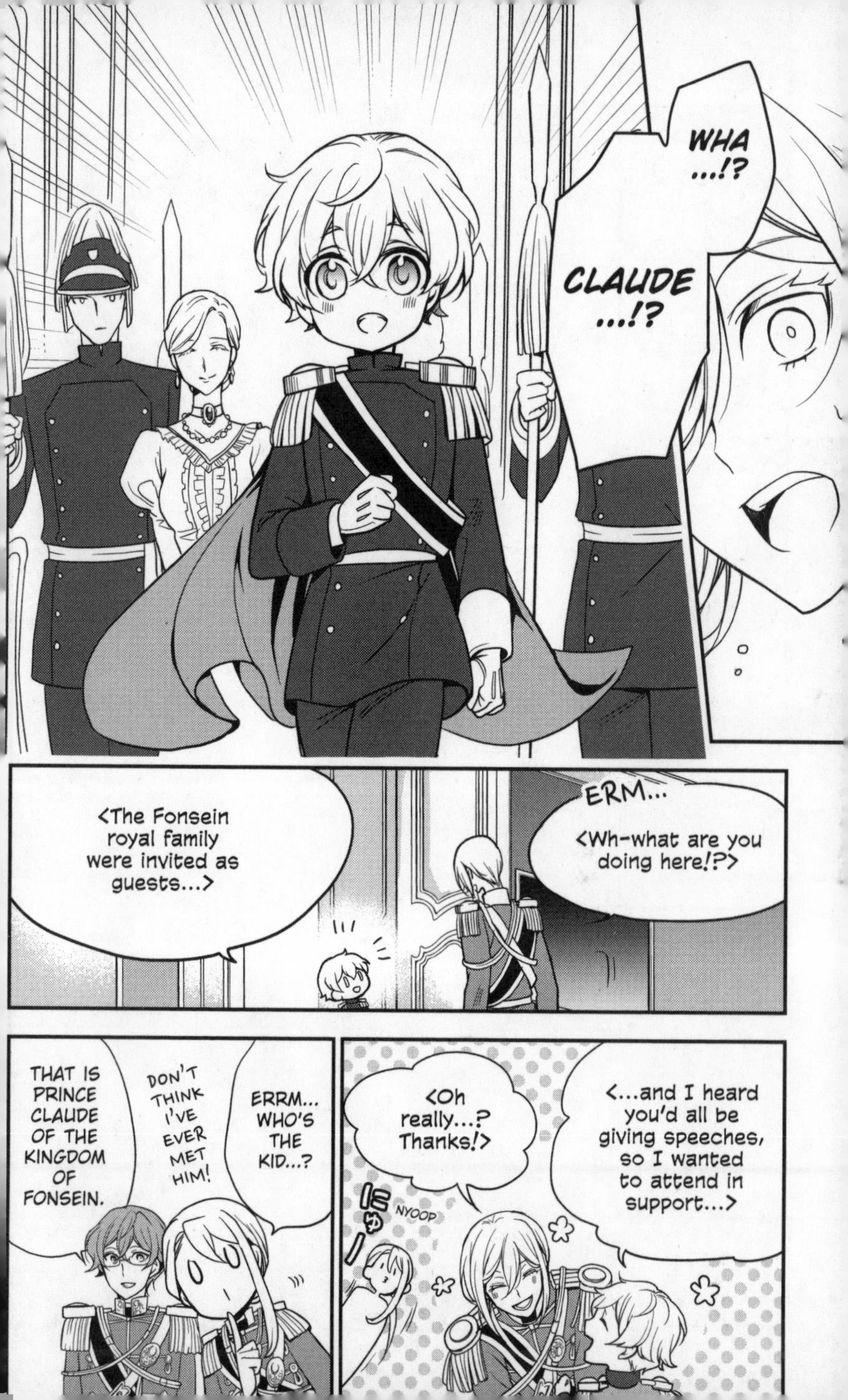
WHA ...!?
CLAUDE ...!?
ERM...
<Wh-what are you doing here!?>
<The Fonsein royal family were invited as guests...>
<...and I heard you'd all be giving speeches, so I wanted to attend in support...>
<Oh really...? Thanks!>
NYOOP
ERRM... WHO'S THE KID...?
DON'T THINK I'VE EVER MET HIM!
THAT IS PRINCE CLAUDE OF THE KINGDOM OF FONSEIN.

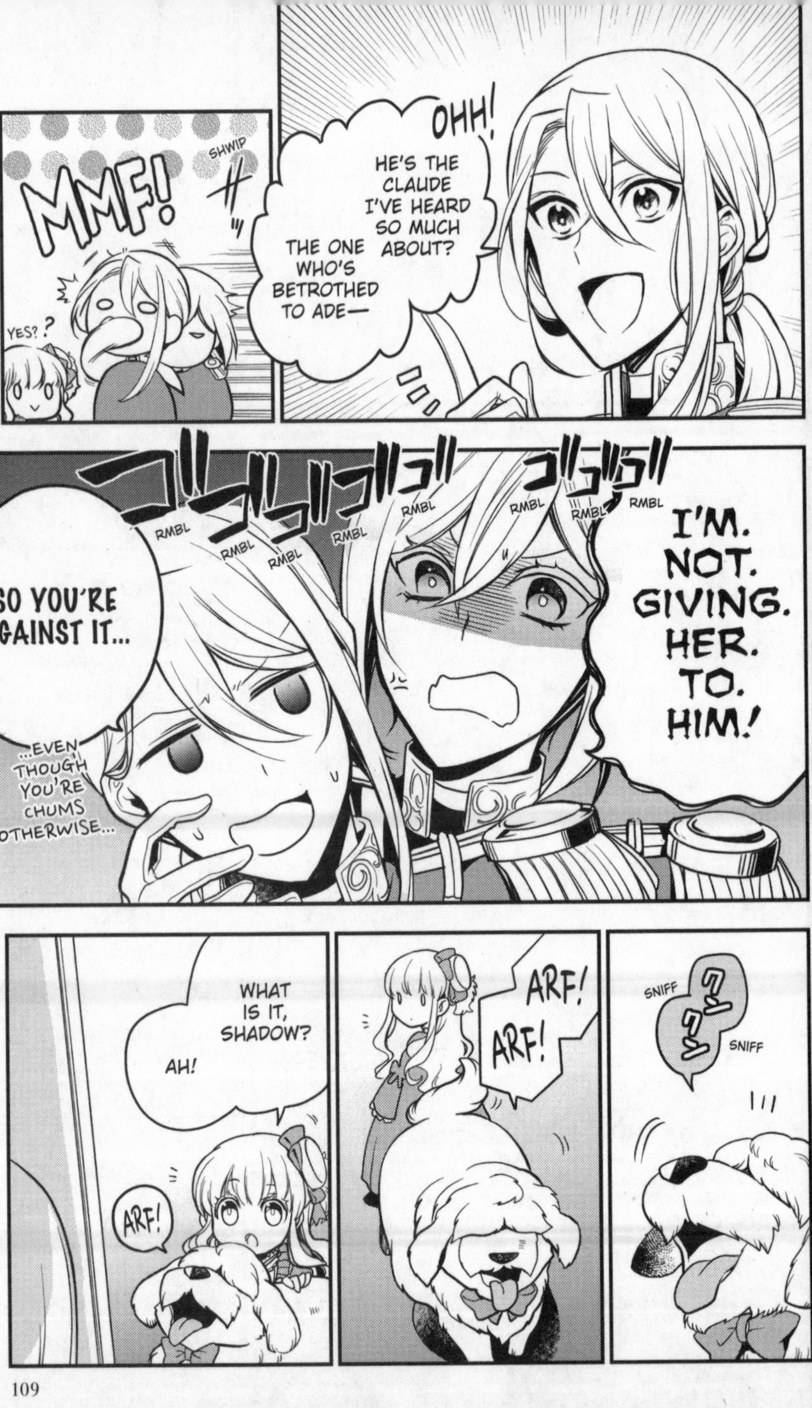
OHH!
HE'S THE CLAUDE I'VE HEARD SO MUCH ABOUT?
THE ONE WHO'S BETROTHED TO ADE—
SHWIP
MMF!
YES??
I'M. NOT. GIVING. HER. TO. HIM!
RMBL RMBL RMBL RMBL RMBL RMBL RMBL RMBL
SO YOU'RE AGAINST IT...
...EVEN THOUGH YOU'RE CHUMS OTHERWISE...
SNIFF
SNIFF
ARF!
ARF!
WHAT IS IT, SHADOW?
AH!
ARF!

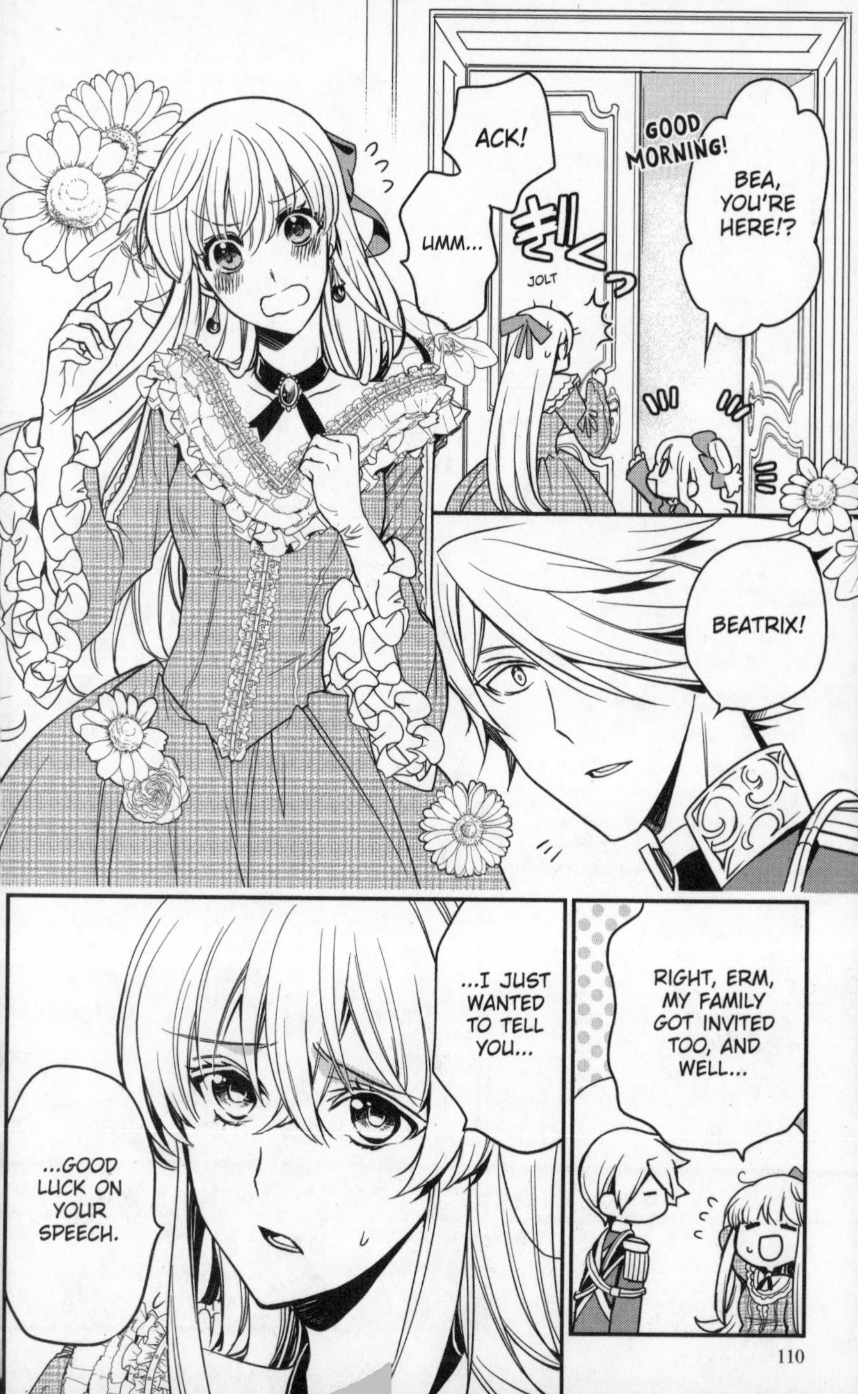
GOOD MORNING!
BEA, YOU'RE HERE!?
ACK!
UMM...
JOLT
BEATRIX!
RIGHT, ERM, MY FAMILY GOT INVITED TOO, AND WELL...
...I JUST WANTED TO TELL YOU...
...GOOD LUCK ON YOUR SPEECH.

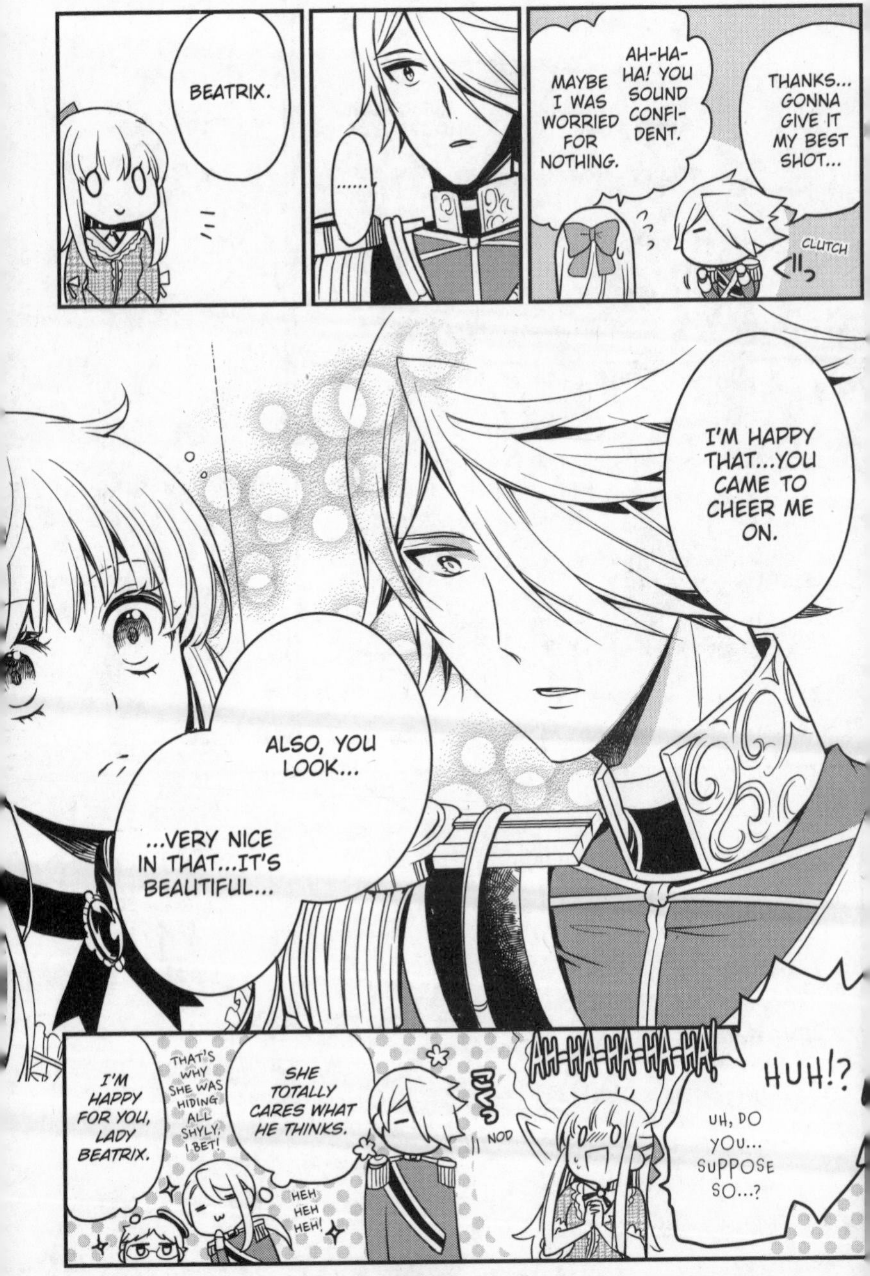
THANKS... GONNA GIVE IT MY BEST SHOT...
AH-HA-HA! YOU SOUND CONFI-DENT.
MAYBE I WAS WORRIED FOR NOTHING.
CLUTCH
......
BEATRIX.
I'M HAPPY THAT...YOU CAME TO CHEER ME ON.
ALSO, YOU LOOK...
...VERY NICE IN THAT...IT'S BEAUTIFUL...
HUH!?
UH, DO YOU... SUPPOSE SO...?
AH-HA-HA-HA-HA!
NOD
SHE TOTALLY CARES WHAT HE THINKS.
HEH HEH HEH!
THAT'S WHY SHE WAS HIDING ALL SHYLY, I BET!
I'M HAPPY FOR YOU, LADY BEATRIX.

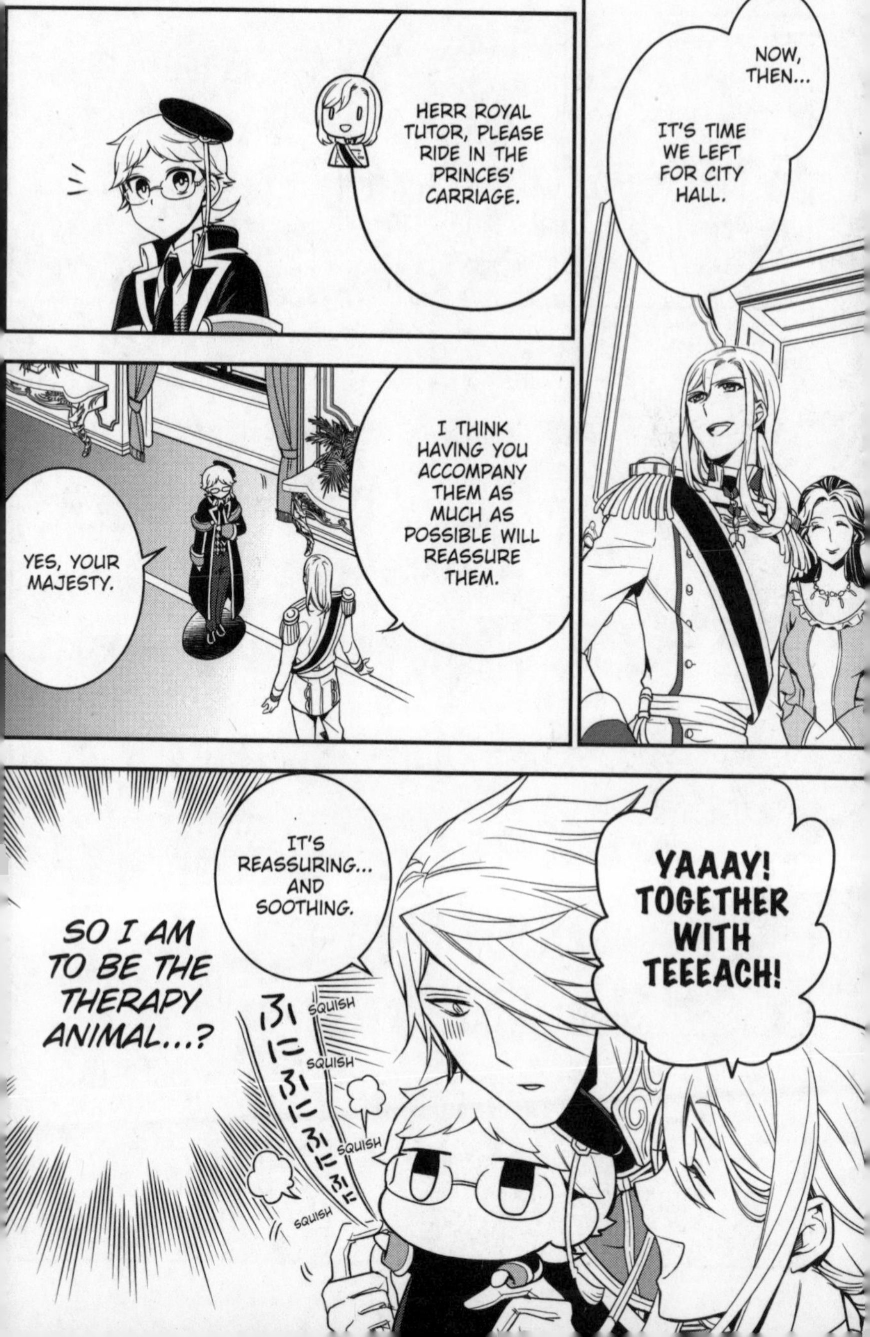
NOW, THEN...
IT'S TIME WE LEFT FOR CITY HALL.
HERR ROYAL TUTOR, PLEASE RIDE IN THE PRINCES' CARRIAGE.
I THINK HAVING YOU ACCOMPANY THEM AS MUCH AS POSSIBLE WILL REASSURE THEM.
YES, YOUR MAJESTY.
YAAAY! TOGETHER WITH TEEEACH!
IT'S REASSURING... AND SOOTHING.
ふにふにふにふにふに
SQUISH
SQUISH
SQUISH
SQUISH
SO I AM TO BE THE THERAPY ANIMAL...?

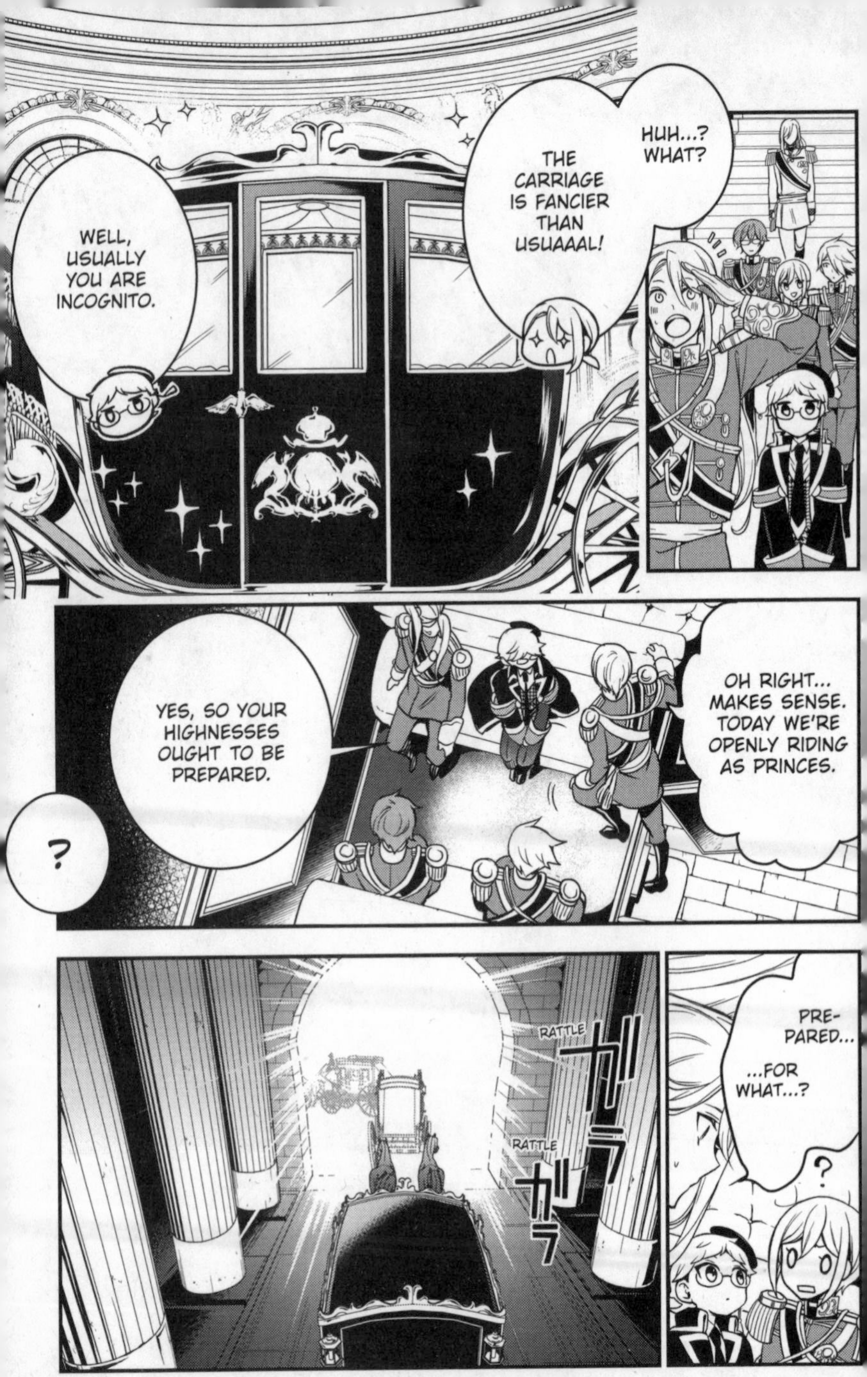
HUH...? WHAT?
THE CARRIAGE IS FANCIER THAN USUAAAL!
WELL, USUALLY YOU ARE INCOGNITO.
OH RIGHT... MAKES SENSE. TODAY WE'RE OPENLY RIDING AS PRINCES.
YES, SO YOUR HIGHNESSES OUGHT TO BE PREPARED.
?
PRE-PARED...
...FOR WHAT...?
?
RATTLE
ガラ
RATTLE
ガラ

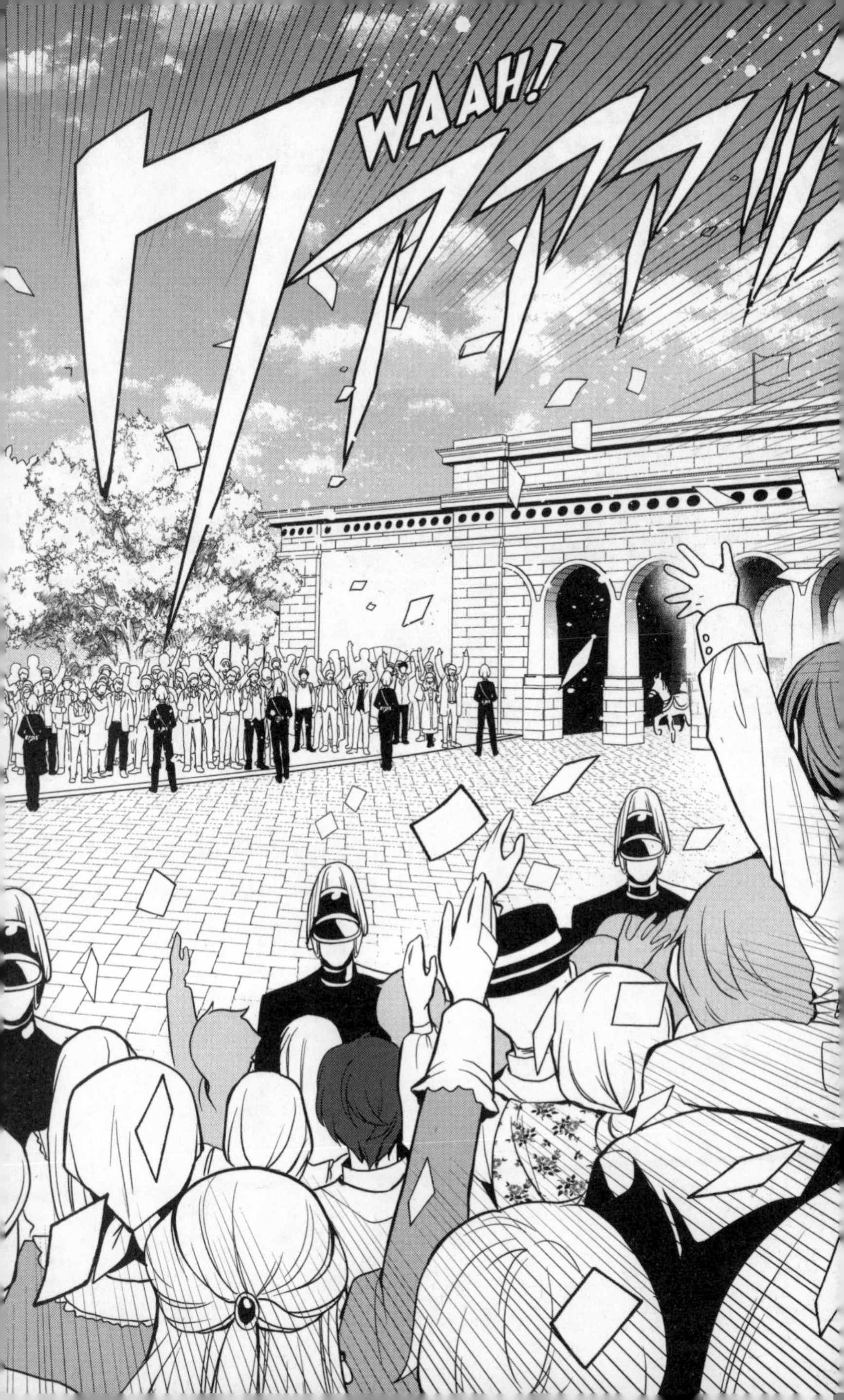
WAAH!!

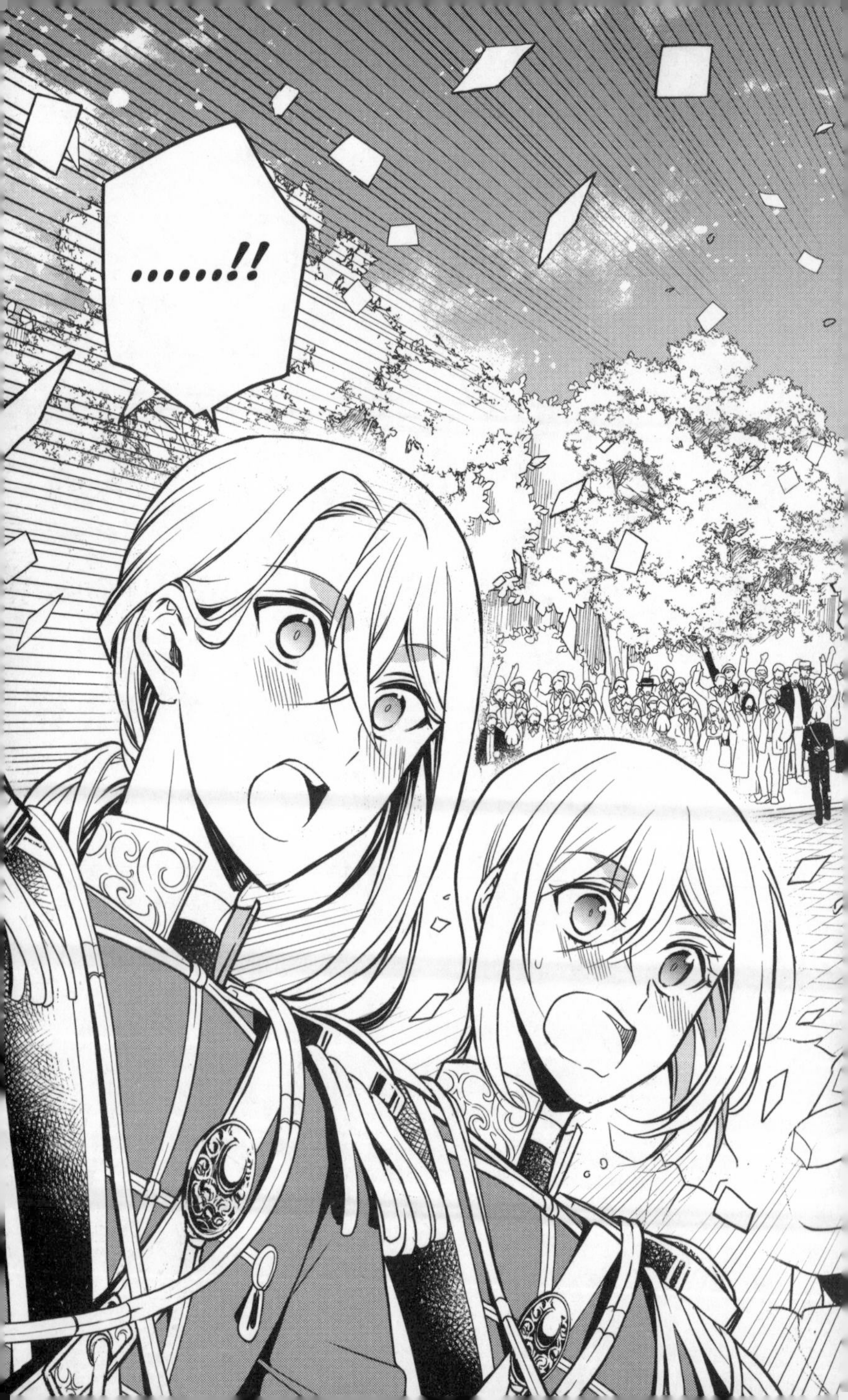
......!!

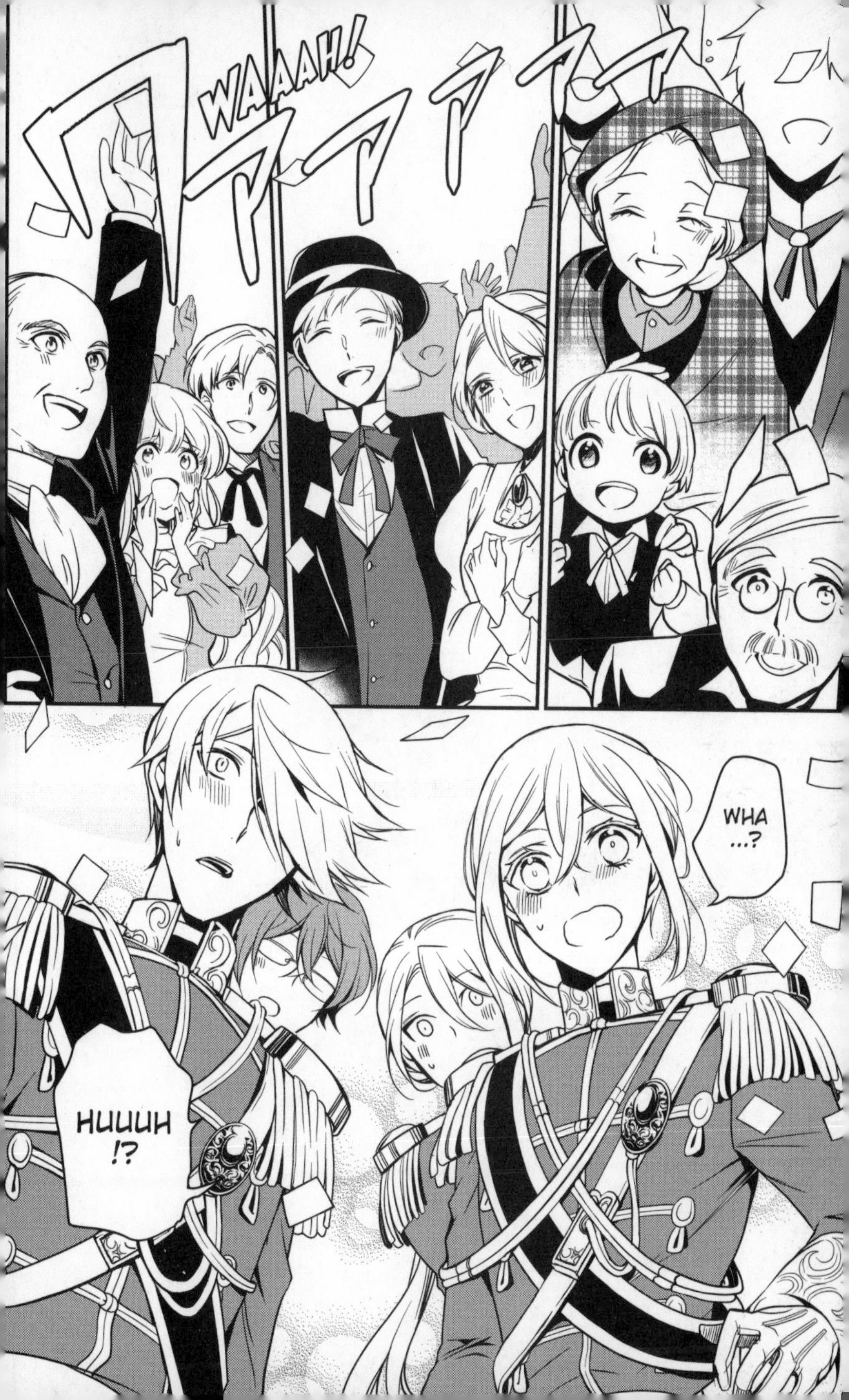
WAAAH!
WHA ...?
HUUUH !?

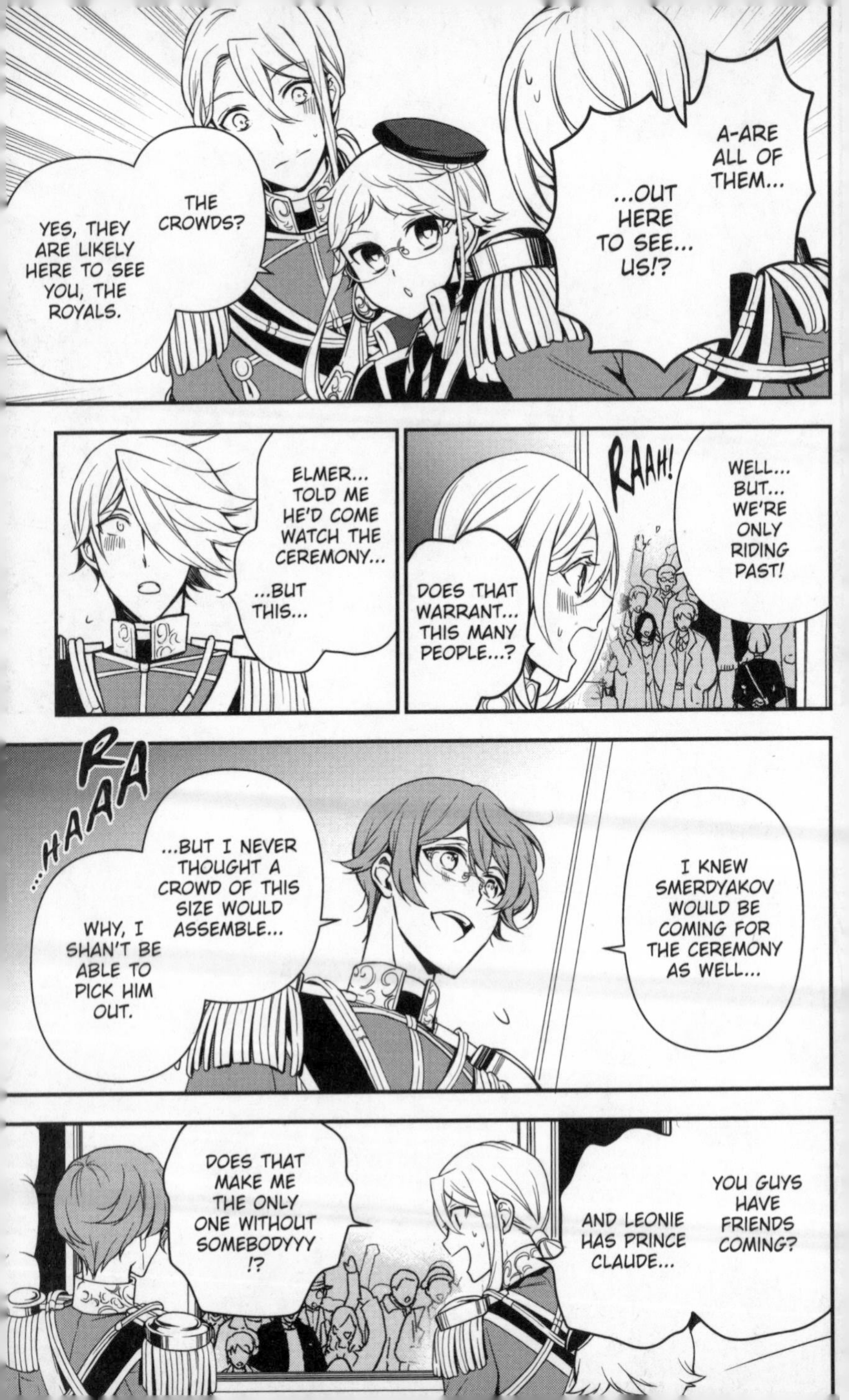
A-ARE ALL OF THEM...
...OUT HERE TO SEE... US!?
THE CROWDS?
YES, THEY ARE LIKELY HERE TO SEE YOU, THE ROYALS.
RAAH!
WELL... BUT... WE'RE ONLY RIDING PAST!
DOES THAT WARRANT... THIS MANY PEOPLE...?
ELMER... TOLD ME HE'D COME WATCH THE CEREMONY...
...BUT THIS...
RAAAAH...
I KNEW SMERDYAKOV WOULD BE COMING FOR THE CEREMONY AS WELL...
...BUT I NEVER THOUGHT A CROWD OF THIS SIZE WOULD ASSEMBLE...
WHY, I SHAN'T BE ABLE TO PICK HIM OUT.
YOU GUYS HAVE FRIENDS COMING?
AND LEONIE HAS PRINCE CLAUDE...
DOES THAT MAKE ME THE ONLY ONE WITHOUT SOMEBODYYY!?

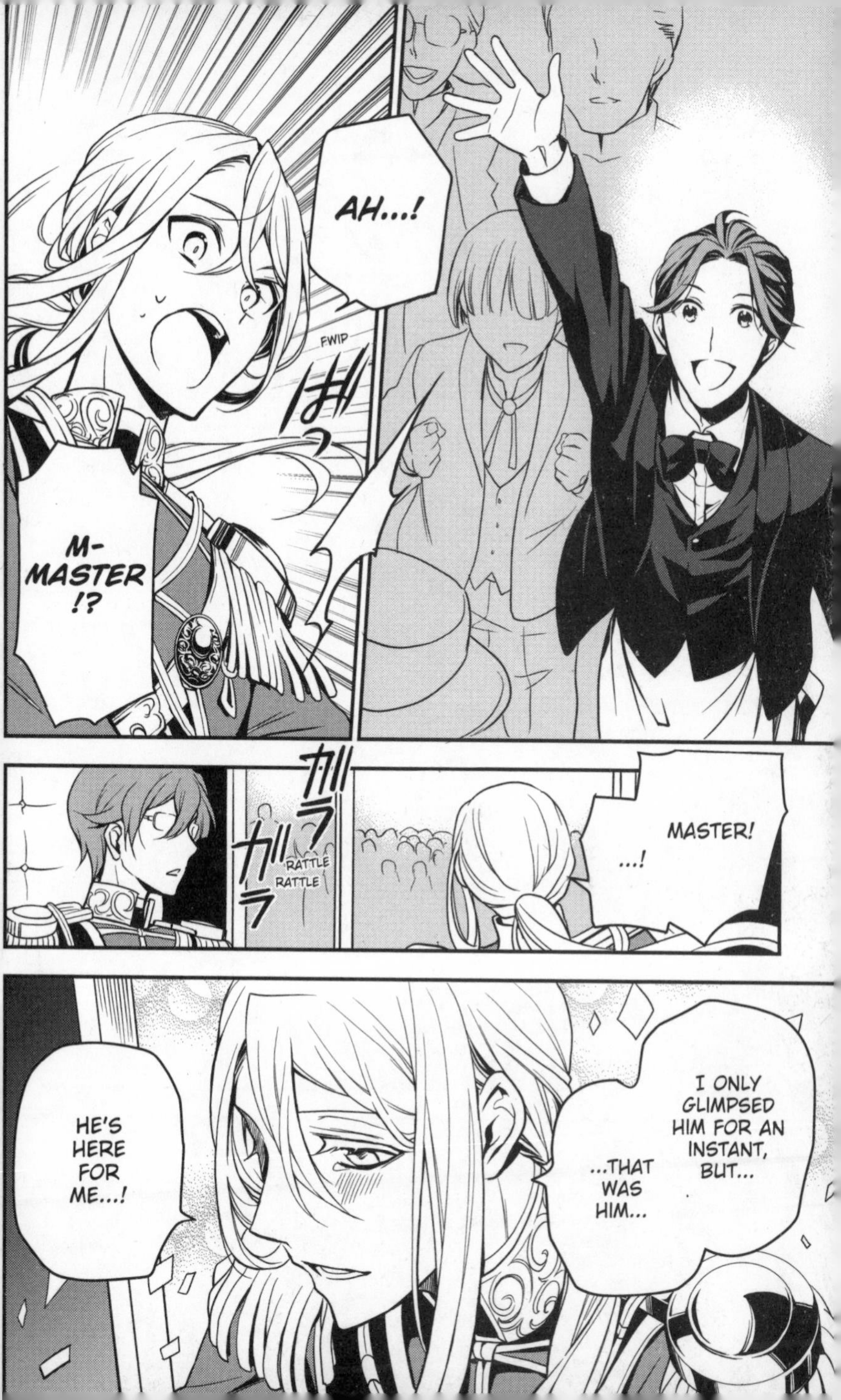
AH...!
FWIP
ぱっ
M-MASTER!?
MASTER!
...!
ガラ
RATTLE
ガラ
RATTLE
I ONLY GLIMPSED HIM FOR AN INSTANT, BUT...
...THAT WAS HIM...
HE'S HERE FOR ME...!

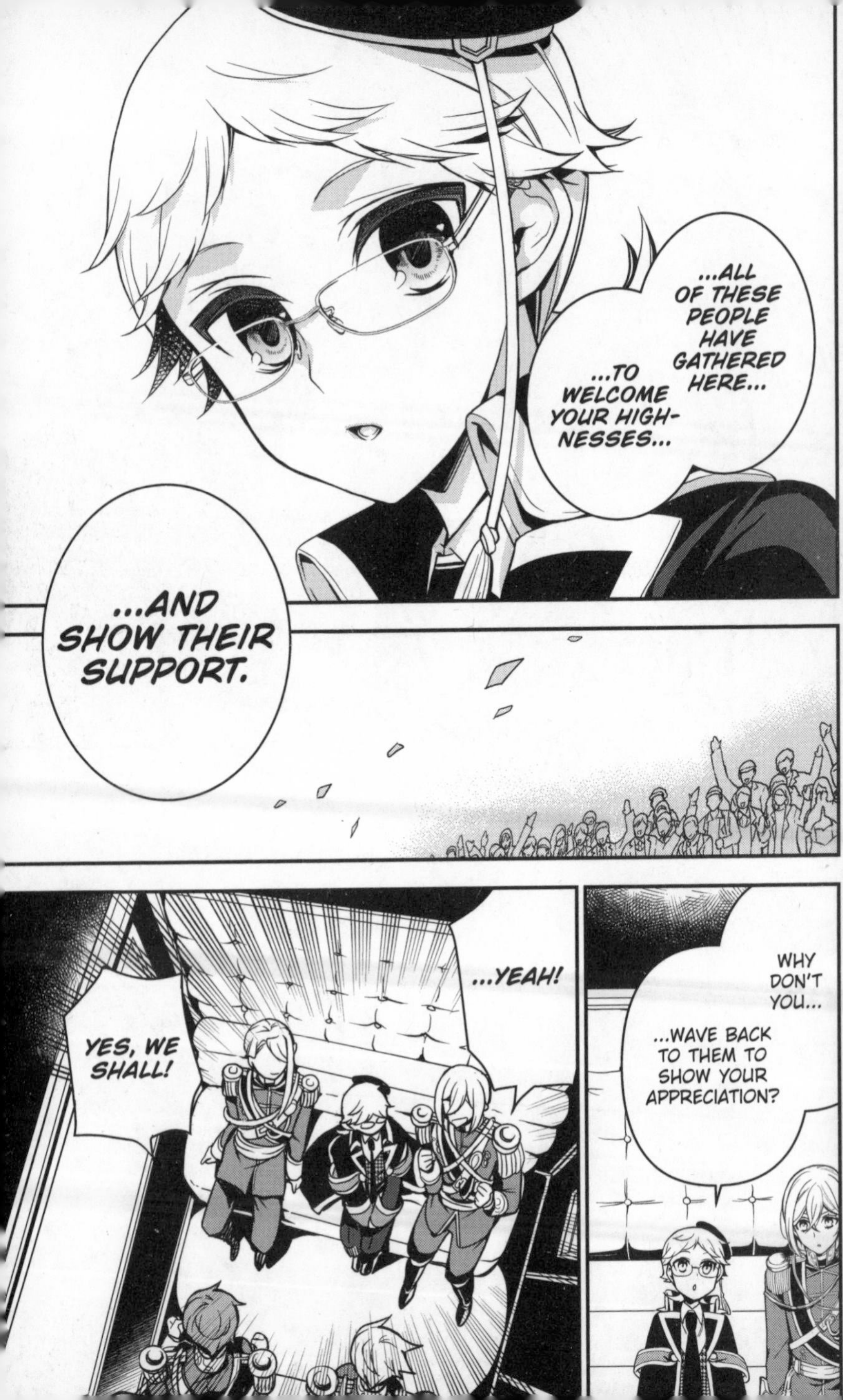
...ALL OF THESE PEOPLE HAVE GATHERED HERE...
...TO WELCOME YOUR HIGH-NESSES...
...AND SHOW THEIR SUPPORT.
WHY DON'T YOU...
...WAVE BACK TO THEM TO SHOW YOUR APPRECIATION?
...YEAH!
YES, WE SHALL!

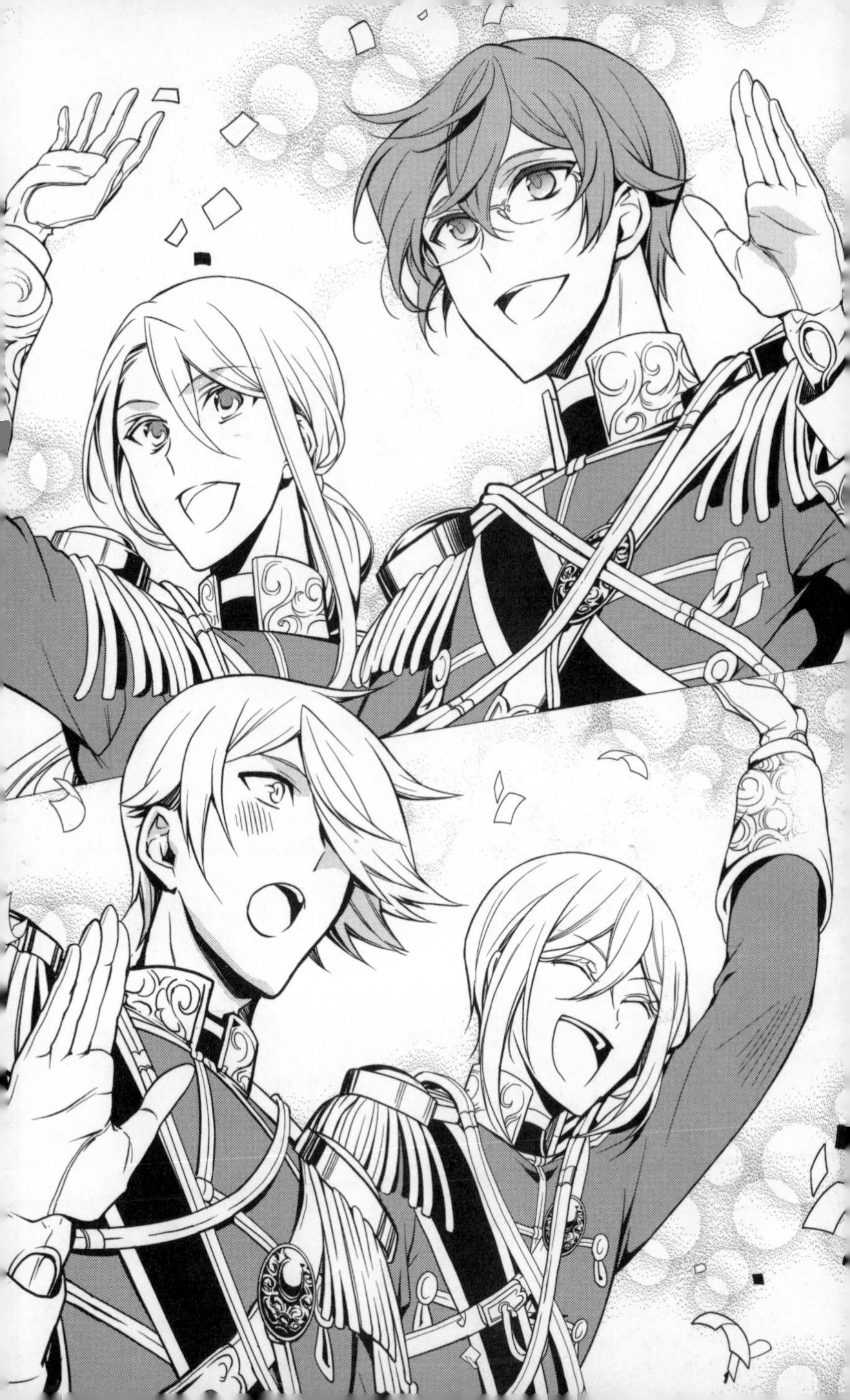

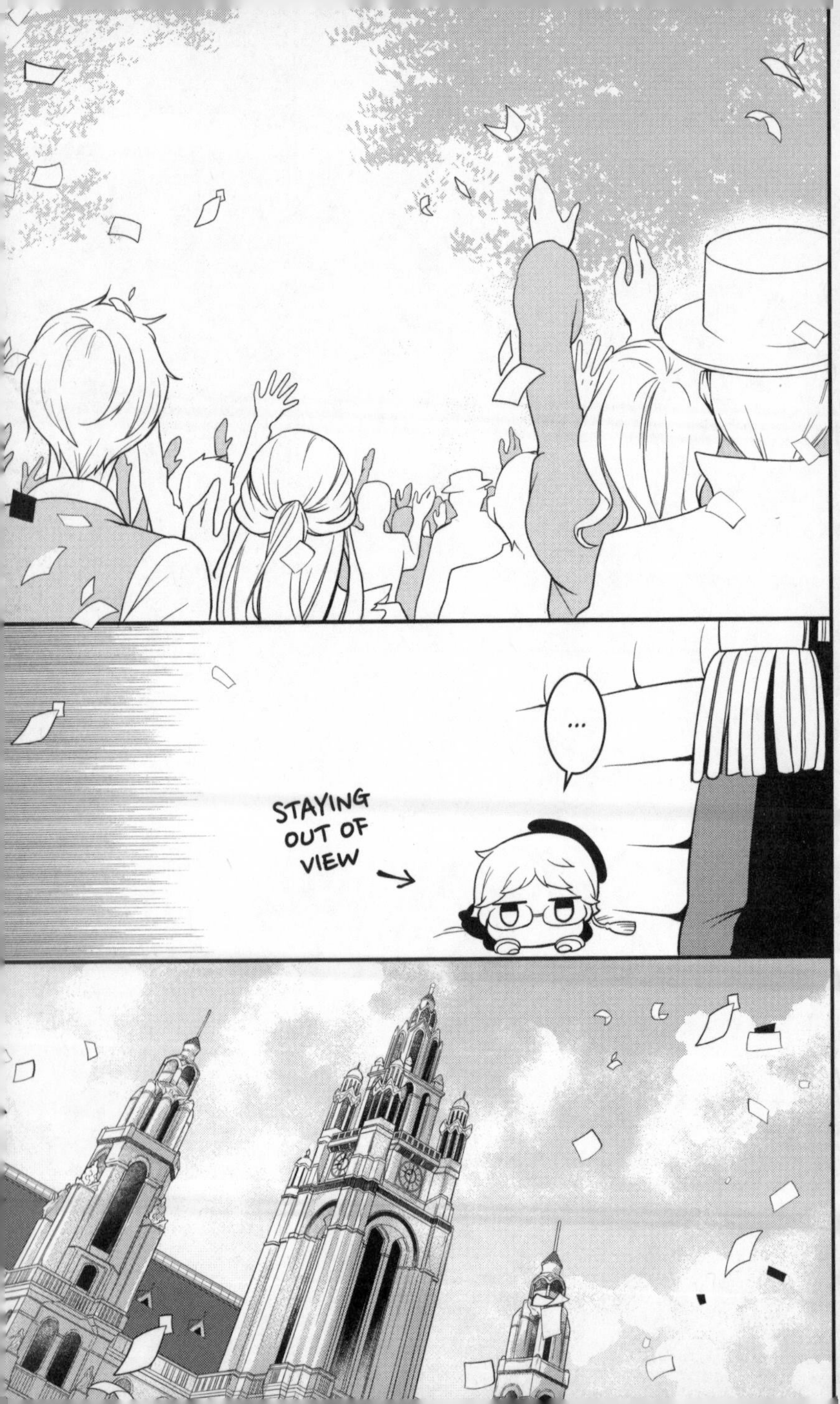
...
STAYING OUT OF VIEW

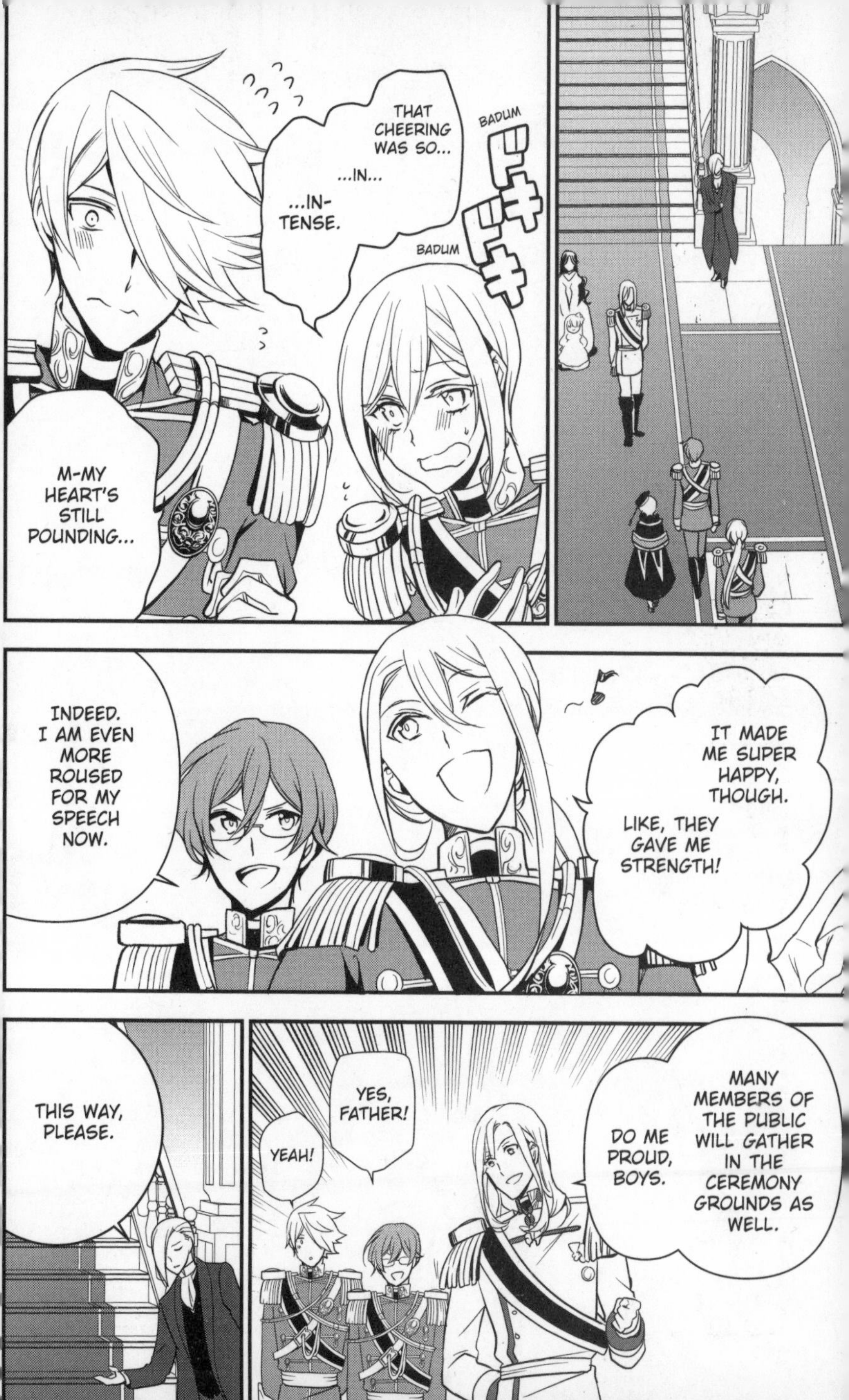
BADUM
ドキ
BADUM
ドキ
THAT CHEERING WAS SO... ...IN... ...IN-TENSE.
M-MY HEART'S STILL POUNDING...
IT MADE ME SUPER HAPPY, THOUGH. LIKE, THEY GAVE ME STRENGTH!
INDEED. I AM EVEN MORE ROUSED FOR MY SPEECH NOW.
MANY MEMBERS OF THE PUBLIC WILL GATHER IN THE CEREMONY GROUNDS AS WELL.
DO ME PROUD, BOYS.
YES, FATHER!
YEAH!
THIS WAY, PLEASE.

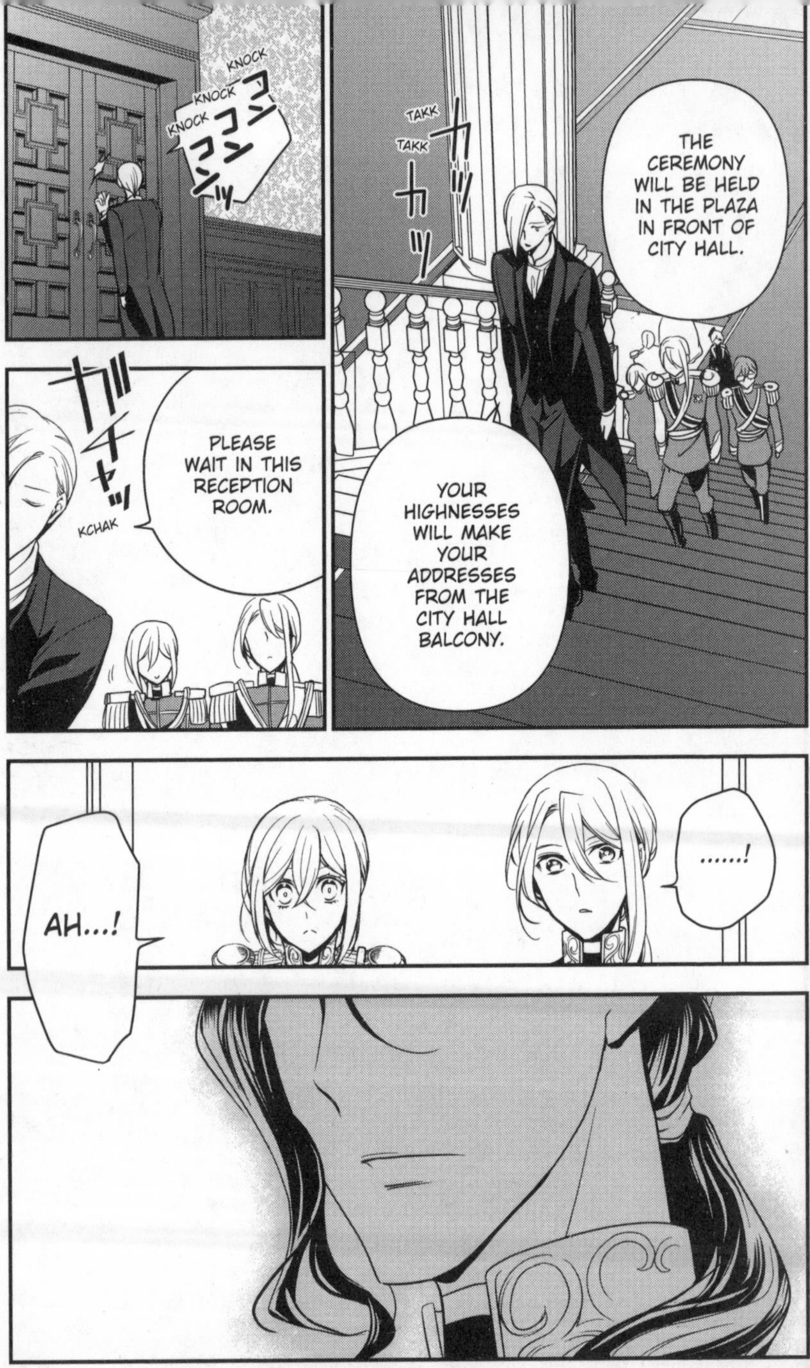
THE CEREMONY WILL BE HELD IN THE PLAZA IN FRONT OF CITY HALL.
TAKK TAKK
カッ カッ
YOUR HIGHNESSES WILL MAKE YOUR ADDRESSES FROM THE CITY HALL BALCONY.
KNOCK KNOCK KNOCK
コン コン コンッ
ガチャッ
KCHAK
PLEASE WAIT IN THIS RECEPTION ROOM.
......!
AH...!

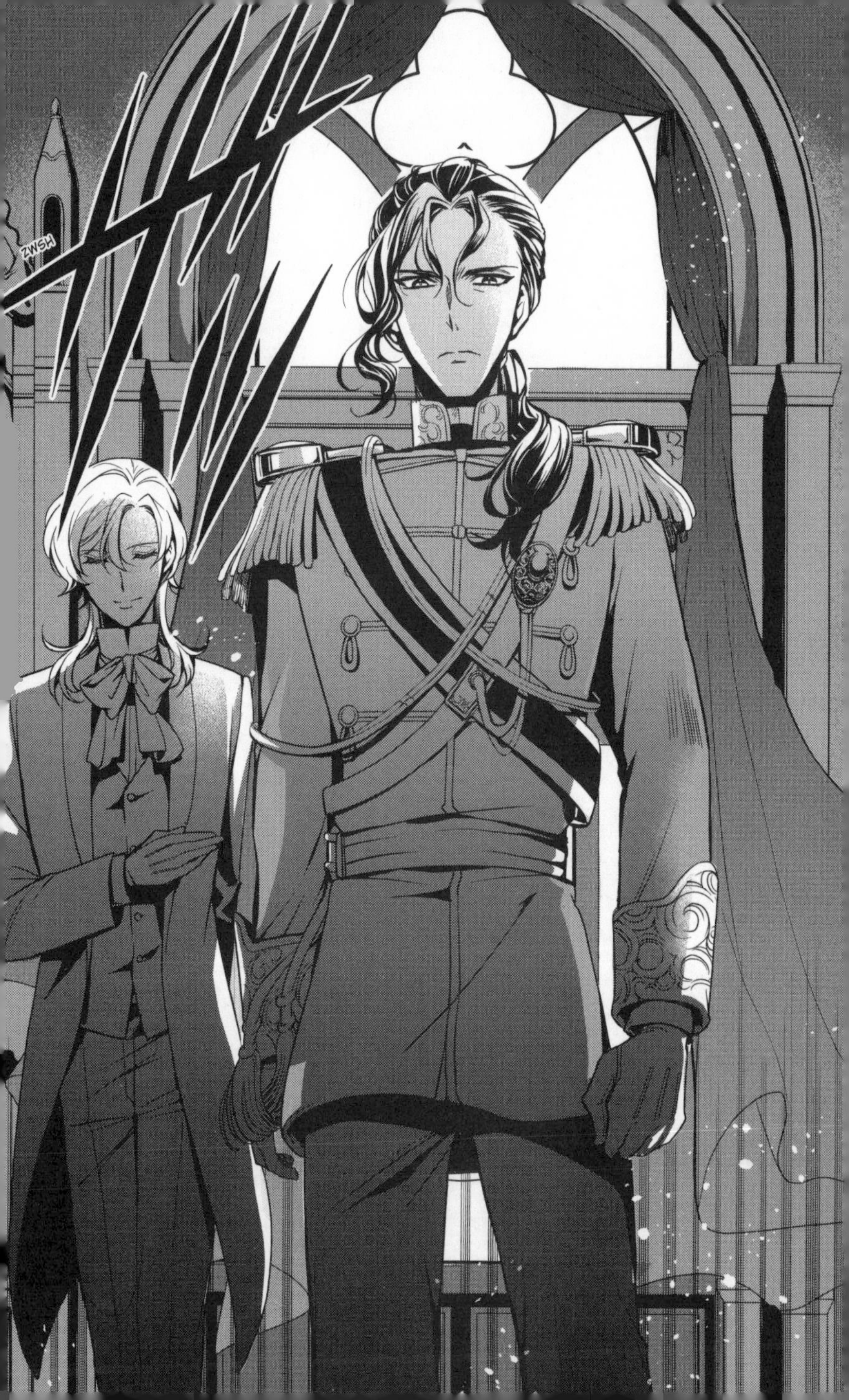
ZWSH

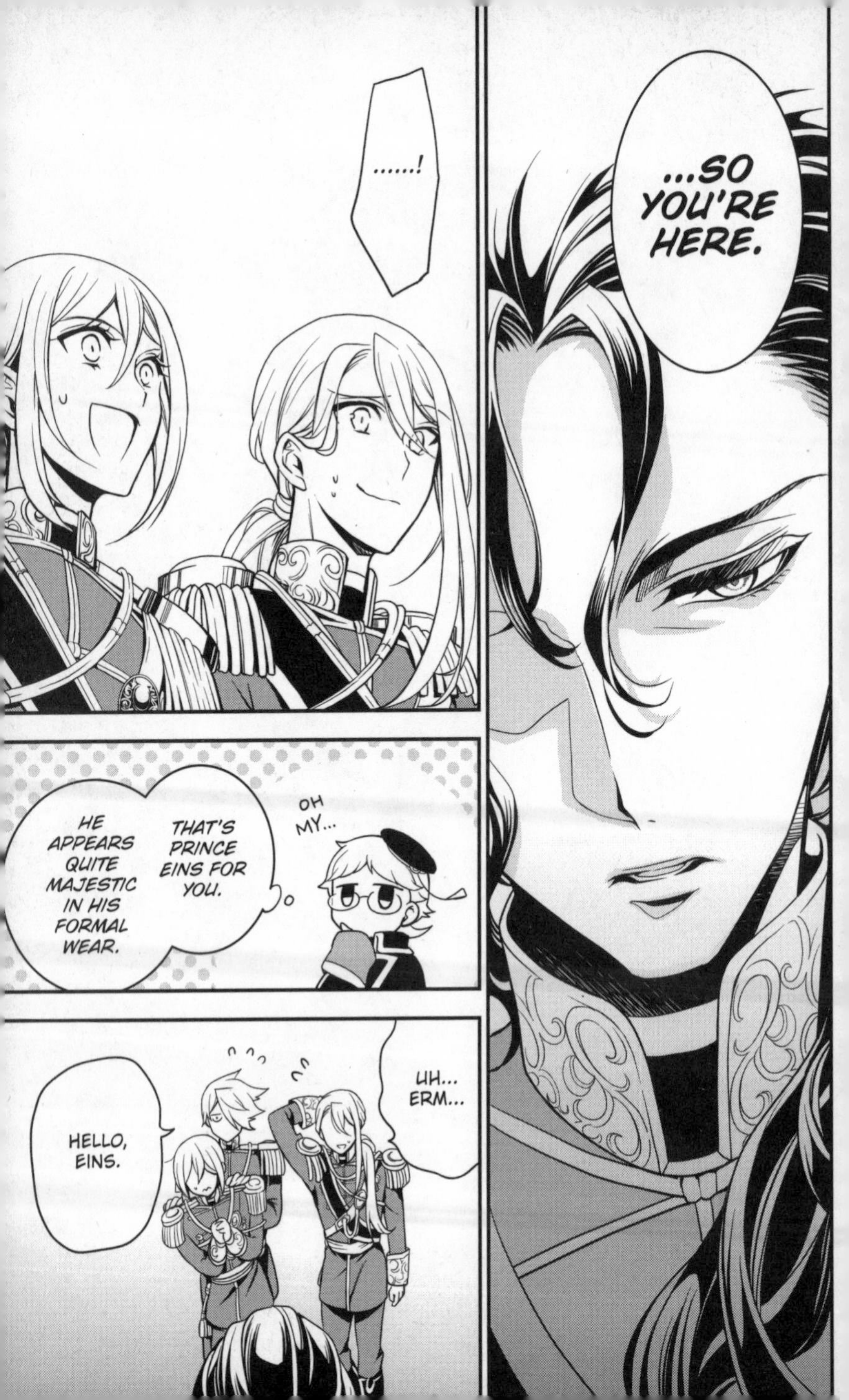
...SO YOU'RE HERE.
......!
OH MY...
THAT'S PRINCE EINS FOR YOU.
HE APPEARS QUITE MAJESTIC IN HIS FORMAL WEAR.
UH... ERM...
HELLO, EINS.

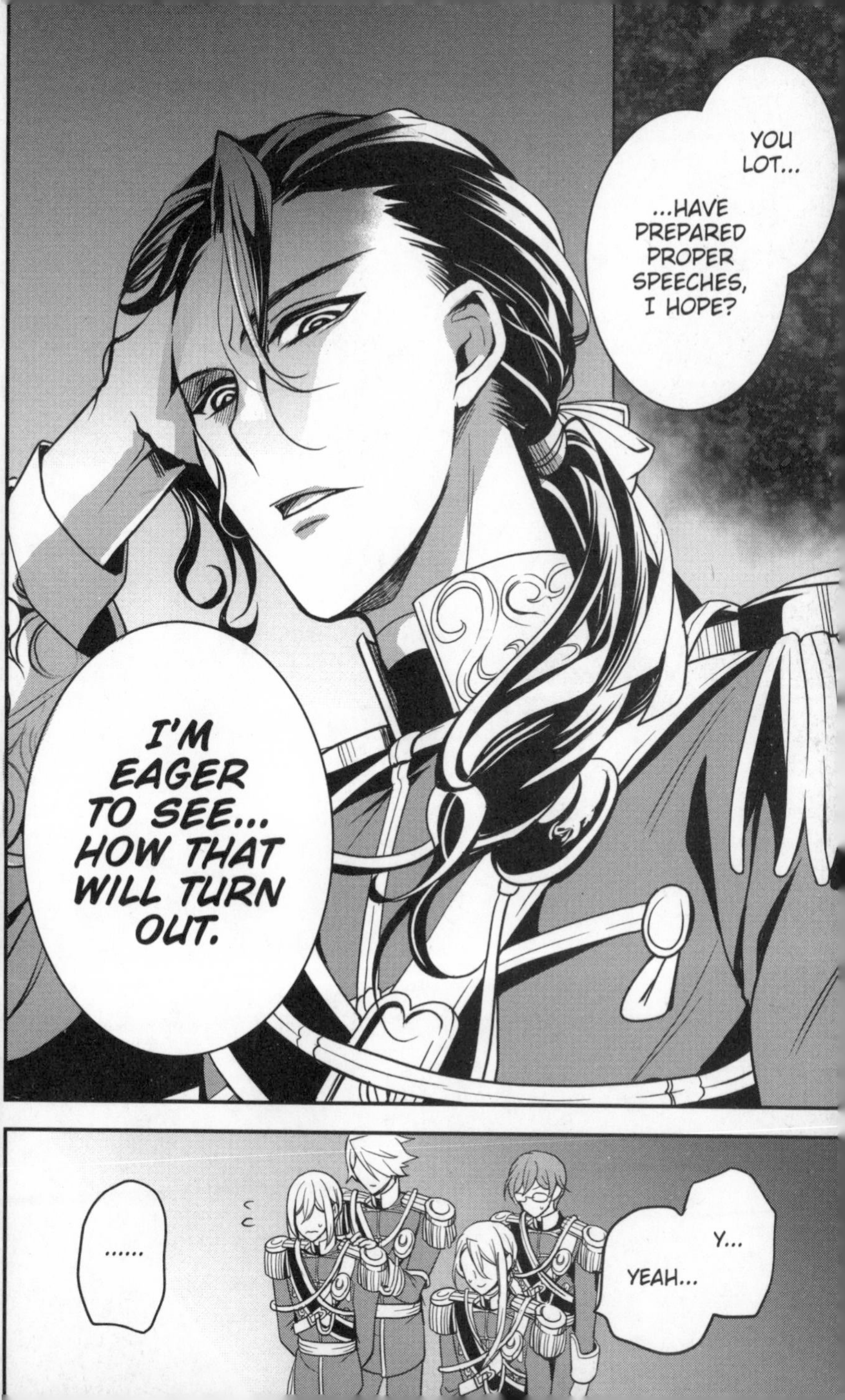
YOU LOT...
...HAVE PREPARED PROPER SPEECHES, I HOPE?
I'M EAGER TO SEE... HOW THAT WILL TURN OUT.
Y... YEAH...
......

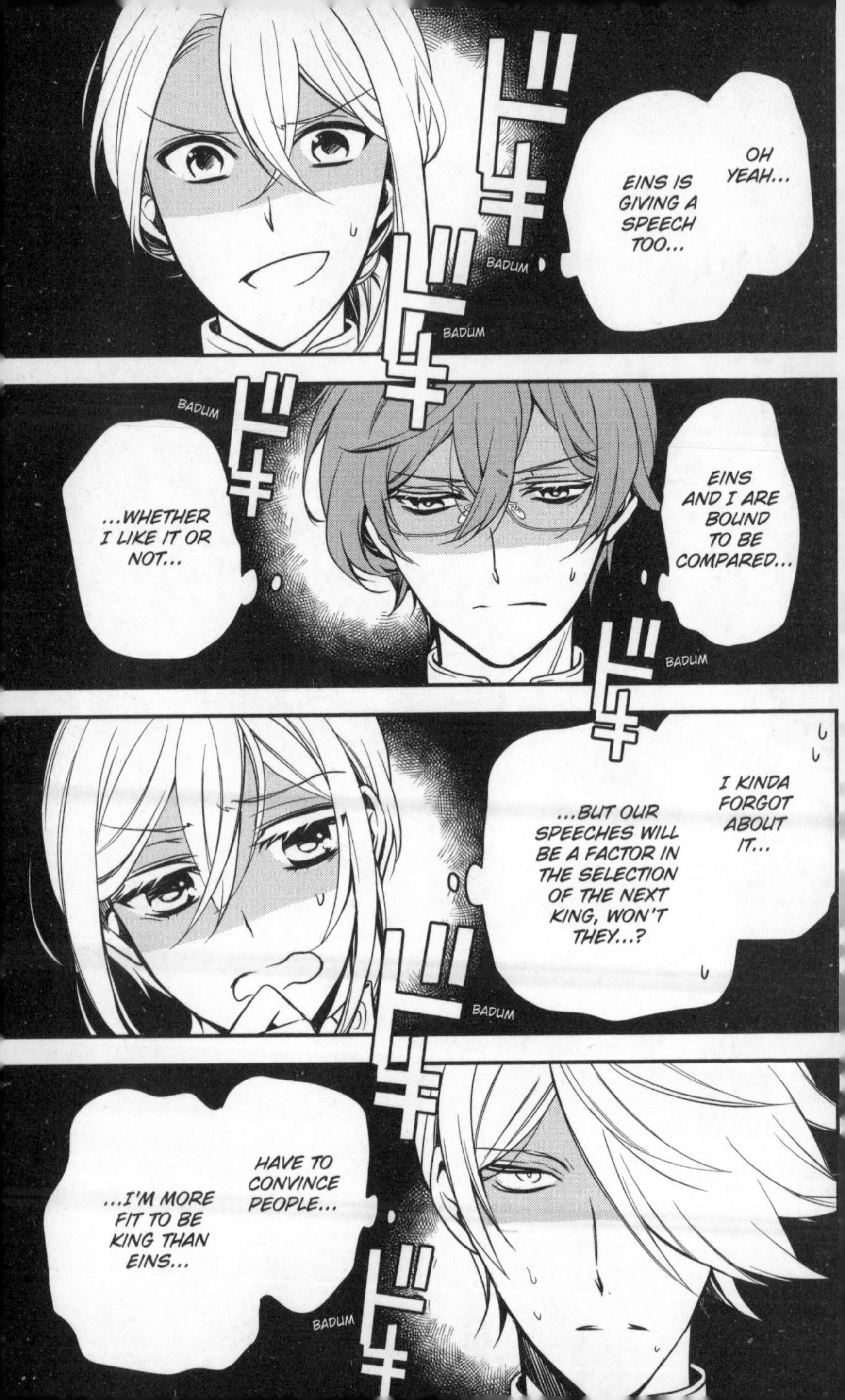
BADUM
BADUM
OH YEAH...
EINS IS GIVING A SPEECH TOO...
BADUM
EINS AND I ARE BOUND TO BE COMPARED...
...WHETHER I LIKE IT OR NOT...
BADUM
I KINDA FORGOT ABOUT IT...
...BUT OUR SPEECHES WILL BE A FACTOR IN THE SELECTION OF THE NEXT KING, WON'T THEY...?
BADUM
HAVE TO CONVINCE PEOPLE...
...I'M MORE FIT TO BE KING THAN EINS...
BADUM

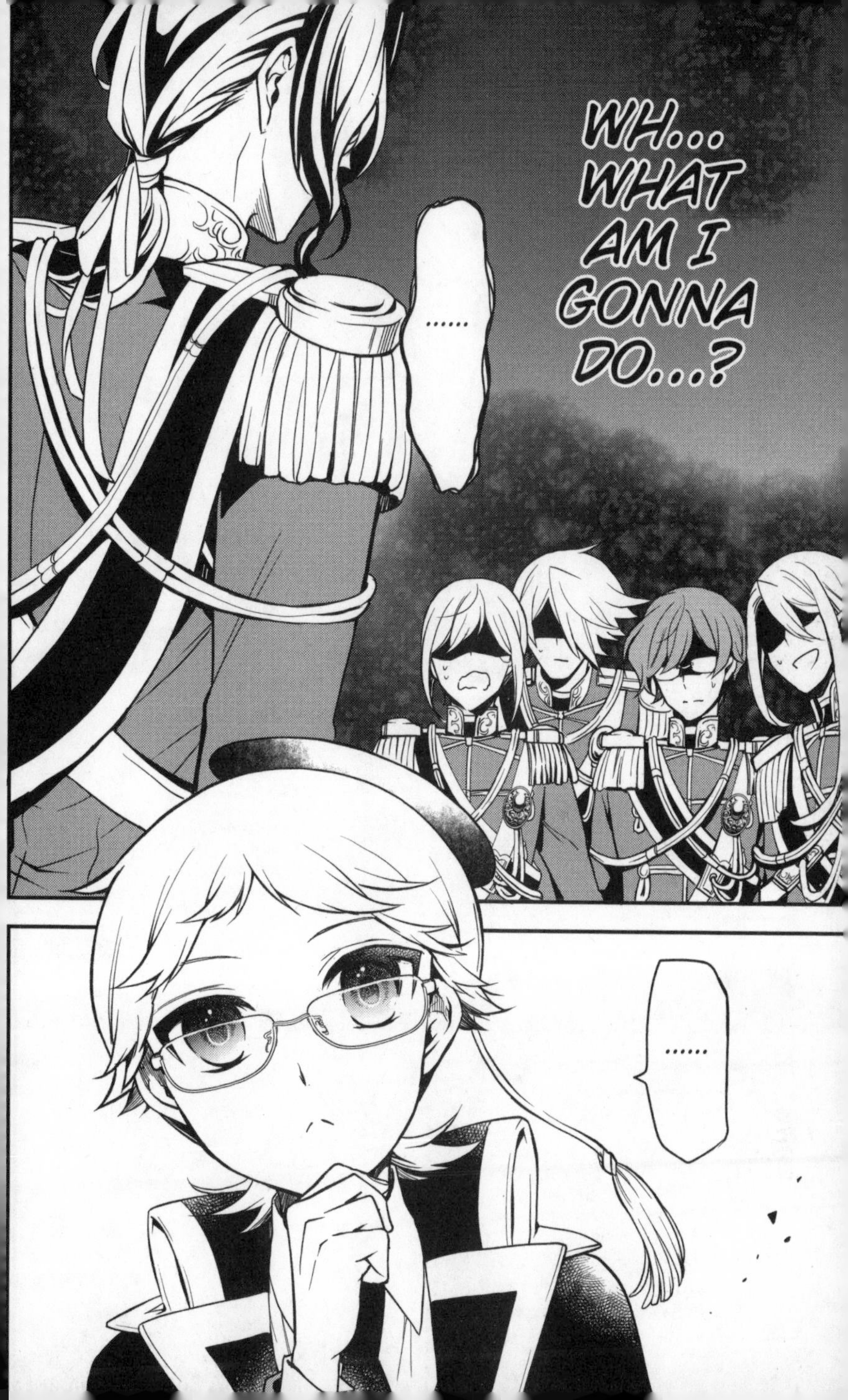
WH... WHAT AM I GONNA DO...?
......
......

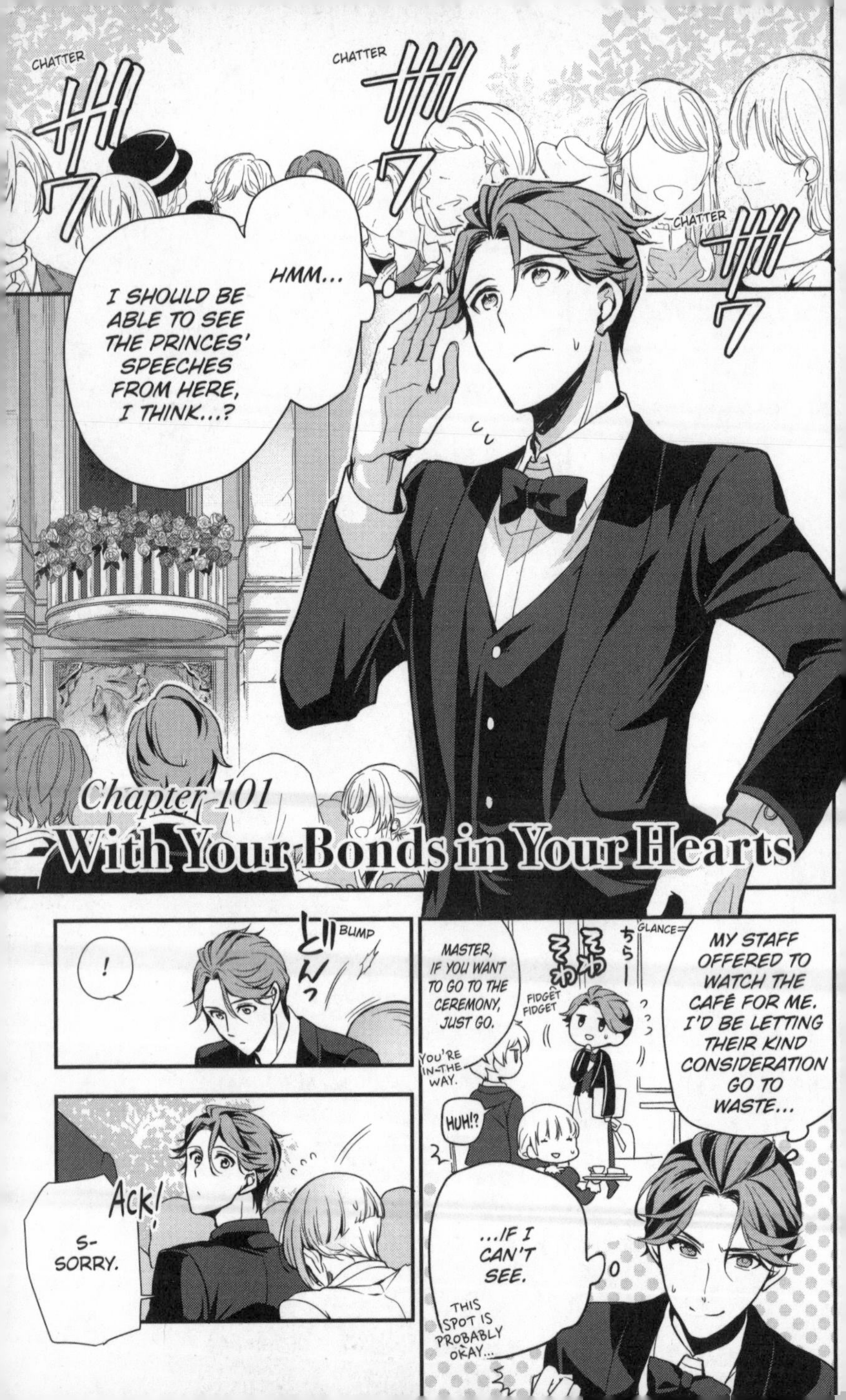
CHATTER
CHATTER
CHATTER
HMM...
I SHOULD BE ABLE TO SEE THE PRINCES' SPEECHES FROM HERE, I THINK...?
Chapter 101
With Your Bonds in Your Hearts
GLANCE
MY STAFF OFFERED TO WATCH THE CAFÉ FOR ME. I'D BE LETTING THEIR KIND CONSIDERATION GO TO WASTE...
MASTER, IF YOU WANT TO GO TO THE CEREMONY, JUST GO.
FIDGET FIDGET
YOU'RE IN THE WAY.
HUH!?
...IF I CAN'T SEE.
THIS SPOT IS PROBABLY OKAY...
BUMP
!
ACK!
S-SORRY.

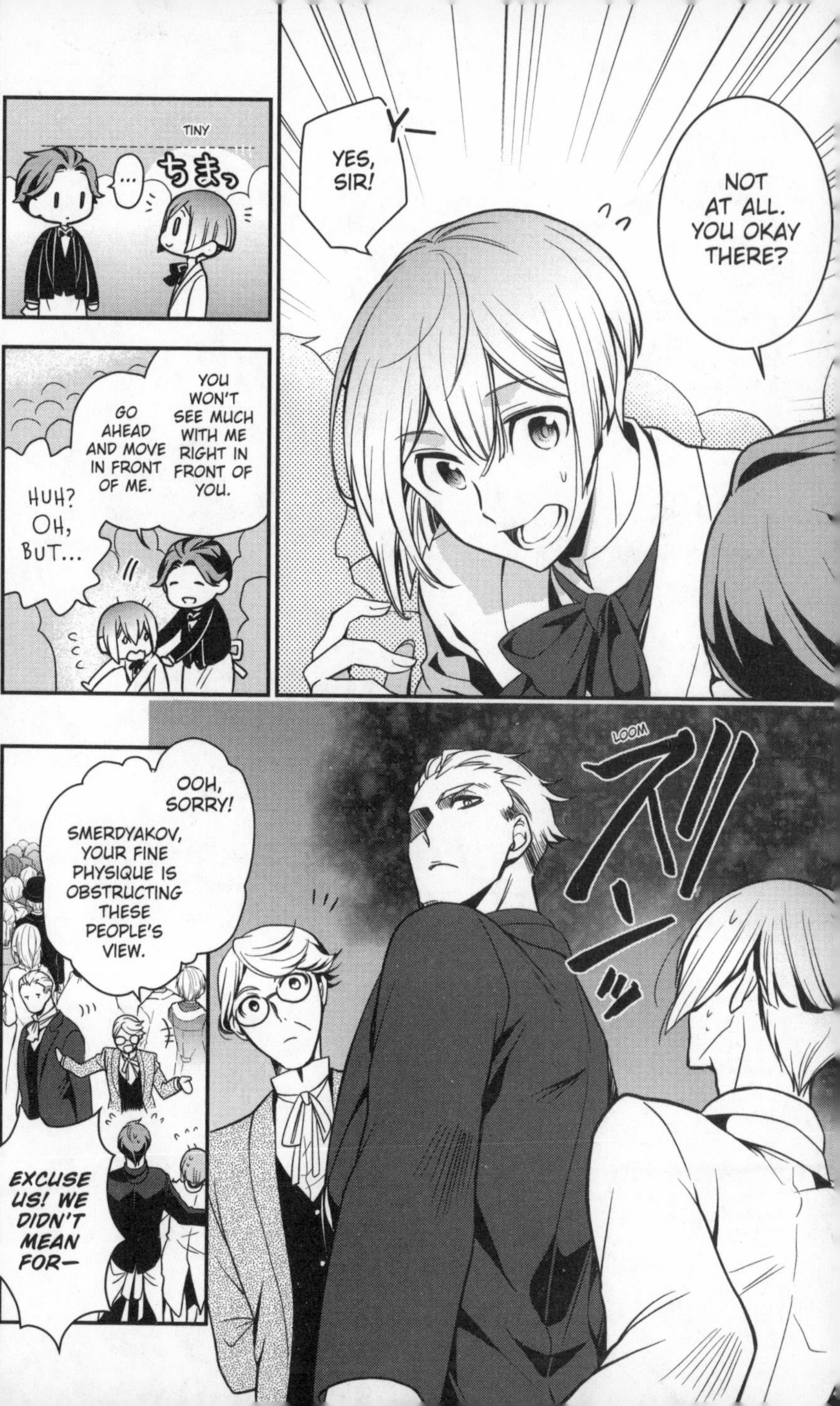
NOT AT ALL. YOU OKAY THERE?
Y—
YES, SIR!
TINY
ちまっ
...
YOU WON'T SEE MUCH WITH ME RIGHT IN FRONT OF YOU.
GO AHEAD AND MOVE IN FRONT OF ME.
HUH? OH, BUT...
LOOM
ズリーッ
OOH, SORRY!
SMERDYAKOV, YOUR FINE PHYSIQUE IS OBSTRUCTING THESE PEOPLE'S VIEW.
EXCUSE US! WE DIDN'T MEAN FOR—

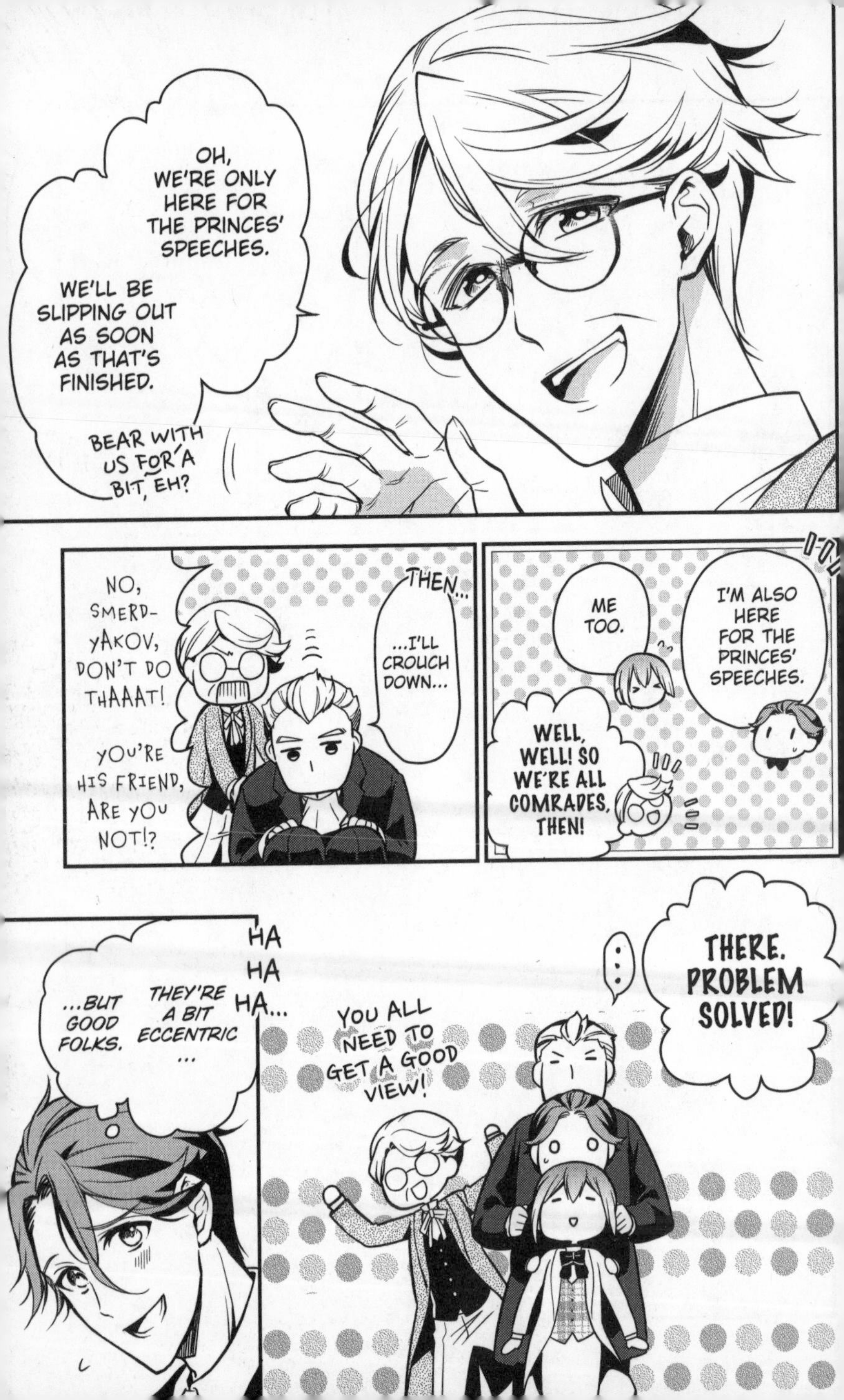
OH, WE'RE ONLY HERE FOR THE PRINCES' SPEECHES.
WE'LL BE SLIPPING OUT AS SOON AS THAT'S FINISHED.
BEAR WITH US FOR A BIT, EH?
I'M ALSO HERE FOR THE PRINCES' SPEECHES.
ME TOO.
WELL, WELL! SO WE'RE ALL COMRADES, THEN!
THEN...
...I'LL CROUCH DOWN...
NO, SMERD-YAKOV, DON'T DO THAAAT!
YOU'RE HIS FRIEND, ARE YOU NOT!?
THERE. PROBLEM SOLVED!
...
YOU ALL NEED TO GET A GOOD VIEW!
HA HA HA...
THEY'RE A BIT ECCENTRIC...
...BUT GOOD FOLKS.

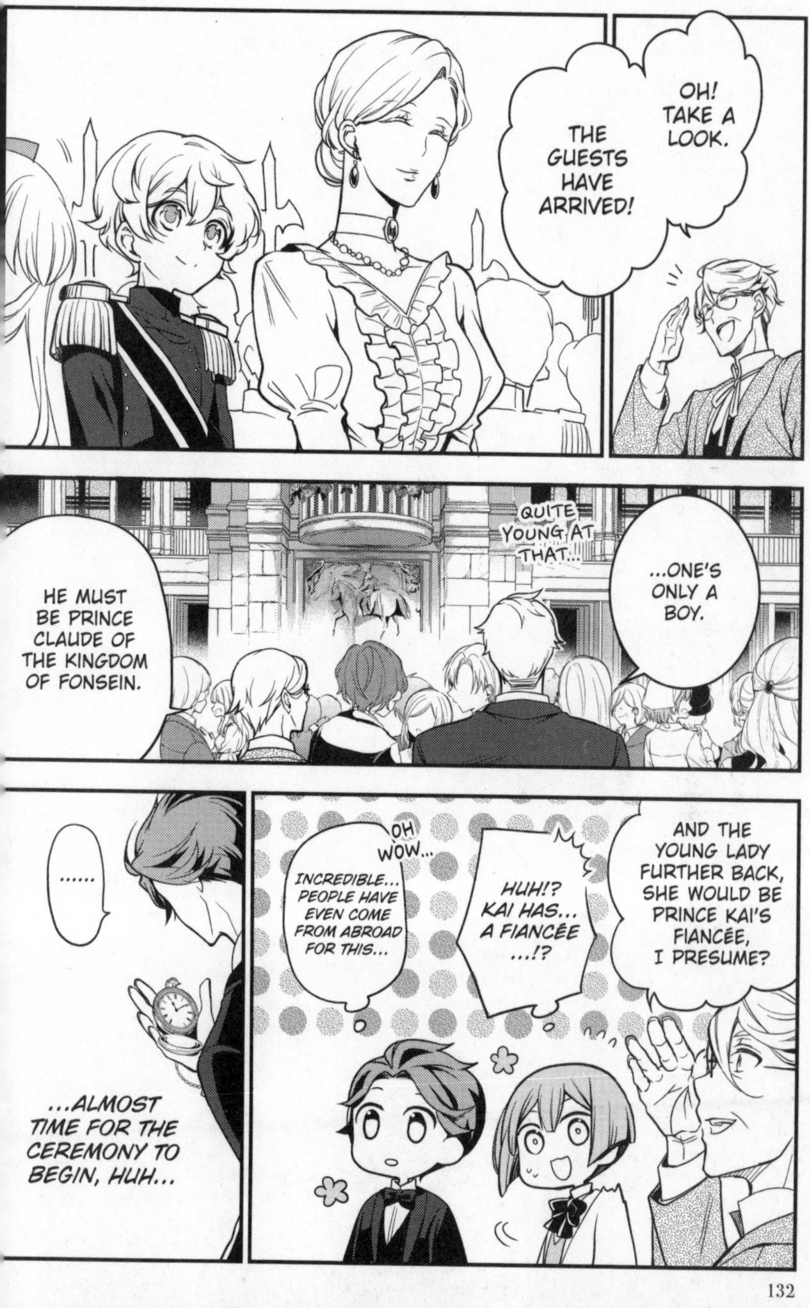
OH! TAKE A LOOK.
THE GUESTS HAVE ARRIVED!
...ONE'S ONLY A BOY.
QUITE YOUNG AT THAT...
HE MUST BE PRINCE CLAUDE OF THE KINGDOM OF FONSEIN.
AND THE YOUNG LADY FURTHER BACK, SHE WOULD BE PRINCE KAI'S FIANCÉE, I PRESUME?
HUH!? KAI HAS... A FIANCÉE ...!?
OH WOW...
INCREDIBLE... PEOPLE HAVE EVEN COME FROM ABROAD FOR THIS...
......
...ALMOST TIME FOR THE CEREMONY TO BEGIN, HUH...

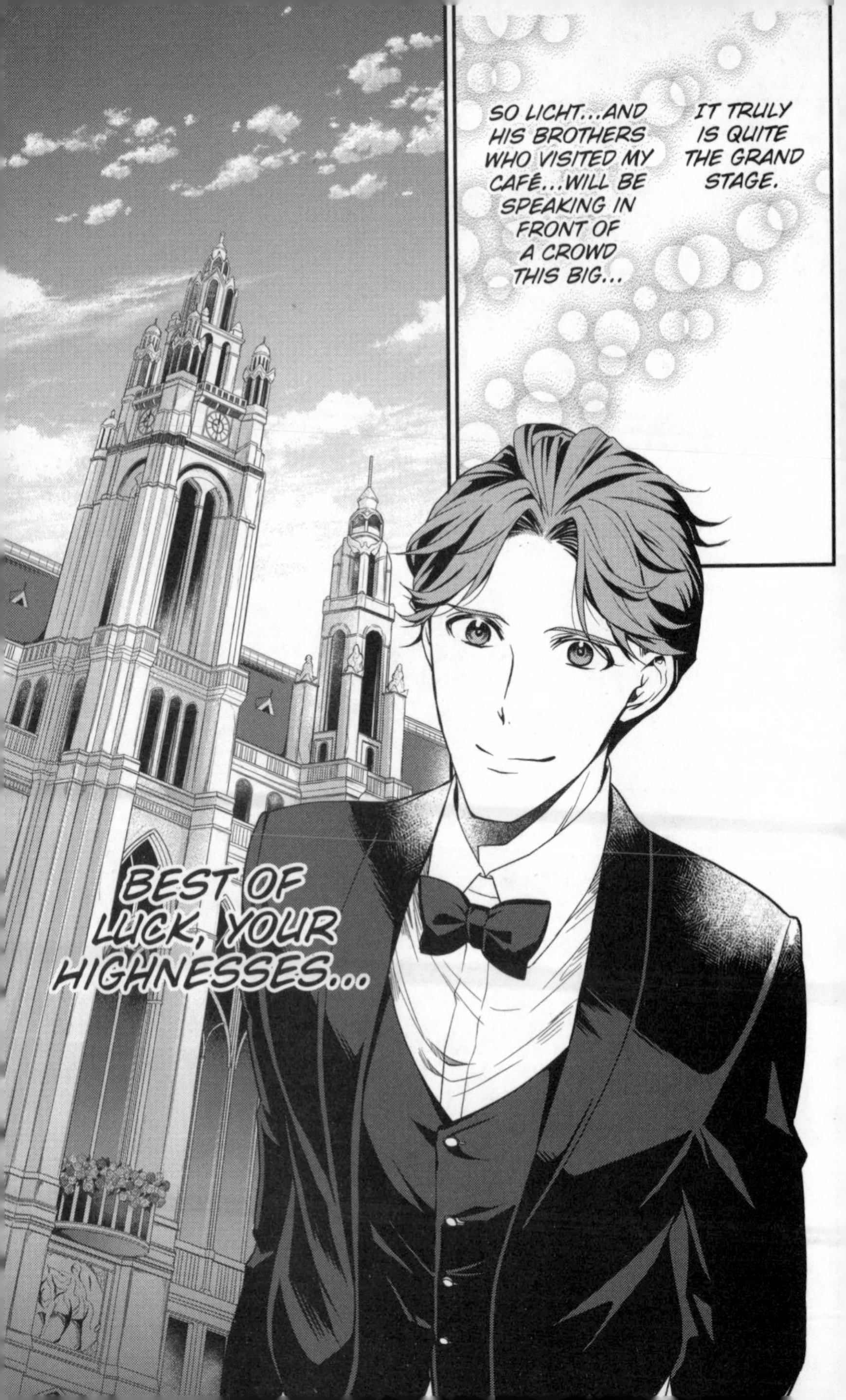
SO LICHT...AND HIS BROTHERS WHO VISITED MY CAFÉ...WILL BE SPEAKING IN FRONT OF A CROWD THIS BIG...
IT TRULY IS QUITE THE GRAND STAGE.
BEST OF LUCK, YOUR HIGHNESSES...

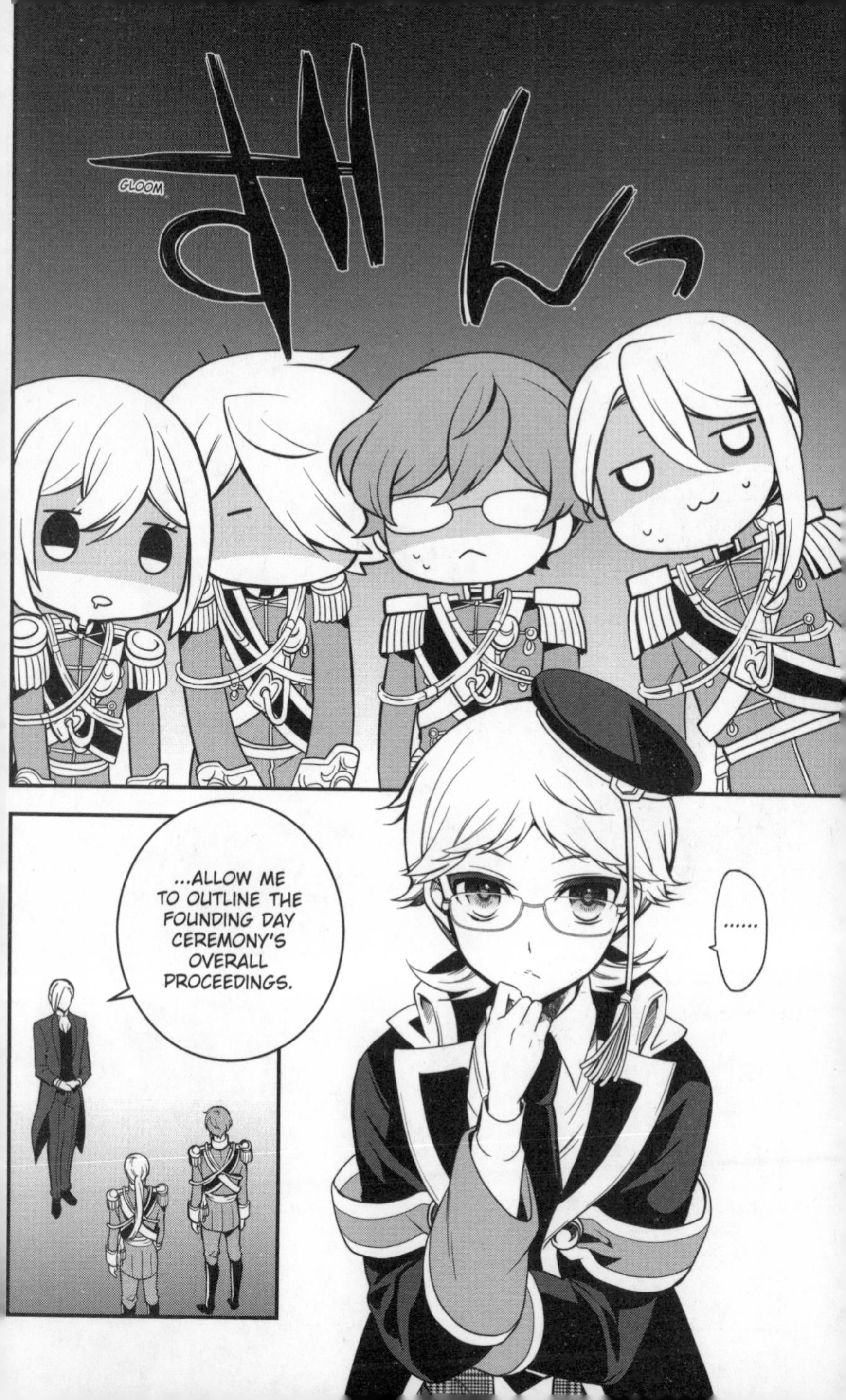
GLOOM
ずーん
......
...ALLOW ME TO OUTLINE THE FOUNDING DAY CEREMONY'S OVERALL PROCEEDINGS.

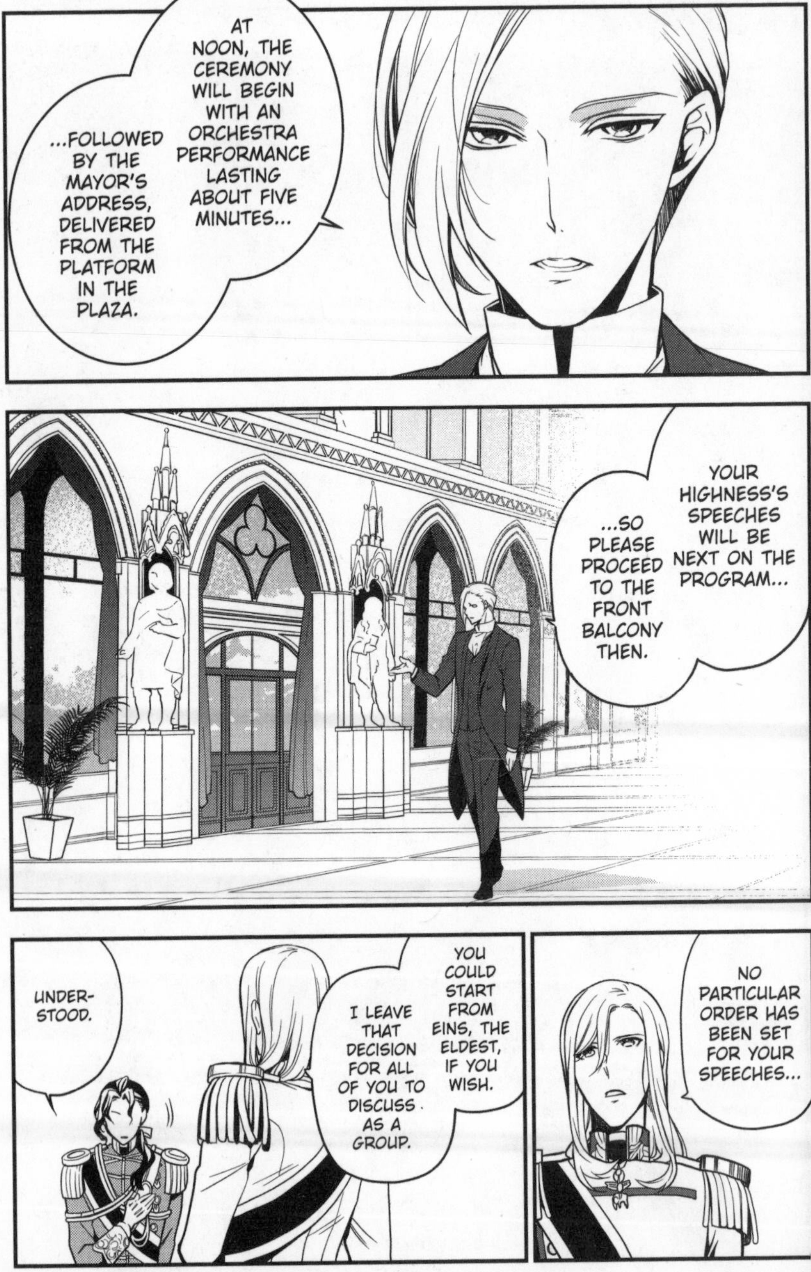
AT NOON, THE CEREMONY WILL BEGIN WITH AN ORCHESTRA PERFORMANCE LASTING ABOUT FIVE MINUTES...
...FOLLOWED BY THE MAYOR'S ADDRESS, DELIVERED FROM THE PLATFORM IN THE PLAZA.
YOUR HIGHNESS'S SPEECHES WILL BE NEXT ON THE PROGRAM...
...SO PLEASE PROCEED TO THE FRONT BALCONY THEN.
NO PARTICULAR ORDER HAS BEEN SET FOR YOUR SPEECHES...
YOU COULD START FROM EINS, THE ELDEST, IF YOU WISH.
I LEAVE THAT DECISION FOR ALL OF YOU TO DISCUSS AS A GROUP.
UNDER-STOOD.

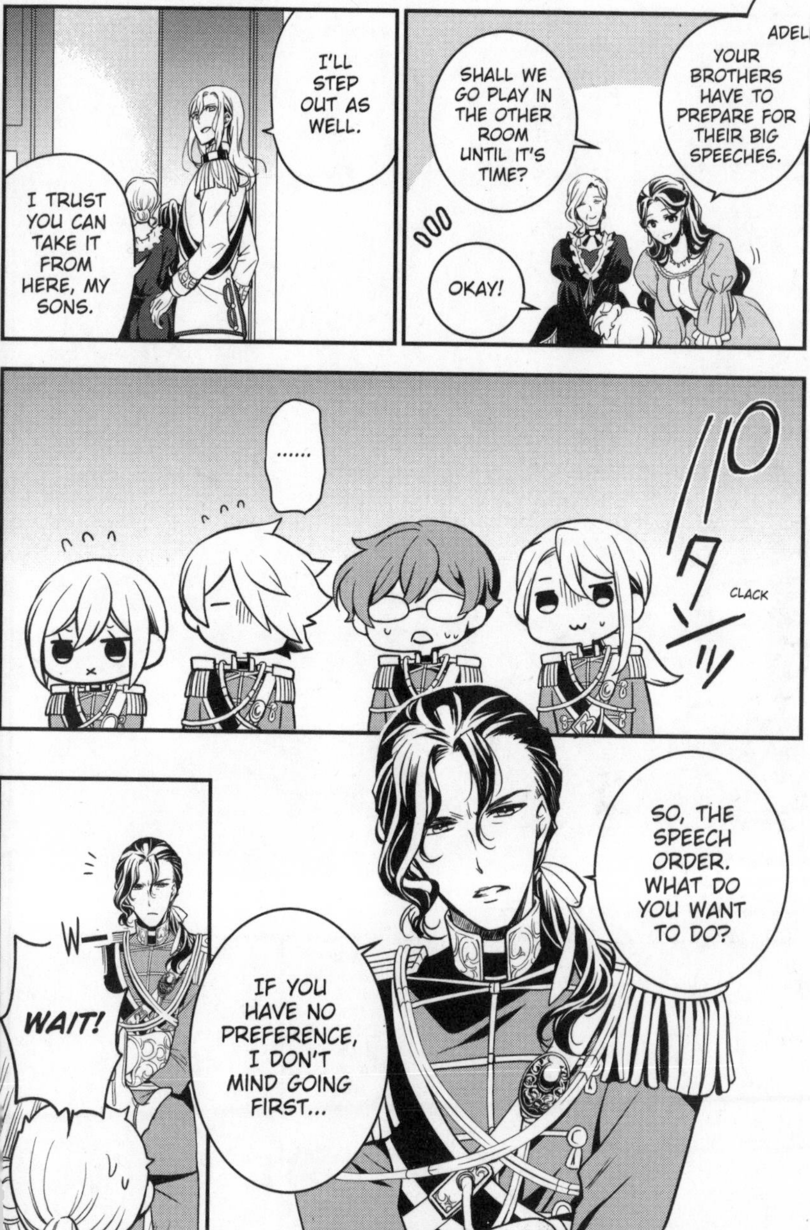
ADELE. YOUR BROTHERS HAVE TO PREPARE FOR THEIR BIG SPEECHES.
SHALL WE GO PLAY IN THE OTHER ROOM UNTIL IT'S TIME?
OKAY!
I'LL STEP OUT AS WELL.
I TRUST YOU CAN TAKE IT FROM HERE, MY SONS.
CLACK
......
SO, THE SPEECH ORDER. WHAT DO YOU WANT TO DO?
IF YOU HAVE NO PREFERENCE, I DON'T MIND GOING FIRST...
W— WAIT!

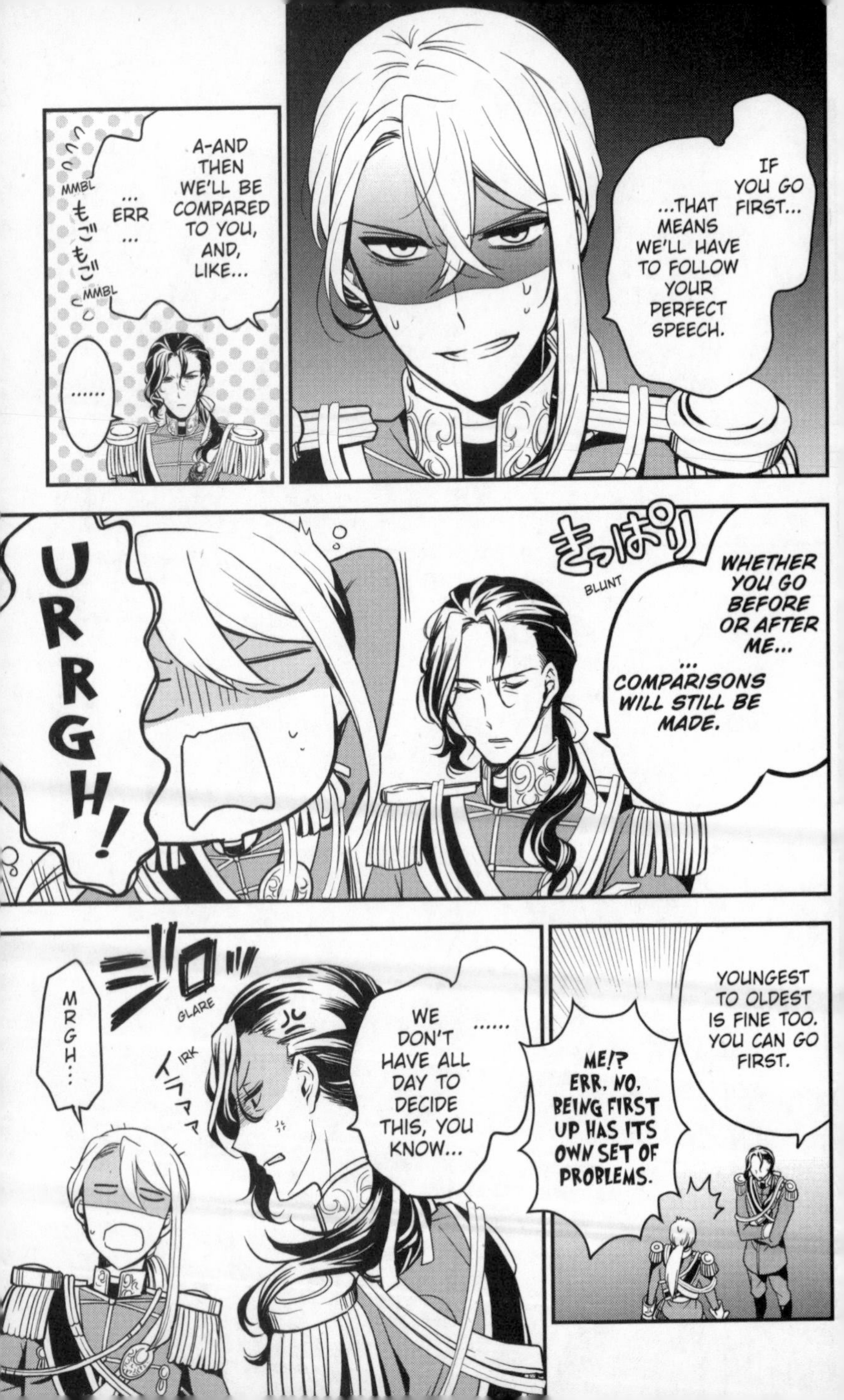
IF YOU GO FIRST...
...THAT MEANS WE'LL HAVE TO FOLLOW YOUR PERFECT SPEECH.
A-AND THEN WE'LL BE COMPARED TO YOU, AND, LIKE...
...ERR...
もごもご
MMBL MMBL
......
きっぱり
BLUNT
WHETHER YOU GO BEFORE OR AFTER ME... ...COMPARISONS WILL STILL BE MADE.
URRGH!
YOUNGEST TO OLDEST IS FINE TOO. YOU CAN GO FIRST.
ME!? ERR, NO, BEING FIRST UP HAS ITS OWN SET OF PROBLEMS.
......
WE DON'T HAVE ALL DAY TO DECIDE THIS, YOU KNOW...
IRK
GLARE
MRGH...

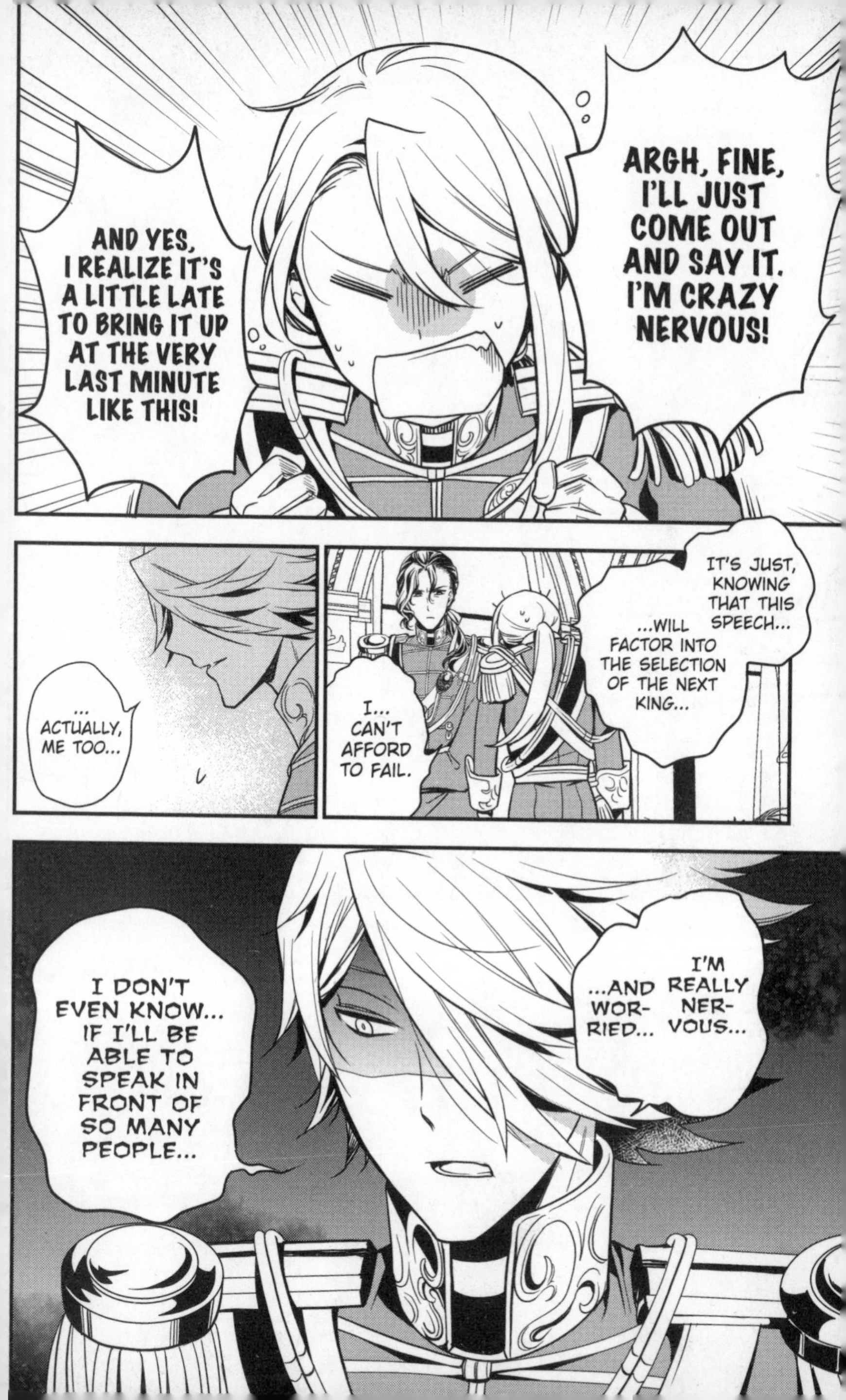
ARGH, FINE, I'LL JUST COME OUT AND SAY IT. I'M CRAZY NERVOUS!
AND YES, I REALIZE IT'S A LITTLE LATE TO BRING IT UP AT THE VERY LAST MINUTE LIKE THIS!
IT'S JUST, KNOWING THAT THIS SPEECH...
...WILL FACTOR INTO THE SELECTION OF THE NEXT KING...
I... CAN'T AFFORD TO FAIL.
... ACTUALLY, ME TOO...
I'M REALLY NER-VOUS...
...AND WOR-RIED...
I DON'T EVEN KNOW... IF I'LL BE ABLE TO SPEAK IN FRONT OF SO MANY PEOPLE...

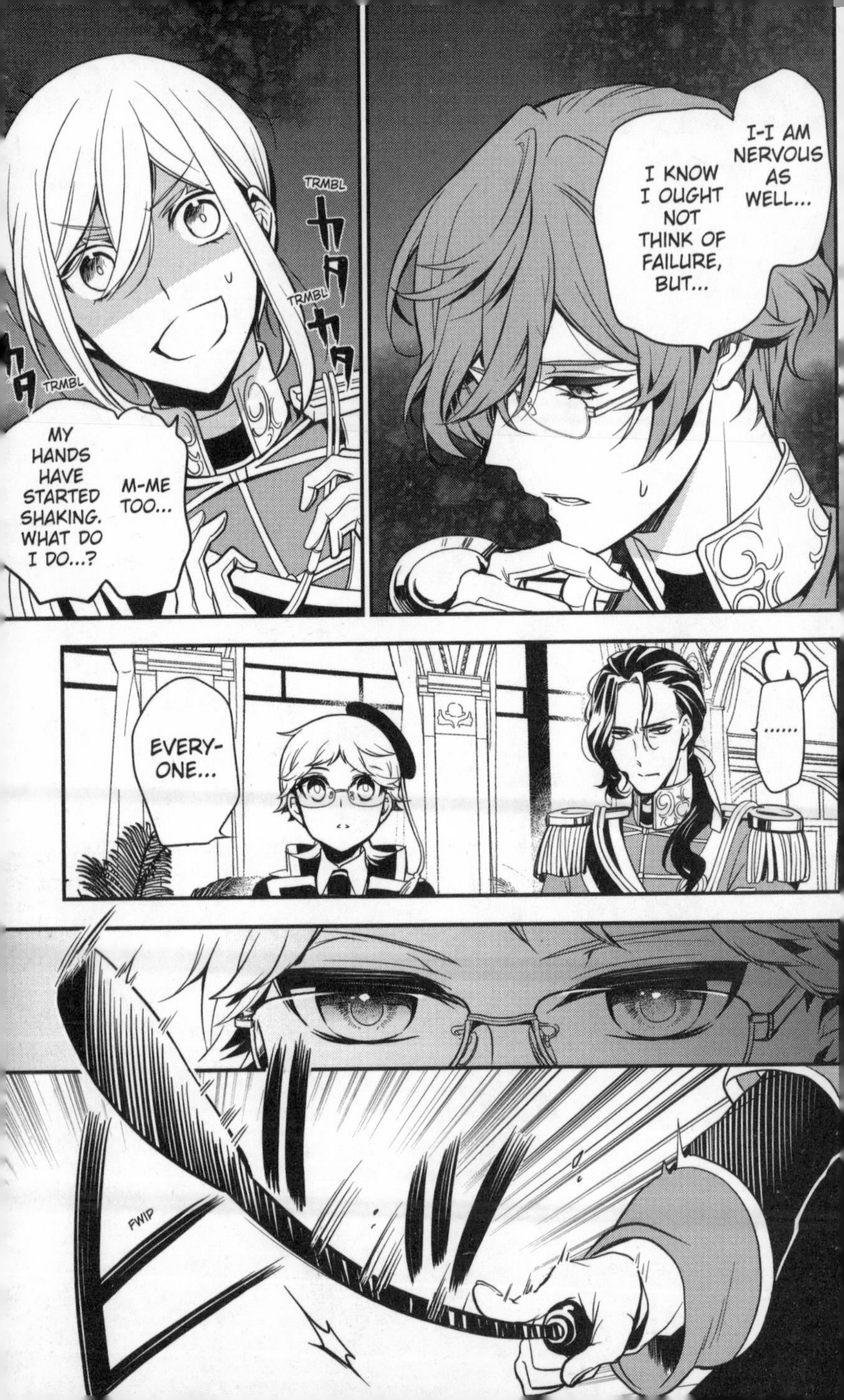
I-I AM NERVOUS AS WELL...
I KNOW I OUGHT NOT THINK OF FAILURE, BUT...
TRMBL
TRMBL
TRMBL
M-ME TOO...
MY HANDS HAVE STARTED SHAKING. WHAT DO I DO...?
......
EVERY-ONE...
FWIP

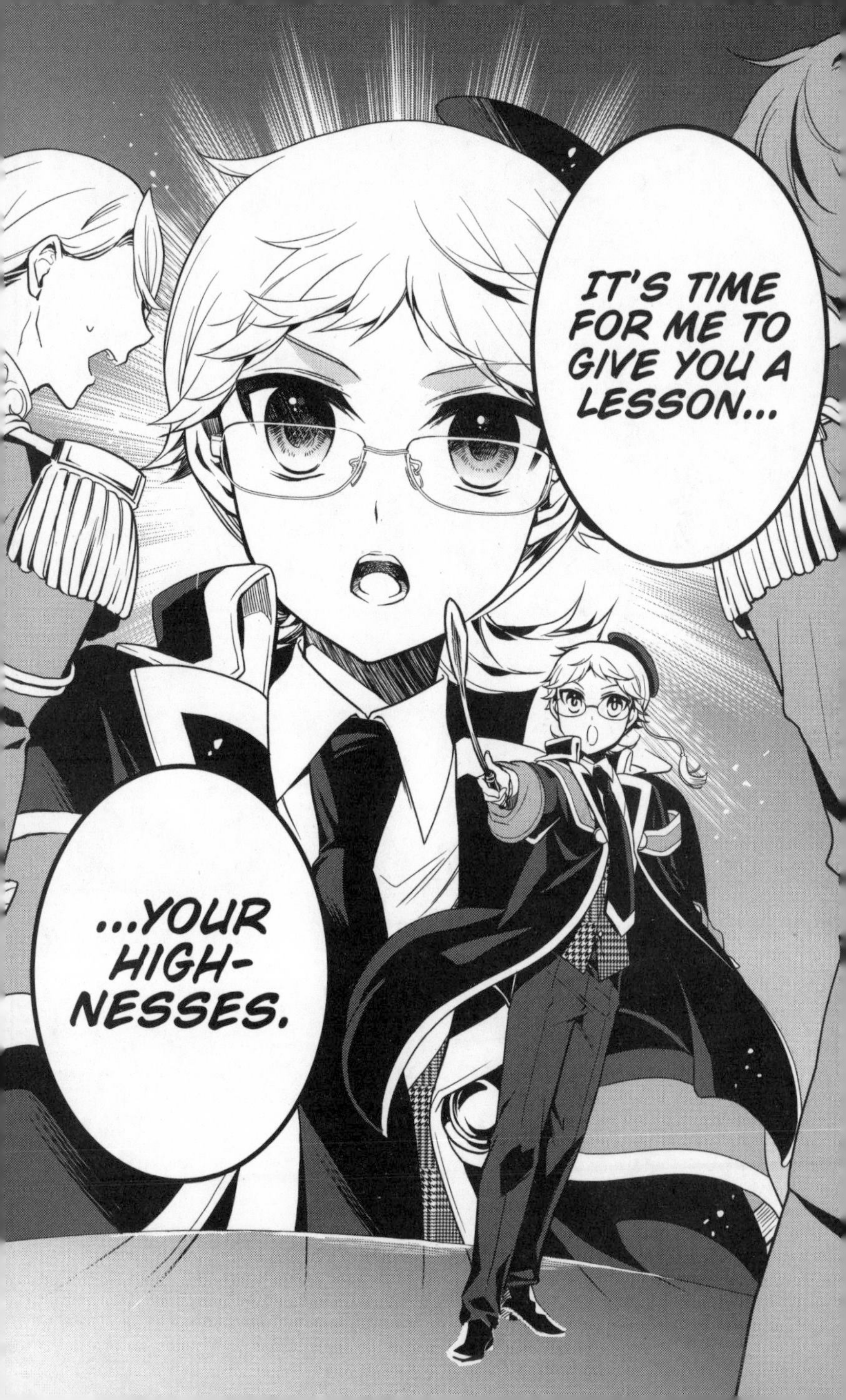
IT'S TIME FOR ME TO GIVE YOU A LESSON...
...YOUR HIGH-NESSES.

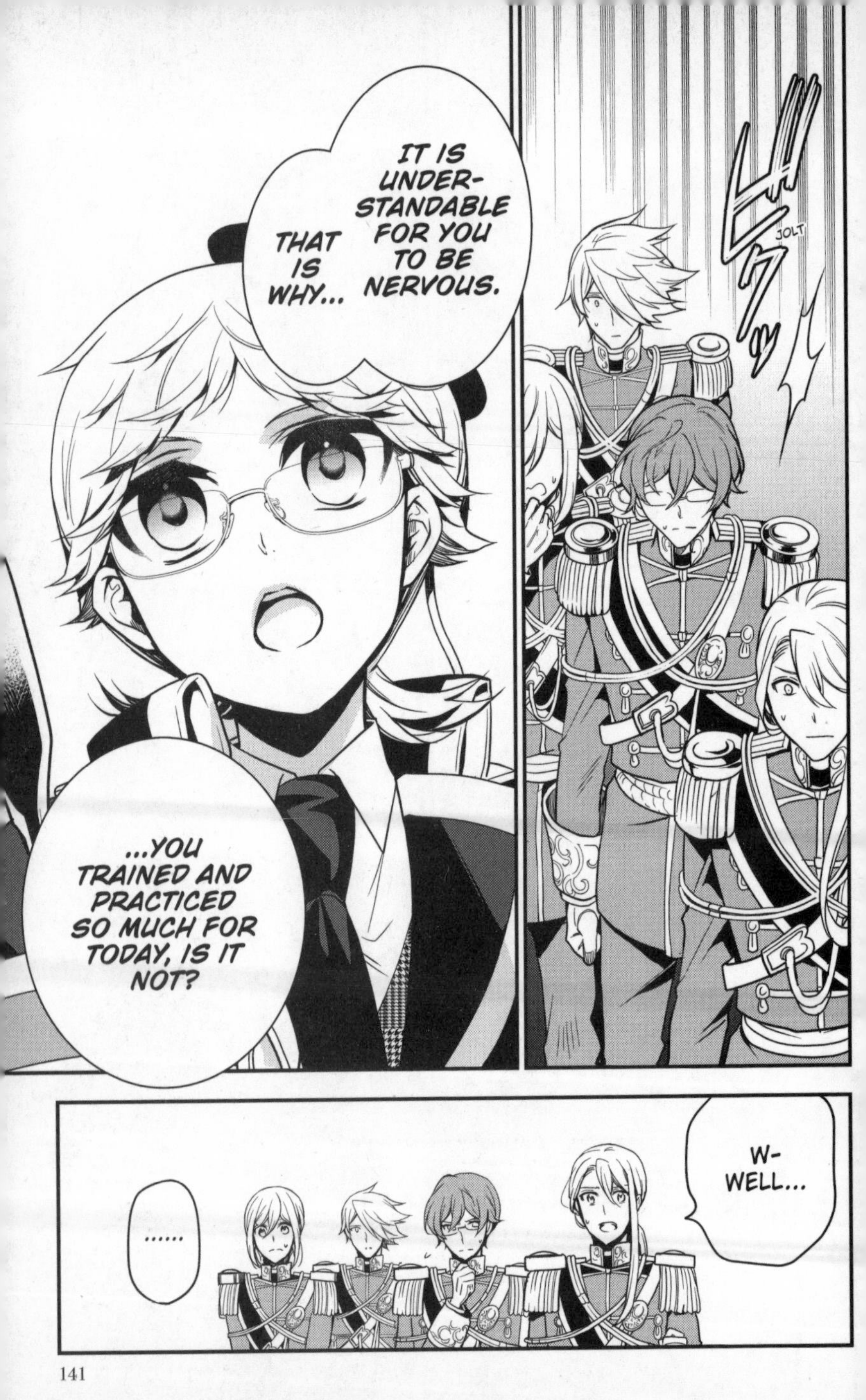
JOLT
IT IS UNDERSTANDABLE FOR YOU TO BE NERVOUS.
THAT IS WHY...
...YOU TRAINED AND PRACTICED SO MUCH FOR TODAY, IS IT NOT?
W-WELL...
......

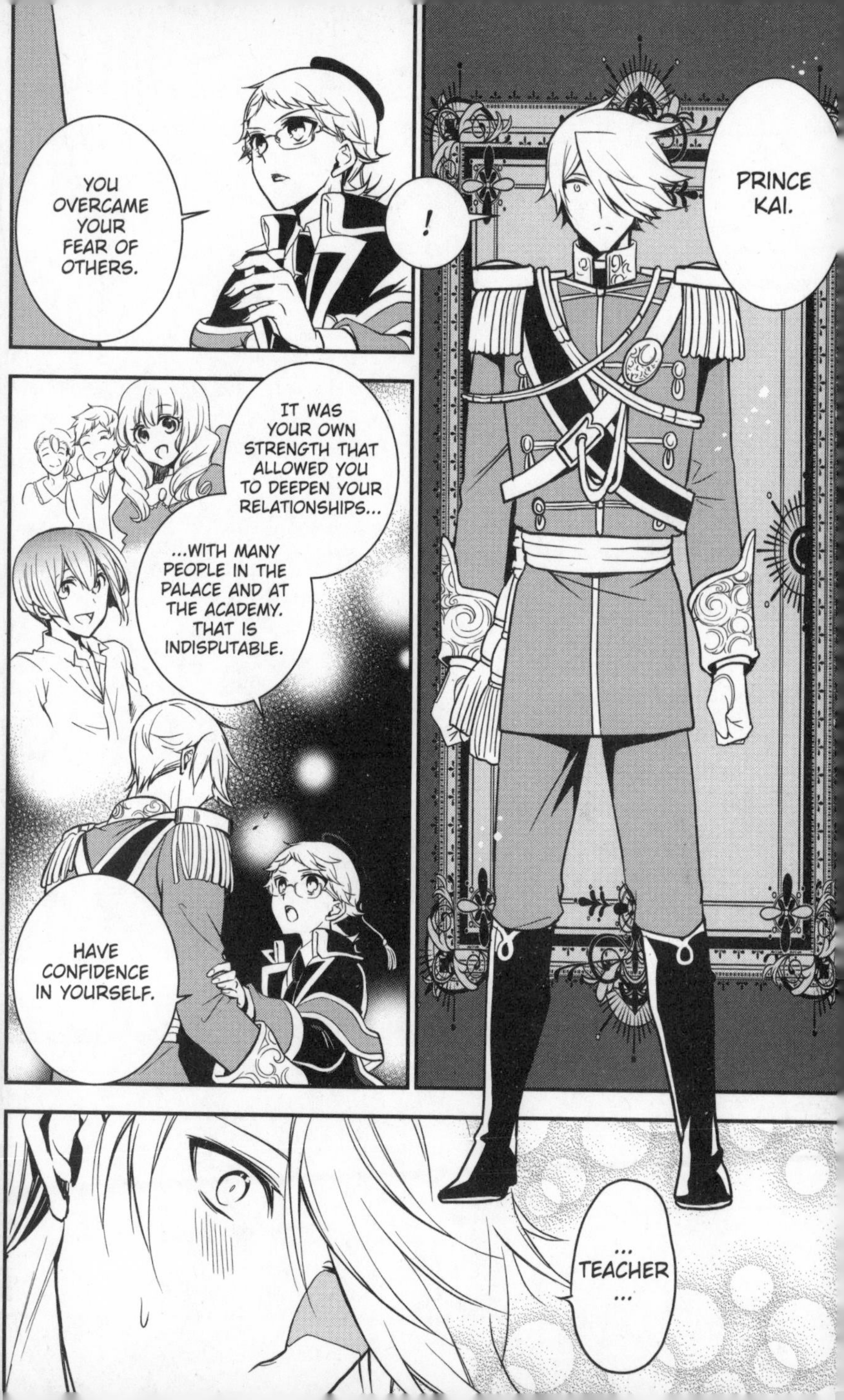
PRINCE KAI.
!
YOU OVERCAME YOUR FEAR OF OTHERS.
IT WAS YOUR OWN STRENGTH THAT ALLOWED YOU TO DEEPEN YOUR RELATIONSHIPS...
...WITH MANY PEOPLE IN THE PALACE AND AT THE ACADEMY. THAT IS INDISPUTABLE.
HAVE CONFIDENCE IN YOURSELF.
...TEACHER...

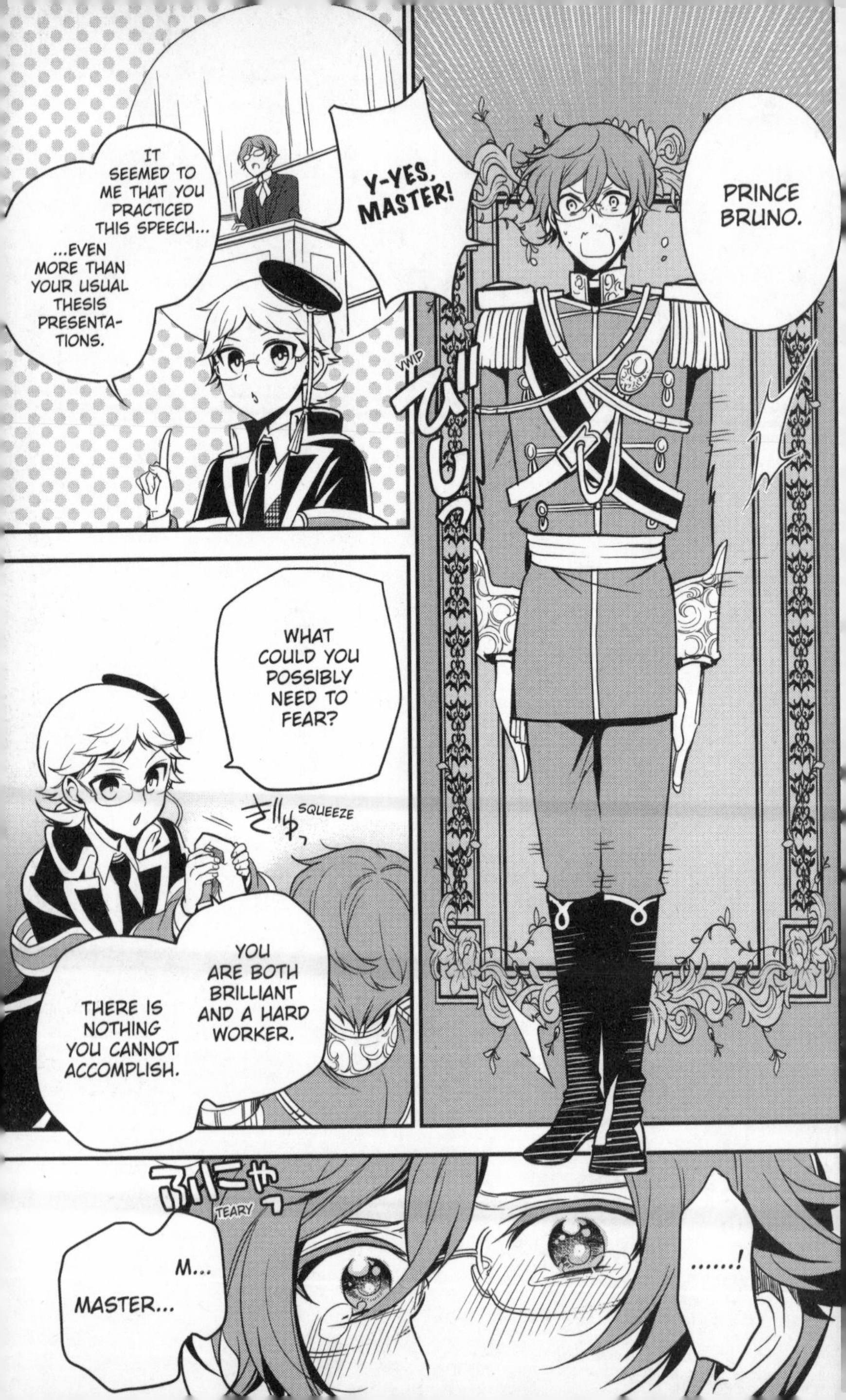

PRINCE BRUNO.
Y-YES, MASTER!
びしっ
VWIP
IT SEEMED TO ME THAT YOU PRACTICED THIS SPEECH...
...EVEN MORE THAN YOUR USUAL THESIS PRESENTATIONS.
WHAT COULD YOU POSSIBLY NEED TO FEAR?
ぎゅっ
SQUEEZE
YOU ARE BOTH BRILLIANT AND A HARD WORKER.
THERE IS NOTHING YOU CANNOT ACCOMPLISH.
......!
ふにゃっ
TEARY
M...
MASTER...

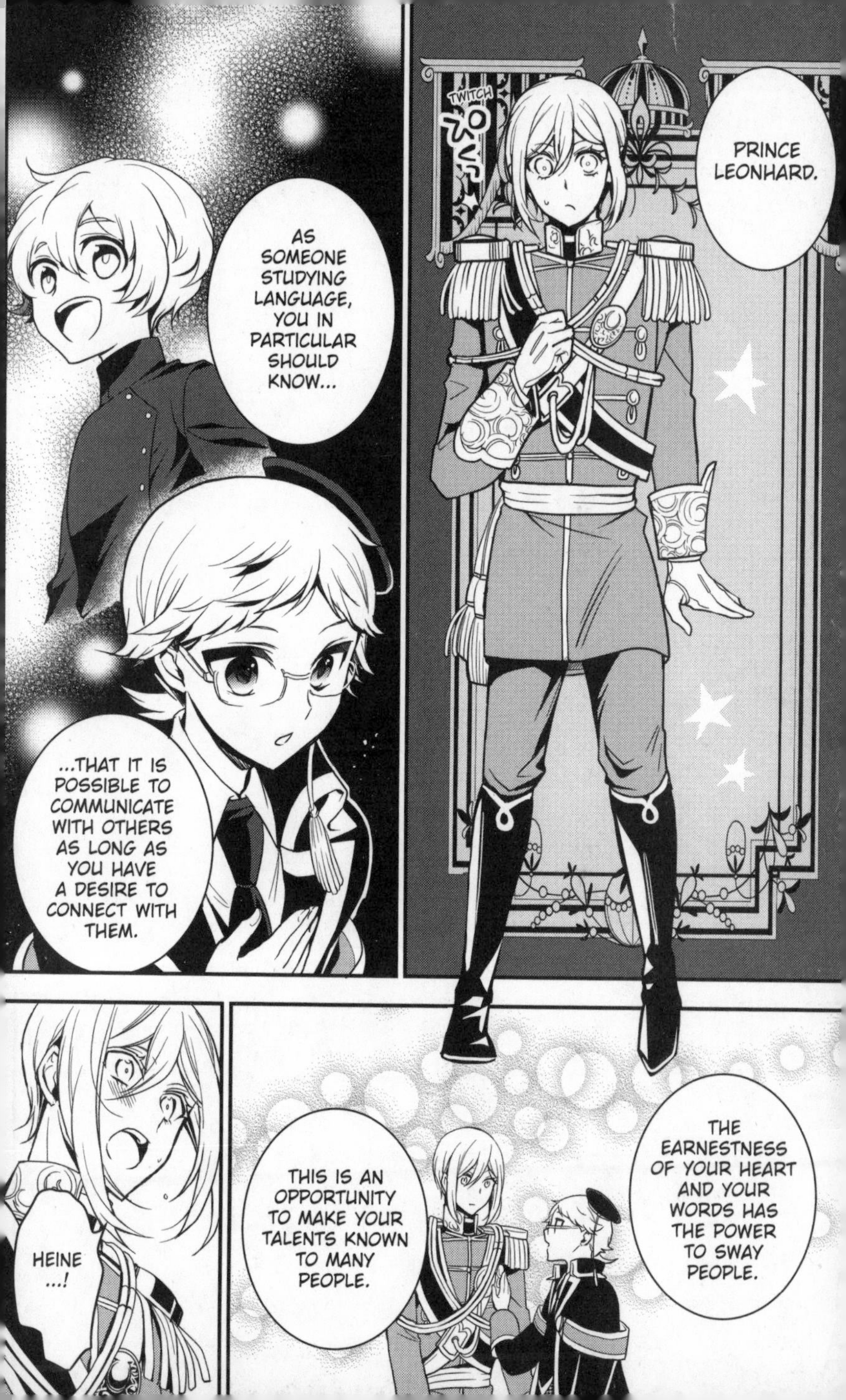
TWITCH
PRINCE LEONHARD.
AS SOMEONE STUDYING LANGUAGE, YOU IN PARTICULAR SHOULD KNOW...
...THAT IT IS POSSIBLE TO COMMUNICATE WITH OTHERS AS LONG AS YOU HAVE A DESIRE TO CONNECT WITH THEM.
THE EARNESTNESS OF YOUR HEART AND YOUR WORDS HAS THE POWER TO SWAY PEOPLE.
THIS IS AN OPPORTUNITY TO MAKE YOUR TALENTS KNOWN TO MANY PEOPLE.
HEINE ...!

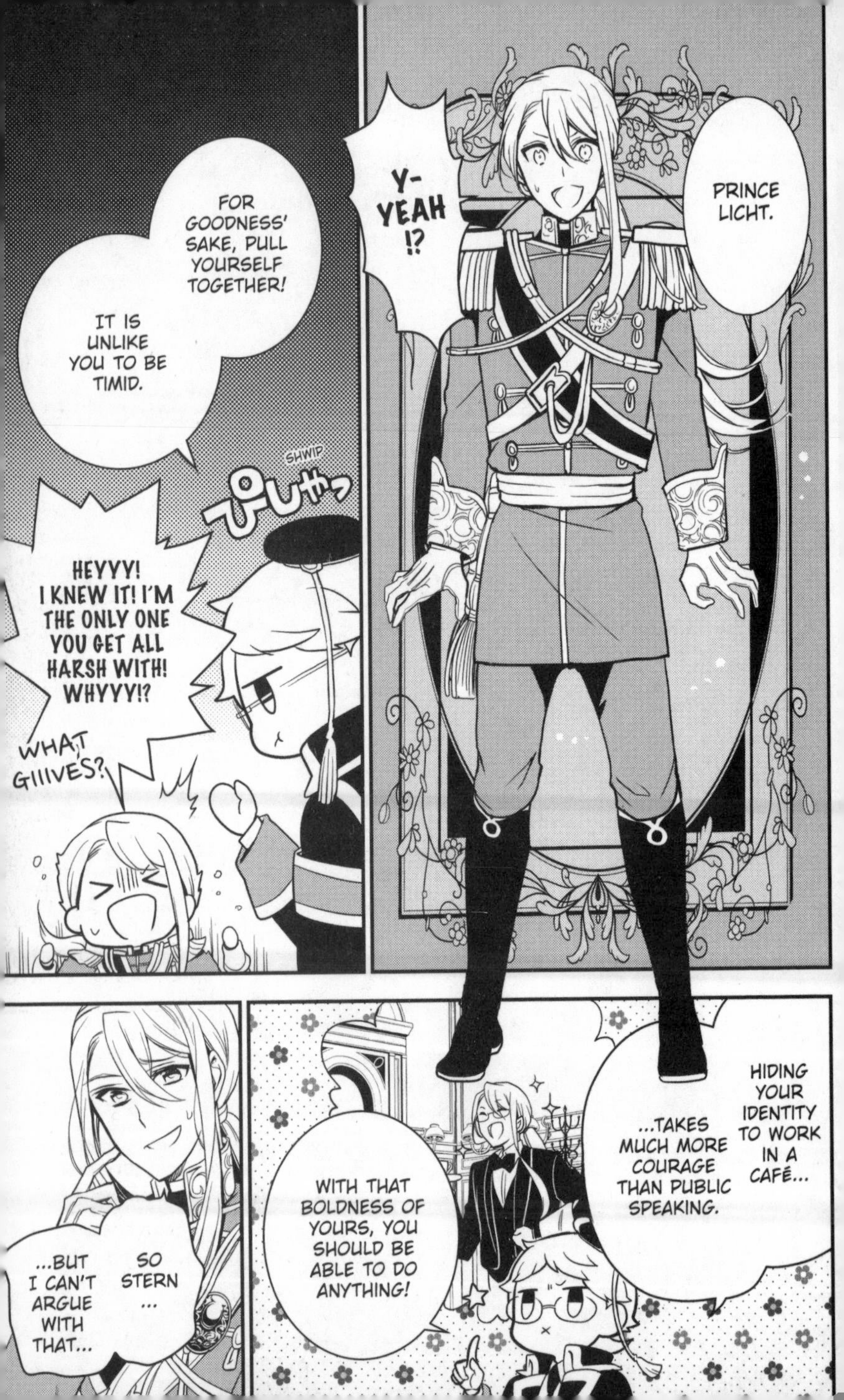
PRINCE LICHT.
Y-YEAH!?
FOR GOODNESS' SAKE, PULL YOURSELF TOGETHER!
IT IS UNLIKE YOU TO BE TIMID.
SHWIP
ぴしゃっ
HEYYY! I KNEW IT! I'M THE ONLY ONE YOU GET ALL HARSH WITH! WHYYY!?
WHAT GIIIVES?
HIDING YOUR IDENTITY TO WORK IN A CAFÉ...
...TAKES MUCH MORE COURAGE THAN PUBLIC SPEAKING.
WITH THAT BOLDNESS OF YOURS, YOU SHOULD BE ABLE TO DO ANYTHING!
SO STERN...
...BUT I CAN'T ARGUE WITH THAT...

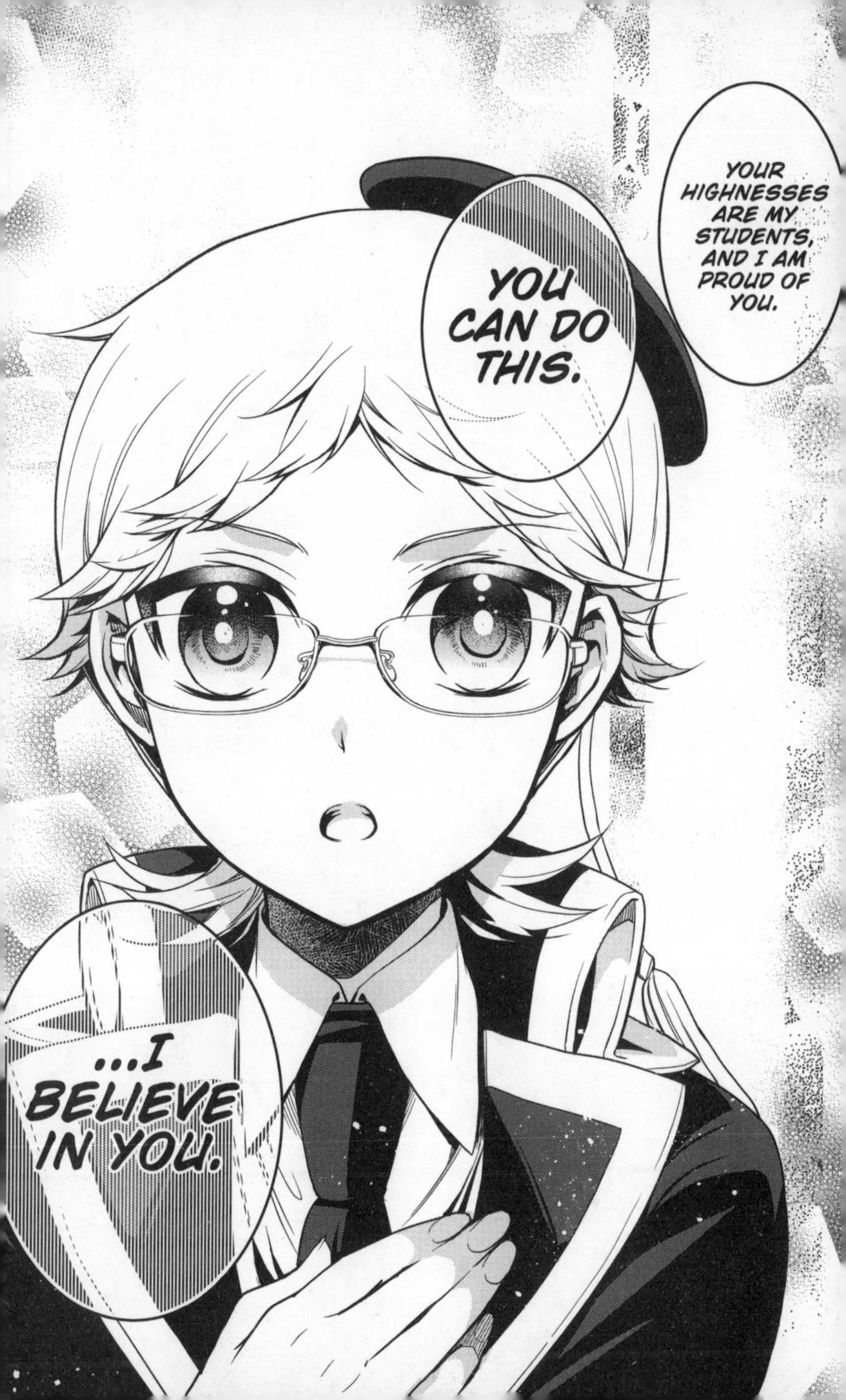
YOUR HIGHNESSES ARE MY STUDENTS, AND I AM PROUD OF YOU.
YOU CAN DO THIS.
...I BELIEVE IN YOU.

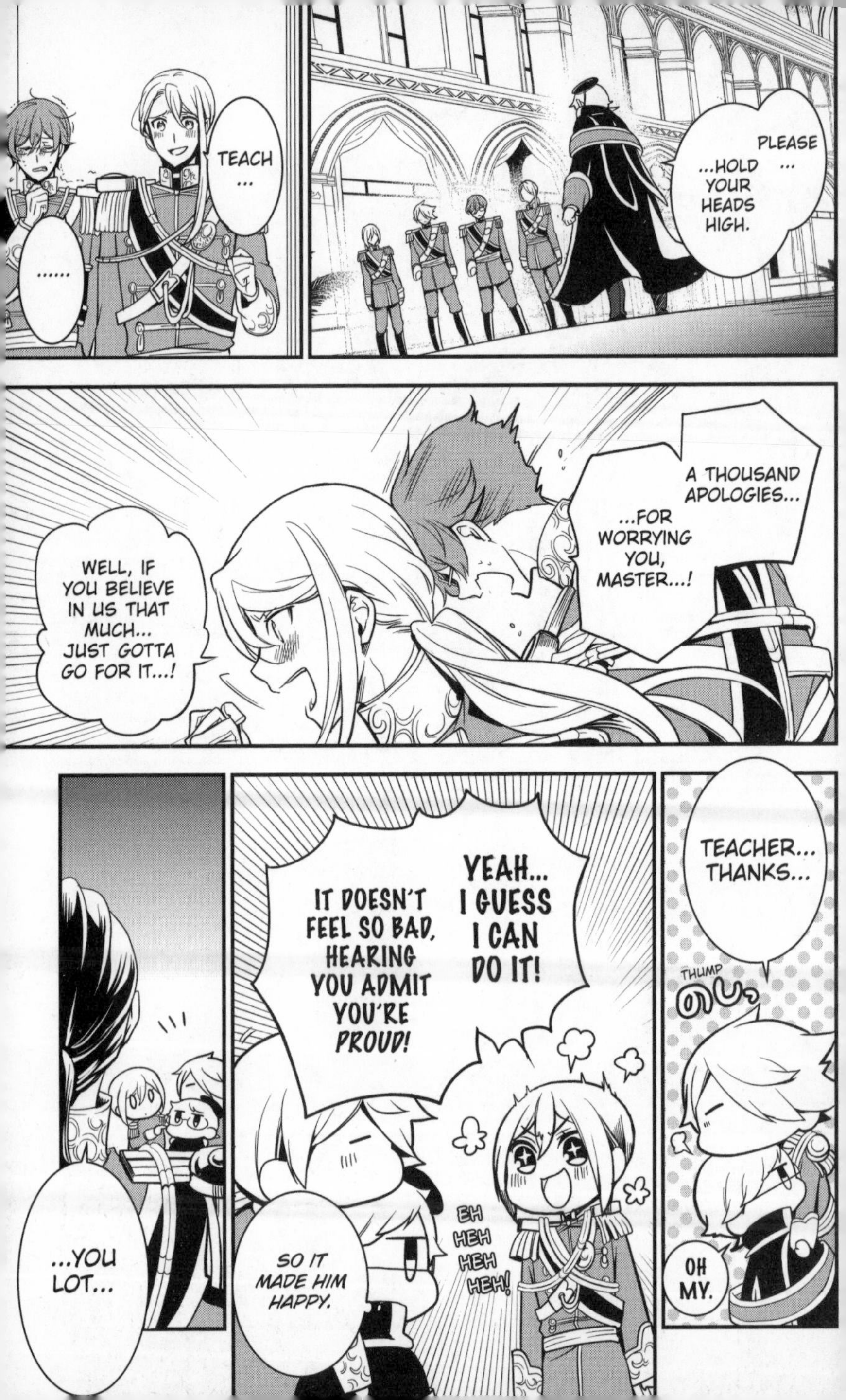
PLEASE ... ...HOLD YOUR HEADS HIGH.
TEACH ...
......
A THOUSAND APOLOGIES...
...FOR WORRYING YOU, MASTER...!
WELL, IF YOU BELIEVE IN US THAT MUCH... JUST GOTTA GO FOR IT...!
TEACHER... THANKS...
THUMP
OH MY.
YEAH... I GUESS I CAN DO IT!
IT DOESN'T FEEL SO BAD, HEARING YOU ADMIT YOU'RE *PROUD*!
EH HEH HEH HEH!
SO IT MADE HIM HAPPY.
...YOU LOT...

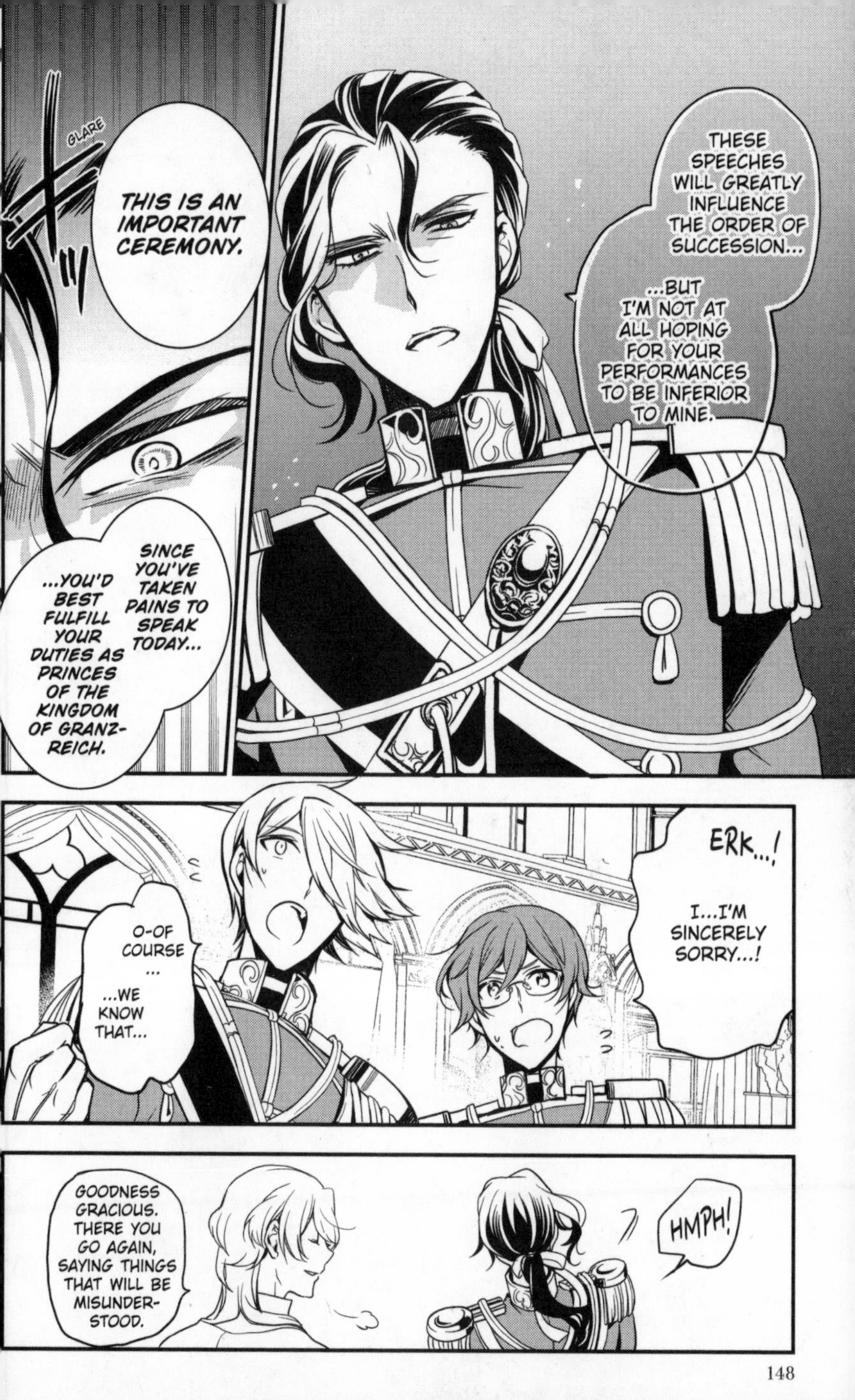
THESE SPEECHES WILL GREATLY INFLUENCE THE ORDER OF SUCCESSION...
...BUT I'M NOT AT ALL HOPING FOR YOUR PERFORMANCES TO BE INFERIOR TO MINE.
GLARE
THIS IS AN IMPORTANT CEREMONY.
SINCE YOU'VE TAKEN PAINS TO SPEAK TODAY...
...YOU'D BEST FULFILL YOUR DUTIES AS PRINCES OF THE KINGDOM OF GRANZ-REICH.
ERK...!
I...I'M SINCERELY SORRY...!
O-OF COURSE ...
...WE KNOW THAT...
HMPH!
GOODNESS GRACIOUS. THERE YOU GO AGAIN, SAYING THINGS THAT WILL BE MISUNDER-STOOD.

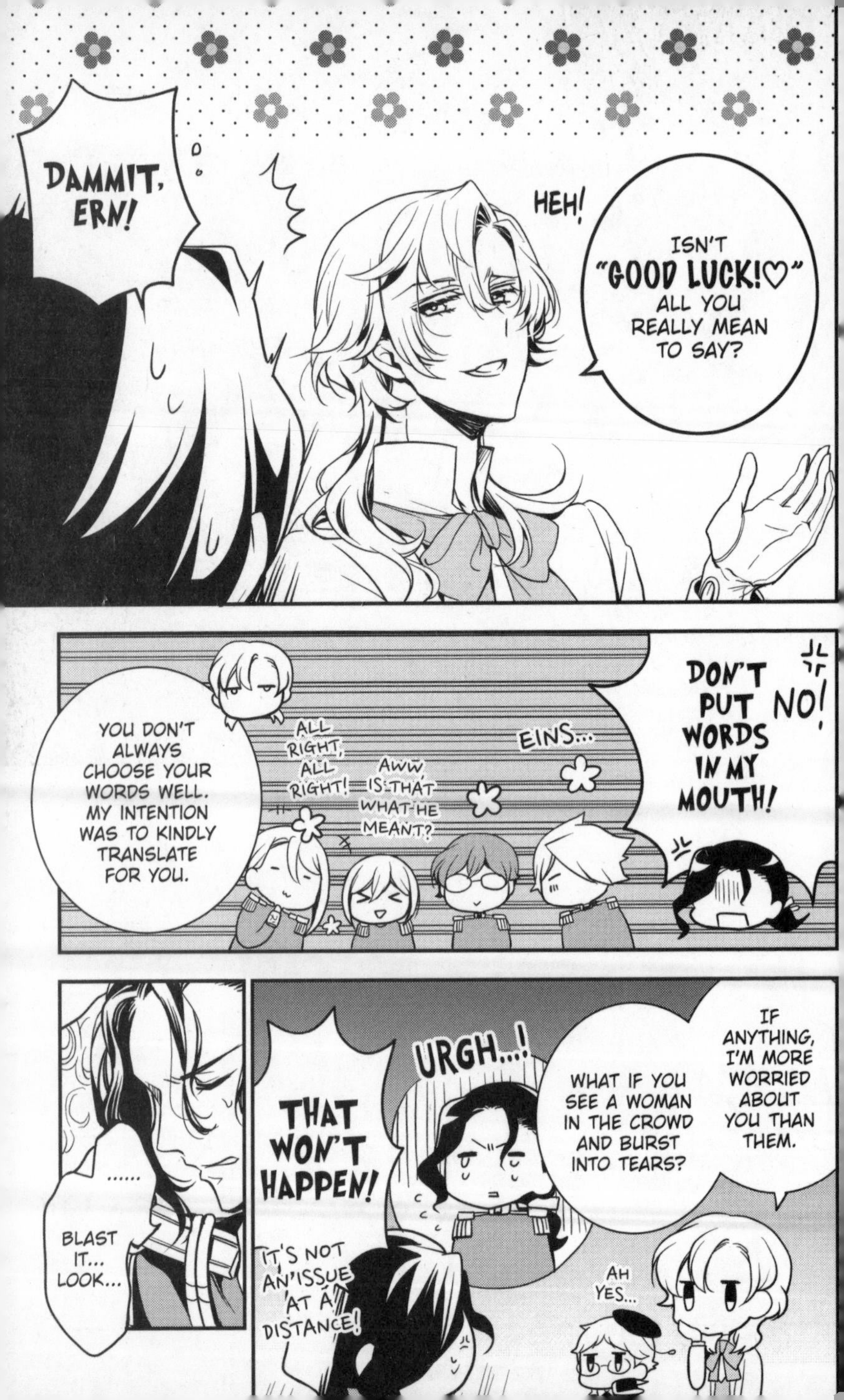
ISN'T "GOOD LUCK!♡" ALL YOU REALLY MEAN TO SAY?
HEH!
DAMMIT, ERN!
NO!
DON'T PUT WORDS IN MY MOUTH!
EINS...
AWW, IS THAT WHAT HE MEANT?
ALL RIGHT, ALL RIGHT!
YOU DON'T ALWAYS CHOOSE YOUR WORDS WELL. MY INTENTION WAS TO KINDLY TRANSLATE FOR YOU.
IF ANYTHING, I'M MORE WORRIED ABOUT YOU THAN THEM.
WHAT IF YOU SEE A WOMAN IN THE CROWD AND BURST INTO TEARS?
URGH...!
THAT WON'T HAPPEN!
AH YES...
IT'S NOT AN ISSUE AT A DISTANCE!
......
BLAST IT... LOOK...

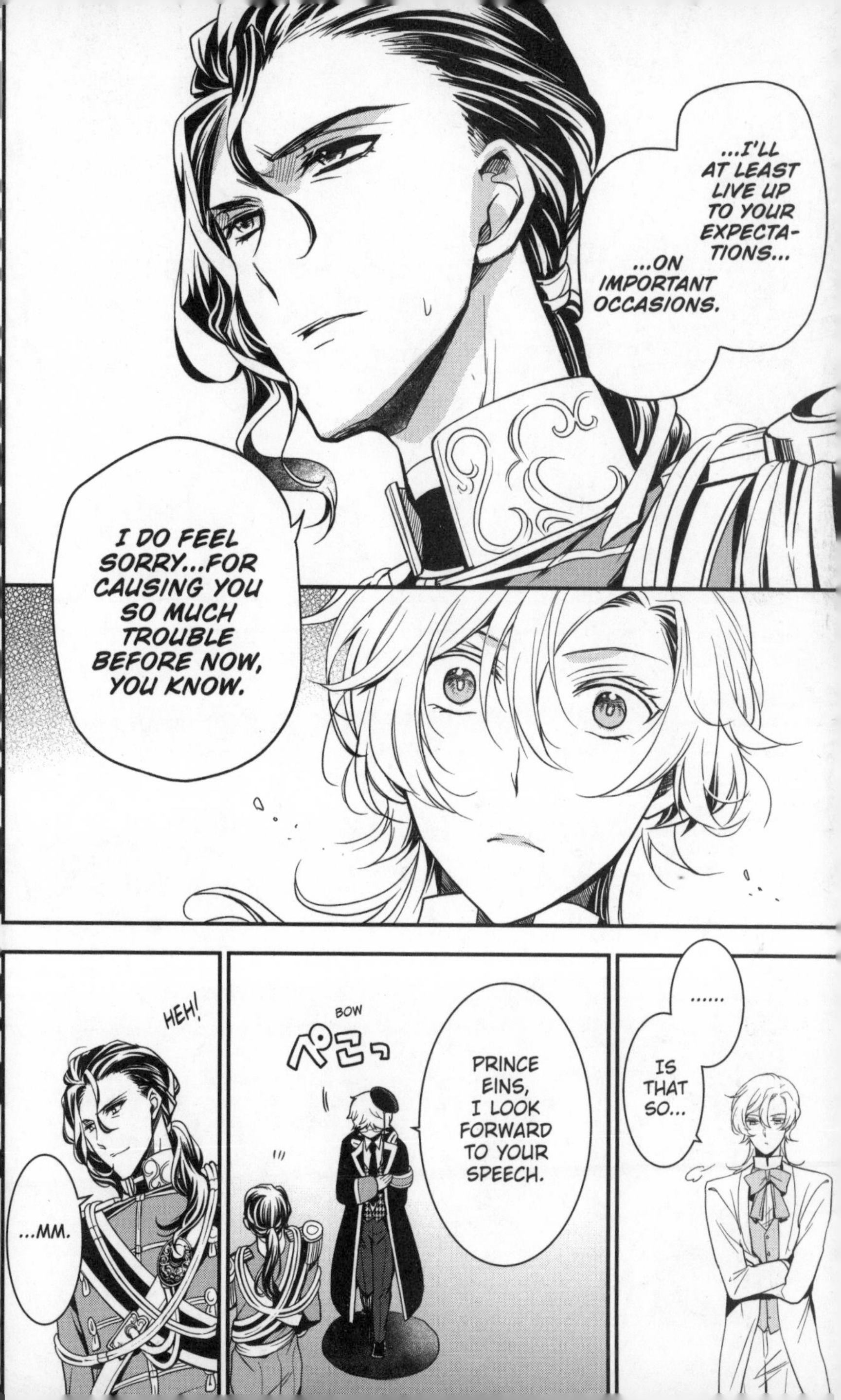
...I'LL AT LEAST LIVE UP TO YOUR EXPECTATIONS...
...ON IMPORTANT OCCASIONS.
I DO FEEL SORRY...FOR CAUSING YOU SO MUCH TROUBLE BEFORE NOW, YOU KNOW.
......
IS THAT SO...
BOW
ペコッ
PRINCE EINS, I LOOK FORWARD TO YOUR SPEECH.
HEH!
...MM.

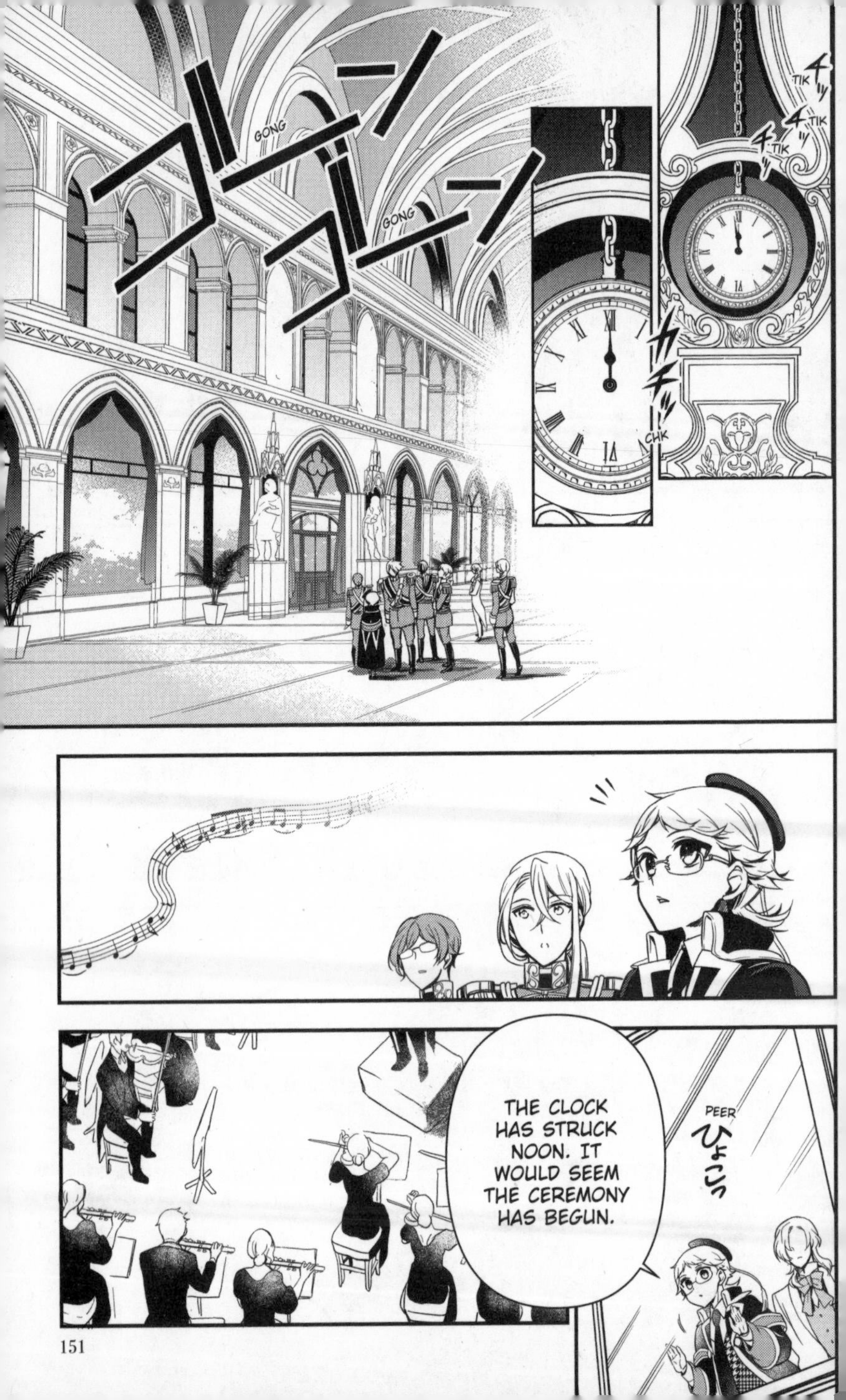
TIK
TIK
TIK
CHK
GONG
GONG
PEER
THE CLOCK HAS STRUCK NOON. IT WOULD SEEM THE CEREMONY HAS BEGUN.

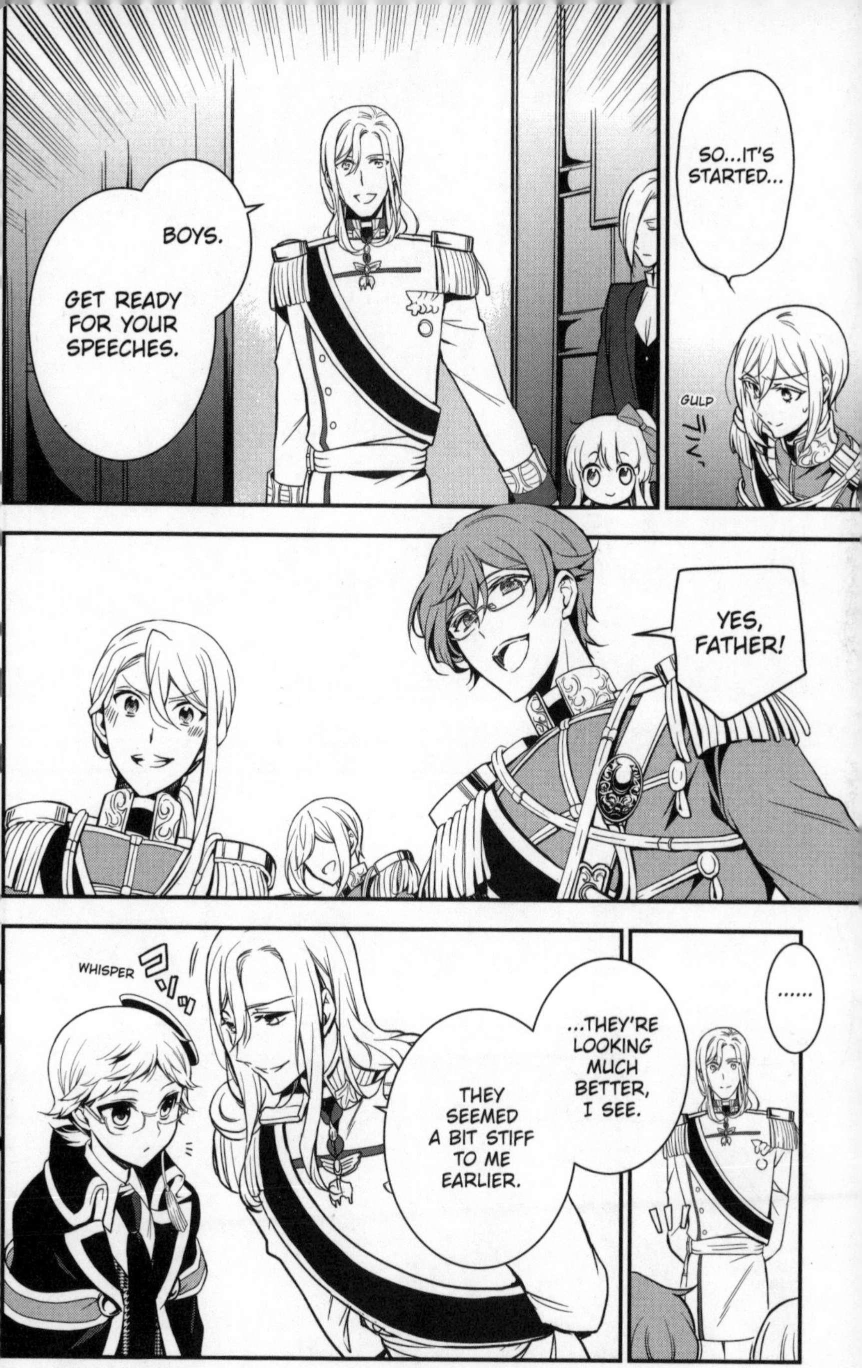
SO...IT'S STARTED...
GULP
BOYS.
GET READY FOR YOUR SPEECHES.
YES, FATHER!
......
...THEY'RE LOOKING MUCH BETTER, I SEE.
THEY SEEMED A BIT STIFF TO ME EARLIER.
WHISPER

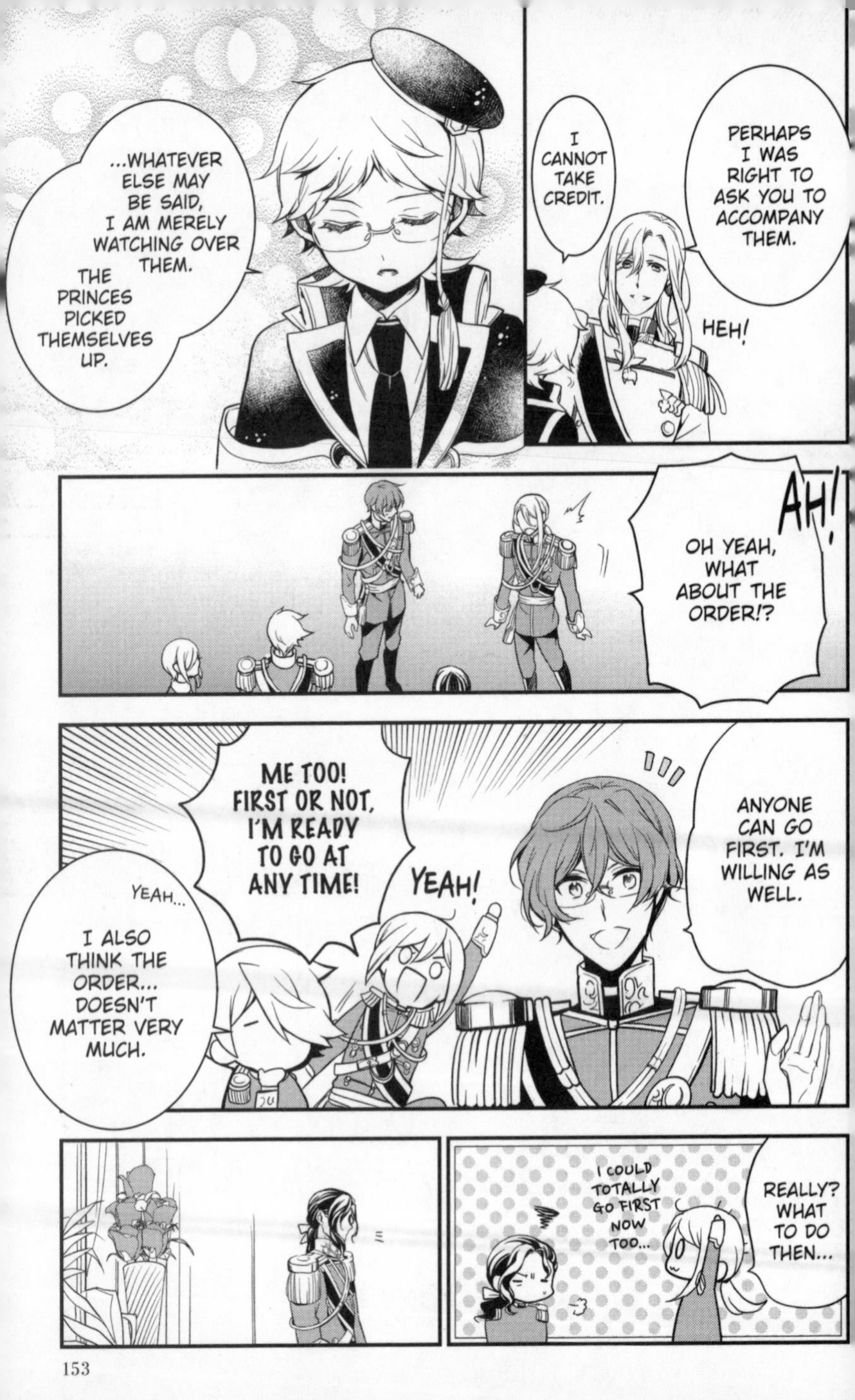
PERHAPS I WAS RIGHT TO ASK YOU TO ACCOMPANY THEM.
HEH!
I CANNOT TAKE CREDIT.
...WHATEVER ELSE MAY BE SAID, I AM MERELY WATCHING OVER THEM.
THE PRINCES PICKED THEMSELVES UP.
AH!
OH YEAH, WHAT ABOUT THE ORDER!?
ANYONE CAN GO FIRST. I'M WILLING AS WELL.
YEAH!
ME TOO! FIRST OR NOT, I'M READY TO GO AT ANY TIME!
YEAH...
I ALSO THINK THE ORDER... DOESN'T MATTER VERY MUCH.
REALLY? WHAT TO DO THEN...
I COULD TOTALLY GO FIRST NOW TOO...

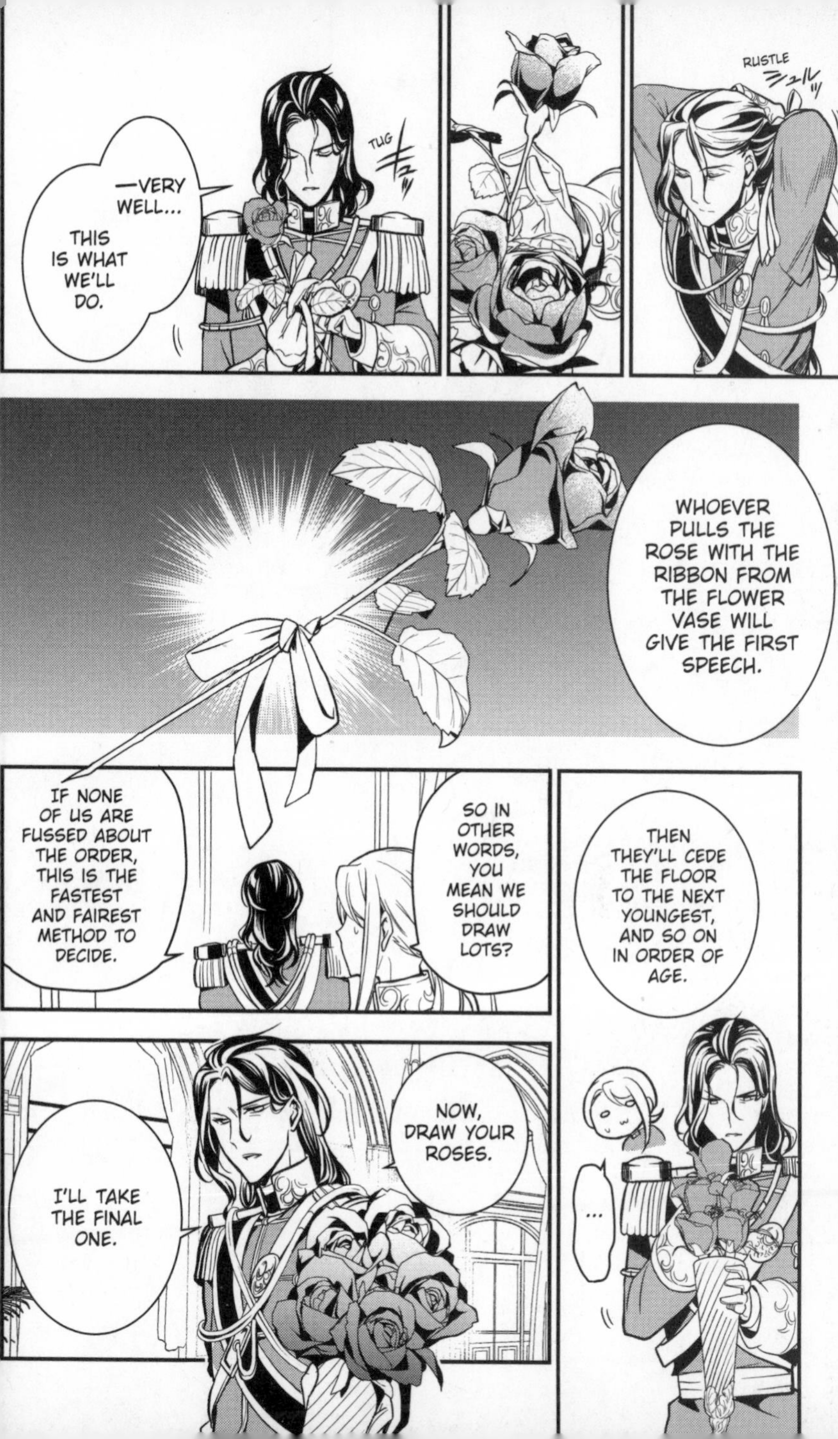
RUSTLE
シュル
TUG
—VERY WELL...
THIS IS WHAT WE'LL DO.
WHOEVER PULLS THE ROSE WITH THE RIBBON FROM THE FLOWER VASE WILL GIVE THE FIRST SPEECH.
THEN THEY'LL CEDE THE FLOOR TO THE NEXT YOUNGEST, AND SO ON IN ORDER OF AGE.
...
SO IN OTHER WORDS, YOU MEAN WE SHOULD DRAW LOTS?
IF NONE OF US ARE FUSSED ABOUT THE ORDER, THIS IS THE FASTEST AND FAIREST METHOD TO DECIDE.
NOW, DRAW YOUR ROSES.
I'LL TAKE THE FINAL ONE.

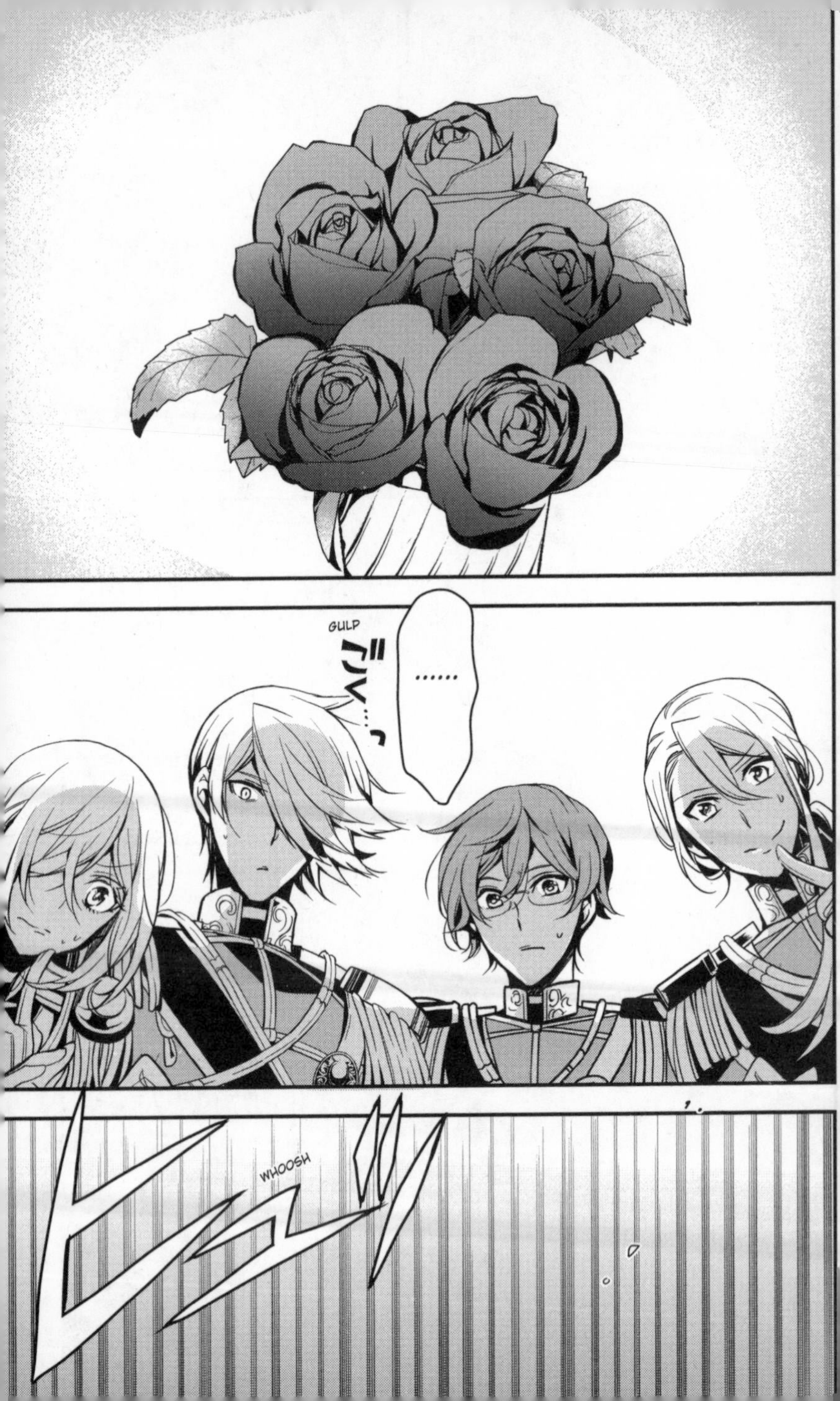

......
GULP
WHOOSH

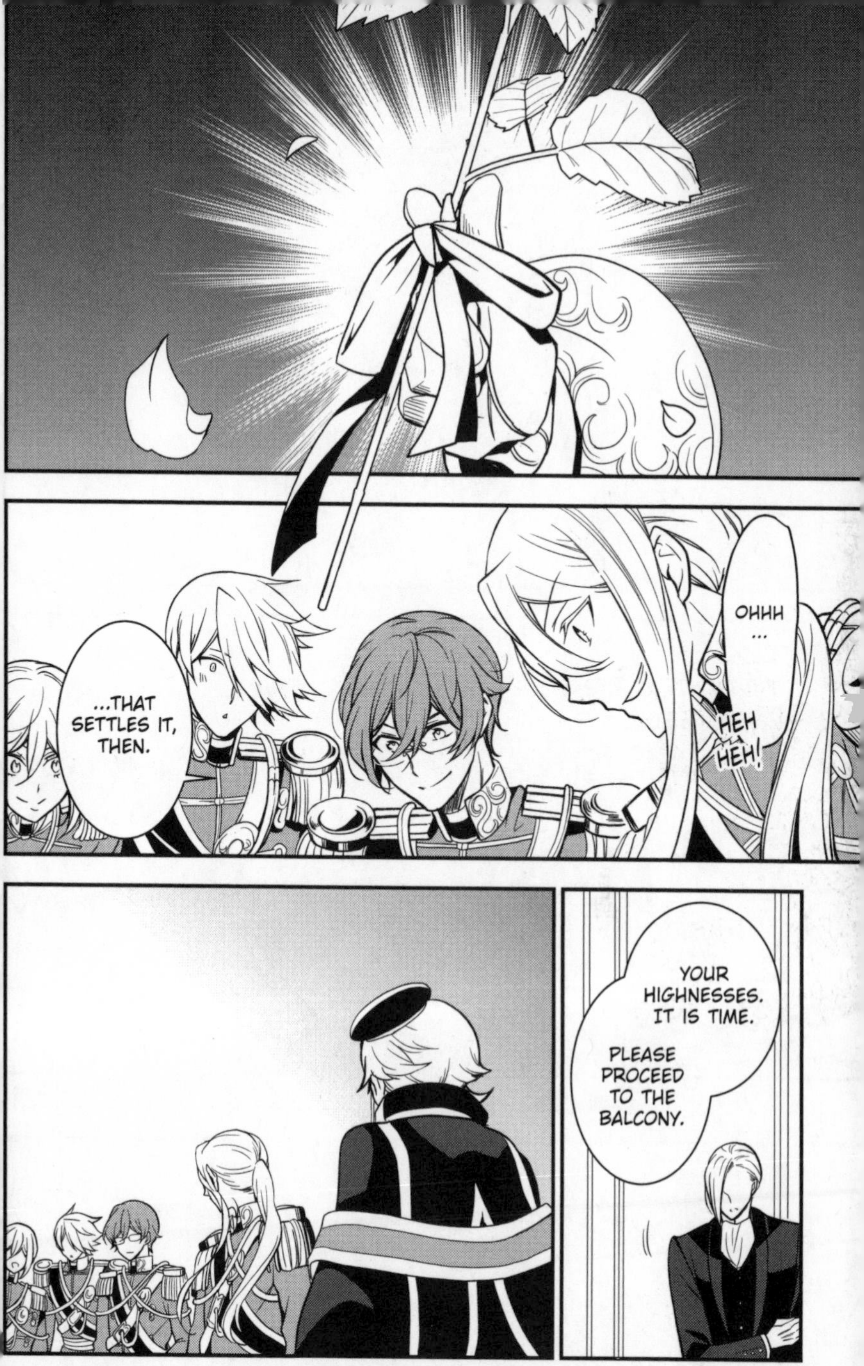
OHHH ...
HEH HEH!
...THAT SETTLES IT, THEN.
YOUR HIGHNESSES. IT IS TIME.
PLEASE PROCEED TO THE BALCONY.

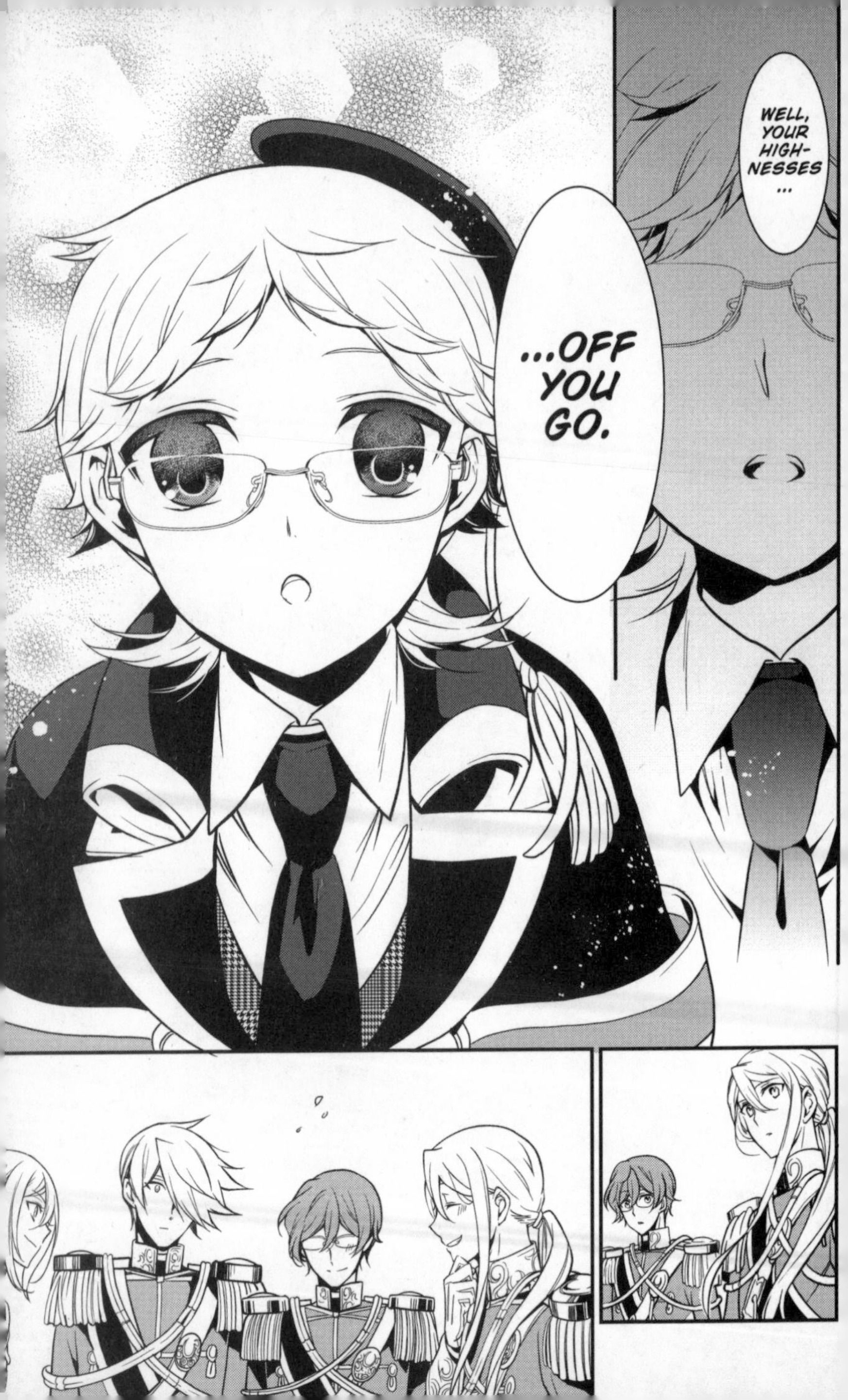
WELL, YOUR HIGH-NESSES ...
...OFF YOU GO.

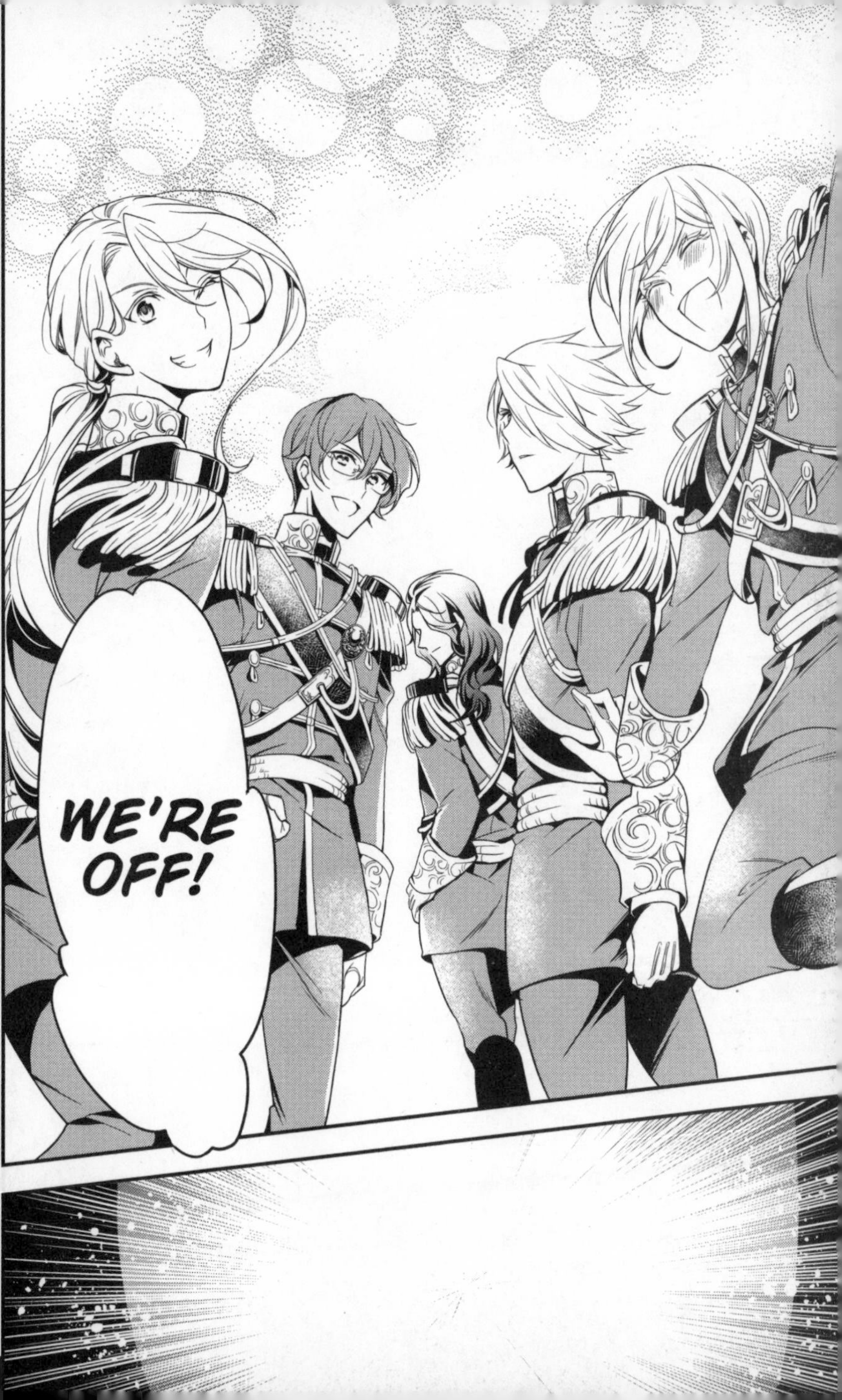
WE'RE OFF!

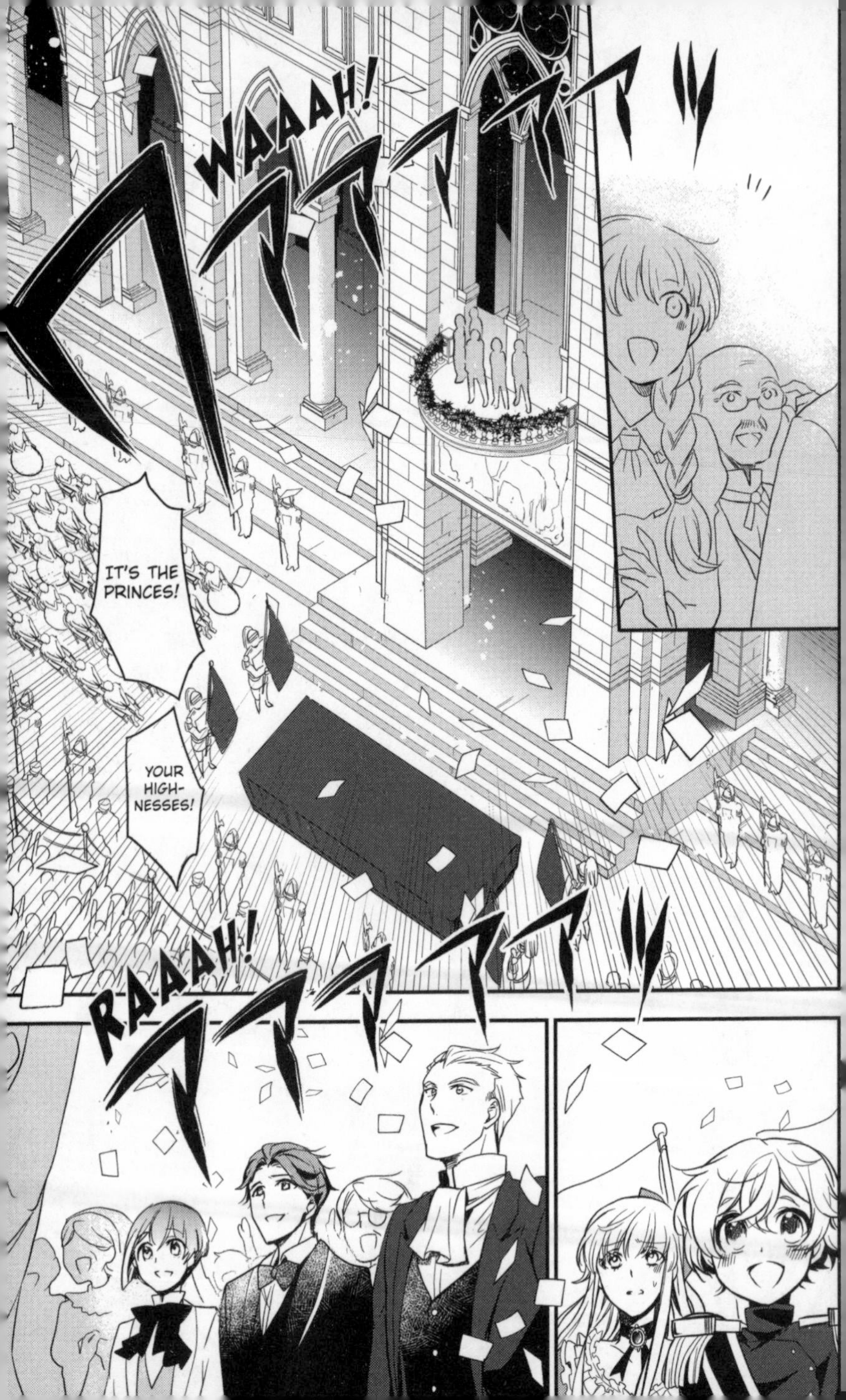
WAAAH!
IT'S THE PRINCES!
YOUR HIGHNESSES!
RAAAH!

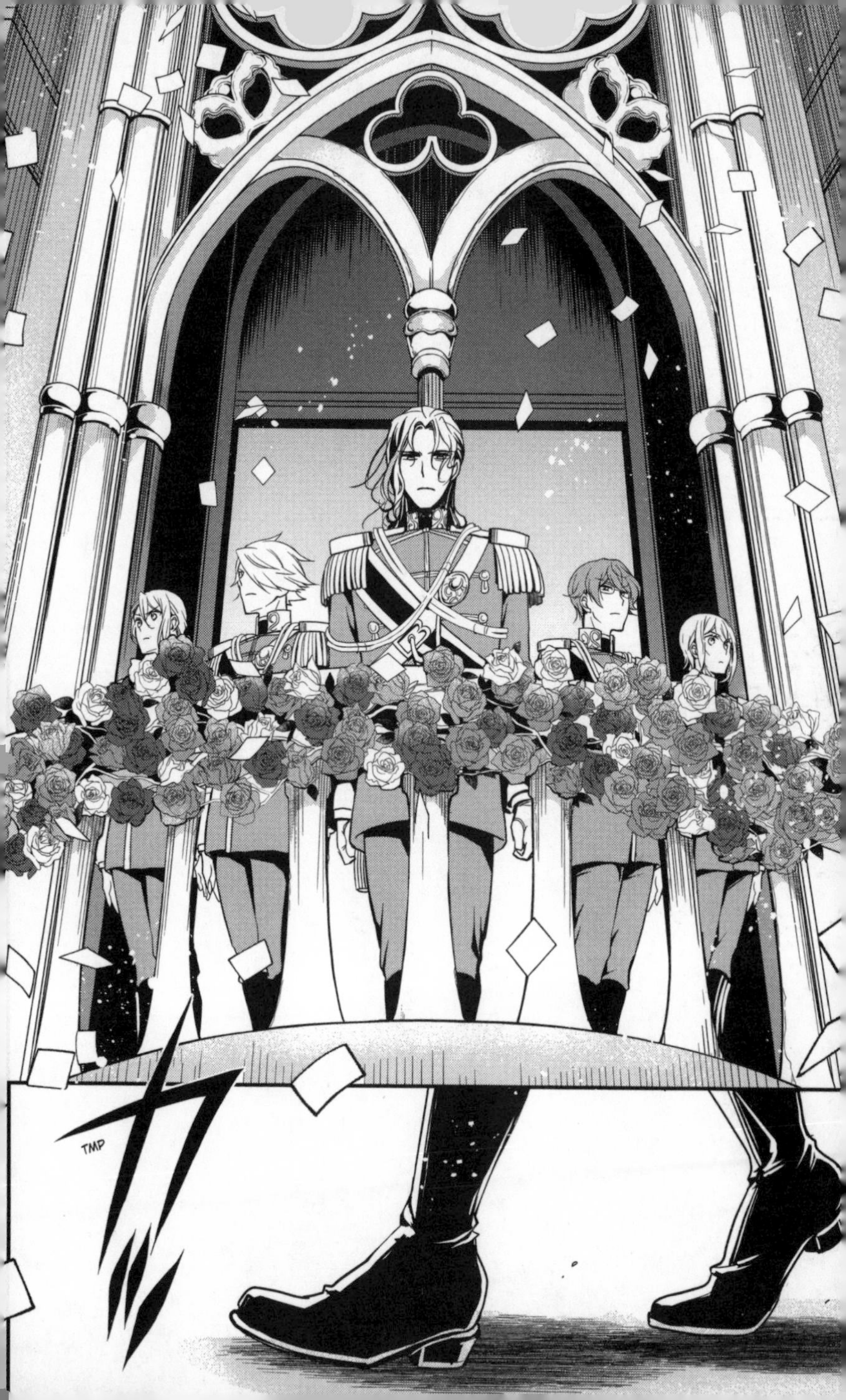
TMP

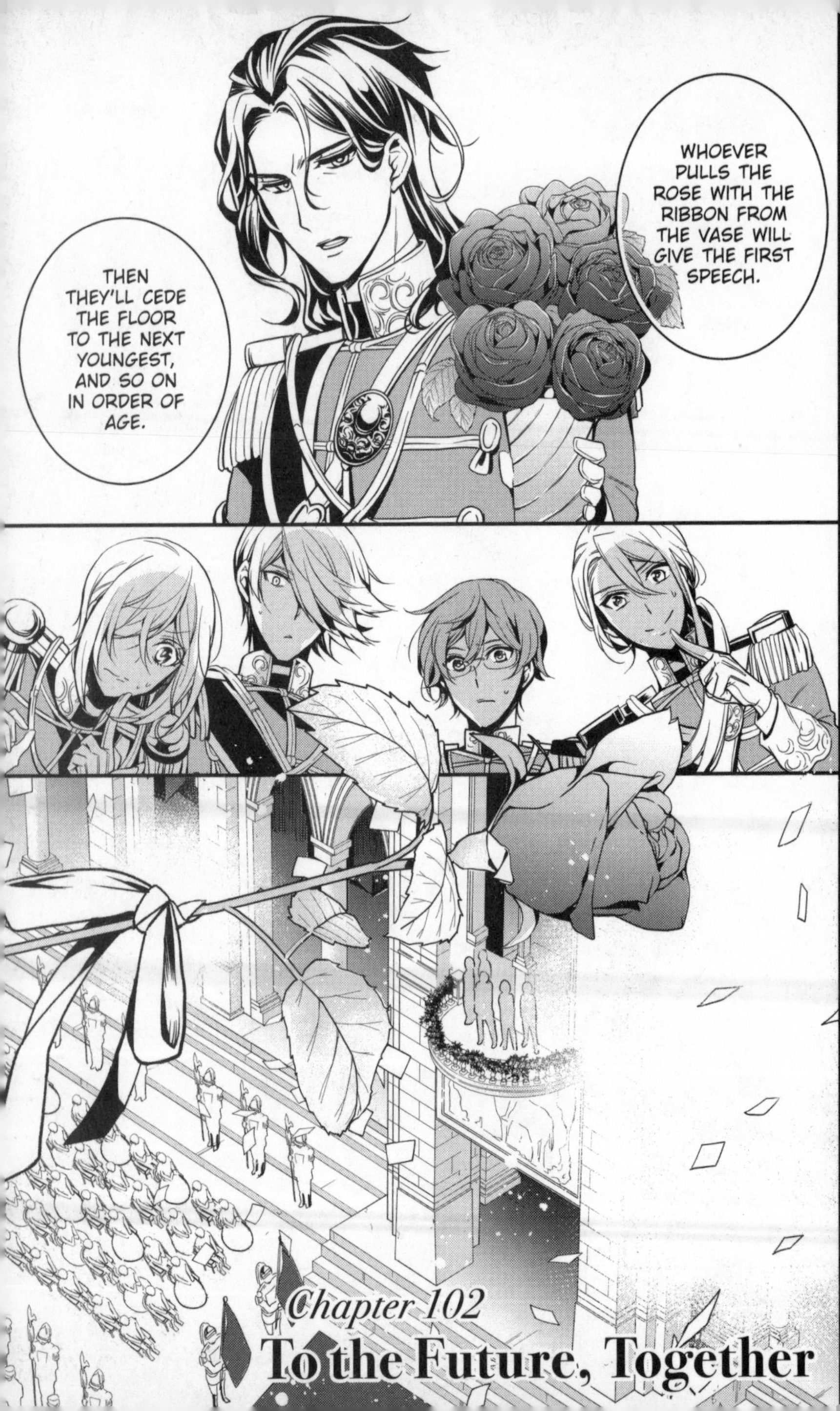
WHOEVER PULLS THE ROSE WITH THE RIBBON FROM THE VASE WILL GIVE THE FIRST SPEECH.
THEN THEY'LL CEDE THE FLOOR TO THE NEXT YOUNGEST, AND SO ON IN ORDER OF AGE.
Chapter 102
To the Future, Together

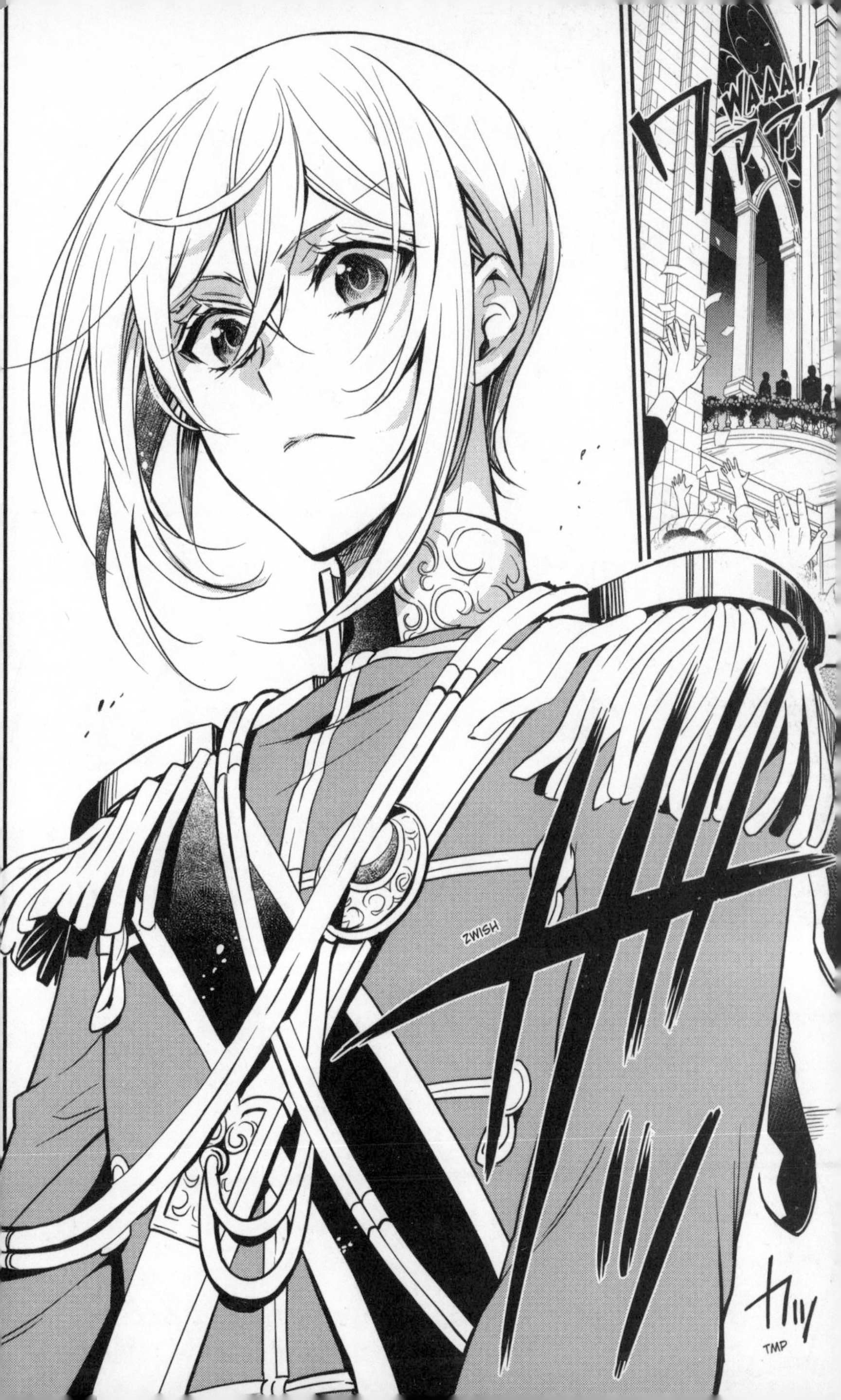
WAAAH!
ZWISH
TMP

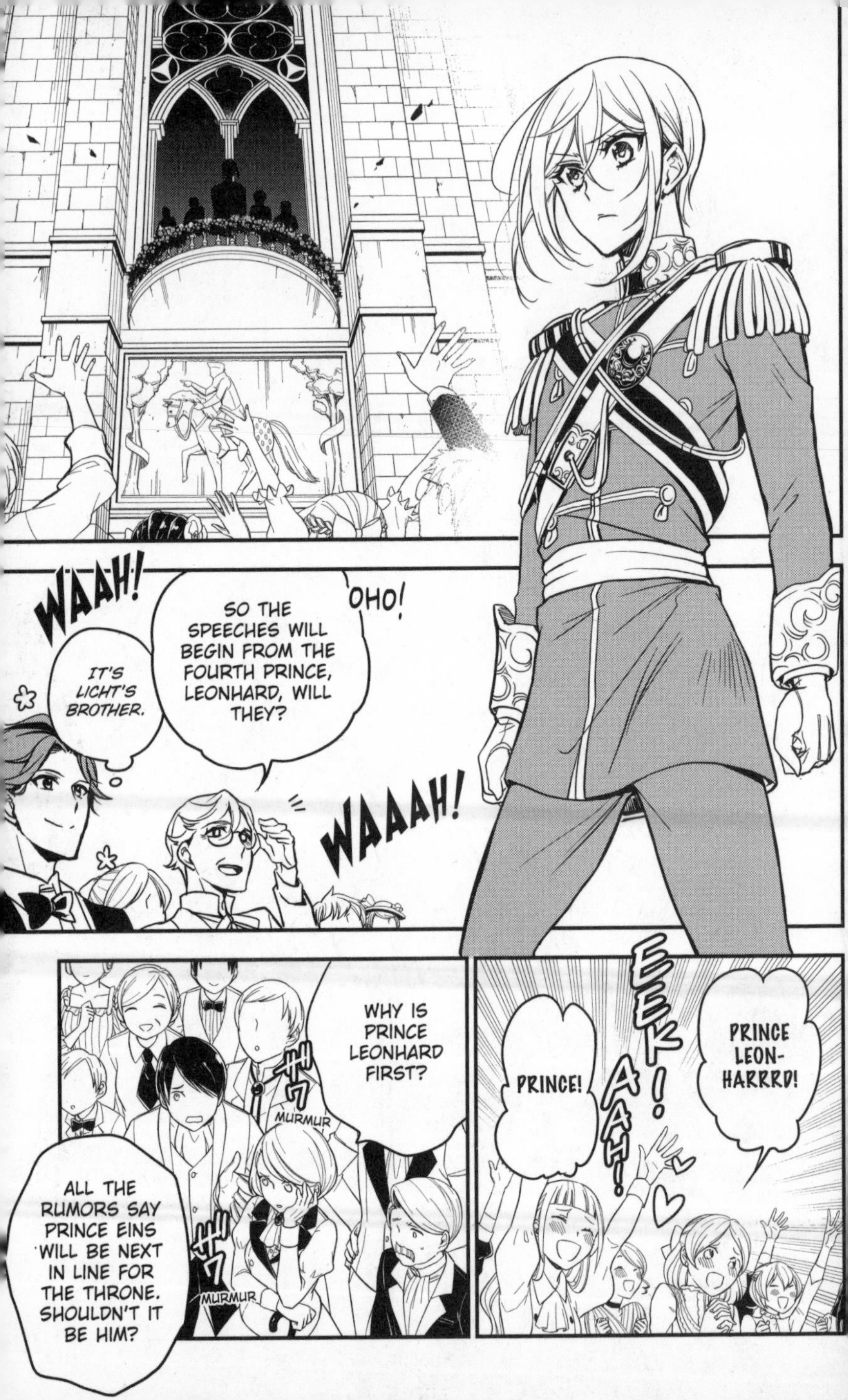
OHO!
SO THE SPEECHES WILL BEGIN FROM THE FOURTH PRINCE, LEONHARD, WILL THEY?
WAAH!
IT'S LICHT'S BROTHER.
WAAAH!
PRINCE LEON-HARRRD!
EEK! AAH!
PRINCE!
WHY IS PRINCE LEONHARD FIRST?
MURMUR
ALL THE RUMORS SAY PRINCE EINS WILL BE NEXT IN LINE FOR THE THRONE. SHOULDN'T IT BE HIM?
MURMUR

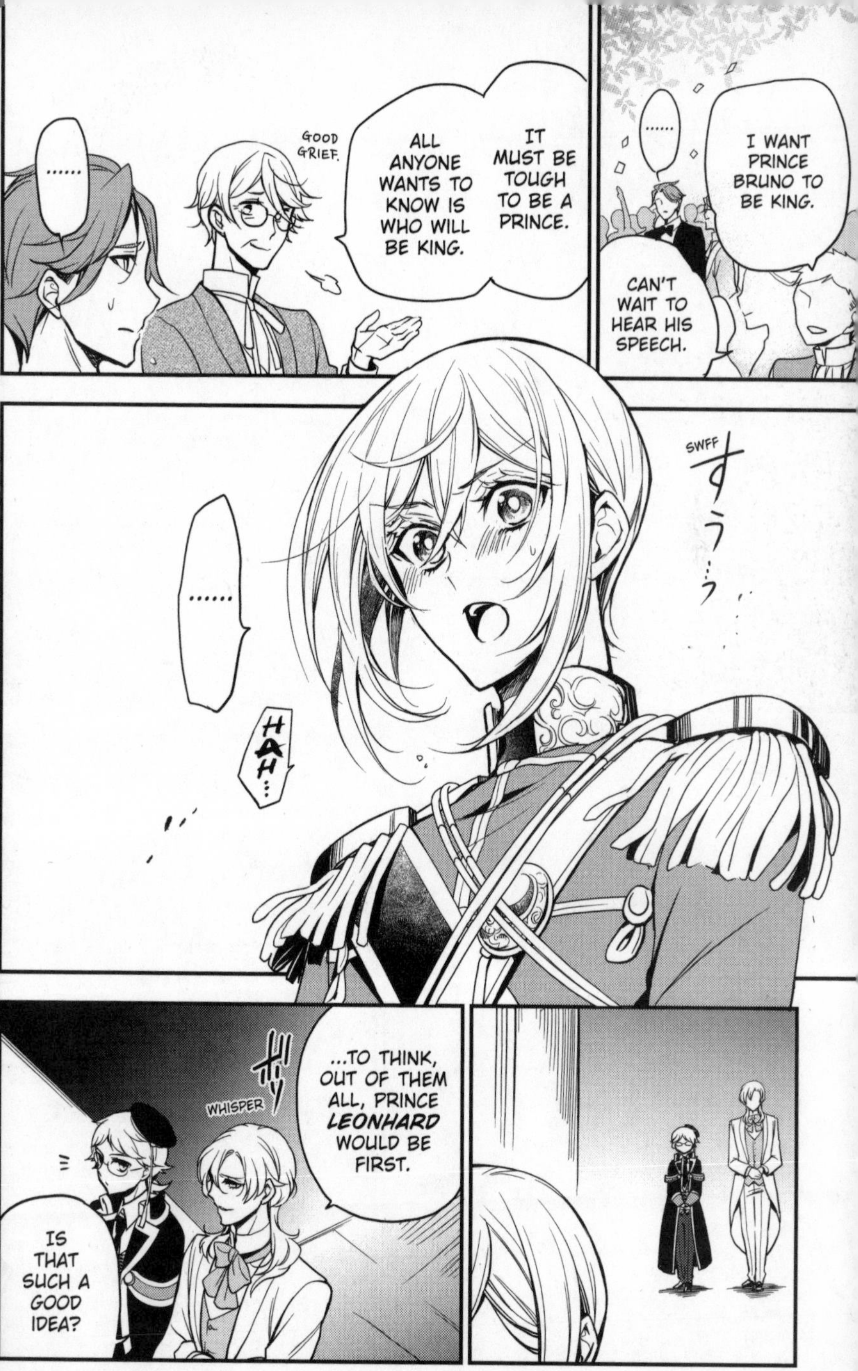
I WANT PRINCE BRUNO TO BE KING.
......
CAN'T WAIT TO HEAR HIS SPEECH.
IT MUST BE TOUGH TO BE A PRINCE.
ALL ANYONE WANTS TO KNOW IS WHO WILL BE KING.
GOOD GRIEF.
......
SWFF
......
HAH...
WHISPER
...TO THINK, OUT OF THEM ALL, PRINCE *LEONHARD* WOULD BE FIRST.
IS THAT SUCH A GOOD IDEA?

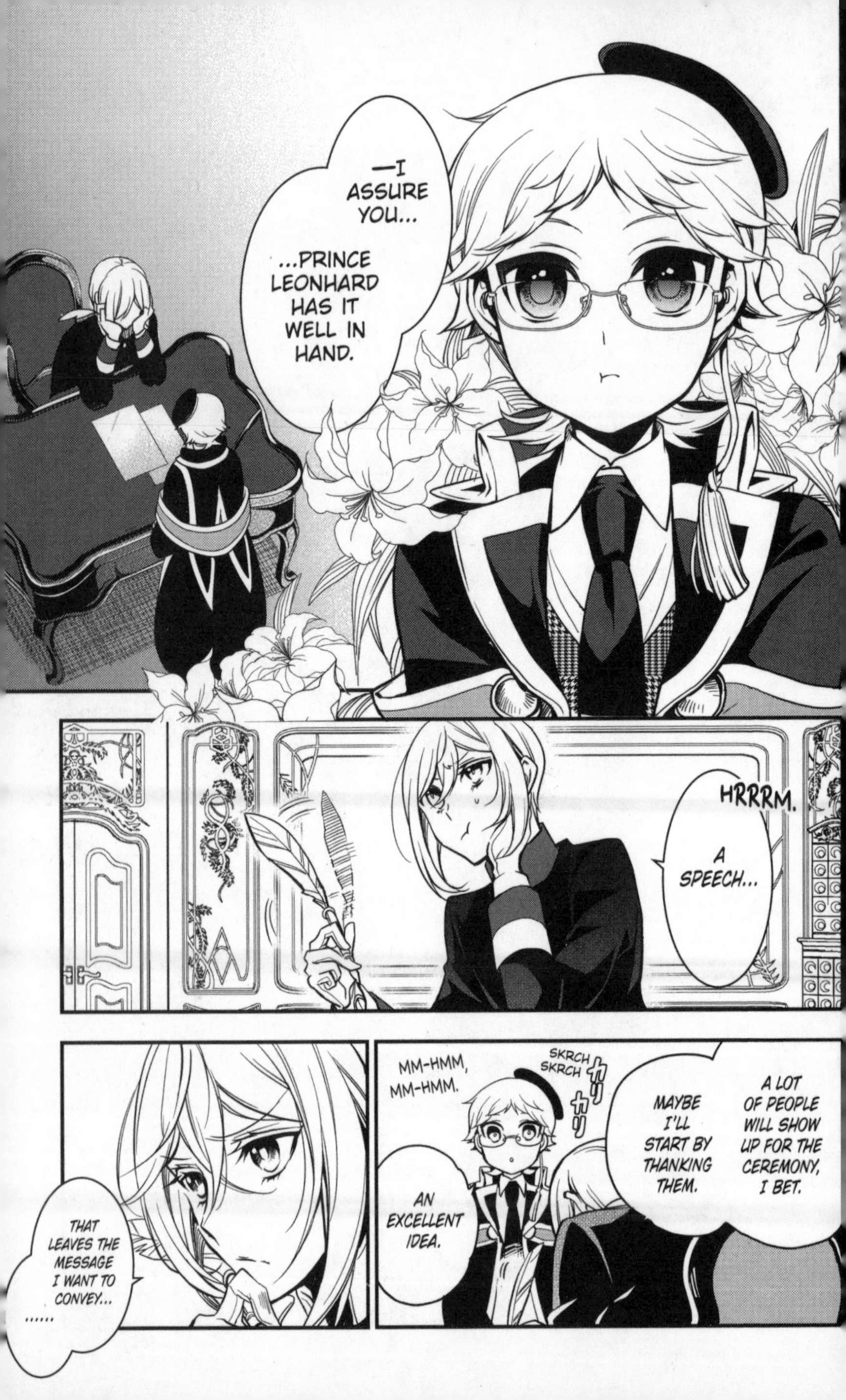
—I ASSURE YOU...
...PRINCE LEONHARD HAS IT WELL IN HAND.
HRRRM.
A SPEECH...
A LOT OF PEOPLE WILL SHOW UP FOR THE CEREMONY, I BET.
MAYBE I'LL START BY THANKING THEM.
SKRCH SKRCH
カリ
カリ
MM-HMM, MM-HMM.
AN EXCELLENT IDEA.
THAT LEAVES THE MESSAGE I WANT TO CONVEY...
......

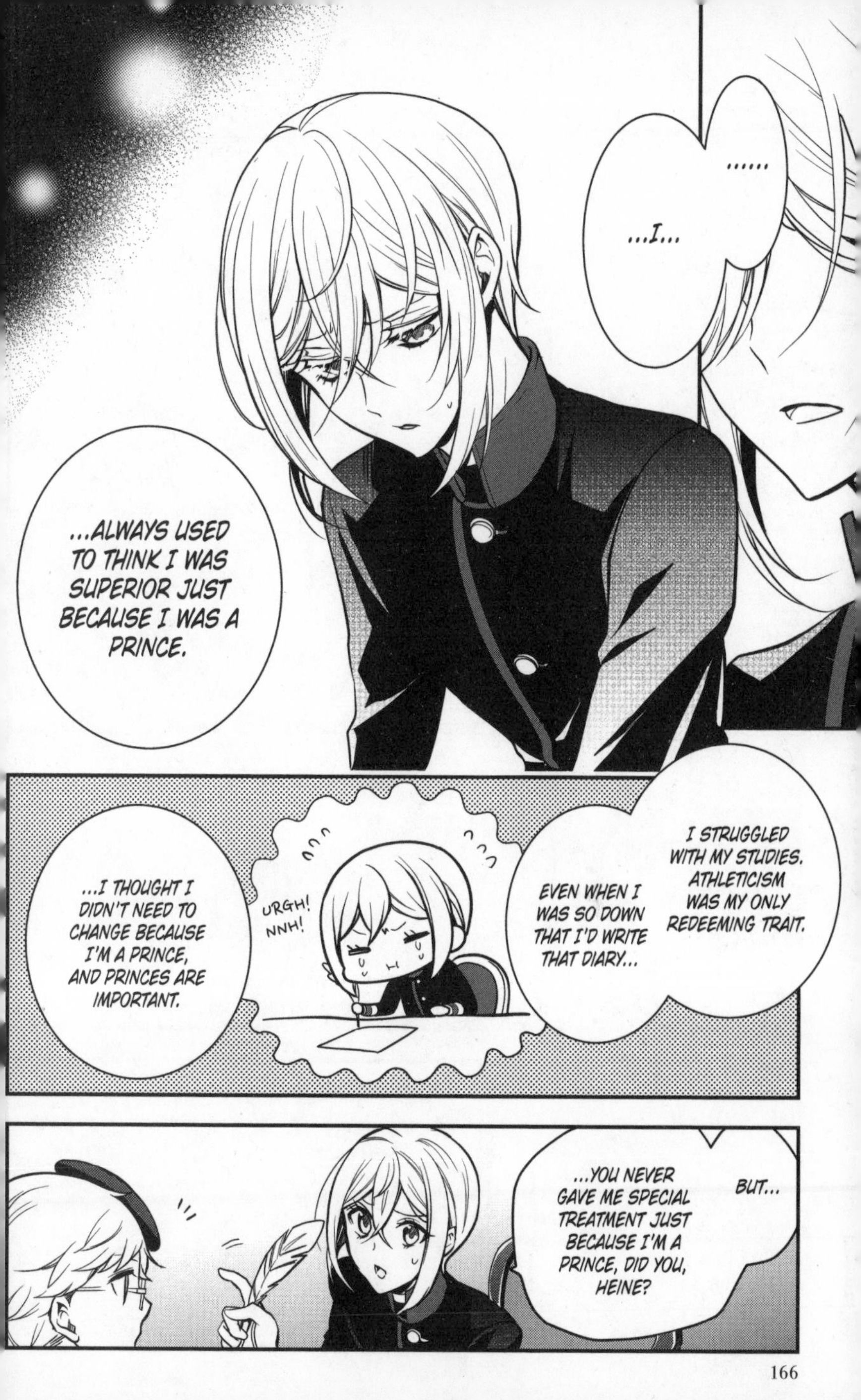
......
...I...
...ALWAYS USED TO THINK I WAS SUPERIOR JUST BECAUSE I WAS A PRINCE.
I STRUGGLED WITH MY STUDIES. ATHLETICISM WAS MY ONLY REDEEMING TRAIT.
EVEN WHEN I WAS SO DOWN THAT I'D WRITE THAT DIARY...
URGH! NNH!
...I THOUGHT I DIDN'T NEED TO CHANGE BECAUSE I'M A PRINCE, AND PRINCES ARE IMPORTANT.
BUT...
...YOU NEVER GAVE ME SPECIAL TREATMENT JUST BECAUSE I'M A PRINCE, DID YOU, HEINE?

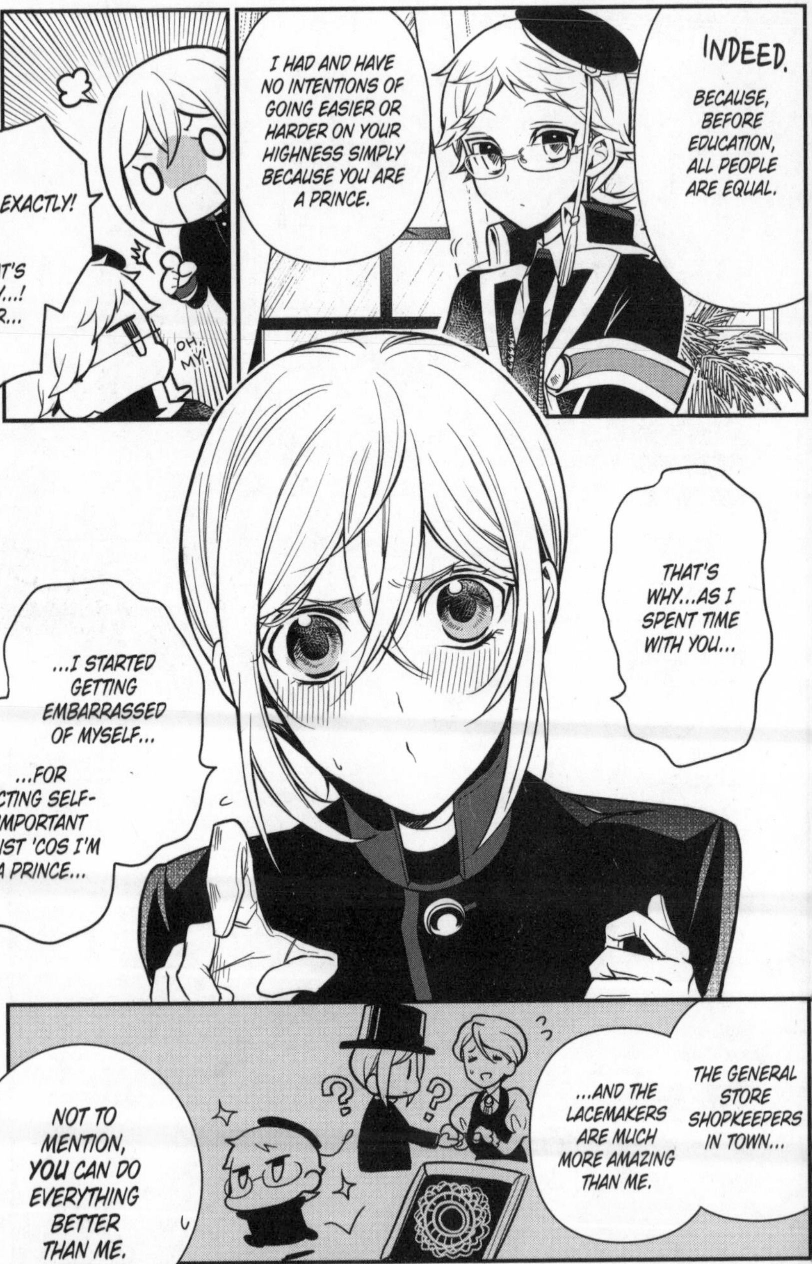
INDEED.
BECAUSE, BEFORE EDUCATION, ALL PEOPLE ARE EQUAL.
I HAD AND HAVE NO INTENTIONS OF GOING EASIER OR HARDER ON YOUR HIGHNESS SIMPLY BECAUSE YOU ARE A PRINCE.
EXACTLY!
THAT'S WHY...! ERR...
OH MY!
THAT'S WHY...AS I SPENT TIME WITH YOU...
...I STARTED GETTING EMBARRASSED OF MYSELF...
...FOR ACTING SELF-IMPORTANT JUST 'COS I'M A PRINCE...
THE GENERAL STORE SHOPKEEPERS IN TOWN...
...AND THE LACEMAKERS ARE MUCH MORE AMAZING THAN ME.
NOT TO MENTION, YOU CAN DO EVERYTHING BETTER THAN ME.

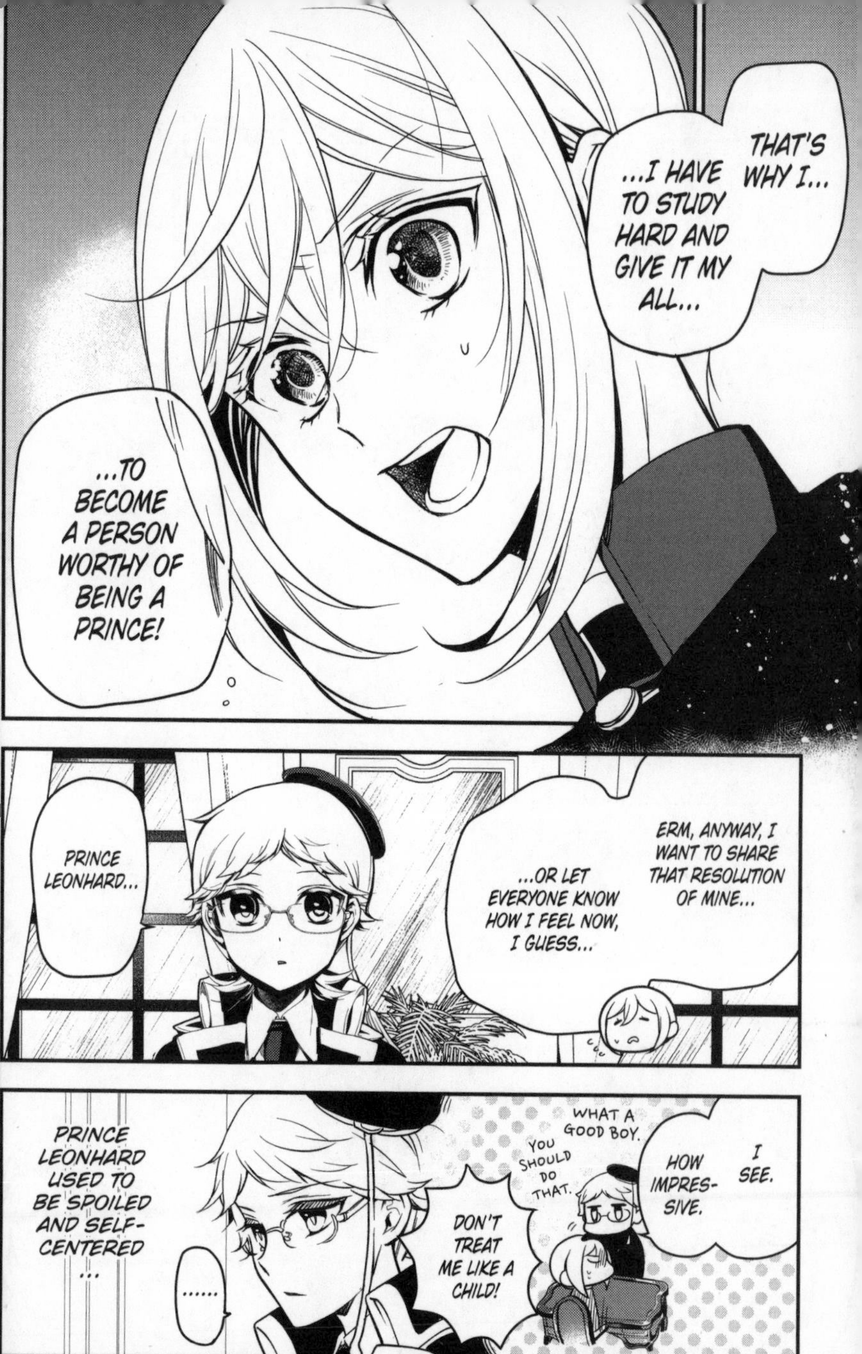
THAT'S WHY I...
...I HAVE TO STUDY HARD AND GIVE IT MY ALL...
...TO BECOME A PERSON WORTHY OF BEING A PRINCE!
ERM, ANYWAY, I WANT TO SHARE THAT RESOLUTION OF MINE...
...OR LET EVERYONE KNOW HOW I FEEL NOW, I GUESS...
PRINCE LEONHARD...
I SEE.
HOW IMPRESSIVE.
WHAT A GOOD BOY.
YOU SHOULD DO THAT.
DON'T TREAT ME LIKE A CHILD!
......
PRINCE LEONHARD USED TO BE SPOILED AND SELF-CENTERED...

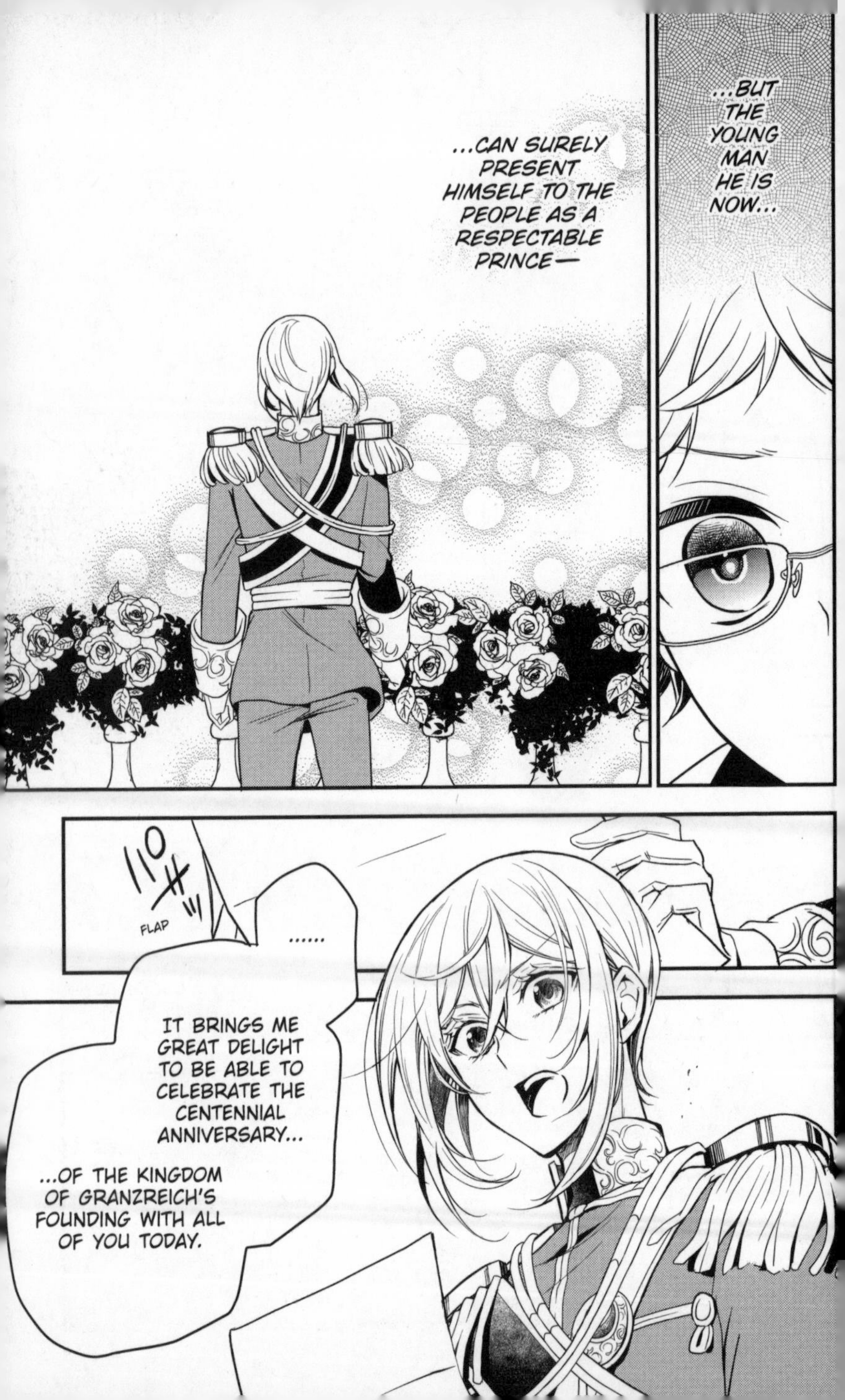
...BUT THE YOUNG MAN HE IS NOW...
...CAN SURELY PRESENT HIMSELF TO THE PEOPLE AS A RESPECTABLE PRINCE—
FLAP
......
IT BRINGS ME GREAT DELIGHT TO BE ABLE TO CELEBRATE THE CENTENNIAL ANNIVERSARY...
...OF THE KINGDOM OF GRANZREICH'S FOUNDING WITH ALL OF YOU TODAY.

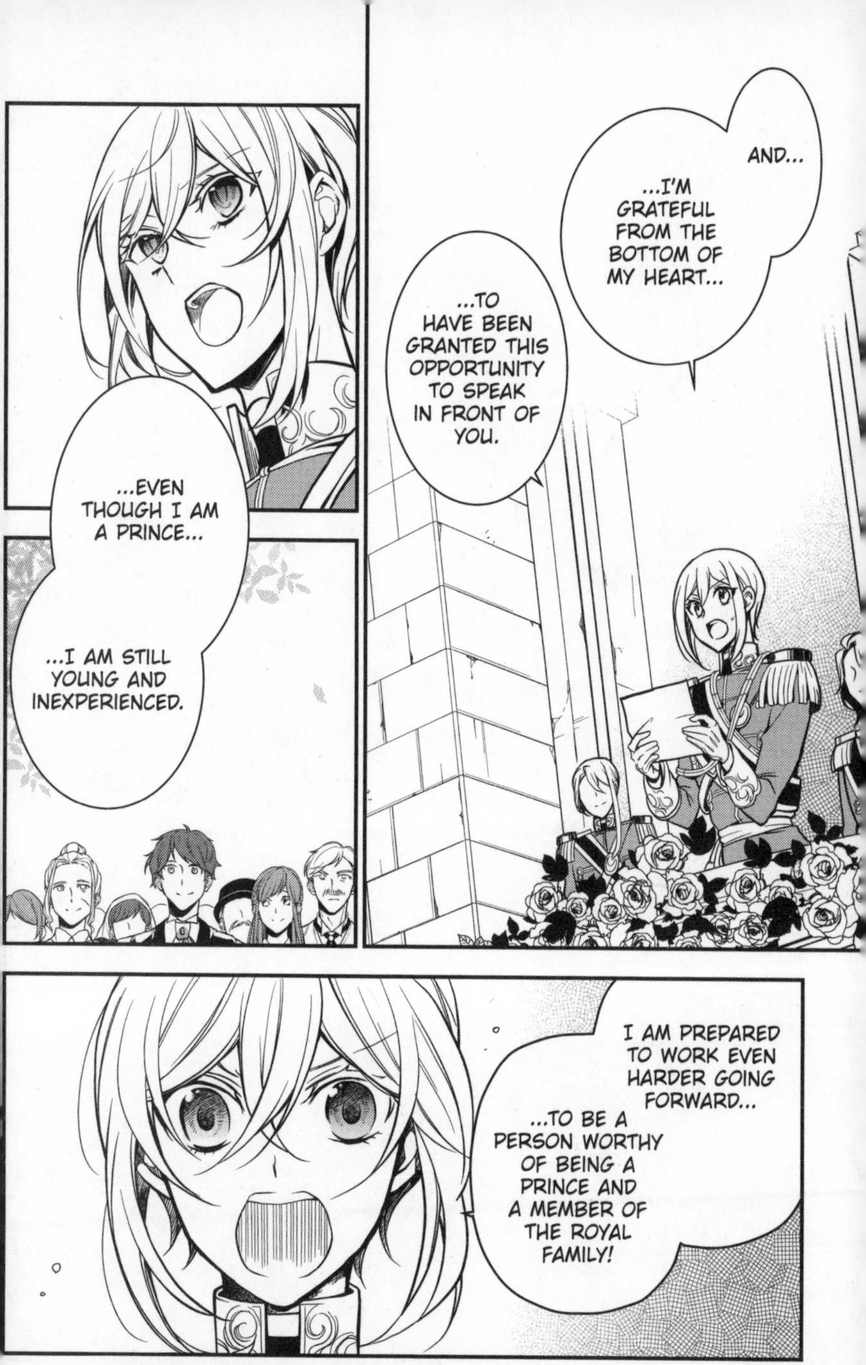
AND...
...I'M GRATEFUL FROM THE BOTTOM OF MY HEART...
...TO HAVE BEEN GRANTED THIS OPPORTUNITY TO SPEAK IN FRONT OF YOU.
...EVEN THOUGH I AM A PRINCE...
...I AM STILL YOUNG AND INEXPERIENCED.
I AM PREPARED TO WORK EVEN HARDER GOING FORWARD...
...TO BE A PERSON WORTHY OF BEING A PRINCE AND A MEMBER OF THE ROYAL FAMILY!

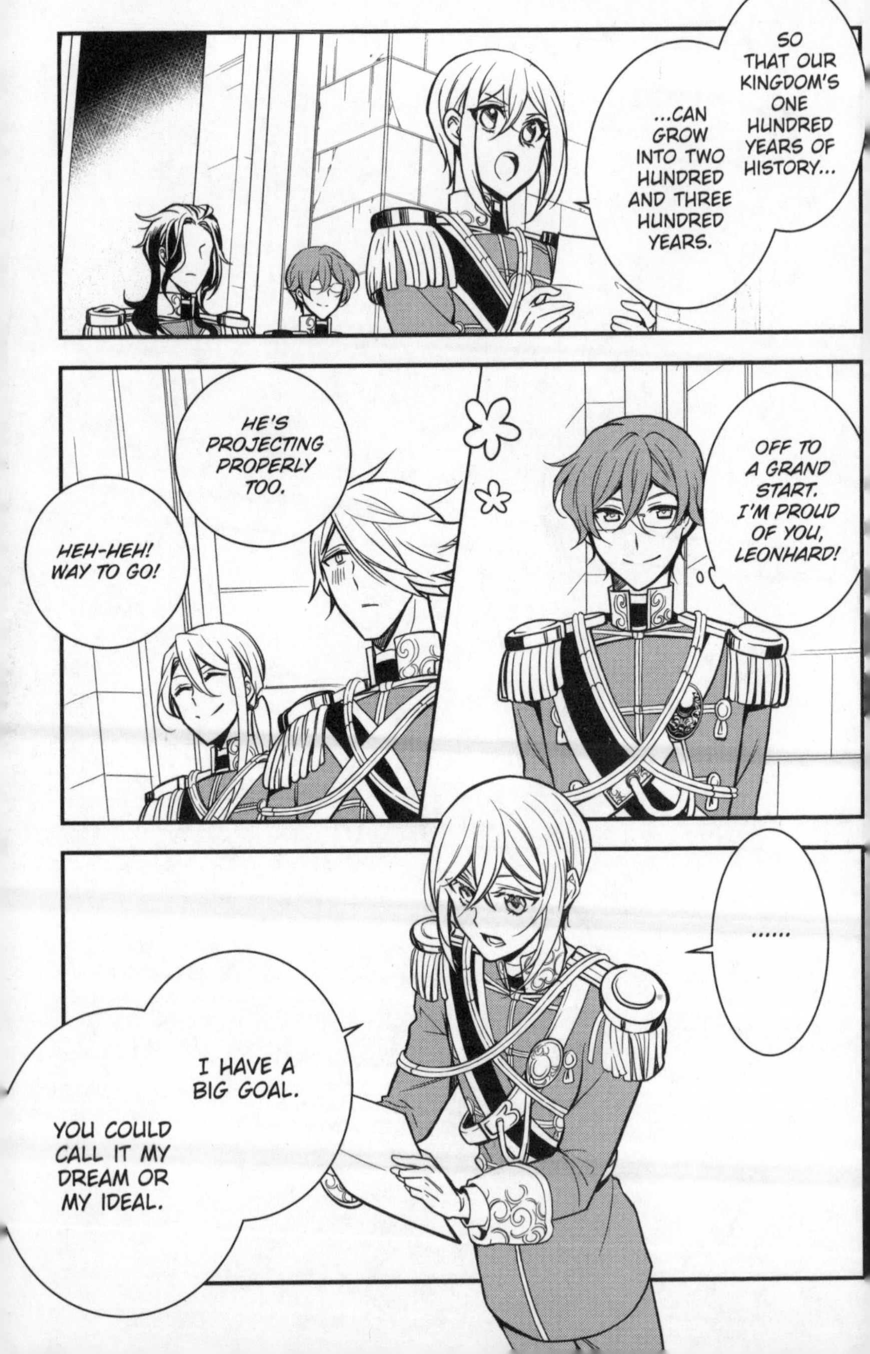
SO THAT OUR KINGDOM'S ONE HUNDRED YEARS OF HISTORY...
...CAN GROW INTO TWO HUNDRED AND THREE HUNDRED YEARS.
OFF TO A GRAND START. I'M PROUD OF YOU, LEONHARD!
HE'S PROJECTING PROPERLY TOO.
HEH-HEH! WAY TO GO!
......
I HAVE A BIG GOAL.
YOU COULD CALL IT MY DREAM OR MY IDEAL.

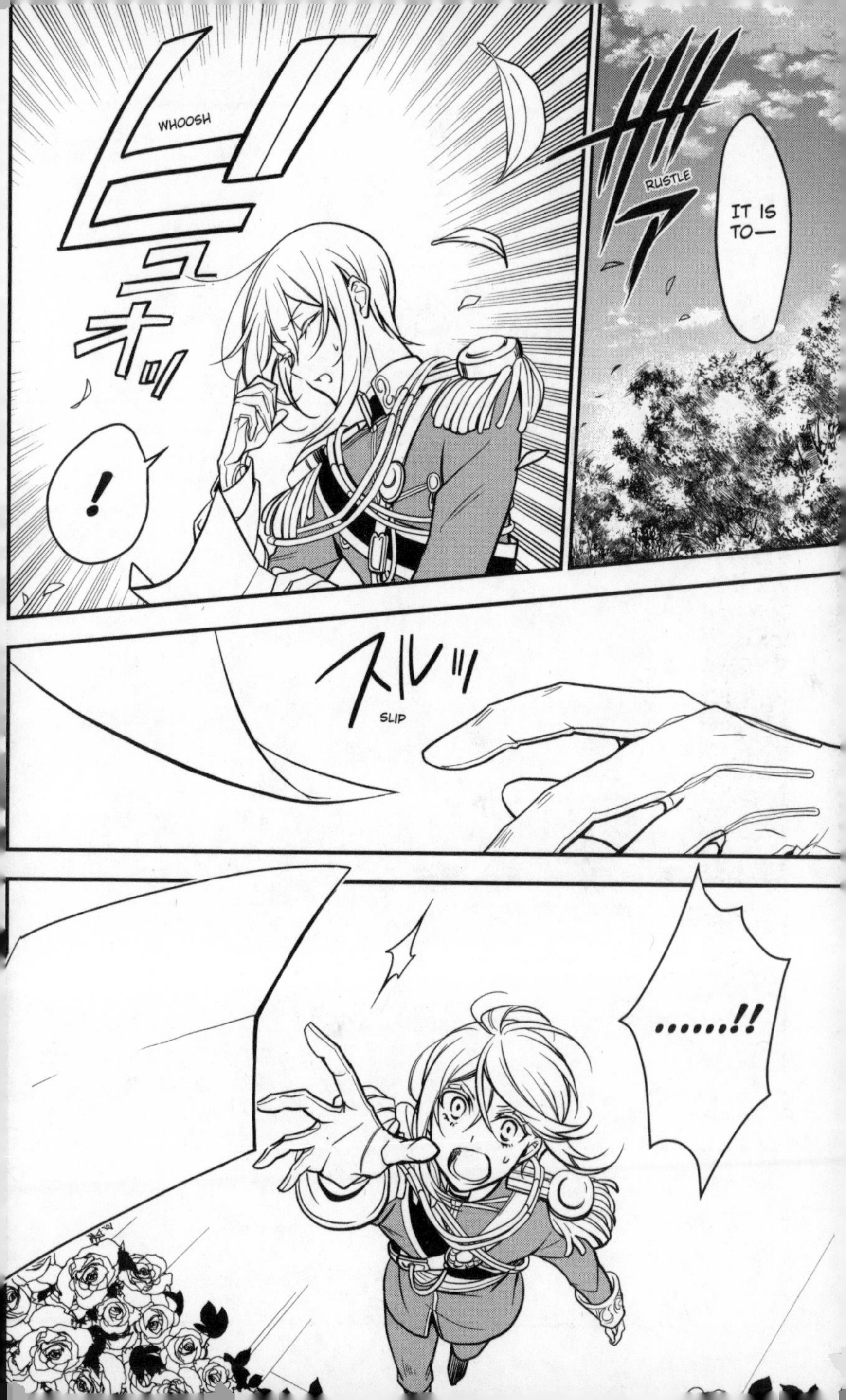

IT IS TO—
ザァ
RUSTLE
ビュオッ
WHOOSH
!
スルッ
SLIP
......!!

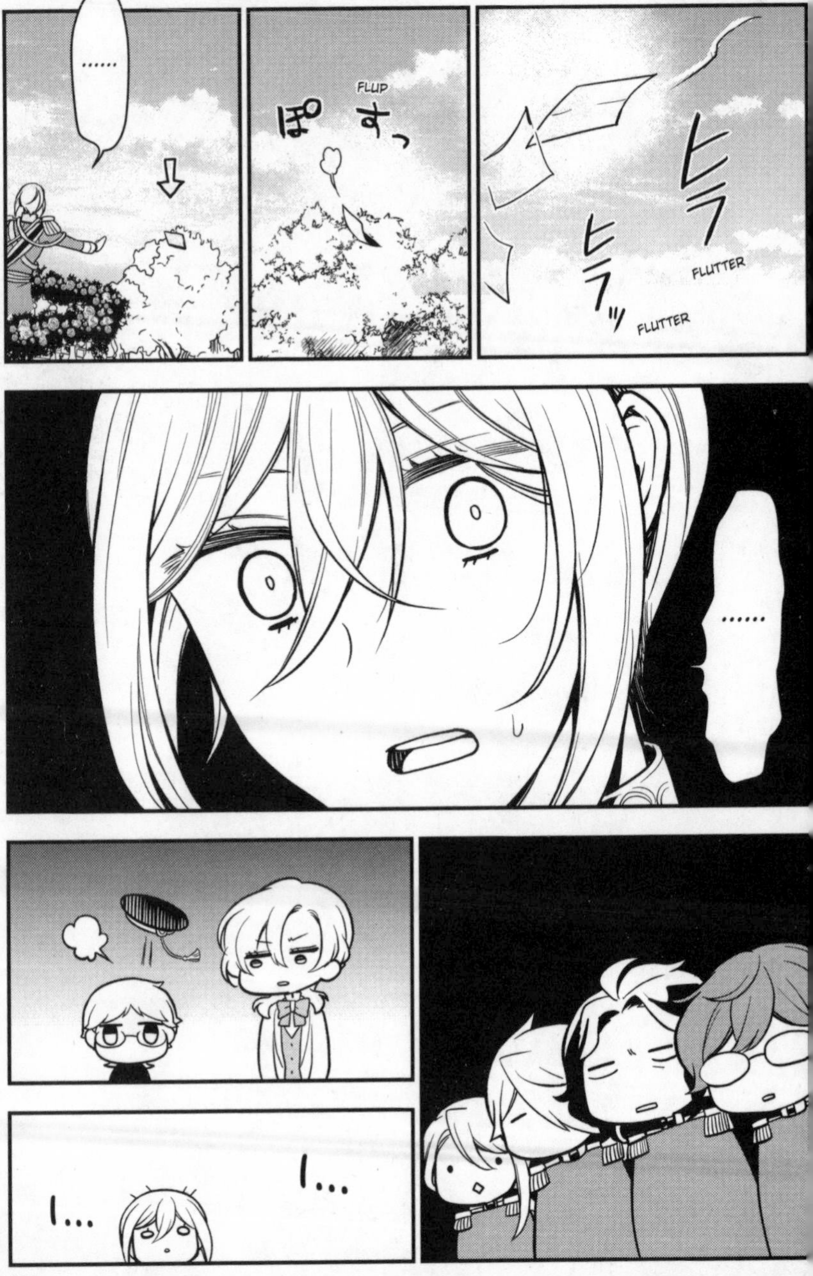
ヒラ
FLUTTER
ヒラッ
FLUTTER
ぽすっ
FLUP
......
......
I...
I...

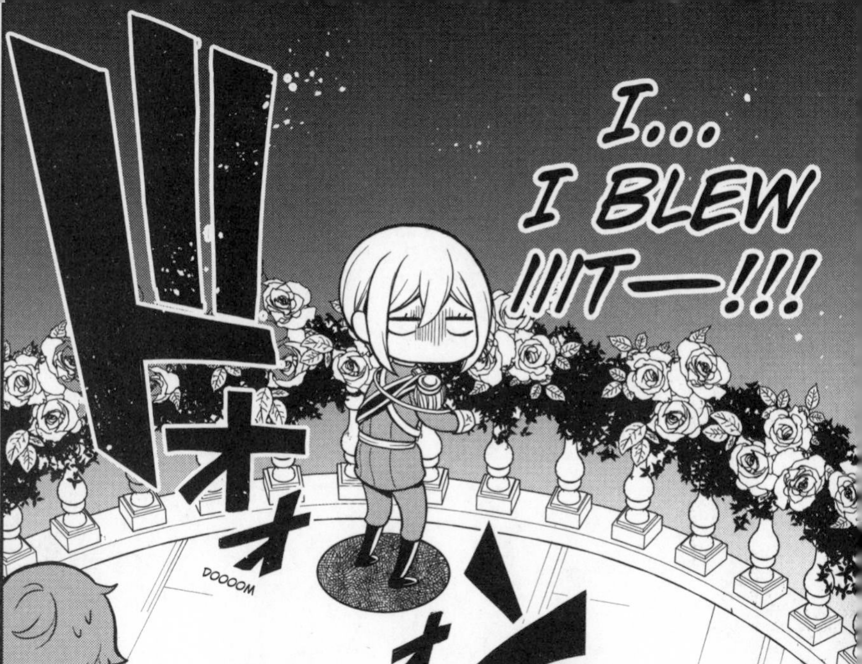
I... I BLEW IIIT—!!!
DOOOOM
ドォォォンッ

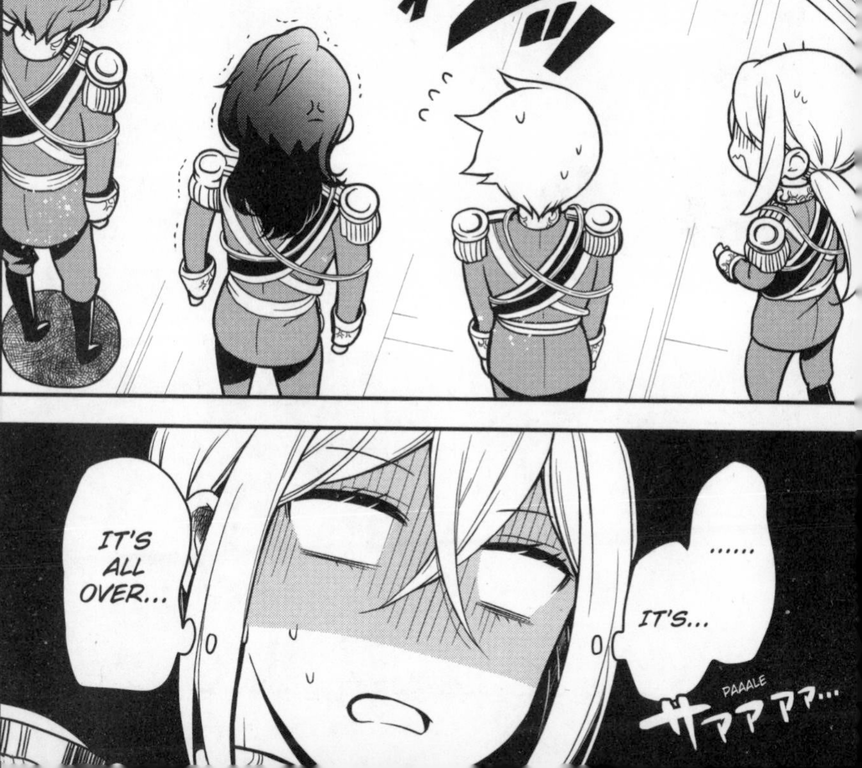
......
IT'S...
IT'S ALL OVER...
PAAALE
サァァァァ…

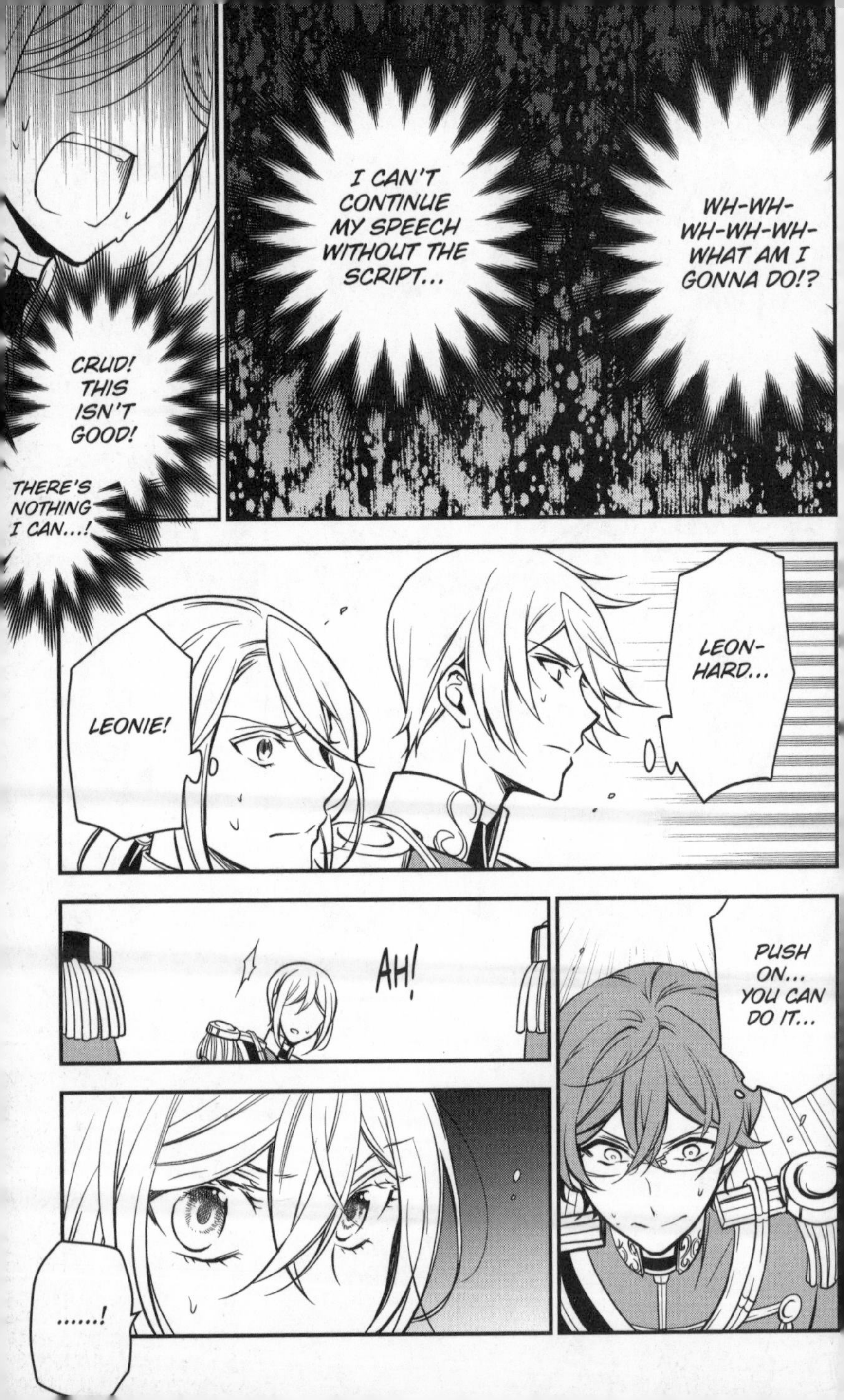
WH-WH-WH-WH-WH-WHAT AM I GONNA DO!?
I CAN'T CONTINUE MY SPEECH WITHOUT THE SCRIPT...
CRUD! THIS ISN'T GOOD!
THERE'S NOTHING I CAN...!
LEON-HARD...
LEONIE!
PUSH ON... YOU CAN DO IT...
AH!
......!

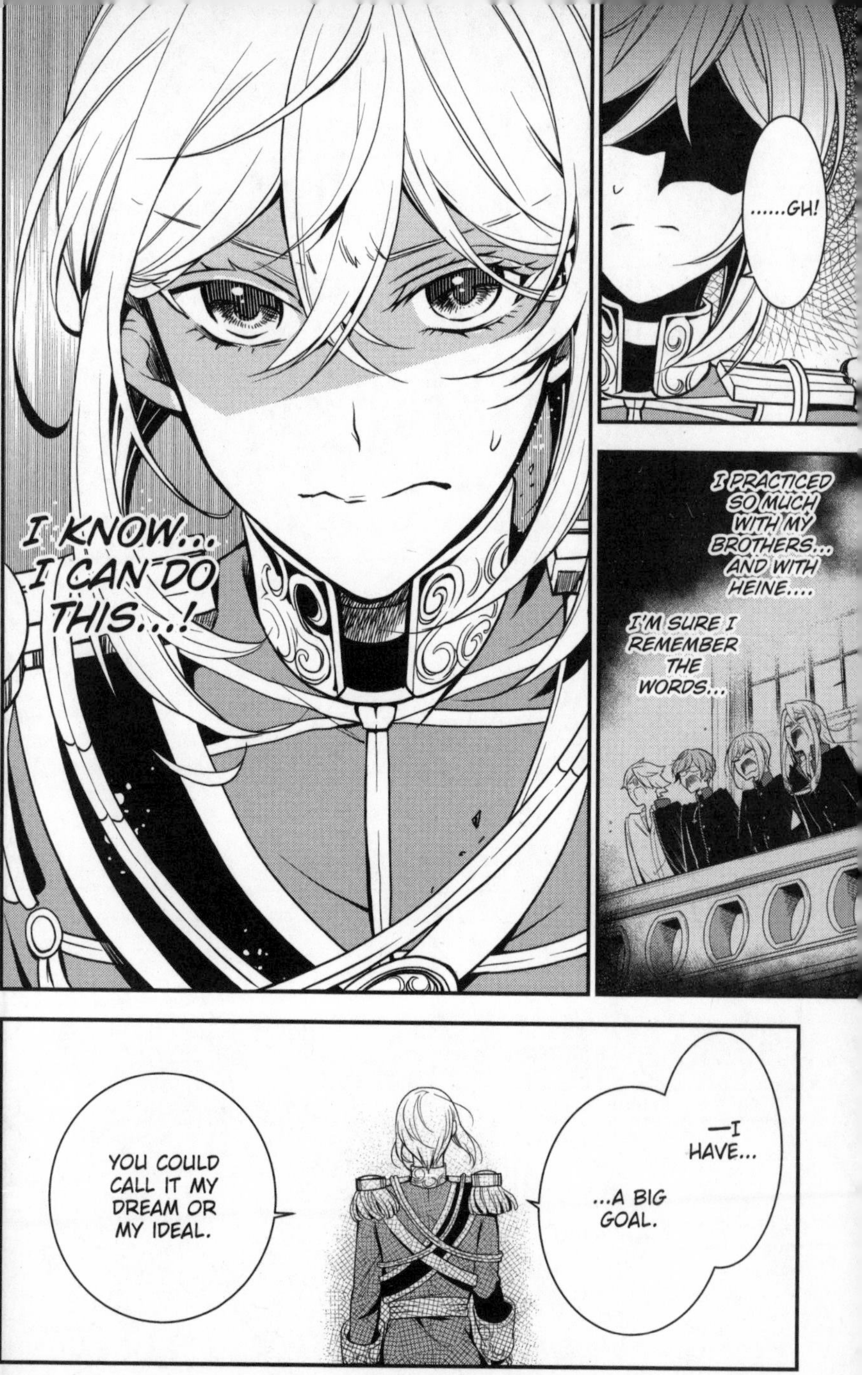
......GH!
I PRACTICED SO MUCH WITH MY BROTHERS... AND WITH HEINE....
I'M SURE I REMEMBER THE WORDS...
I KNOW... I CAN DO THIS...!
—I HAVE...
...A BIG GOAL.
YOU COULD CALL IT MY DREAM OR MY IDEAL.

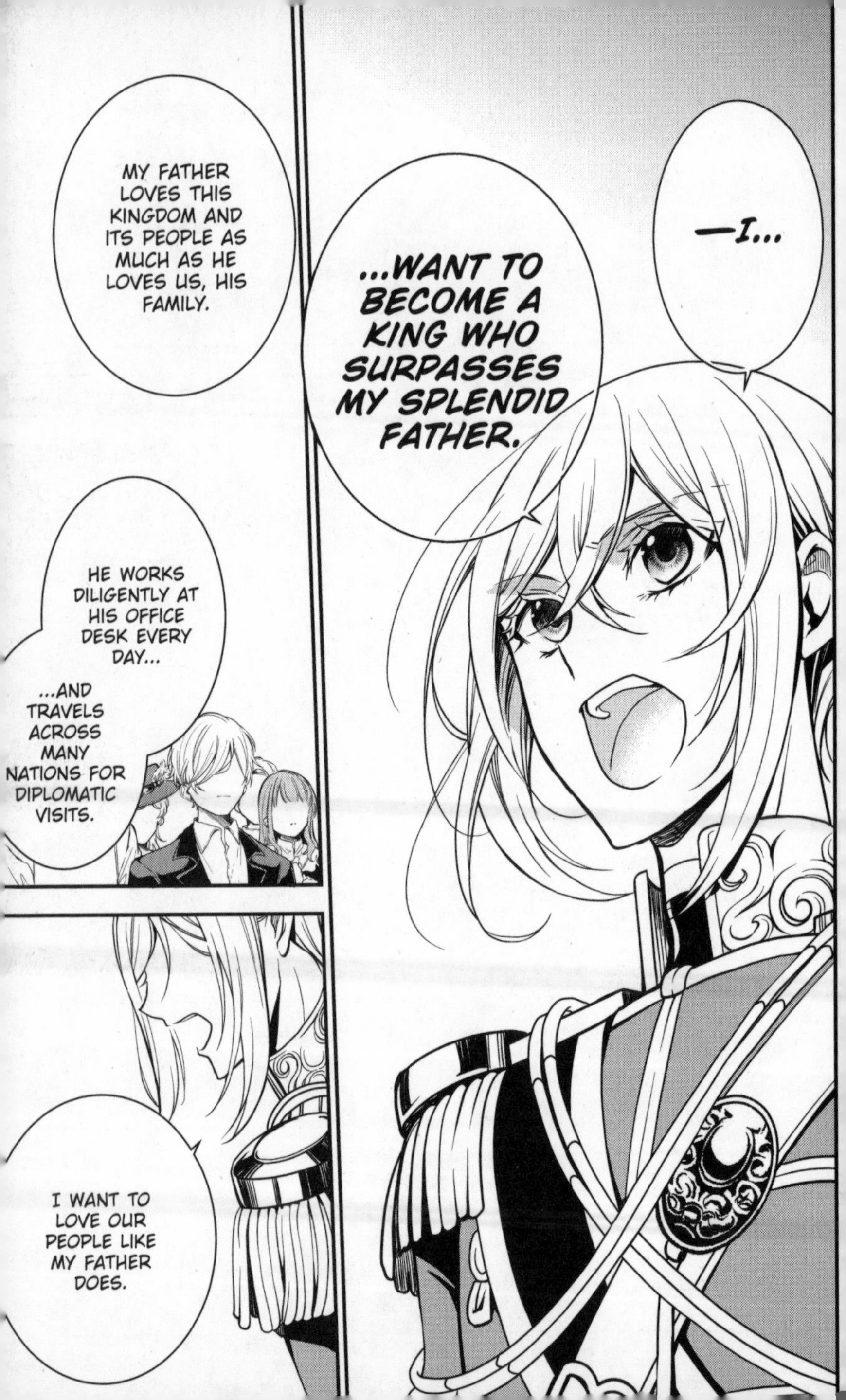
—I...
...WANT TO BECOME A KING WHO SURPASSES MY SPLENDID FATHER.
MY FATHER LOVES THIS KINGDOM AND ITS PEOPLE AS MUCH AS HE LOVES US, HIS FAMILY.
HE WORKS DILIGENTLY AT HIS OFFICE DESK EVERY DAY...
...AND TRAVELS ACROSS MANY NATIONS FOR DIPLOMATIC VISITS.
I WANT TO LOVE OUR PEOPLE LIKE MY FATHER DOES.

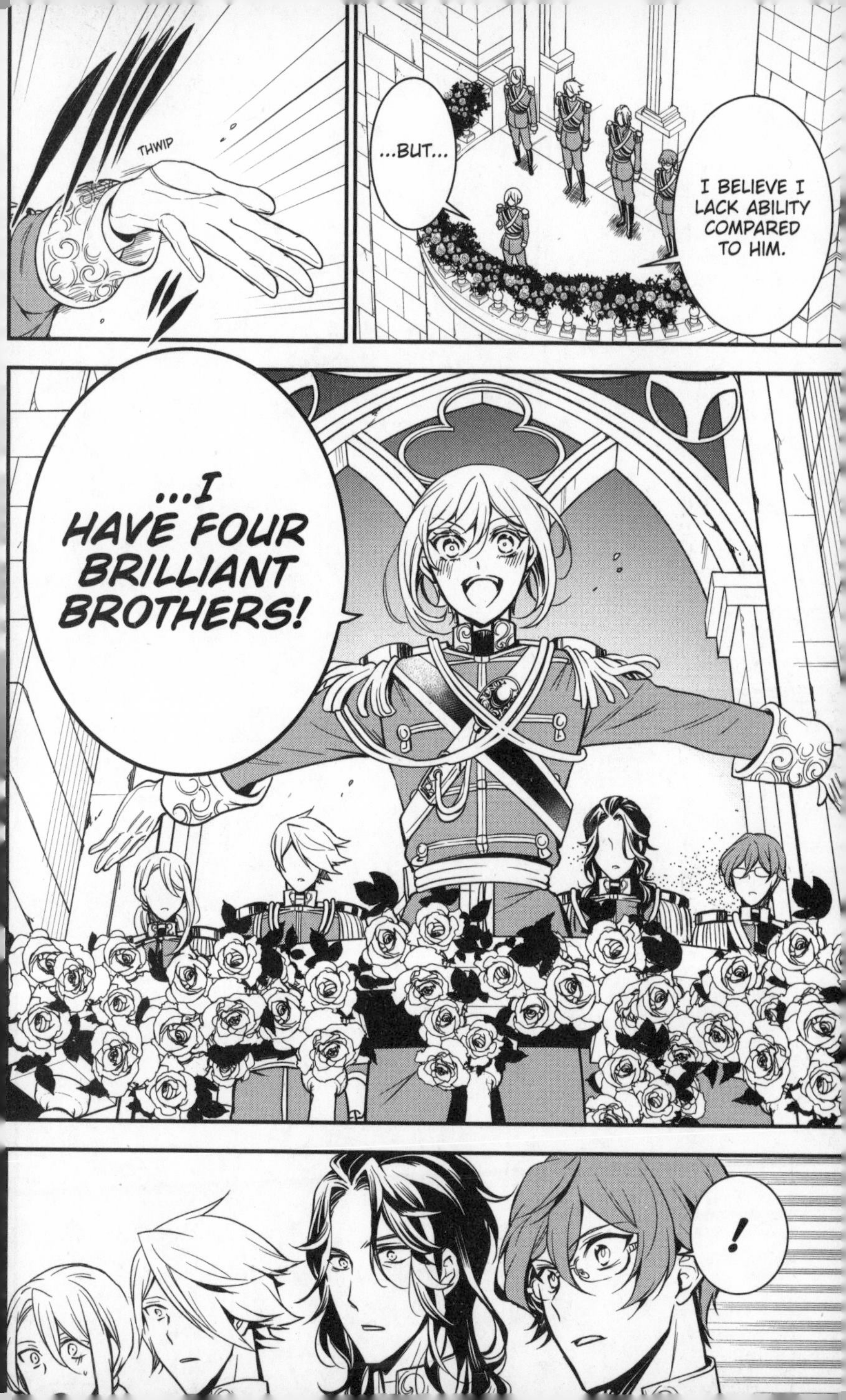
I BELIEVE I LACK ABILITY COMPARED TO HIM.
...BUT...
THWIP
...I HAVE FOUR BRILLIANT BROTHERS!
!

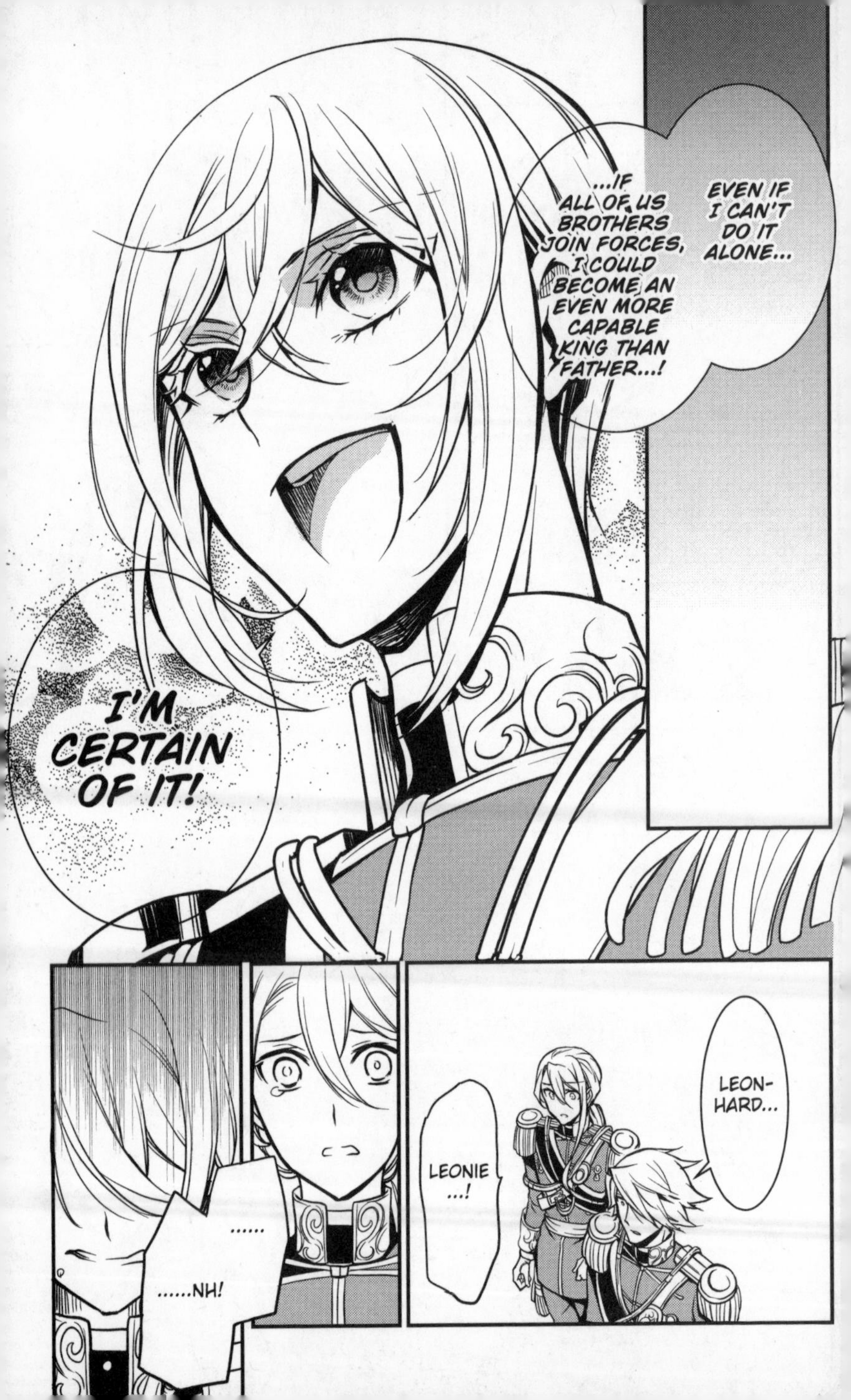
EVEN IF I CAN'T DO IT ALONE...
...IF ALL OF US BROTHERS JOIN FORCES, I COULD BECOME AN EVEN MORE CAPABLE KING THAN FATHER...!
I'M CERTAIN OF IT!
LEON-HARD...
LEONIE ...!
......
......NH!

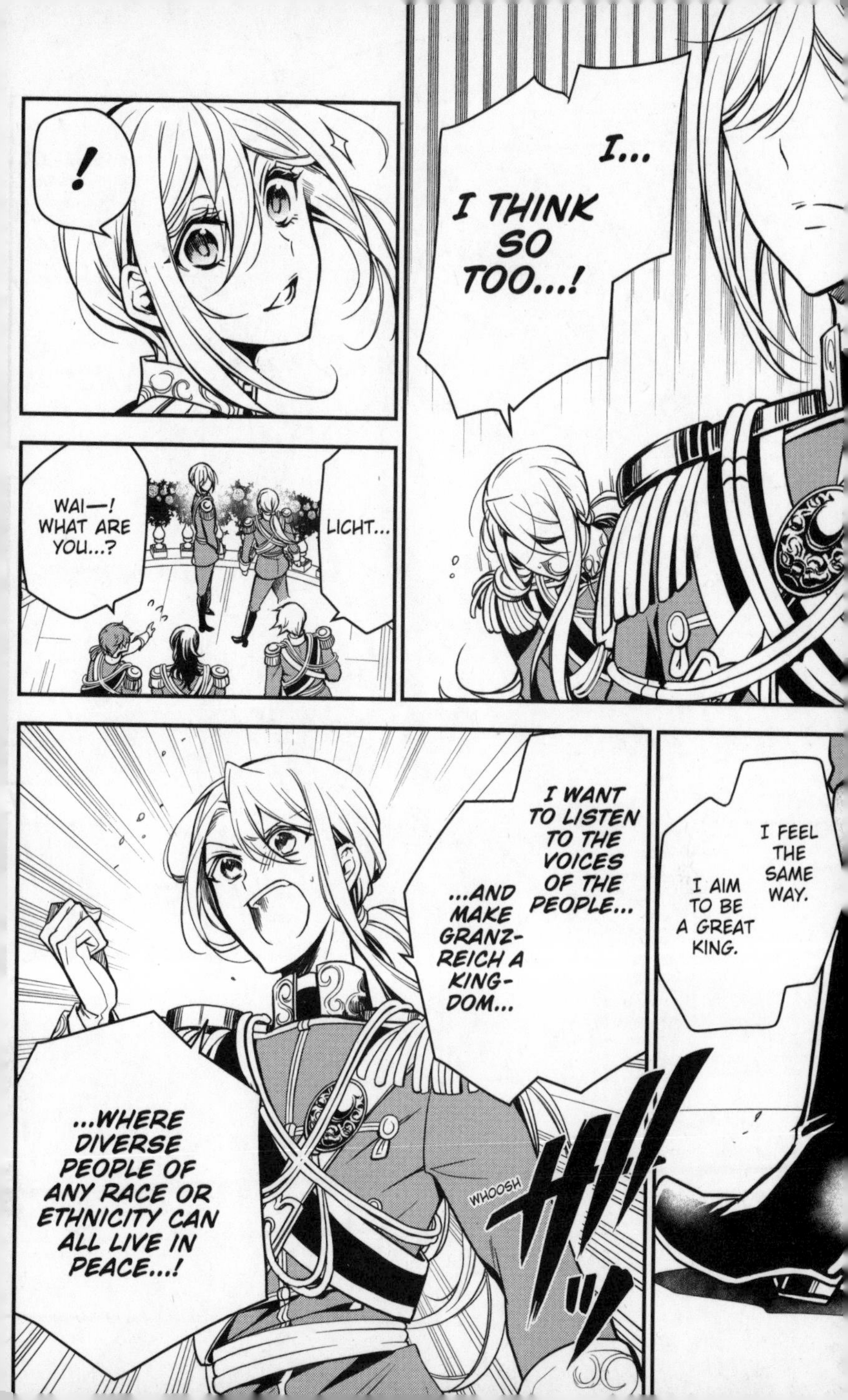
I...
I THINK SO TOO...!
!
LICHT...
WAI—! WHAT ARE YOU...?
I FEEL THE SAME WAY.
I AIM TO BE A GREAT KING.
I WANT TO LISTEN TO THE VOICES OF THE PEOPLE...
...AND MAKE GRANZ-REICH A KING-DOM...
...WHERE DIVERSE PEOPLE OF ANY RACE OR ETHNICITY CAN ALL LIVE IN PEACE...!
WHOOSH

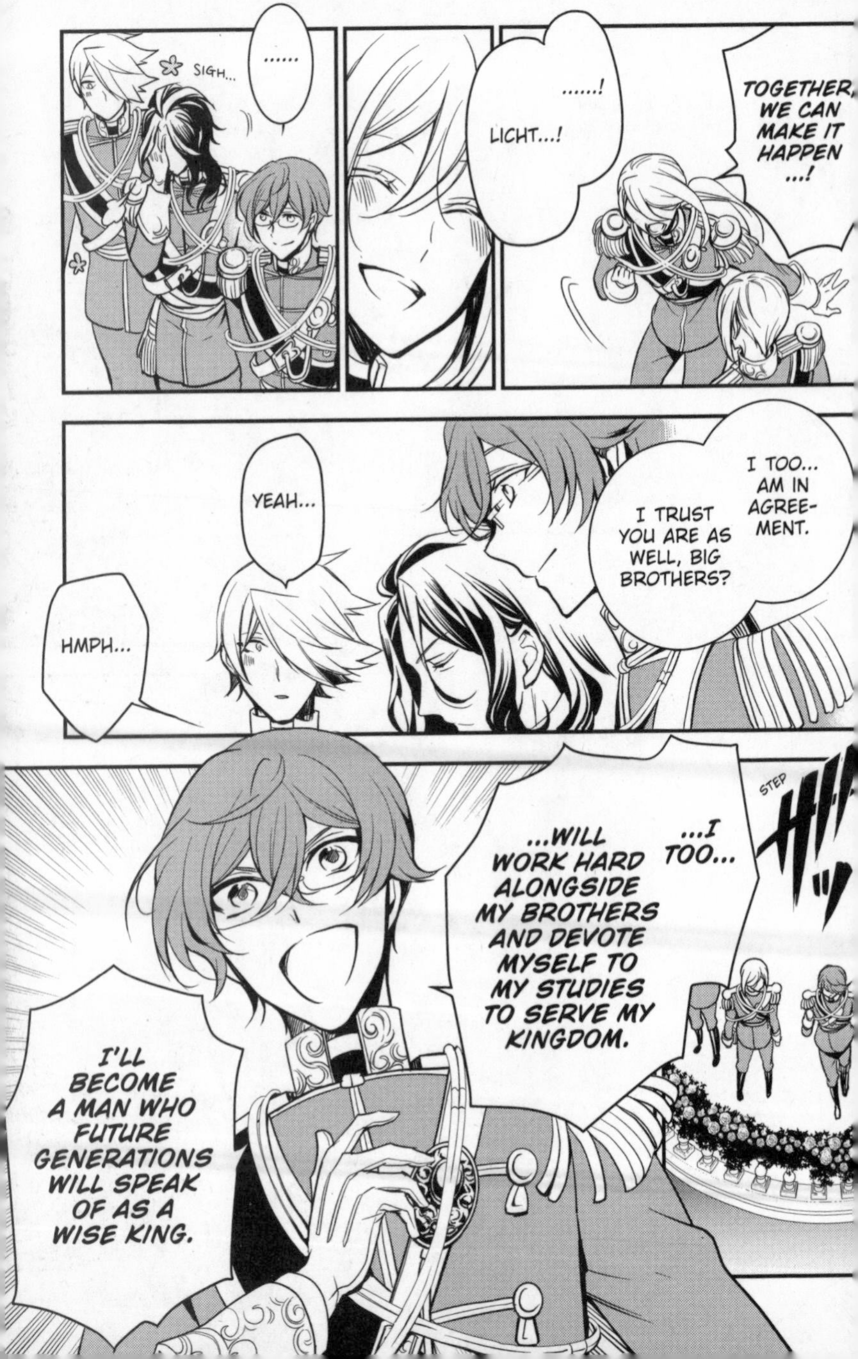
TOGETHER, WE CAN MAKE IT HAPPEN ...!
......!
LICHT...!
......
SIGH...
I TOO... AM IN AGREE-MENT.
I TRUST YOU ARE AS WELL, BIG BROTHERS?
YEAH...
HMPH...
STEP
...I TOO...
...WILL WORK HARD ALONGSIDE MY BROTHERS AND DEVOTE MYSELF TO MY STUDIES TO SERVE MY KINGDOM.
I'LL BECOME A MAN WHO FUTURE GENERATIONS WILL SPEAK OF AS A WISE KING.

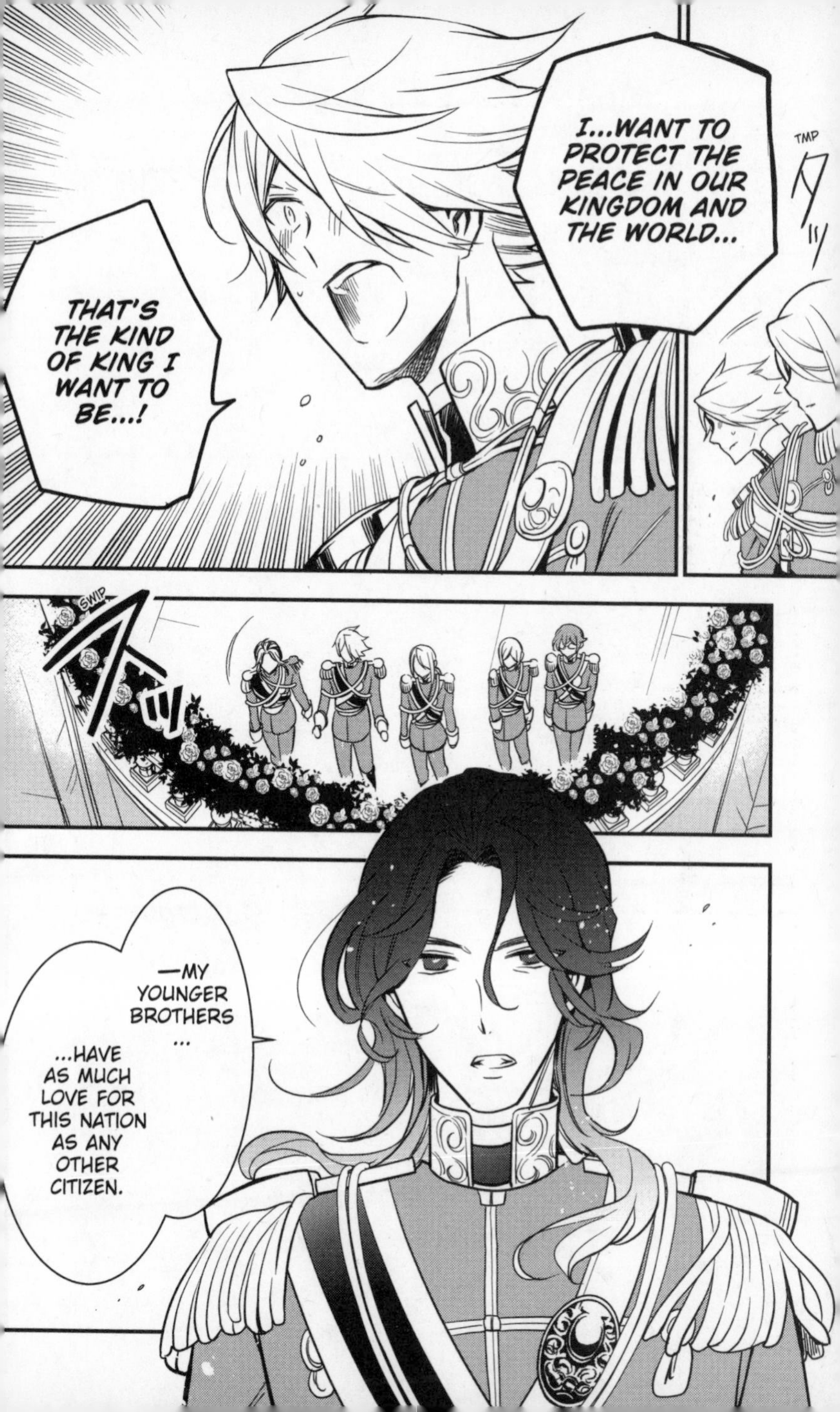
TMP
I...WANT TO PROTECT THE PEACE IN OUR KINGDOM AND THE WORLD...
THAT'S THE KIND OF KING I WANT TO BE...!
SWIP
—MY YOUNGER BROTHERS ...
...HAVE AS MUCH LOVE FOR THIS NATION AS ANY OTHER CITIZEN.

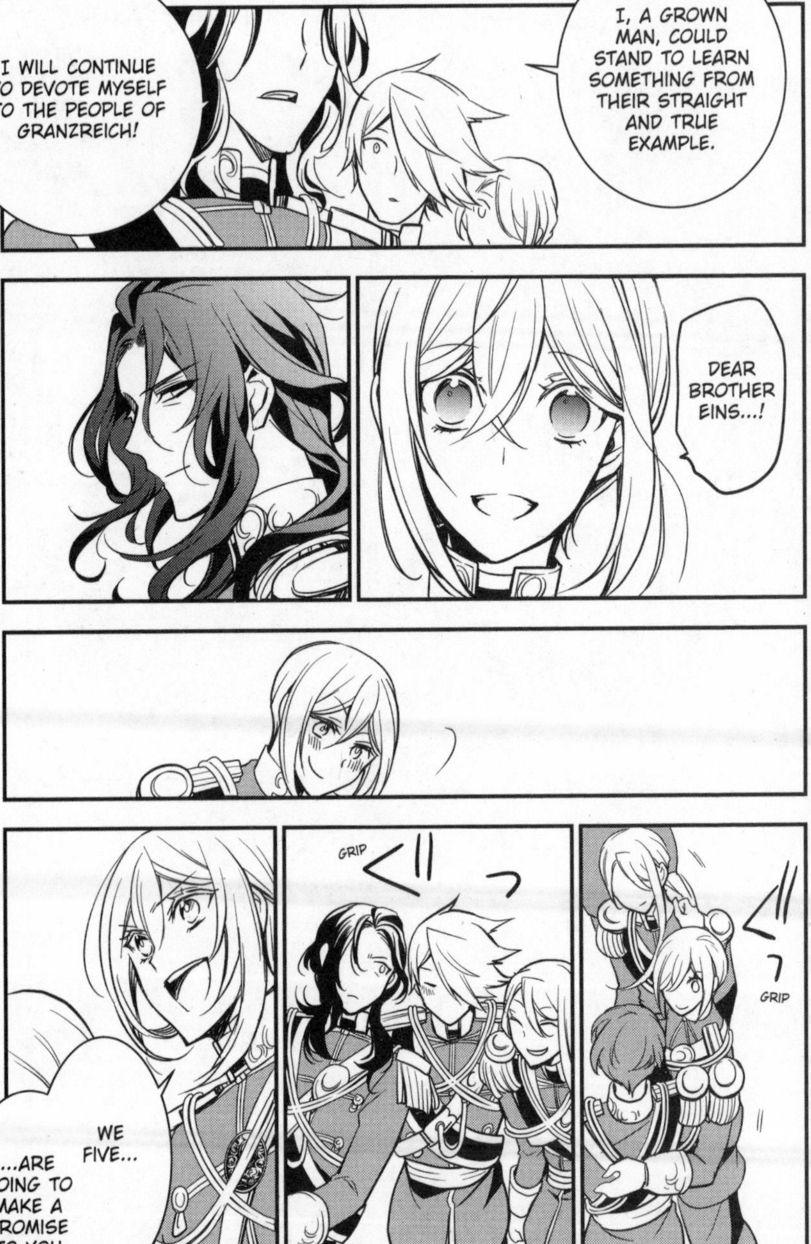
I, A GROWN MAN, COULD STAND TO LEARN SOMETHING FROM THEIR STRAIGHT AND TRUE EXAMPLE.
I WILL CONTINUE TO DEVOTE MYSELF TO THE PEOPLE OF GRANZREICH!
DEAR BROTHER EINS...!
GRIP
GRIP
WE FIVE...
...ARE GOING TO MAKE A PROMISE TO YOU ALL.

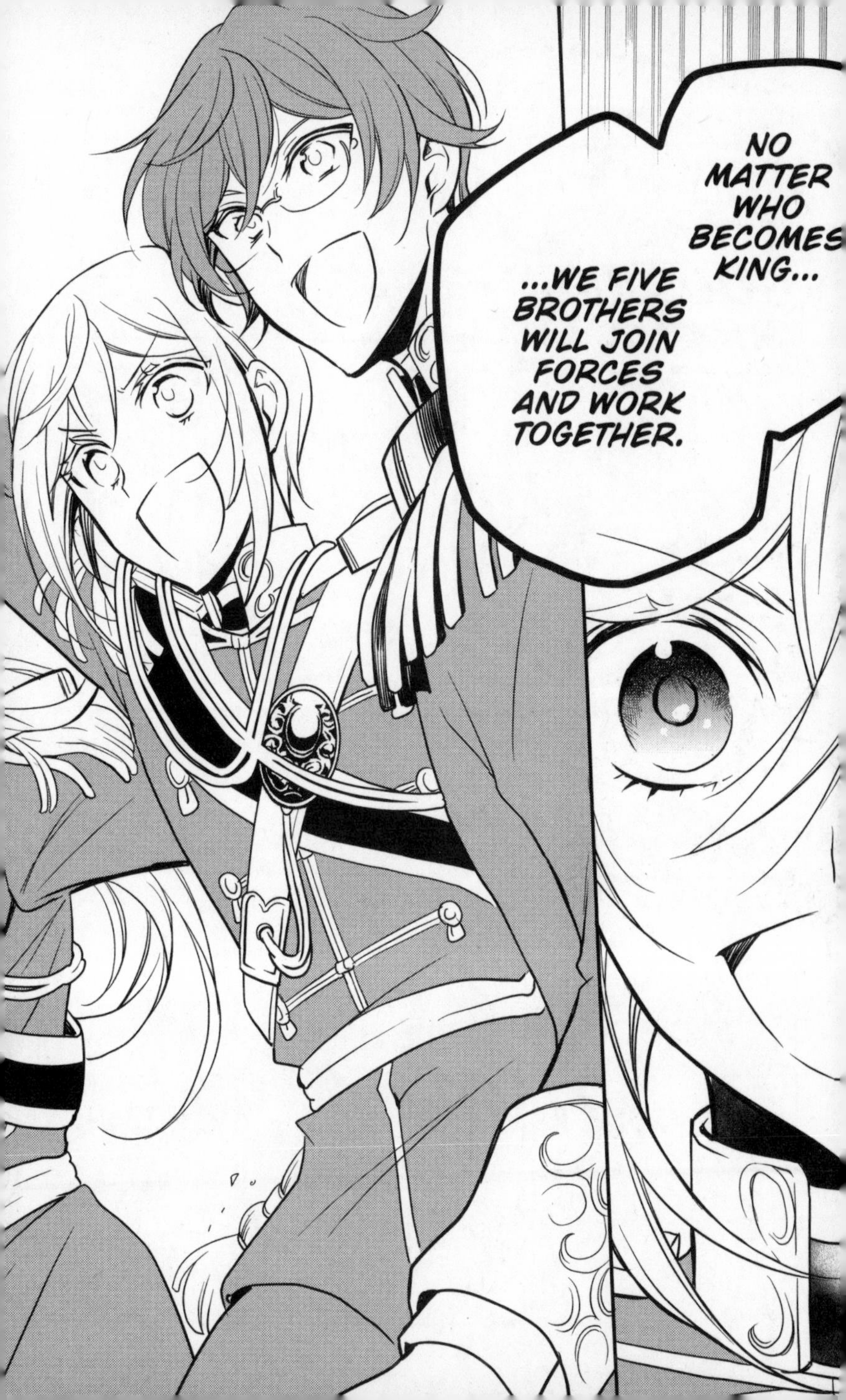
NO MATTER WHO BECOMES KING...
...WE FIVE BROTHERS WILL JOIN FORCES AND WORK TOGETHER.

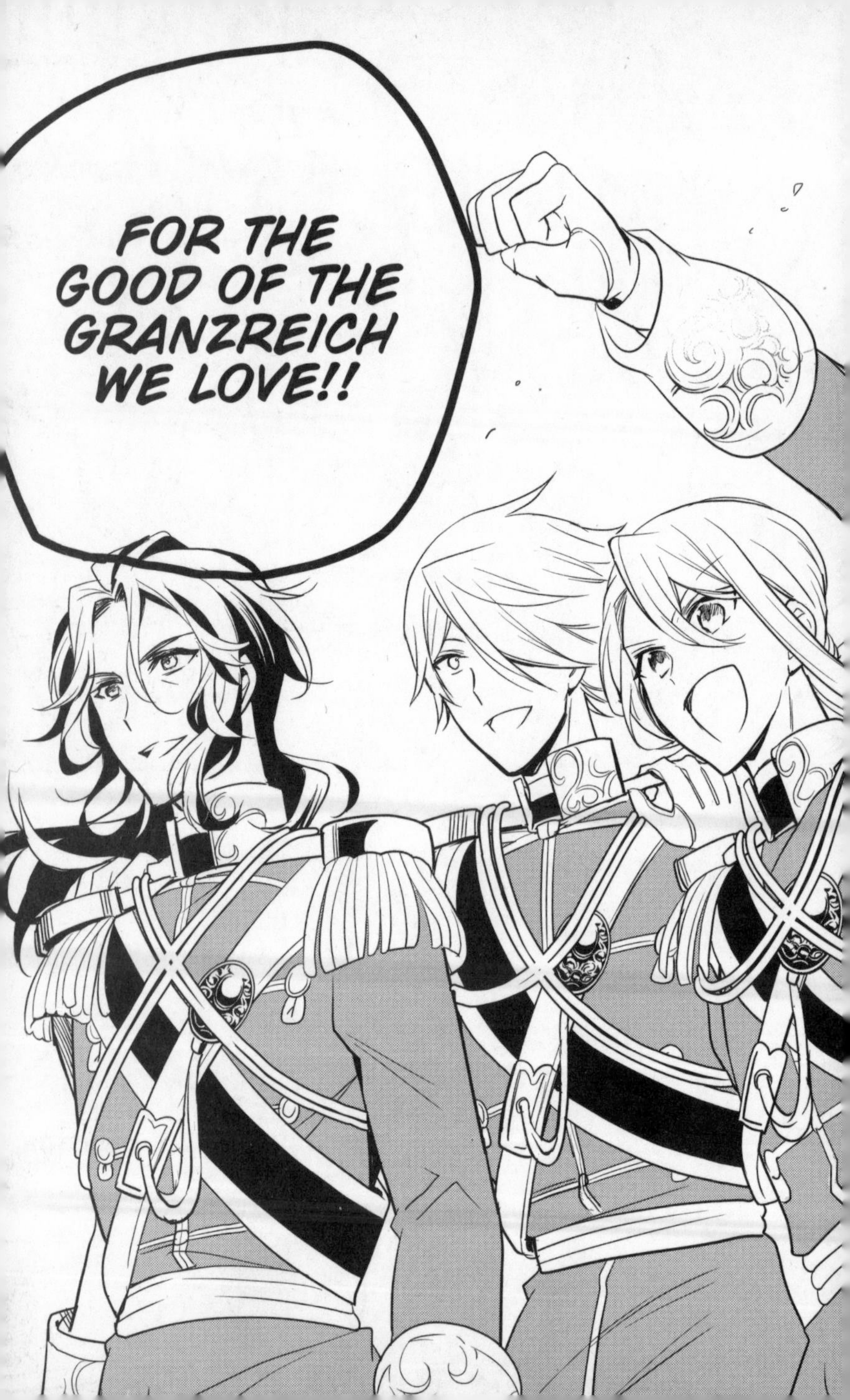
FOR THE GOOD OF THE GRANZREICH WE LOVE!!

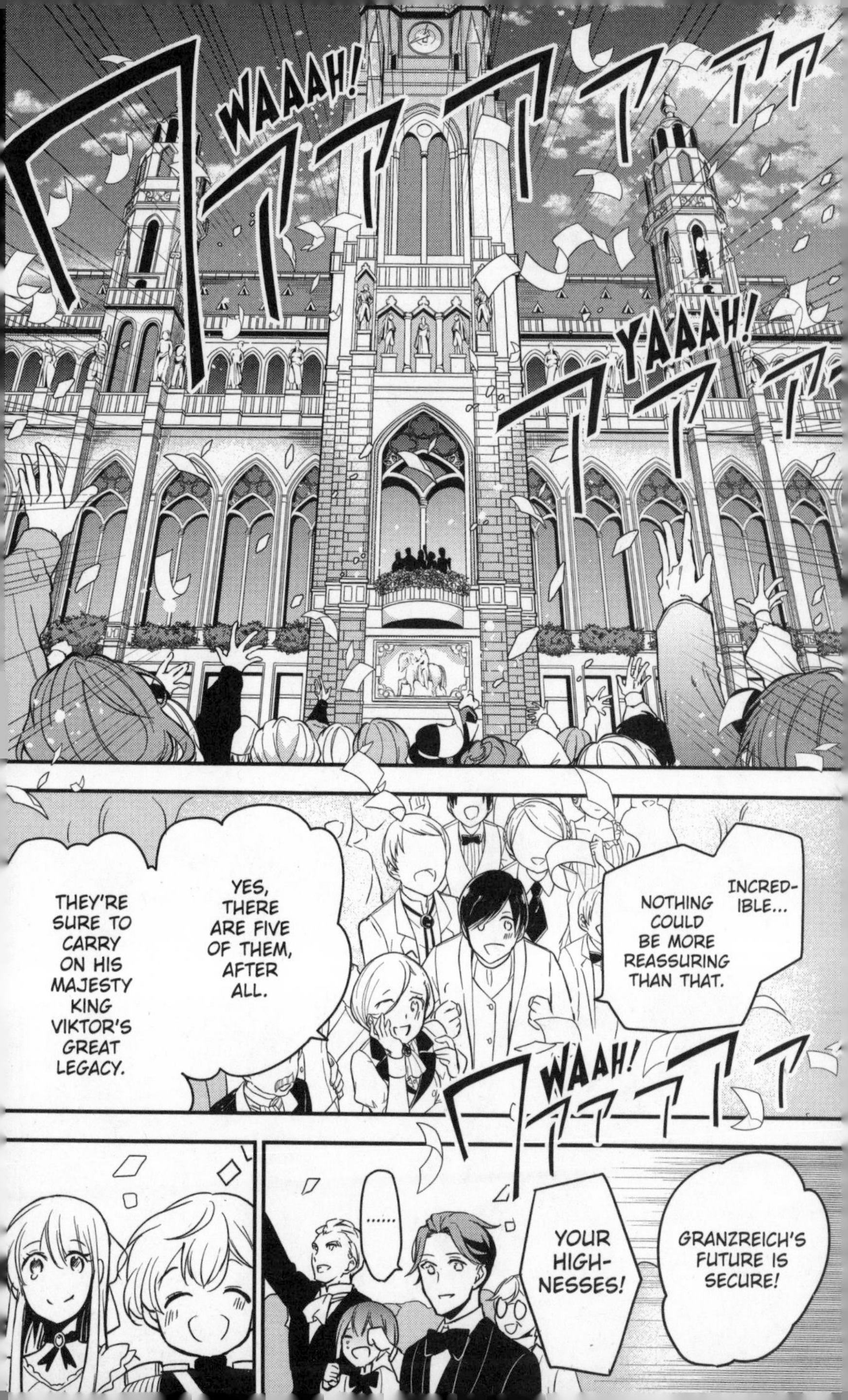
WAAAH!
YAAAH!
INCREDIBLE... NOTHING COULD BE MORE REASSURING THAN THAT.
YES, THERE ARE FIVE OF THEM, AFTER ALL.
THEY'RE SURE TO CARRY ON HIS MAJESTY KING VIKTOR'S GREAT LEGACY.
WAAH!
GRANZREICH'S FUTURE IS SECURE!
YOUR HIGHNESSES!
......

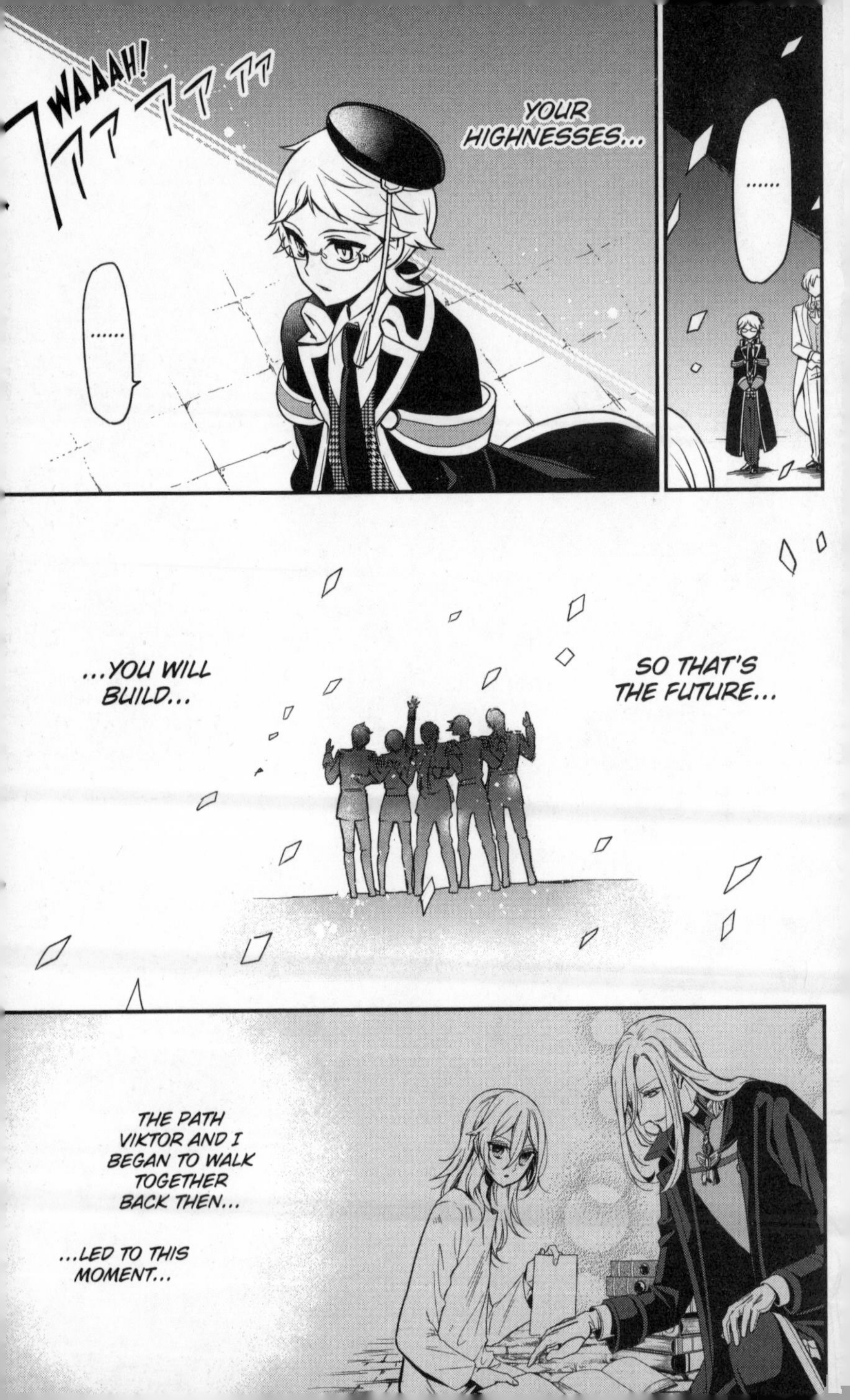
......
YOUR HIGHNESSES...
WAAAH!
......
SO THAT'S THE FUTURE...
...YOU WILL BUILD...
THE PATH VIKTOR AND I BEGAN TO WALK TOGETHER BACK THEN...
...LED TO THIS MOMENT...

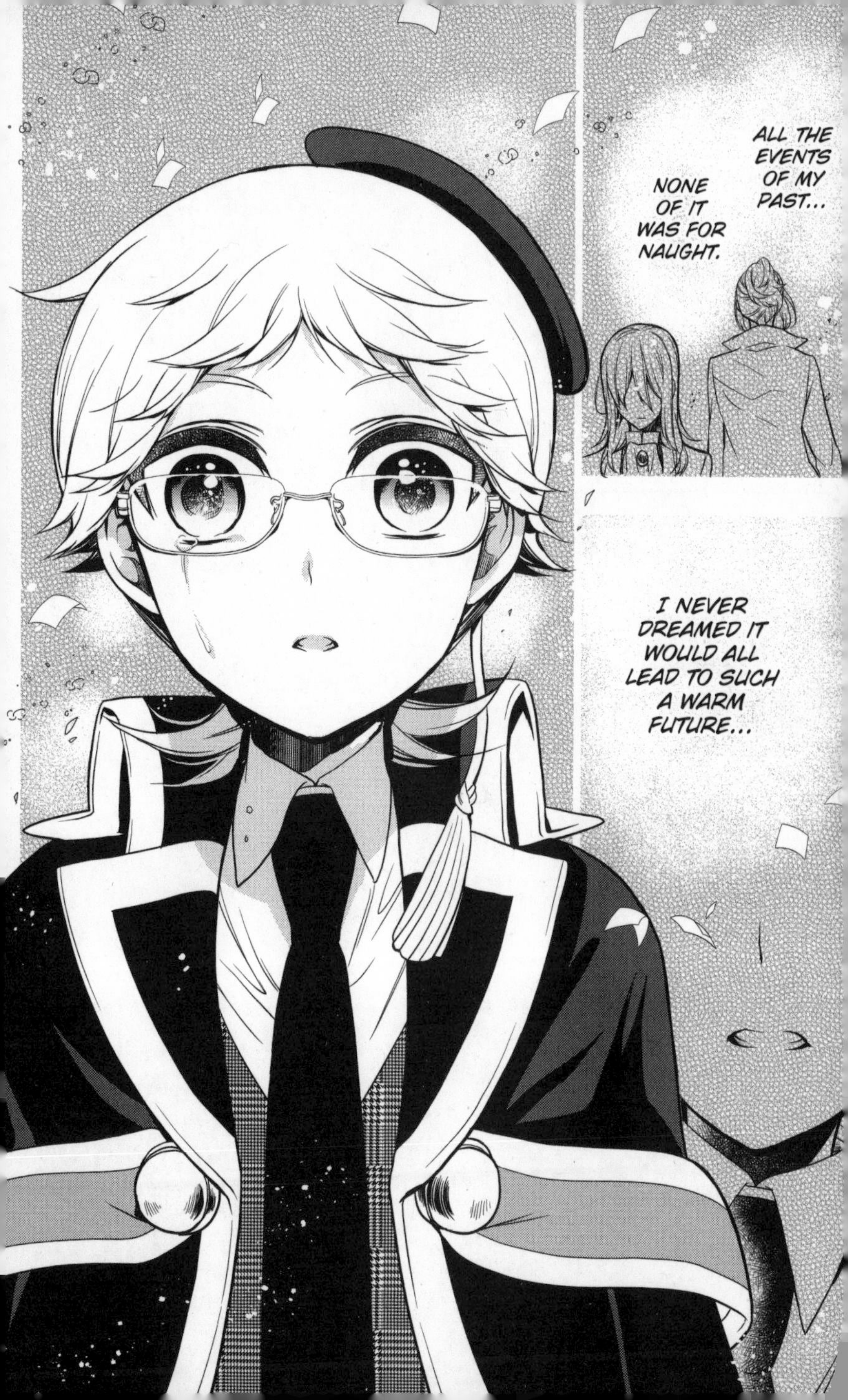
ALL THE EVENTS OF MY PAST...
NONE OF IT WAS FOR NAUGHT.
I NEVER DREAMED IT WOULD ALL LEAD TO SUCH A WARM FUTURE...

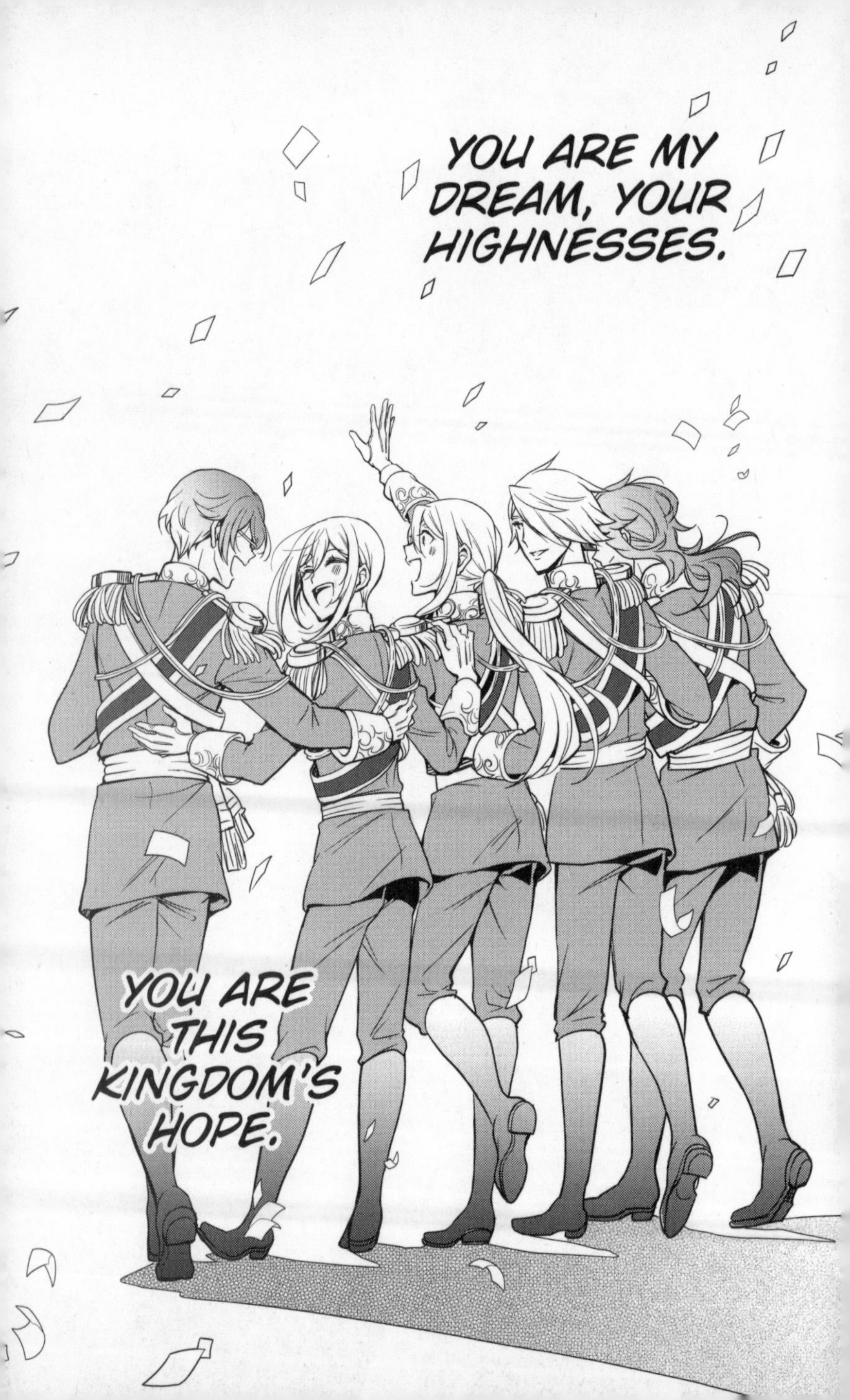
YOU ARE MY DREAM, YOUR HIGHNESSES.
YOU ARE THIS KINGDOM'S HOPE.

THE
ROYAL
TUTOR

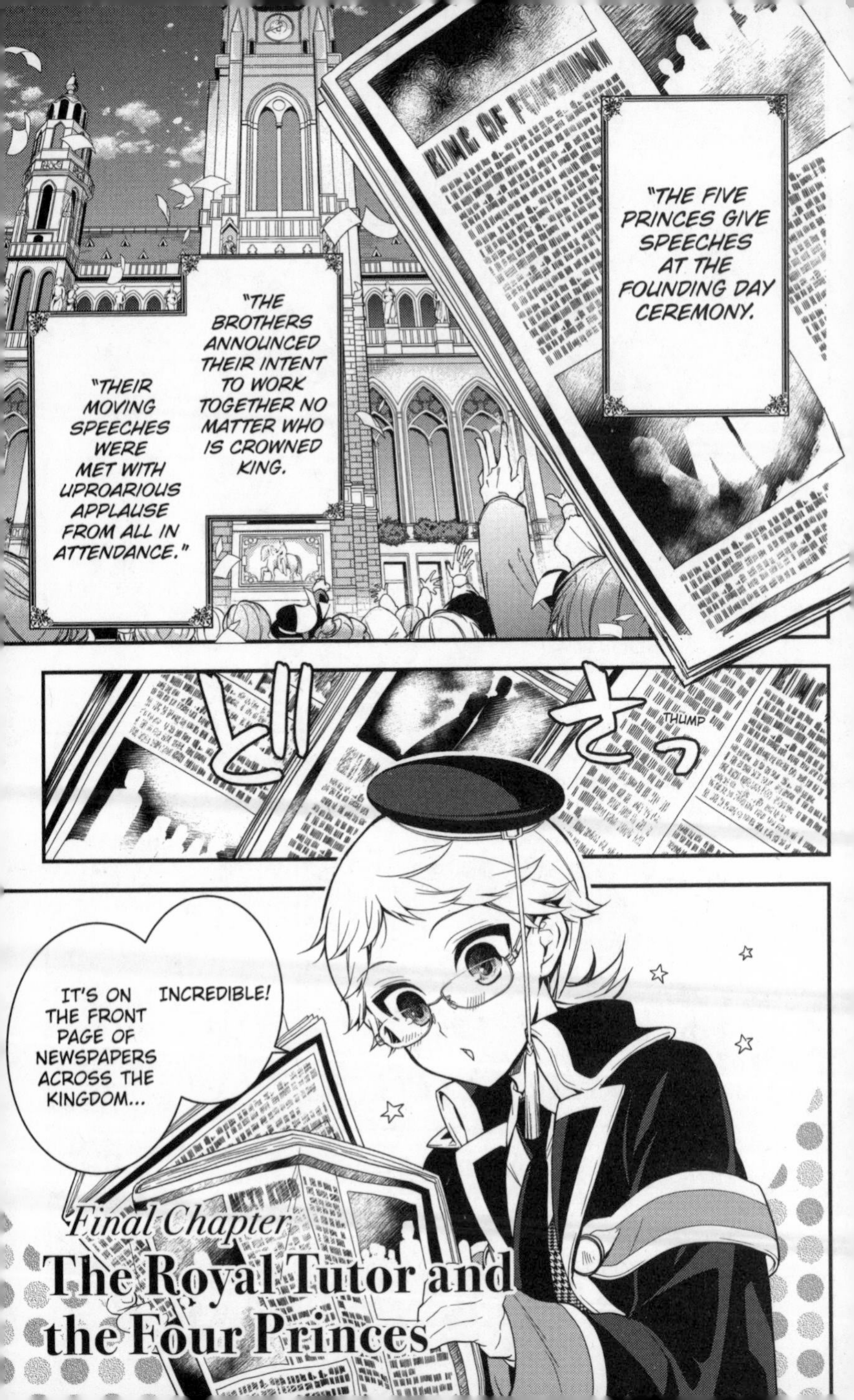
"THE FIVE PRINCES GIVE SPEECHES AT THE FOUNDING DAY CEREMONY.
"THE BROTHERS ANNOUNCED THEIR INTENT TO WORK TOGETHER NO MATTER WHO IS CROWNED KING.
"THEIR MOVING SPEECHES WERE MET WITH UPROARIOUS APPLAUSE FROM ALL IN ATTENDANCE."
THUMP
INCREDIBLE!
IT'S ON THE FRONT PAGE OF NEWSPAPERS ACROSS THE KINGDOM...
Final Chapter
The Royal Tutor and the Four Princes

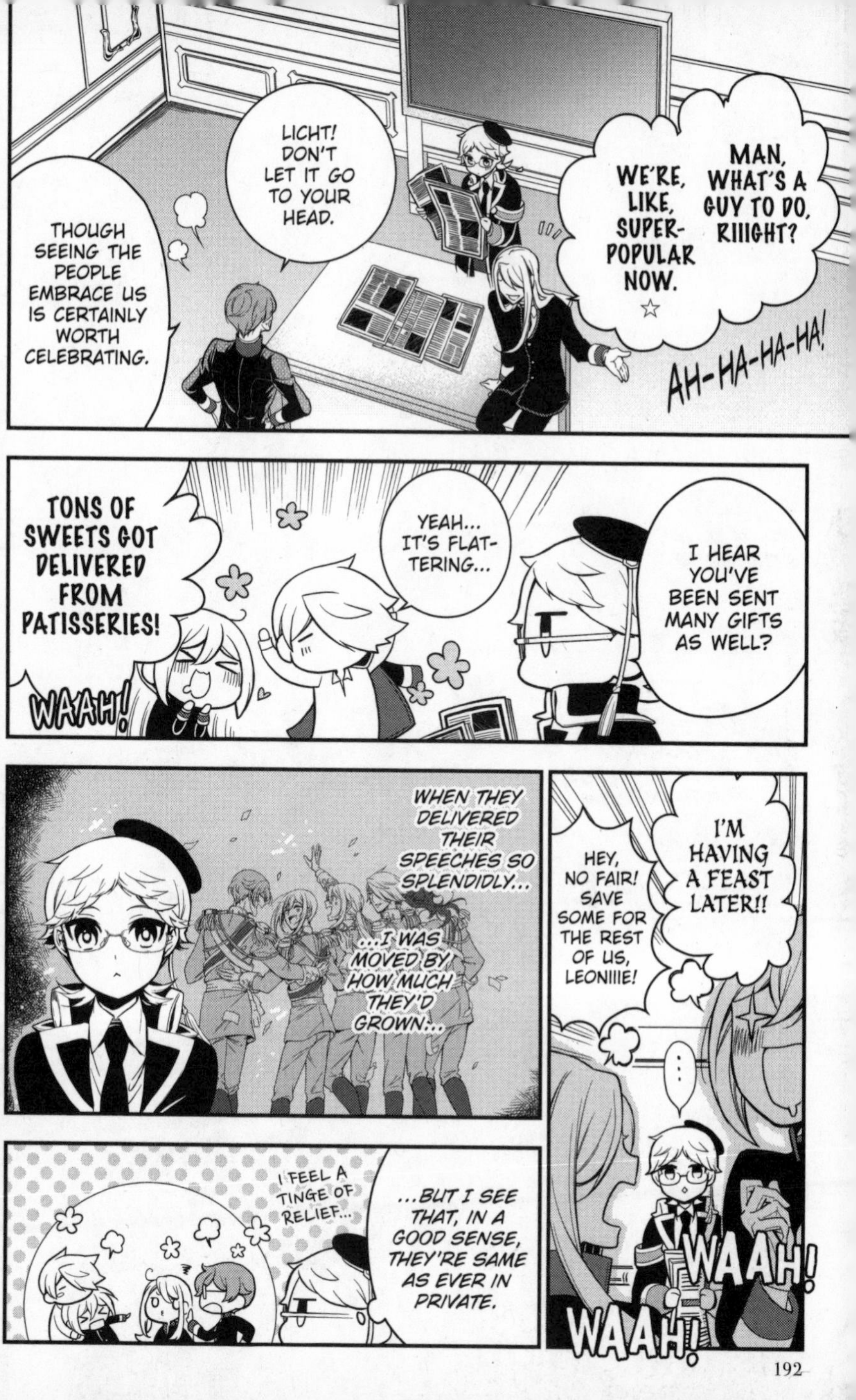
MAN, WHAT'S A GUY TO DO, RIIIGHT?
WE'RE, LIKE, SUPER-POPULAR NOW. ☆
AH-HA-HA-HA!
LICHT! DON'T LET IT GO TO YOUR HEAD.
THOUGH SEEING THE PEOPLE EMBRACE US IS CERTAINLY WORTH CELEBRATING.
I HEAR YOU'VE BEEN SENT MANY GIFTS AS WELL?
YEAH... IT'S FLAT-TERING...
TONS OF SWEETS GOT DELIVERED FROM PATISSERIES!
WAAH!
I'M HAVING A FEAST LATER!!
HEY, NO FAIR! SAVE SOME FOR THE REST OF US, LEONIIIE!
...
WAAH!
WAAH!
WHEN THEY DELIVERED THEIR SPEECHES SO SPLENDIDLY...
...I WAS MOVED BY HOW MUCH THEY'D GROWN...
...BUT I SEE THAT, IN A GOOD SENSE, THEY'RE SAME AS EVER IN PRIVATE.
I FEEL A TINGE OF RELIEF...

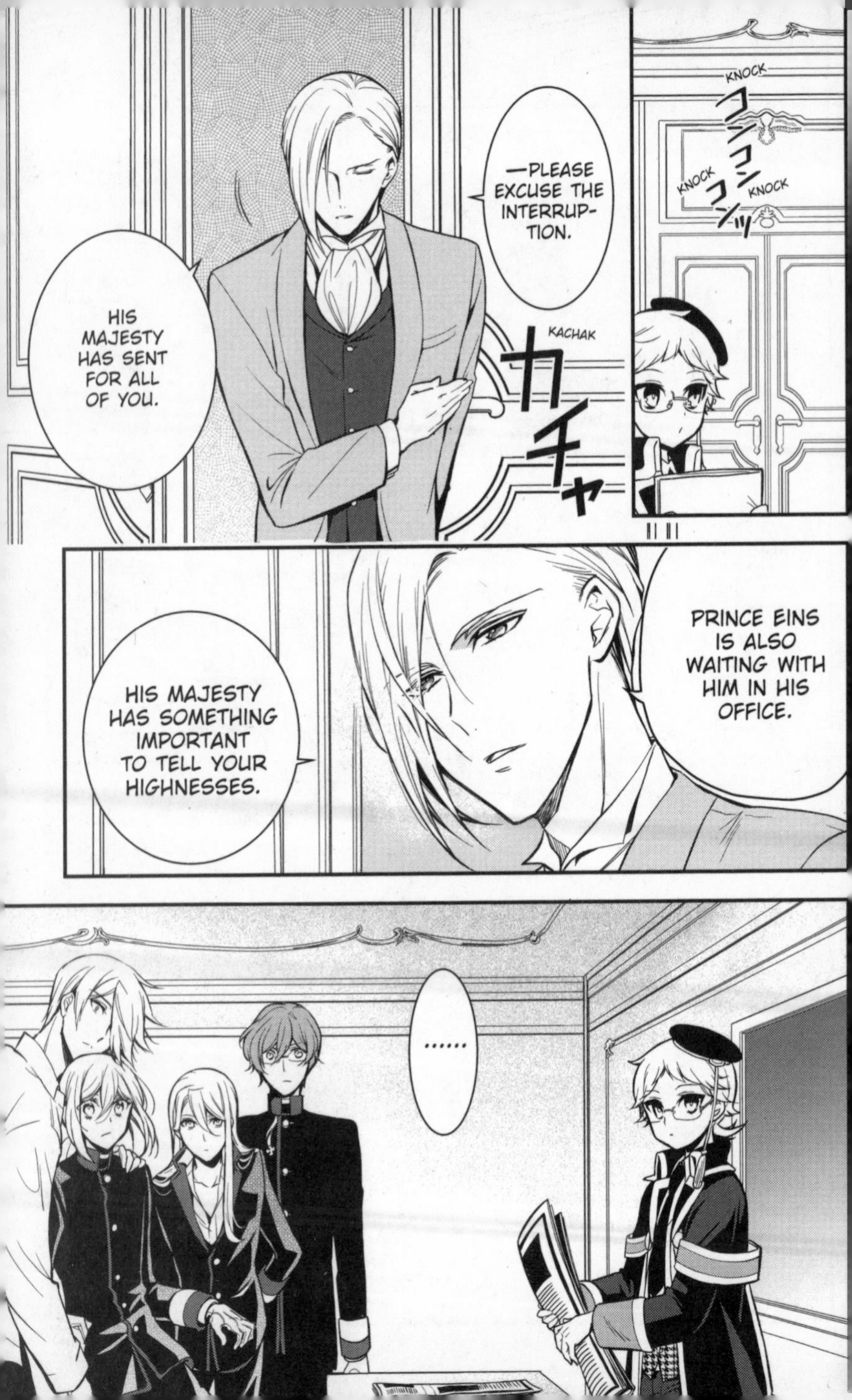
KNOCK
KNOCK
KNOCK
コンコンコンッ
KACHAK
カチャ
—PLEASE EXCUSE THE INTERRUP-TION.
HIS MAJESTY HAS SENT FOR ALL OF YOU.
PRINCE EINS IS ALSO WAITING WITH HIM IN HIS OFFICE.
HIS MAJESTY HAS SOMETHING IMPORTANT TO TELL YOUR HIGHNESSES.
......

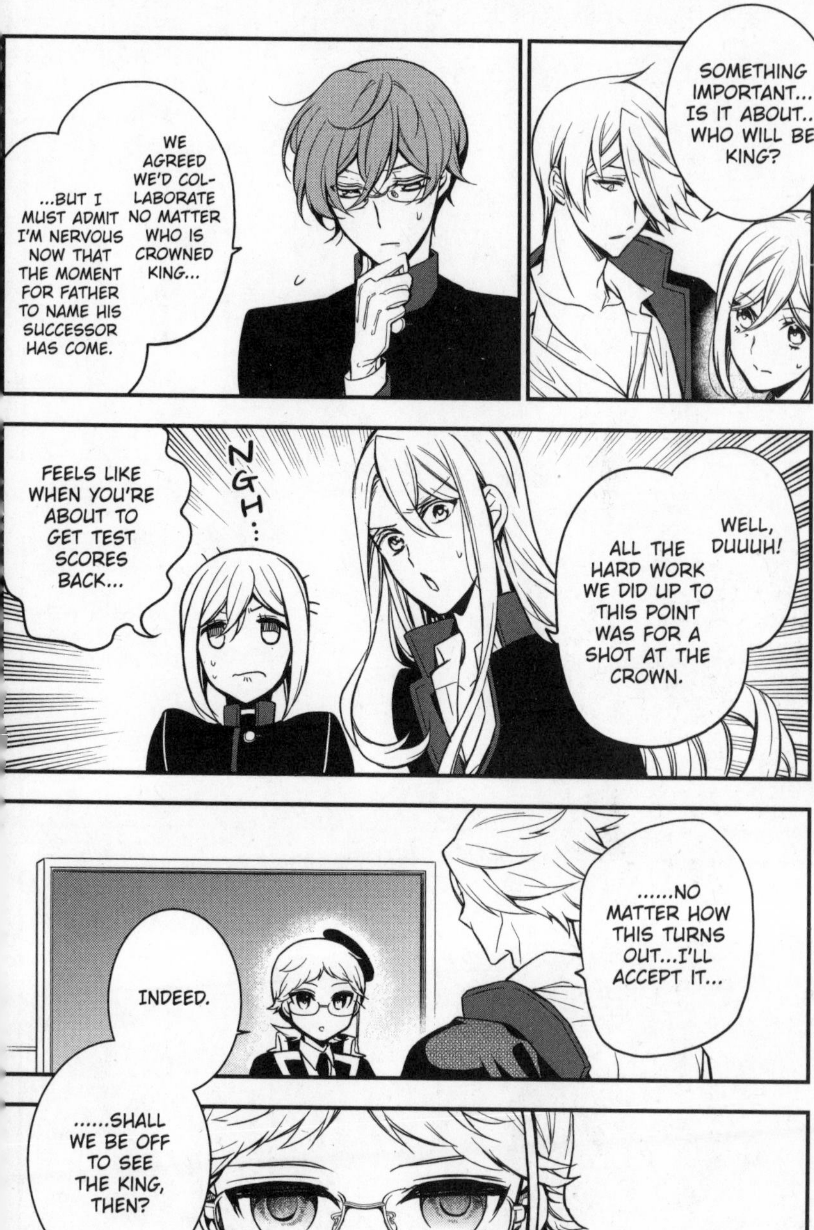
SOMETHING IMPORTANT... IS IT ABOUT... WHO WILL BE KING?
WE AGREED WE'D COL-LABORATE NO MATTER WHO IS CROWNED KING...
...BUT I MUST ADMIT I'M NERVOUS NOW THAT THE MOMENT FOR FATHER TO NAME HIS SUCCESSOR HAS COME.
WELL, DUUUH!
ALL THE HARD WORK WE DID UP TO THIS POINT WAS FOR A SHOT AT THE CROWN.
NGH...
FEELS LIKE WHEN YOU'RE ABOUT TO GET TEST SCORES BACK...
......NO MATTER HOW THIS TURNS OUT...I'LL ACCEPT IT...
INDEED.
......SHALL WE BE OFF TO SEE THE KING, THEN?

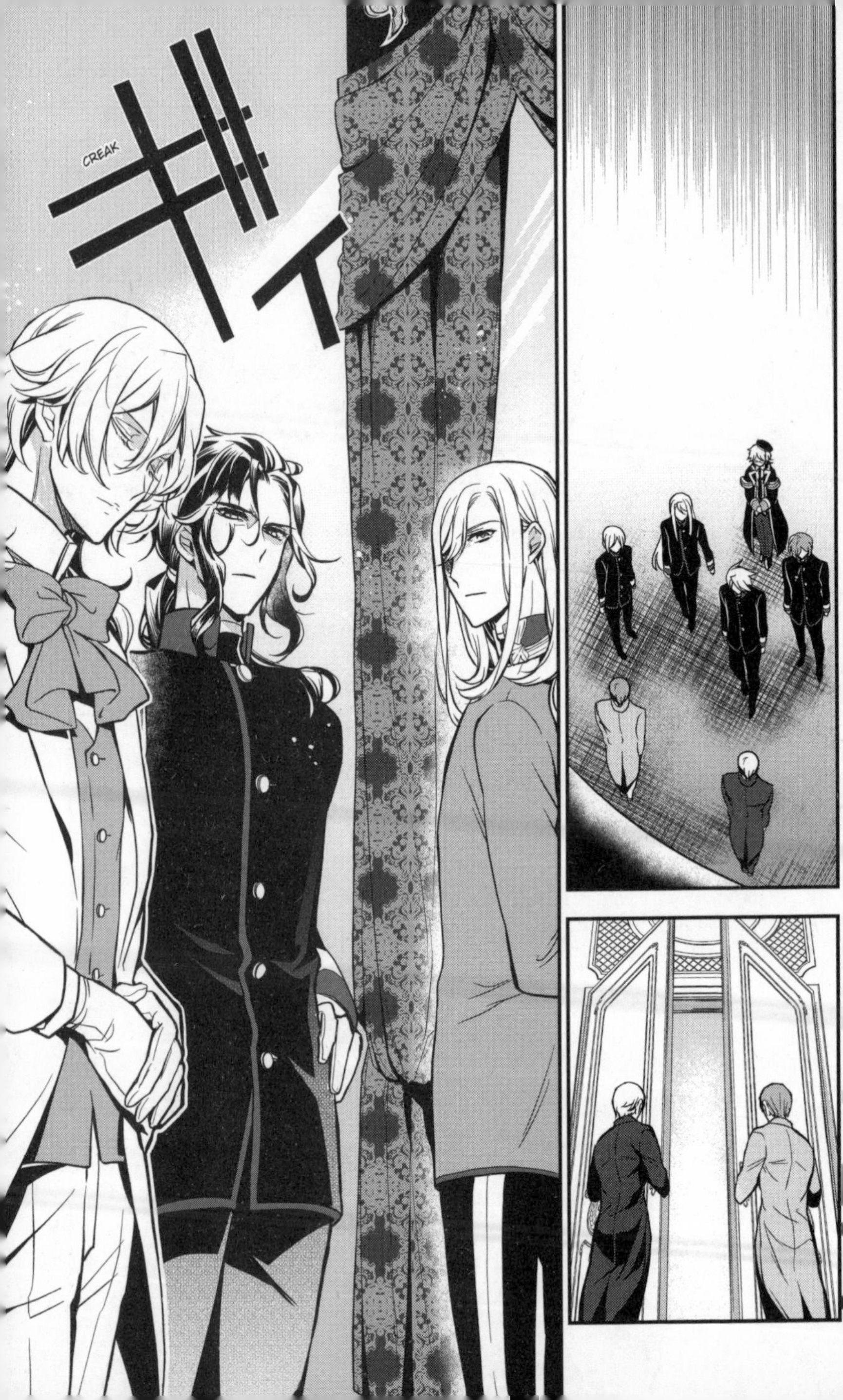
ギイ
CREAK

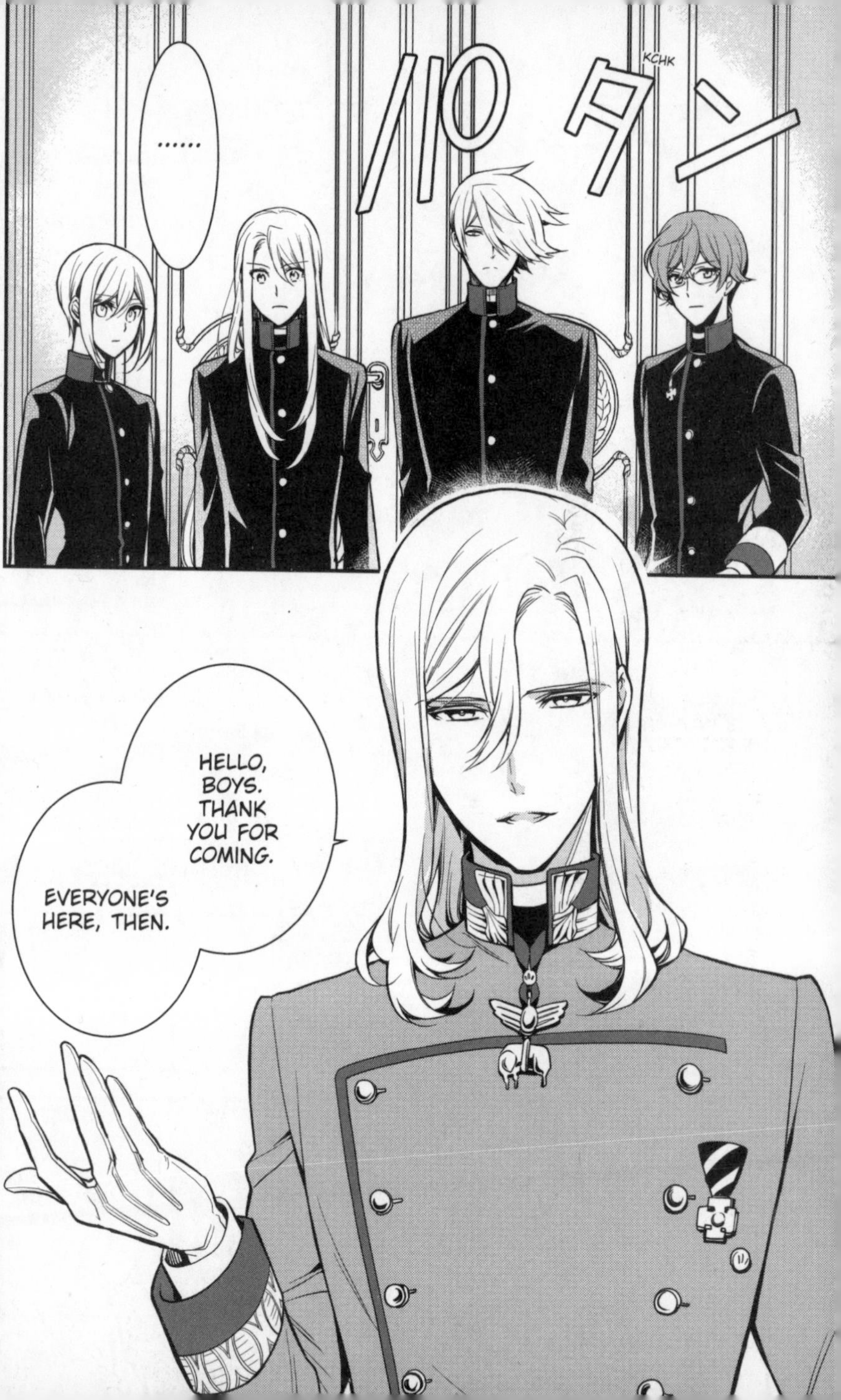
パタン
KCHK
......
HELLO, BOYS. THANK YOU FOR COMING.
EVERYONE'S HERE, THEN.

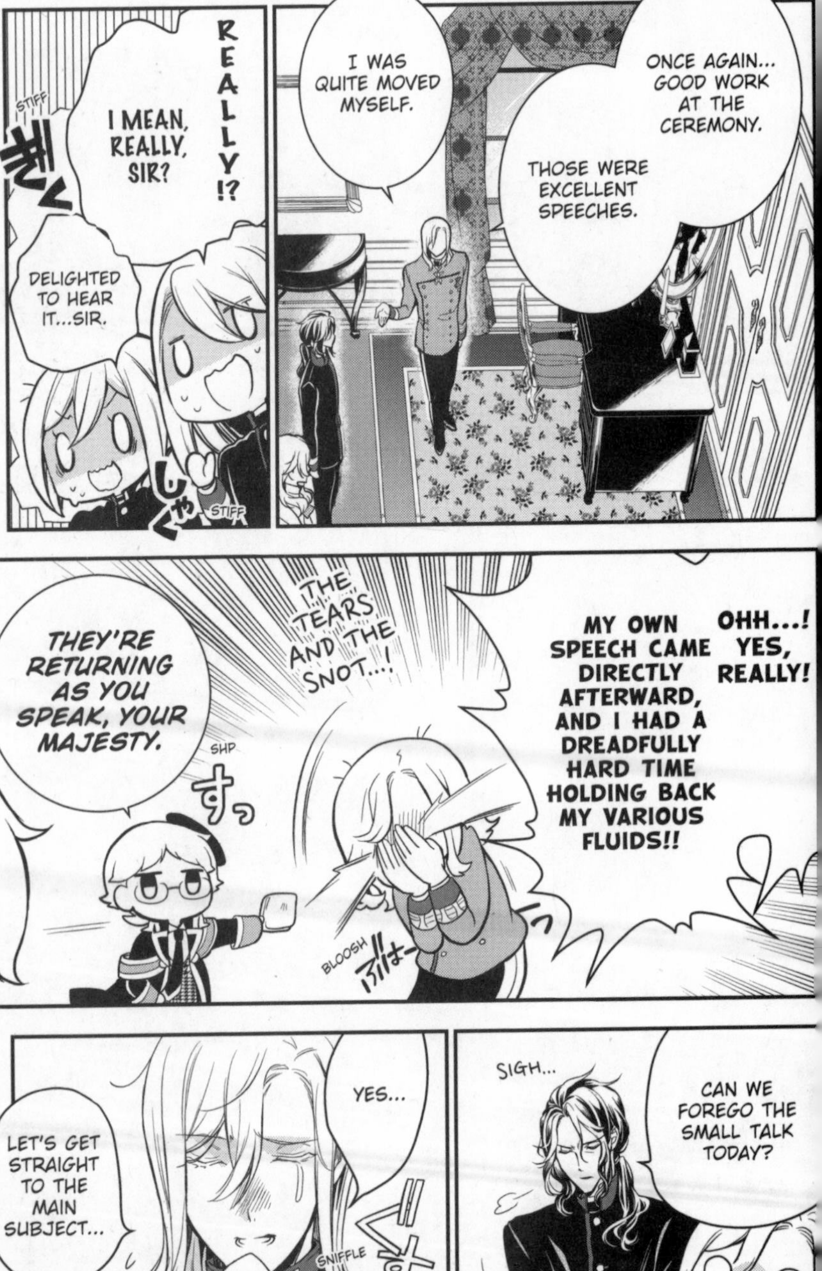
ONCE AGAIN... GOOD WORK AT THE CEREMONY.
THOSE WERE EXCELLENT SPEECHES.
I WAS QUITE MOVED MYSELF.
REALLY!?
I MEAN, REALLY, SIR?
STIFF
DELIGHTED TO HEAR IT...SIR.
STIFF
OHH...! YES, REALLY!
MY OWN SPEECH CAME DIRECTLY AFTERWARD, AND I HAD A DREADFULLY HARD TIME HOLDING BACK MY VARIOUS FLUIDS!!
THE TEARS AND THE SNOT...!
BLOOSH
THEY'RE RETURNING AS YOU SPEAK, YOUR MAJESTY.
SHP
CAN WE FOREGO THE SMALL TALK TODAY?
SIGH...
YES...
SNIFFLE
LET'S GET STRAIGHT TO THE MAIN SUBJECT...

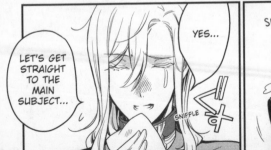

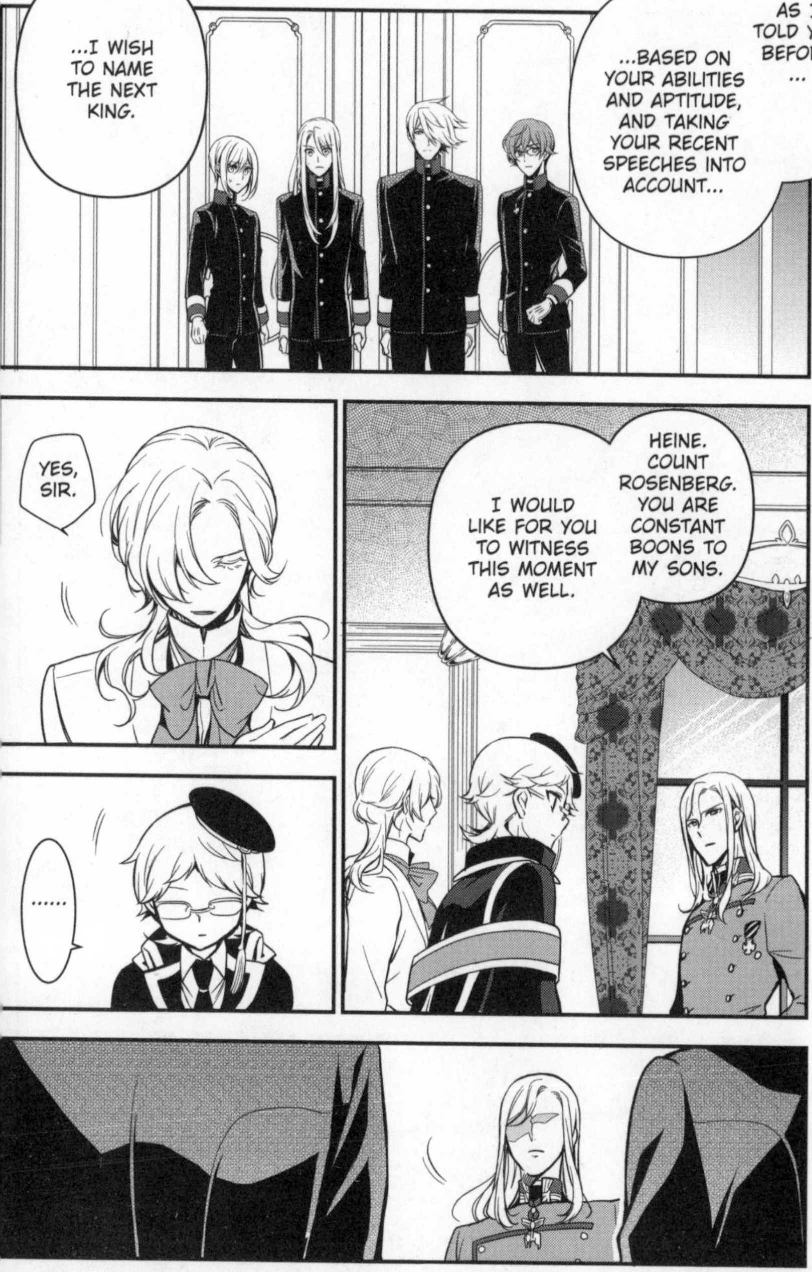
AS I TOLD YOU BEFORE...
...BASED ON YOUR ABILITIES AND APTITUDE, AND TAKING YOUR RECENT SPEECHES INTO ACCOUNT...
...I WISH TO NAME THE NEXT KING.
HEINE. COUNT ROSENBERG. YOU ARE CONSTANT BOONS TO MY SONS.
I WOULD LIKE FOR YOU TO WITNESS THIS MOMENT AS WELL.
YES, SIR.
......

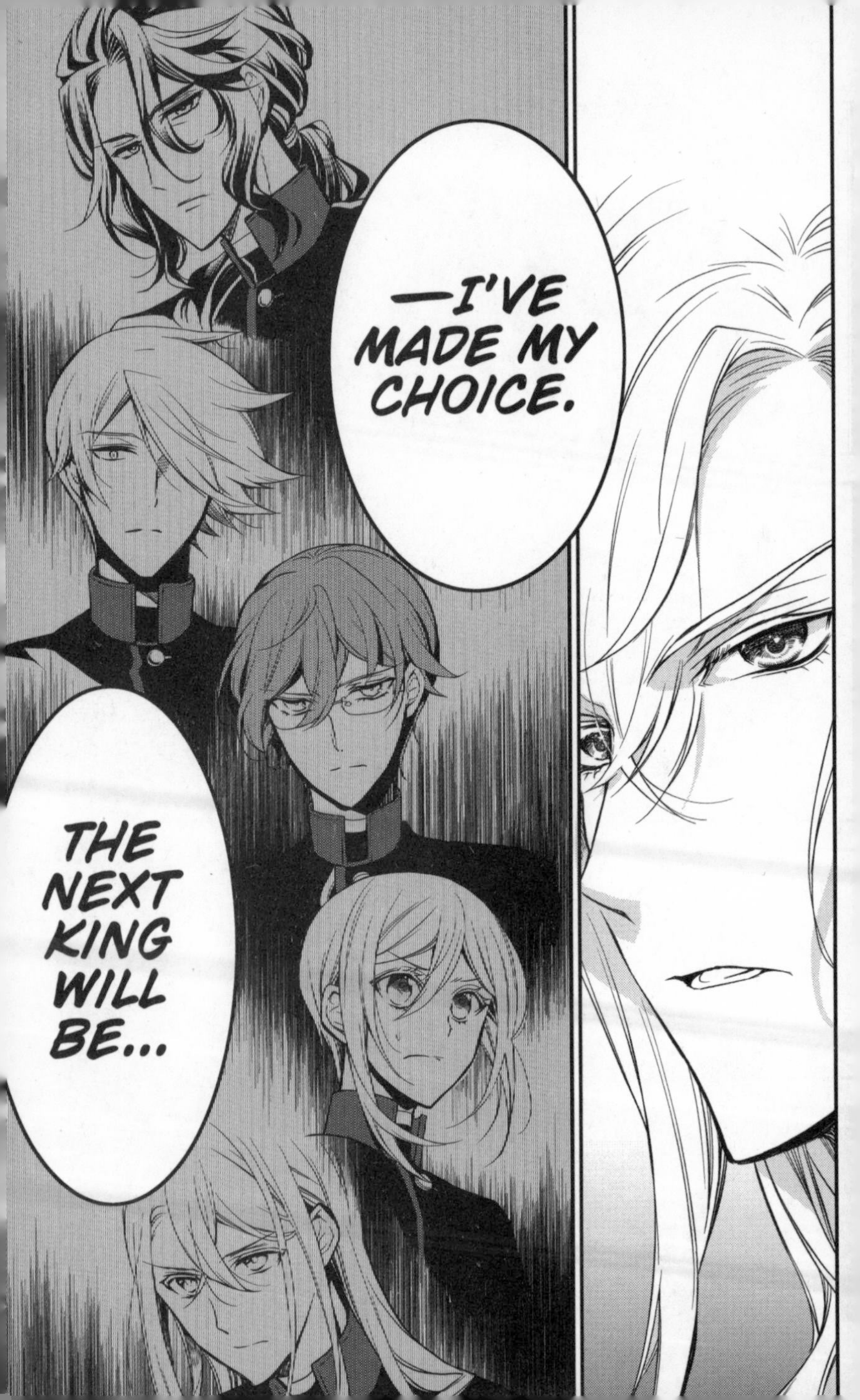
—I'VE MADE MY CHOICE.
THE NEXT KING WILL BE...

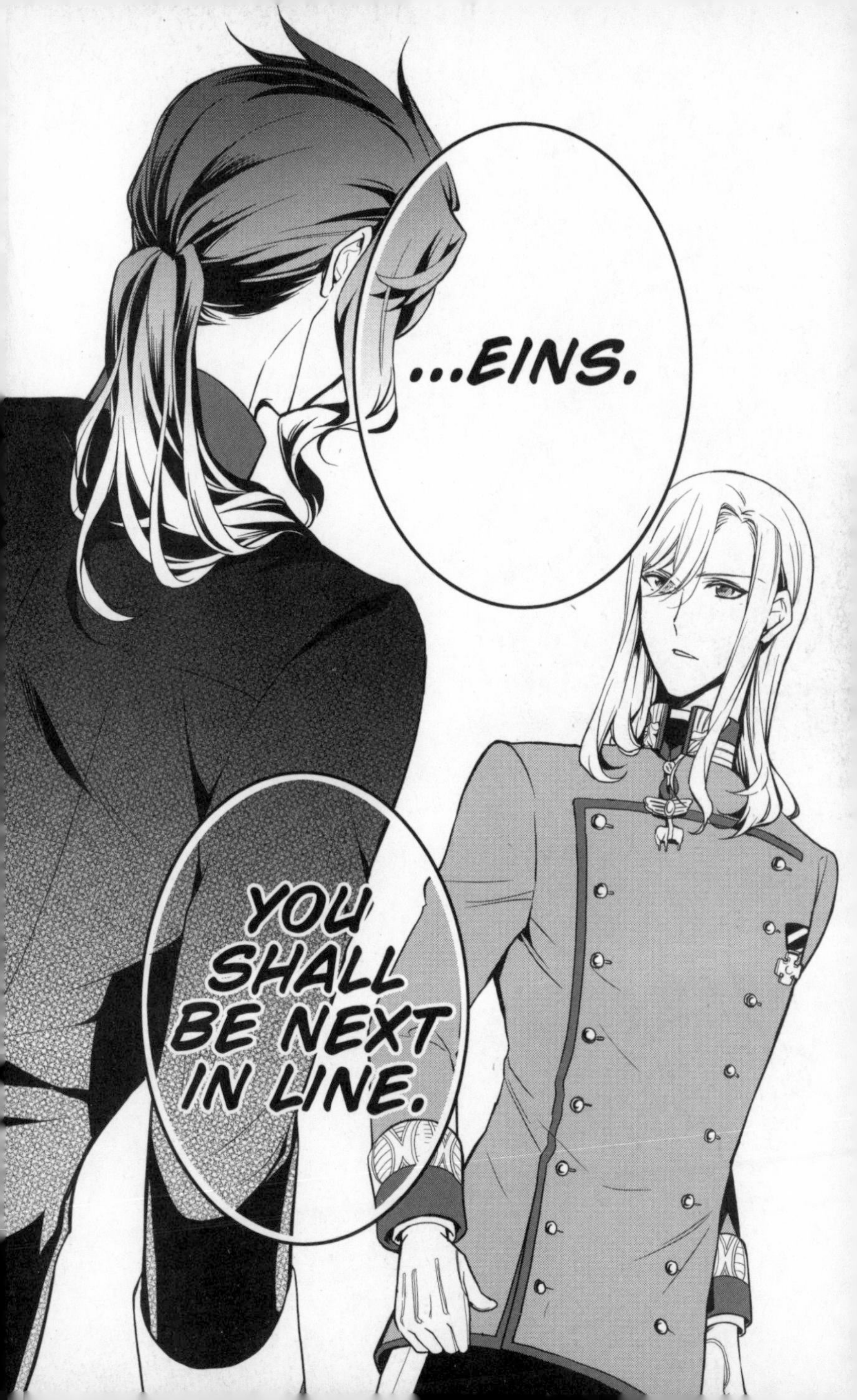
...EINS.
YOU SHALL BE NEXT IN LINE.

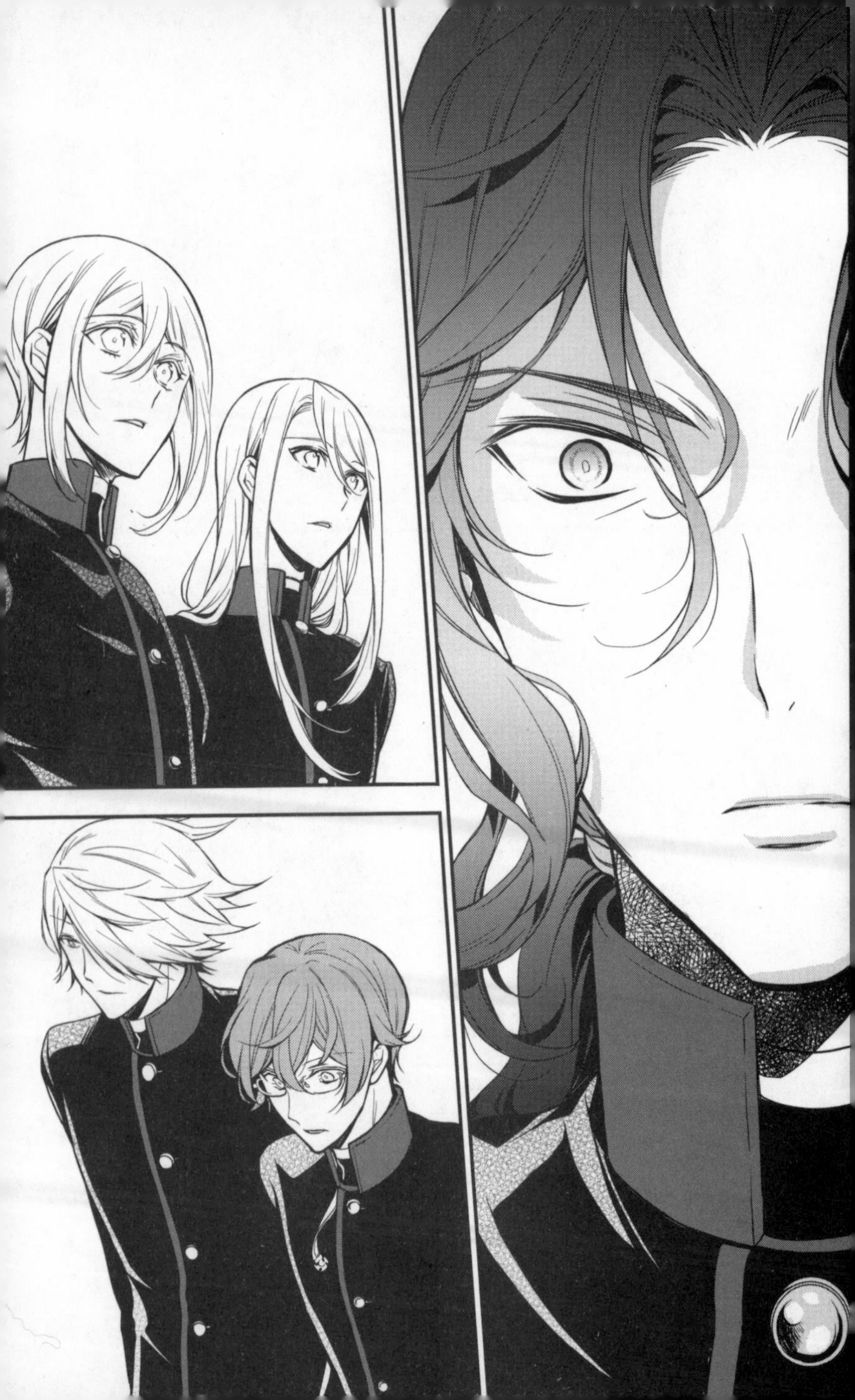

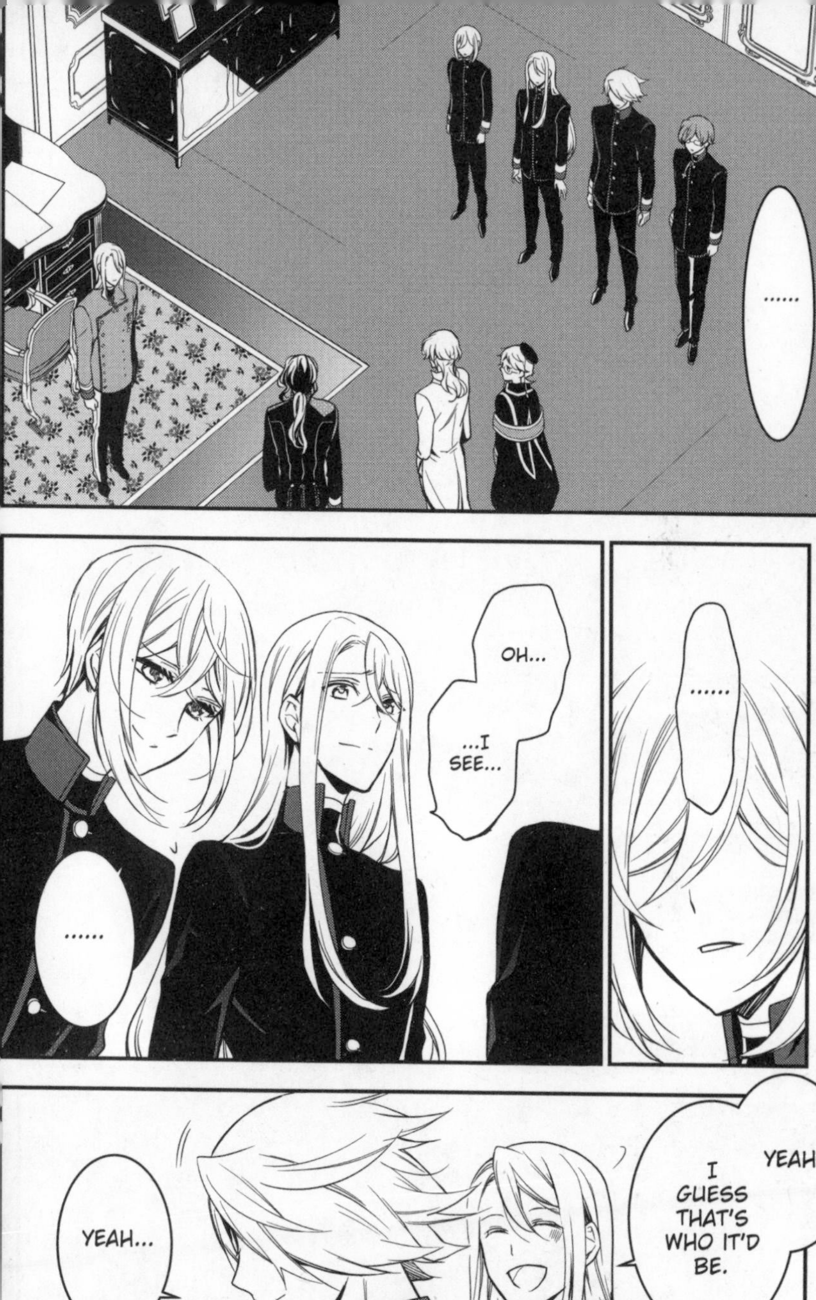
......
......
OH... ...I SEE...
......
YEAH. I GUESS THAT'S WHO IT'D BE.
YEAH...

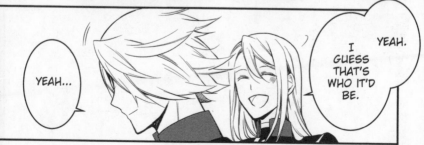

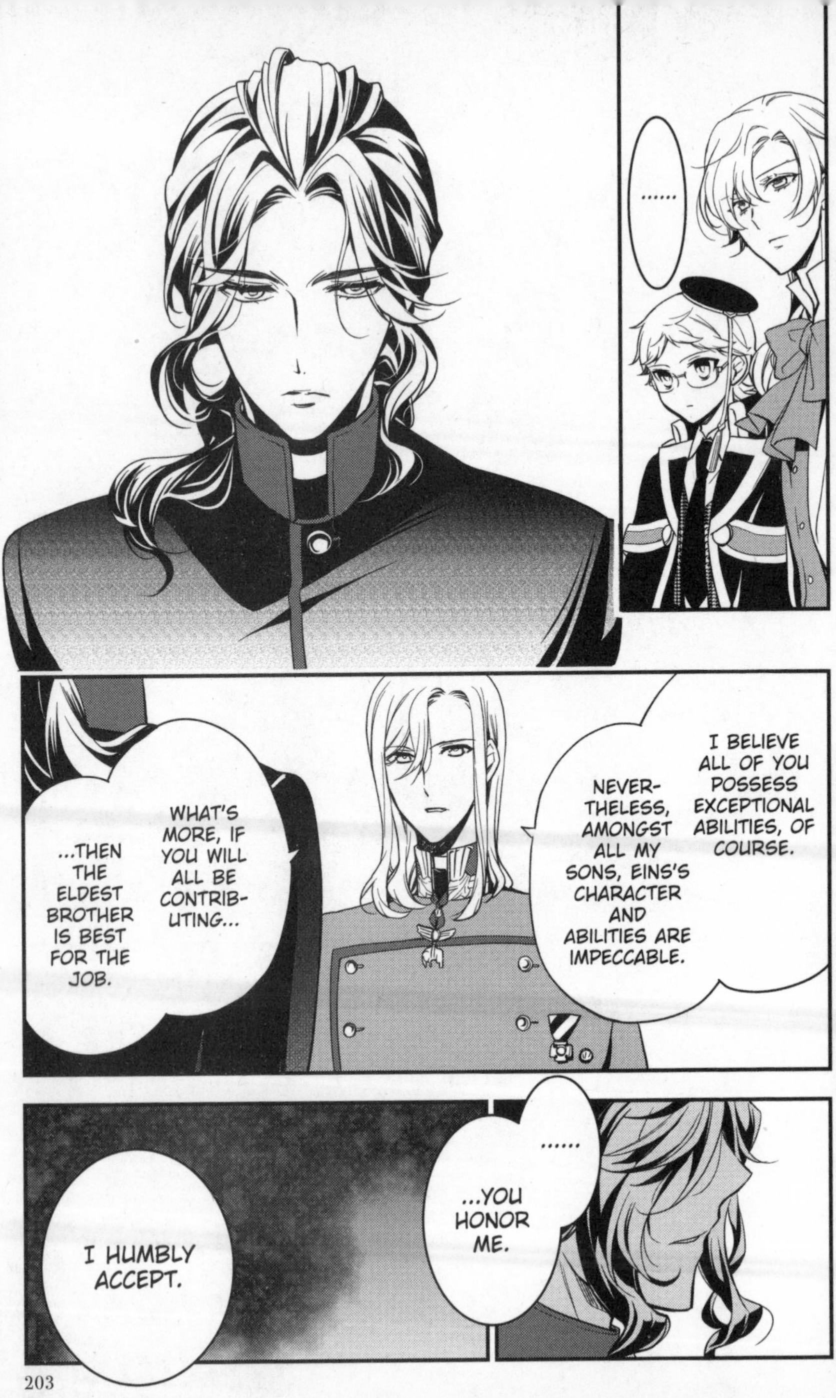
......
I BELIEVE ALL OF YOU POSSESS EXCEPTIONAL ABILITIES, OF COURSE.
NEVER-THELESS, AMONGST ALL MY SONS, EINS'S CHARACTER AND ABILITIES ARE IMPECCABLE.
WHAT'S MORE, IF YOU WILL ALL BE CONTRIB-UTING...
...THEN THE ELDEST BROTHER IS BEST FOR THE JOB.
......
...YOU HONOR ME.
I HUMBLY ACCEPT.

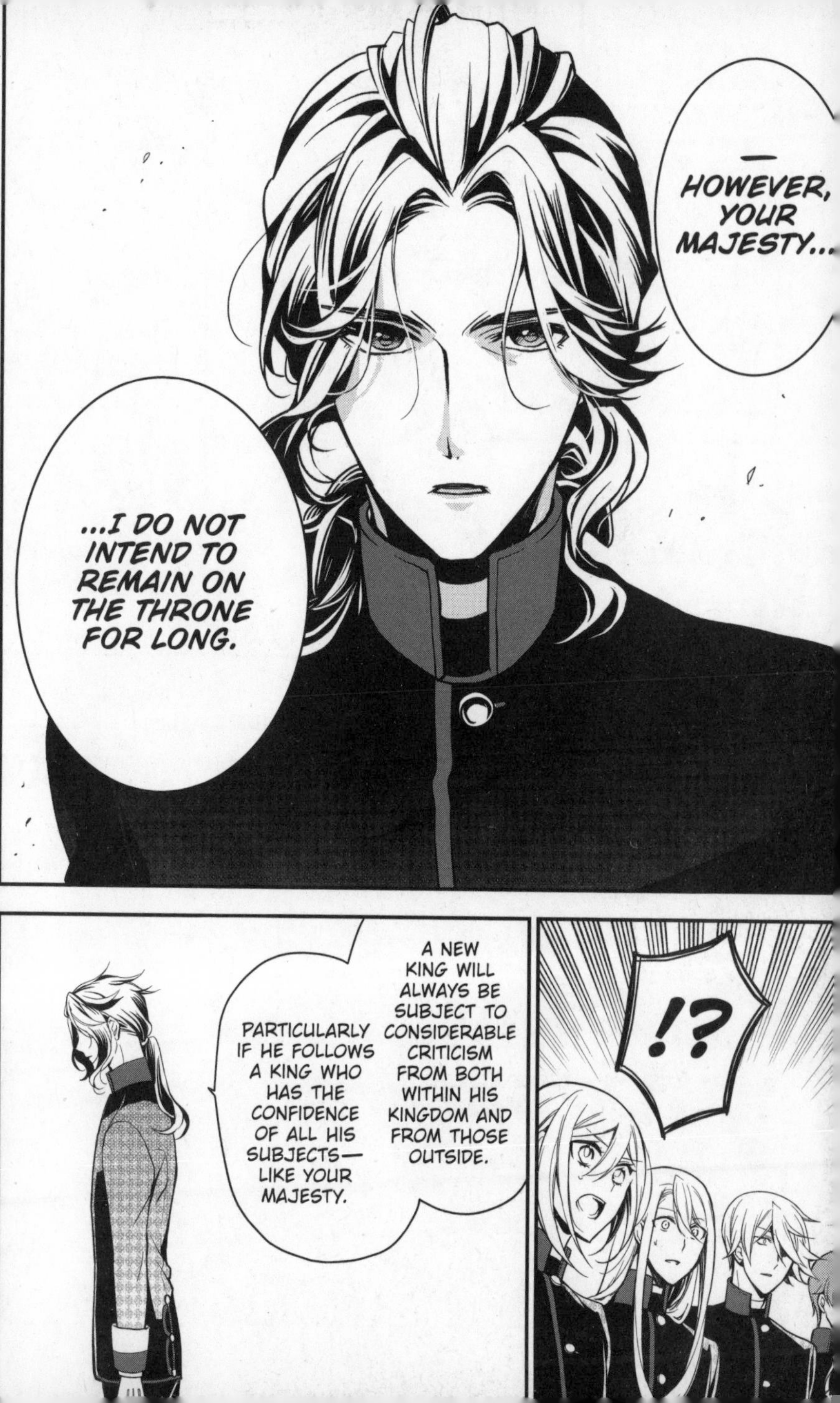
—HOWEVER, YOUR MAJESTY...
...I DO NOT INTEND TO REMAIN ON THE THRONE FOR LONG.
!?
A NEW KING WILL ALWAYS BE SUBJECT TO CONSIDERABLE CRITICISM FROM BOTH WITHIN HIS KINGDOM AND FROM THOSE OUTSIDE.
PARTICULARLY IF HE FOLLOWS A KING WHO HAS THE CONFIDENCE OF ALL HIS SUBJECTS— LIKE YOUR MAJESTY.

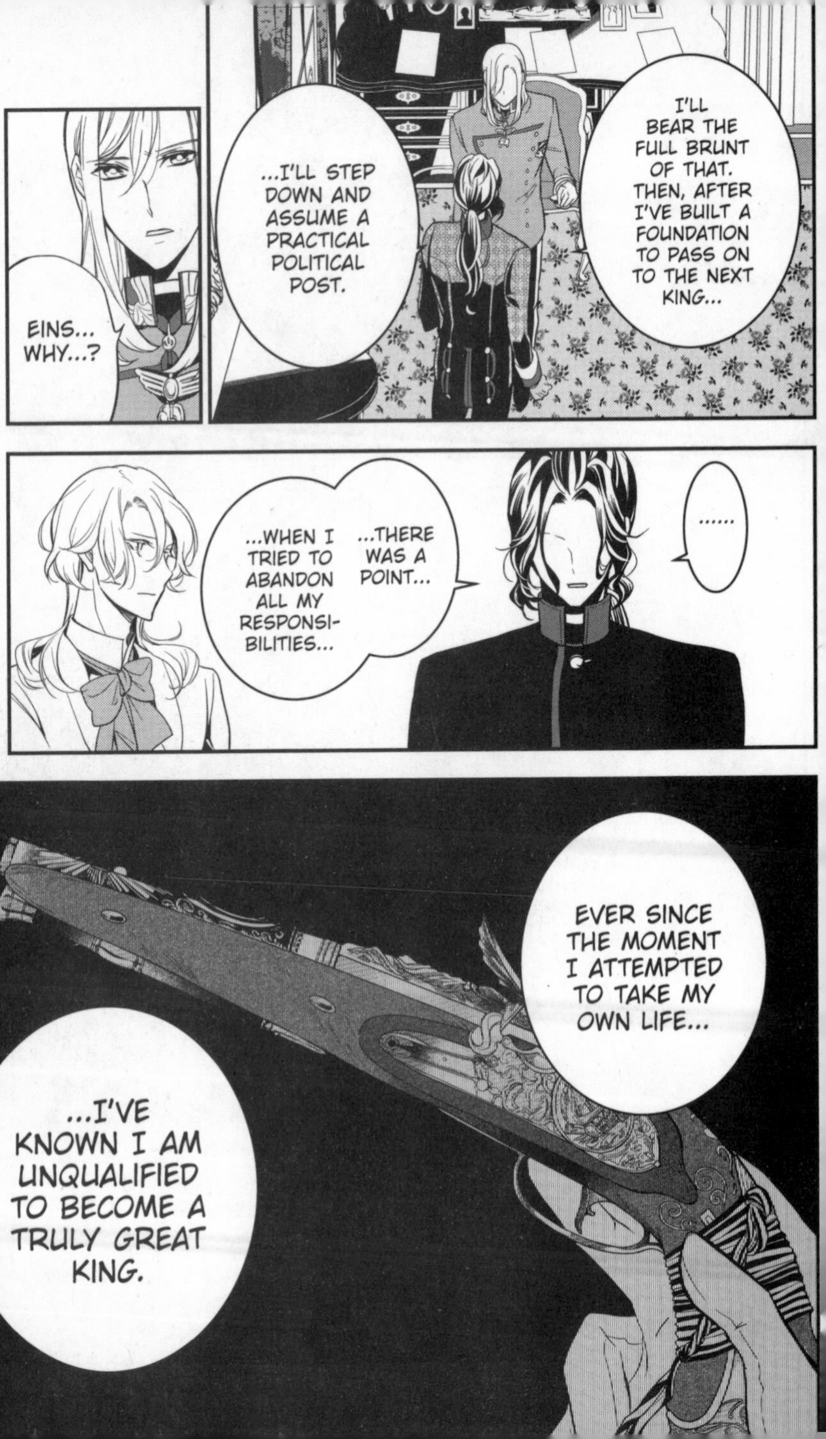
...I'LL STEP DOWN AND ASSUME A PRACTICAL POLITICAL POST.
I'LL BEAR THE FULL BRUNT OF THAT. THEN, AFTER I'VE BUILT A FOUNDATION TO PASS ON TO THE NEXT KING...
EINS... WHY...?
......
...THERE WAS A POINT...
...WHEN I TRIED TO ABANDON ALL MY RESPONSI-BILITIES...
EVER SINCE THE MOMENT I ATTEMPTED TO TAKE MY OWN LIFE...
...I'VE KNOWN I AM UNQUALIFIED TO BECOME A TRULY GREAT KING.

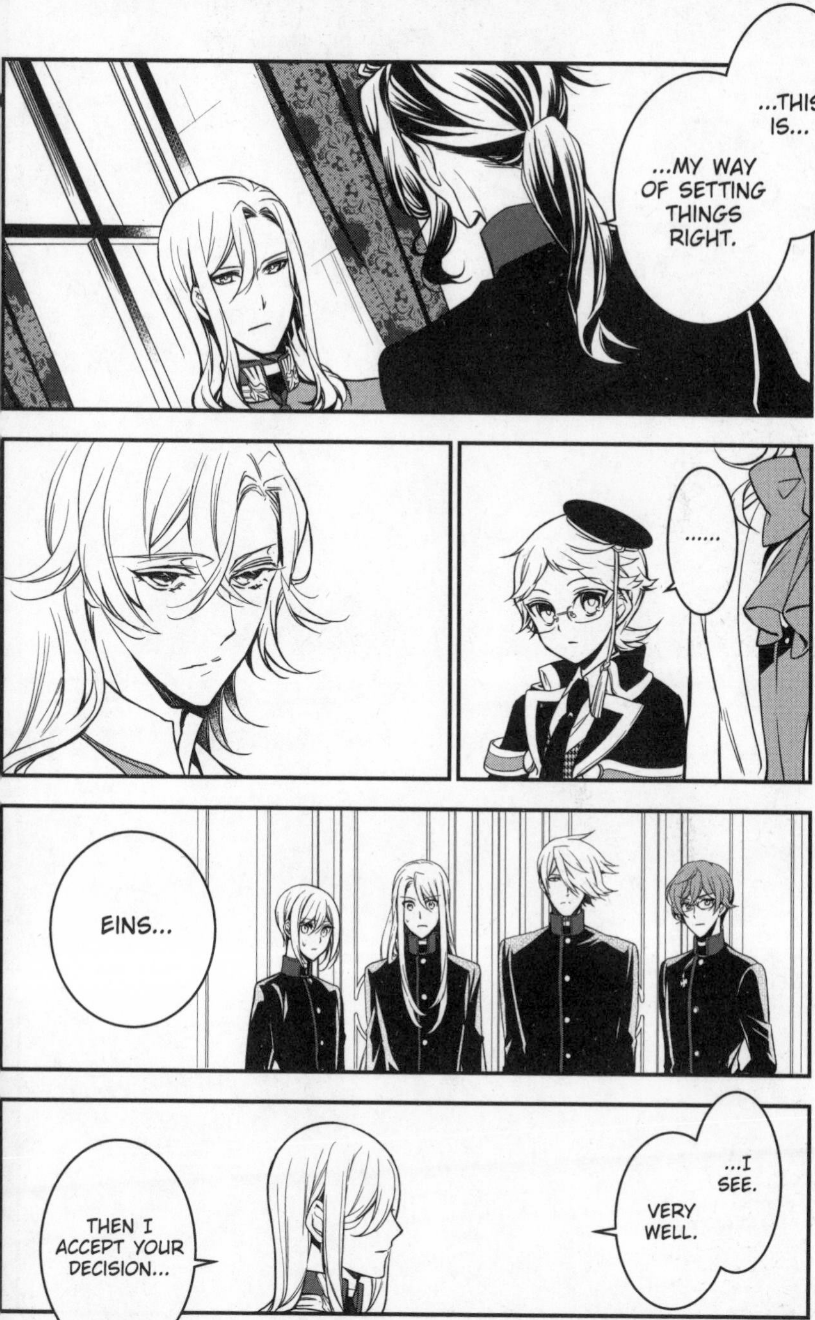
...THIS IS...
...MY WAY OF SETTING THINGS RIGHT.
......
EINS...
...I SEE.
VERY WELL.
THEN I ACCEPT YOUR DECISION...

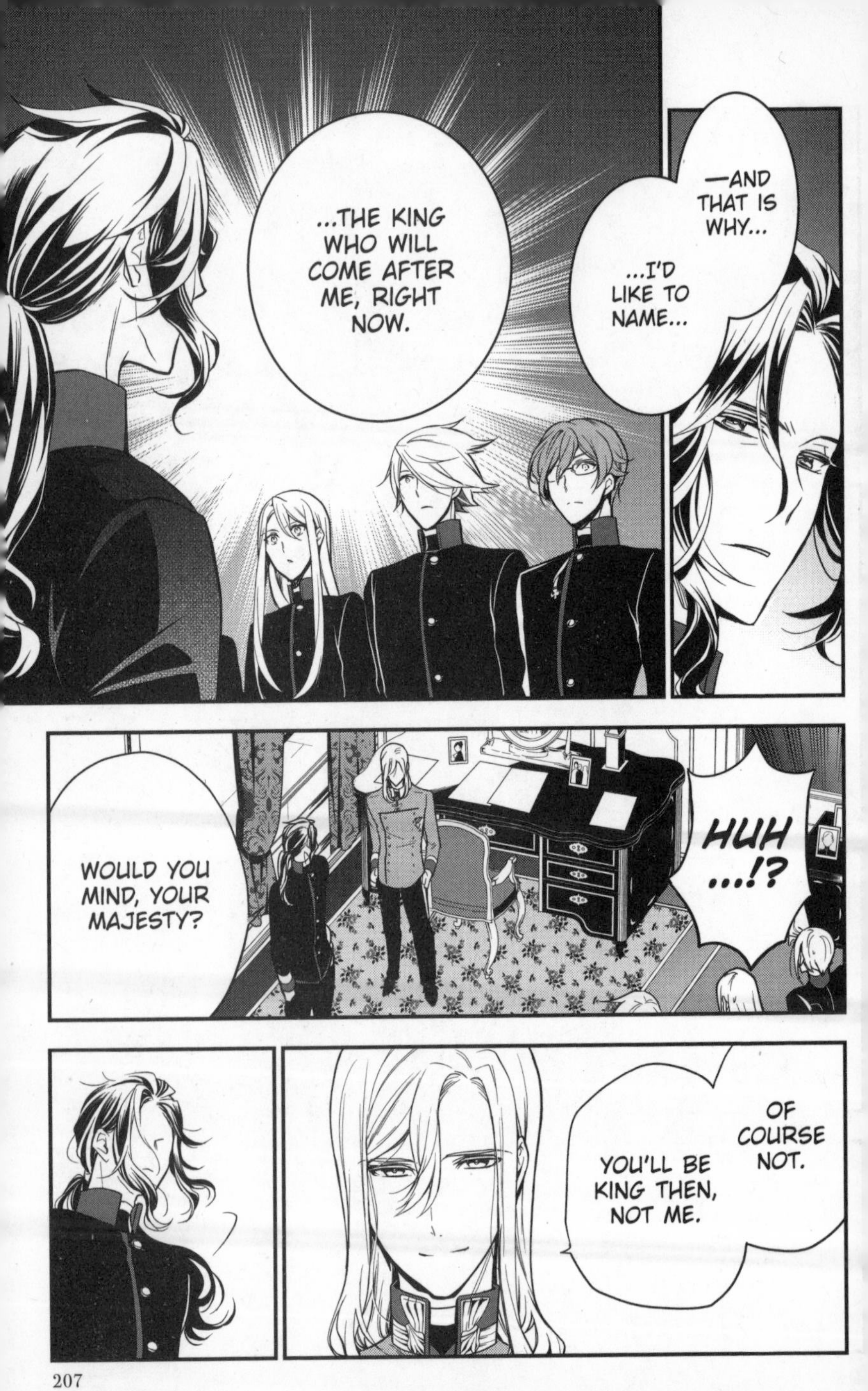
—AND THAT IS WHY...
...I'D LIKE TO NAME...
...THE KING WHO WILL COME AFTER ME, RIGHT NOW.
HUH ...!?
WOULD YOU MIND, YOUR MAJESTY?
OF COURSE NOT.
YOU'LL BE KING THEN, NOT ME.

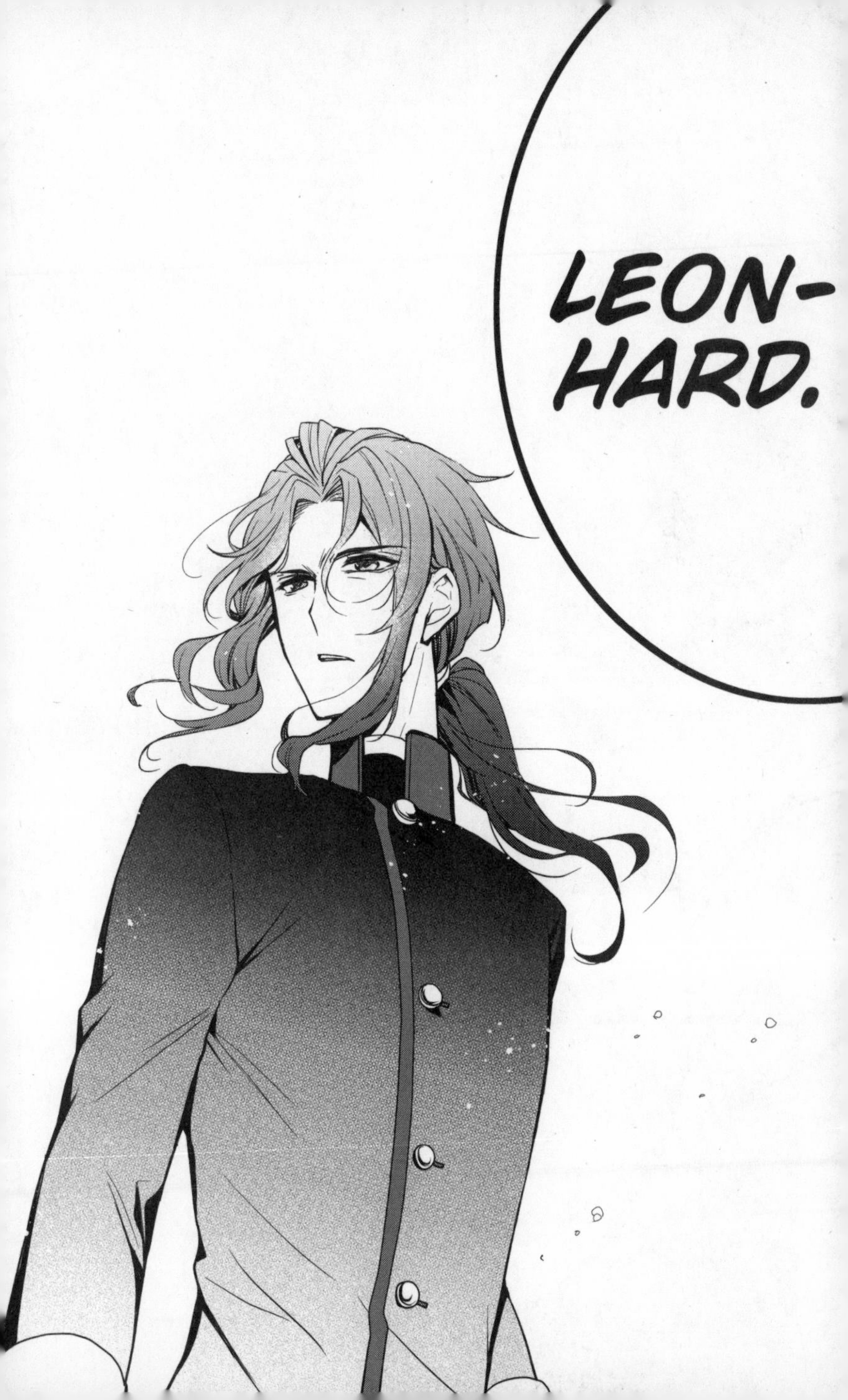
LEON-
HARD.

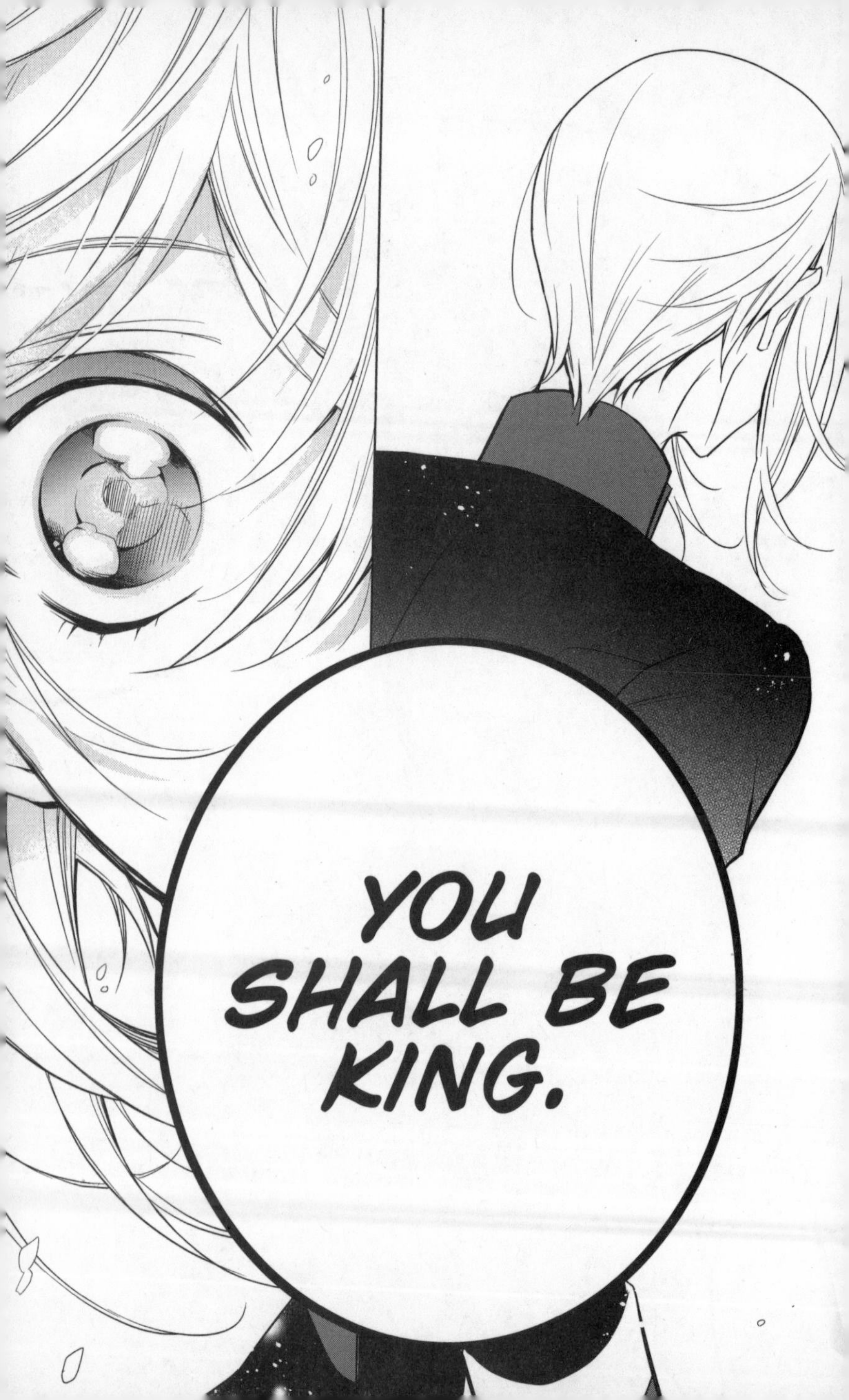
YOU SHALL BE KING.

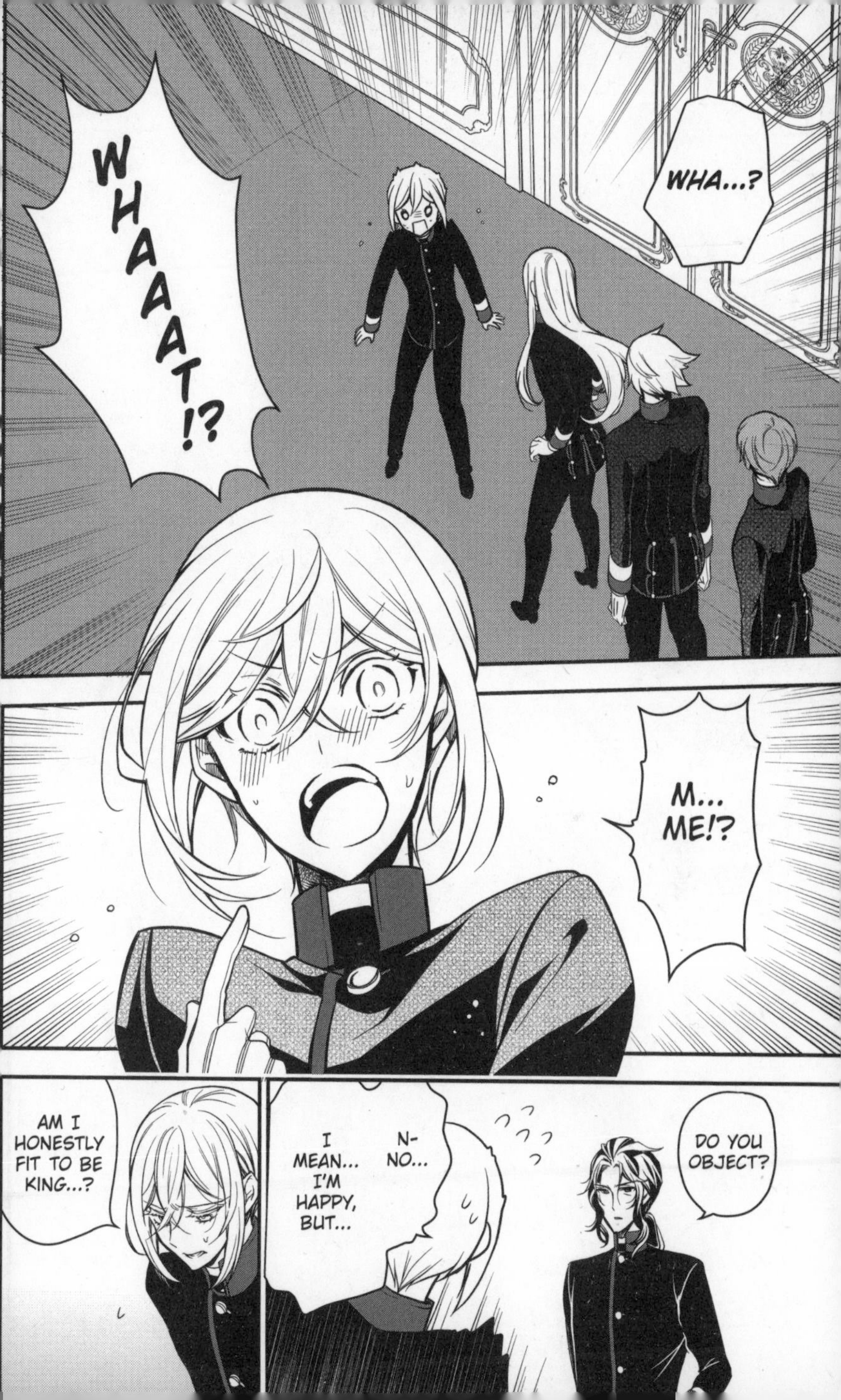
WHA...?
WHAAAT!?
M... ME!?
DO YOU OBJECT?
N- NO...
I MEAN... I'M HAPPY, BUT...
AM I HONESTLY FIT TO BE KING...?

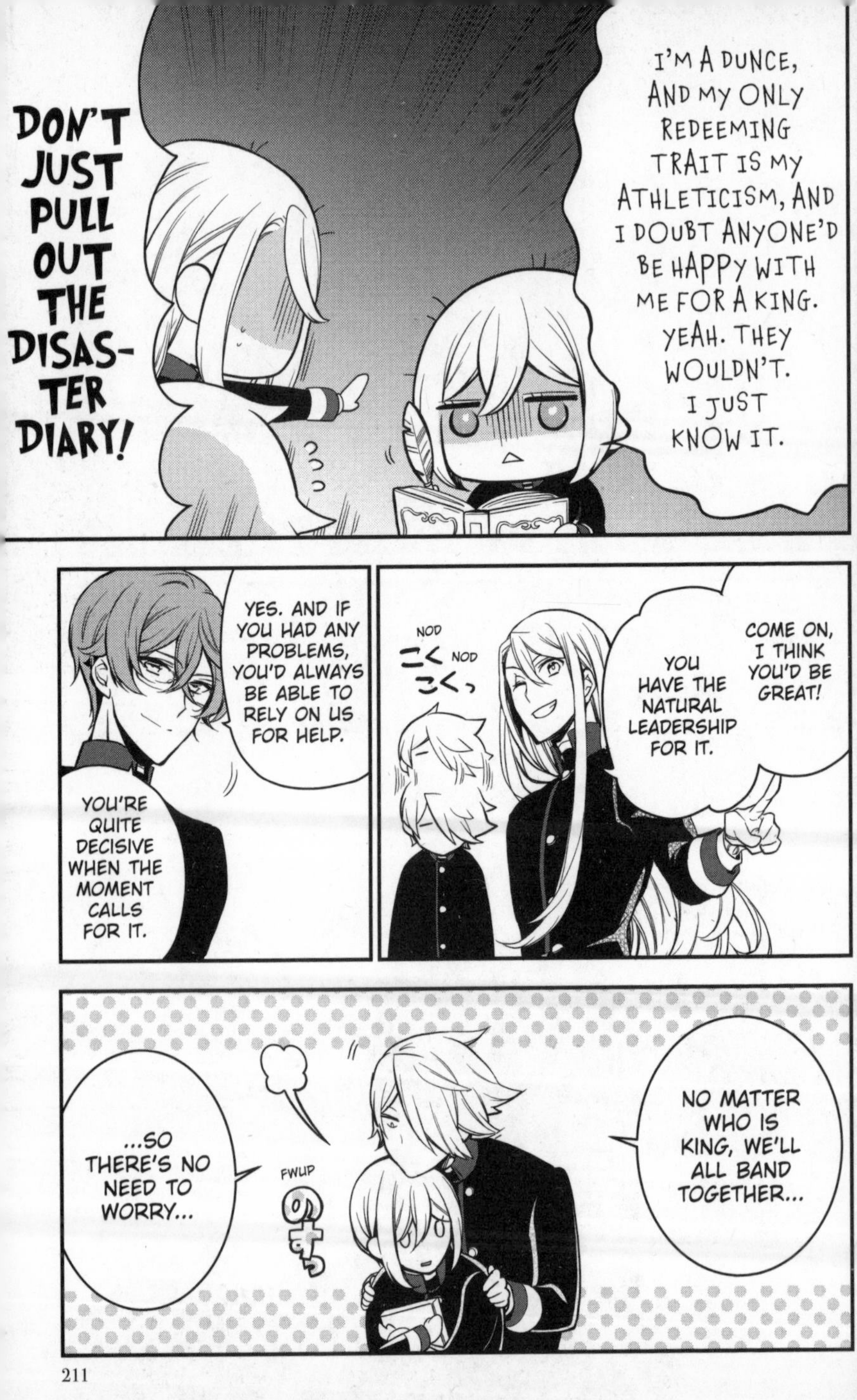
I'M A DUNCE, AND MY ONLY REDEEMING TRAIT IS MY ATHLETICISM, AND I DOUBT ANYONE'D BE HAPPY WITH ME FOR A KING. YEAH. THEY WOULDN'T. I JUST KNOW IT.
DON'T JUST PULL OUT THE DISASTER DIARY!
NOD NOD
COME ON, I THINK YOU'D BE GREAT!
YOU HAVE THE NATURAL LEADERSHIP FOR IT.
YES. AND IF YOU HAD ANY PROBLEMS, YOU'D ALWAYS BE ABLE TO RELY ON US FOR HELP.
YOU'RE QUITE DECISIVE WHEN THE MOMENT CALLS FOR IT.
NO MATTER WHO IS KING, WE'LL ALL BAND TOGETHER...
FWUP
...SO THERE'S NO NEED TO WORRY...

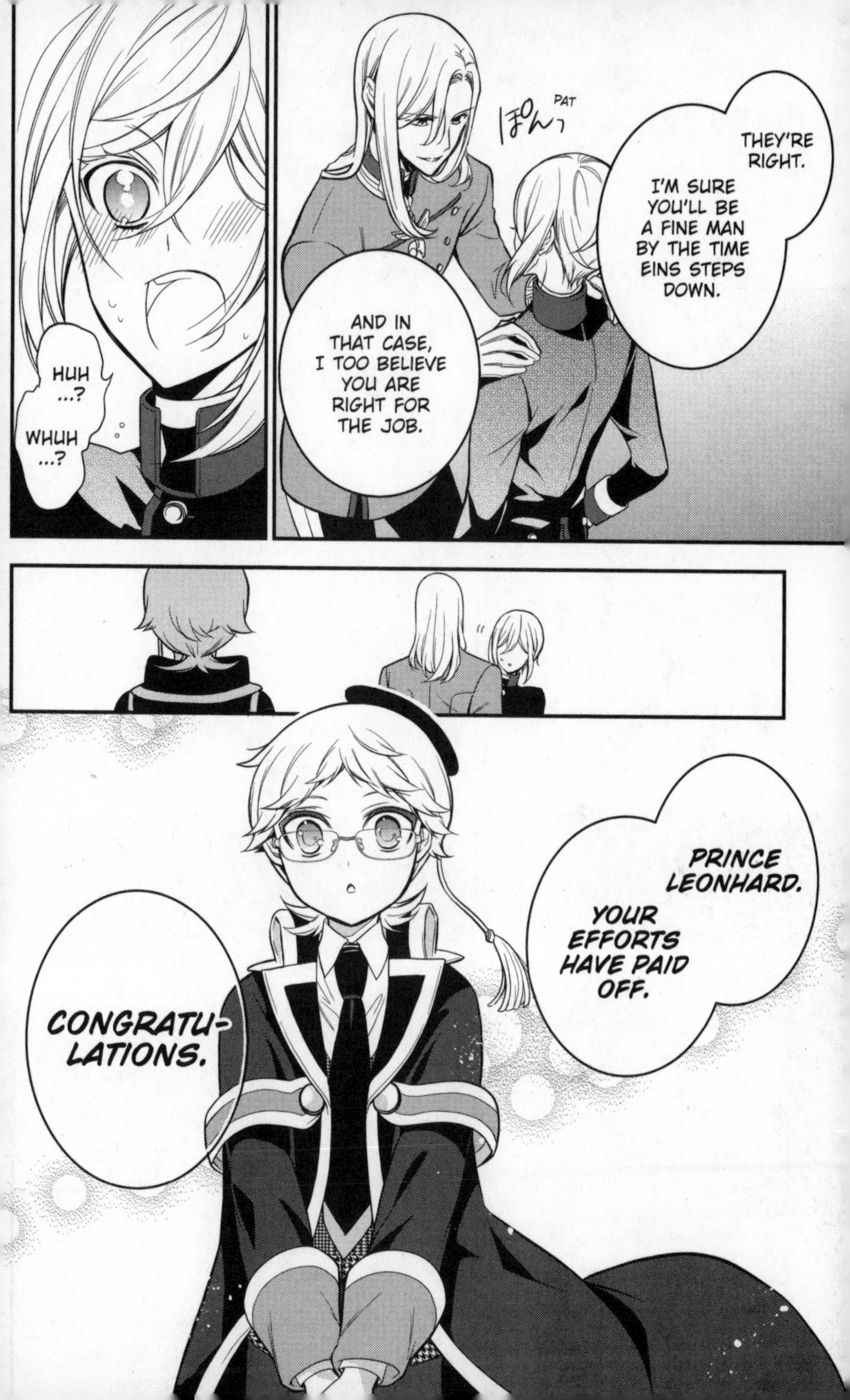
PAT
ぽんっ
THEY'RE RIGHT.
I'M SURE YOU'LL BE A FINE MAN BY THE TIME EINS STEPS DOWN.
AND IN THAT CASE, I TOO BELIEVE YOU ARE RIGHT FOR THE JOB.
HUH ...?
WHUH ...?
PRINCE LEONHARD.
YOUR EFFORTS HAVE PAID OFF.
CONGRATU-LATIONS.

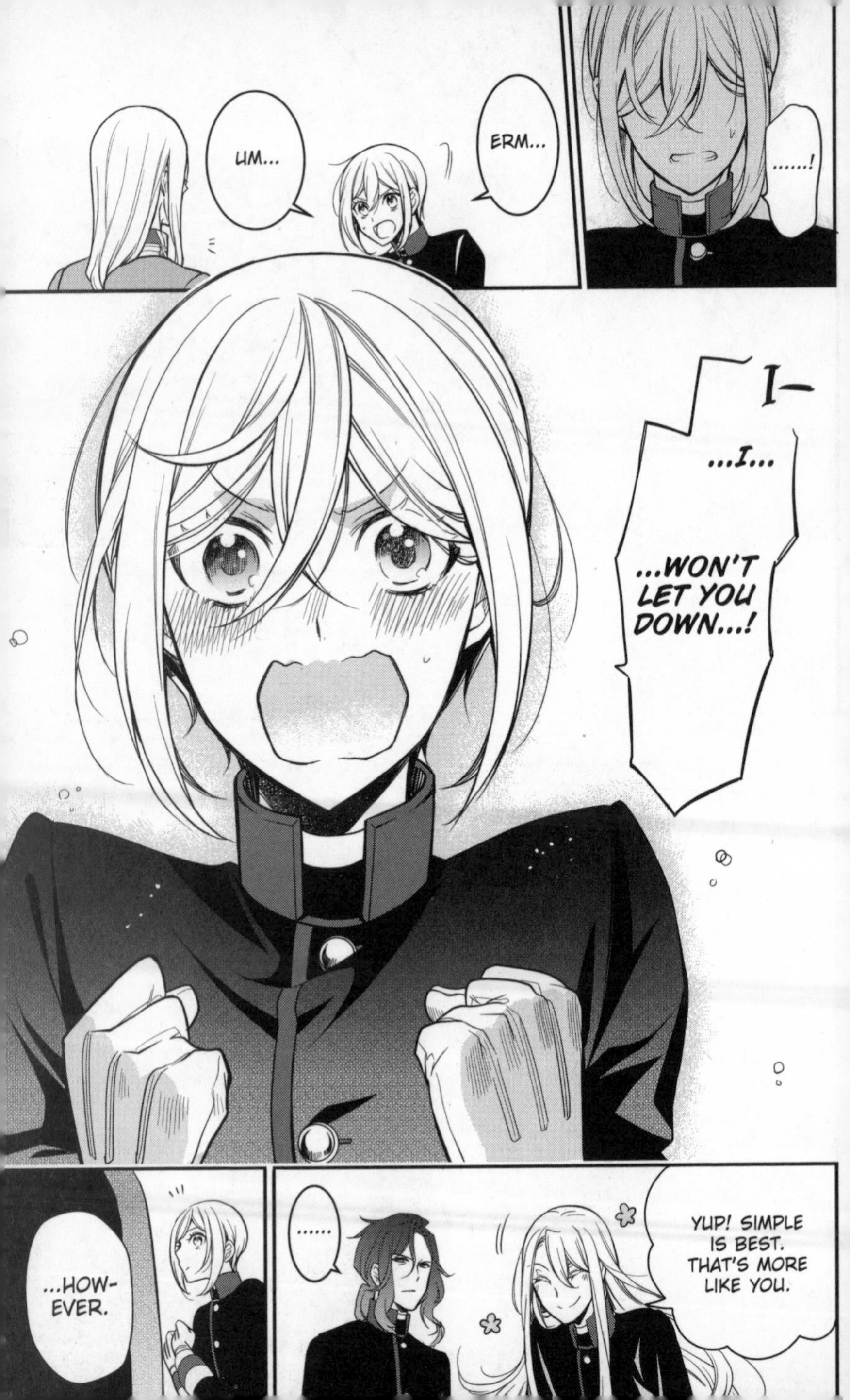
......!
ERM...
UM...
I—
...I...
...WON'T LET YOU DOWN...!
YUP! SIMPLE IS BEST. THAT'S MORE LIKE YOU.
......
...HOW-EVER.

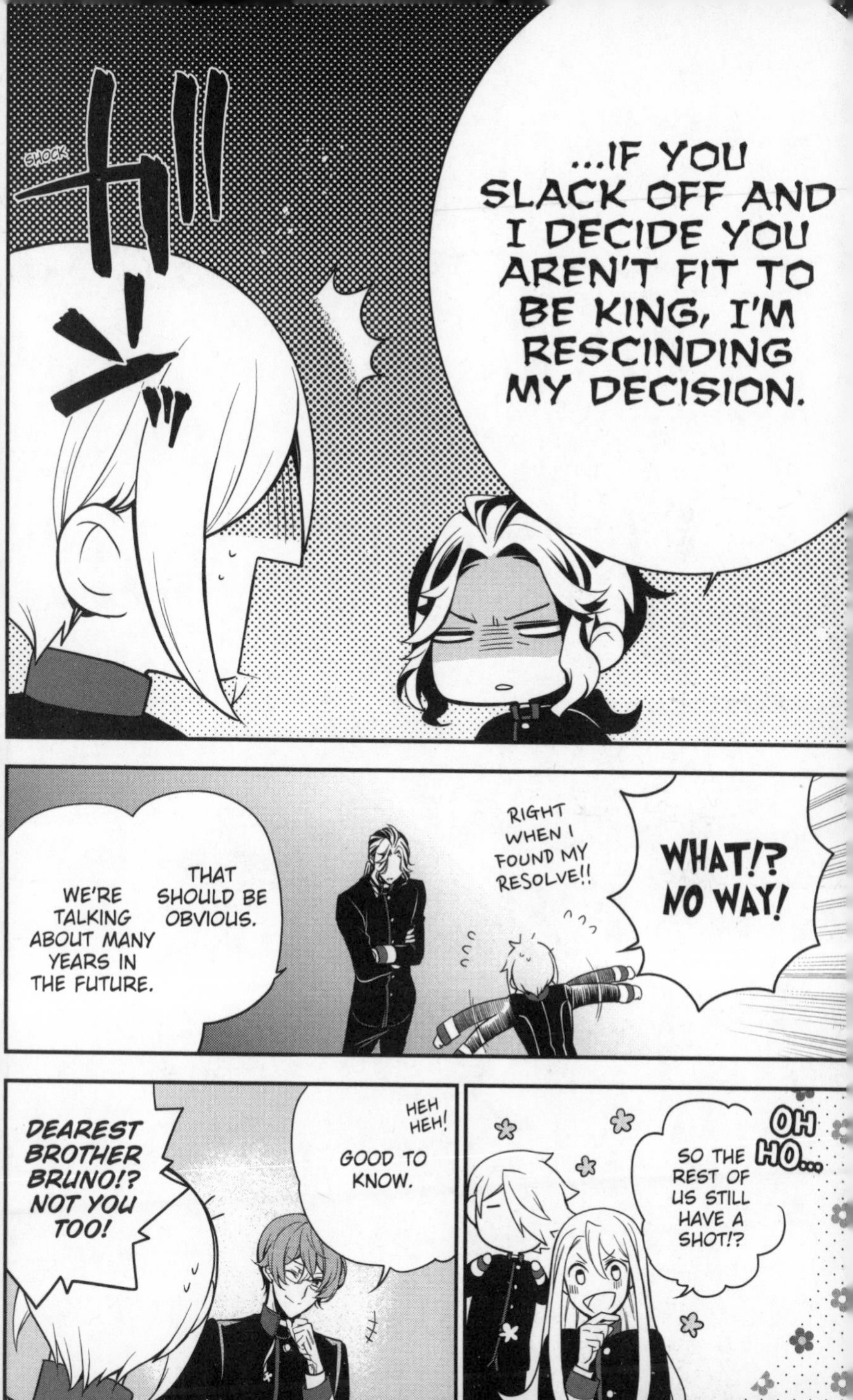
...IF YOU SLACK OFF AND I DECIDE YOU AREN'T FIT TO BE KING, I'M RESCINDING MY DECISION.
SHOCK
WHAT!? NO WAY!
RIGHT WHEN I FOUND MY RESOLVE!!
THAT SHOULD BE OBVIOUS.
WE'RE TALKING ABOUT MANY YEARS IN THE FUTURE.
OH HO...
SO THE REST OF US STILL HAVE A SHOT!?
HEH HEH!
GOOD TO KNOW.
DEAREST BROTHER BRUNO!? NOT YOU TOO!

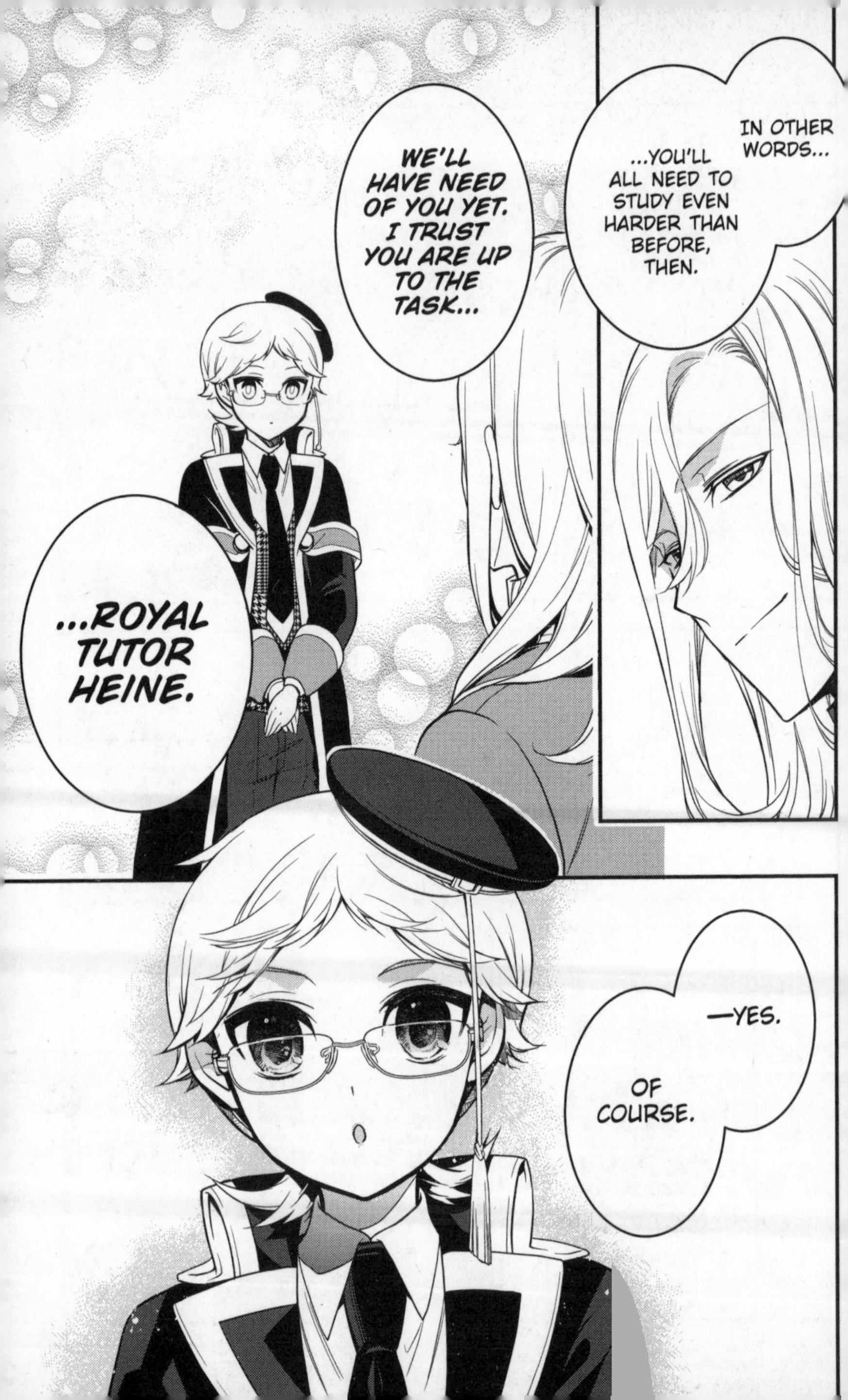
IN OTHER WORDS...
...YOU'LL ALL NEED TO STUDY EVEN HARDER THAN BEFORE, THEN.
WE'LL HAVE NEED OF YOU YET. I TRUST YOU ARE UP TO THE TASK...
...ROYAL TUTOR HEINE.
—YES.
OF COURSE.

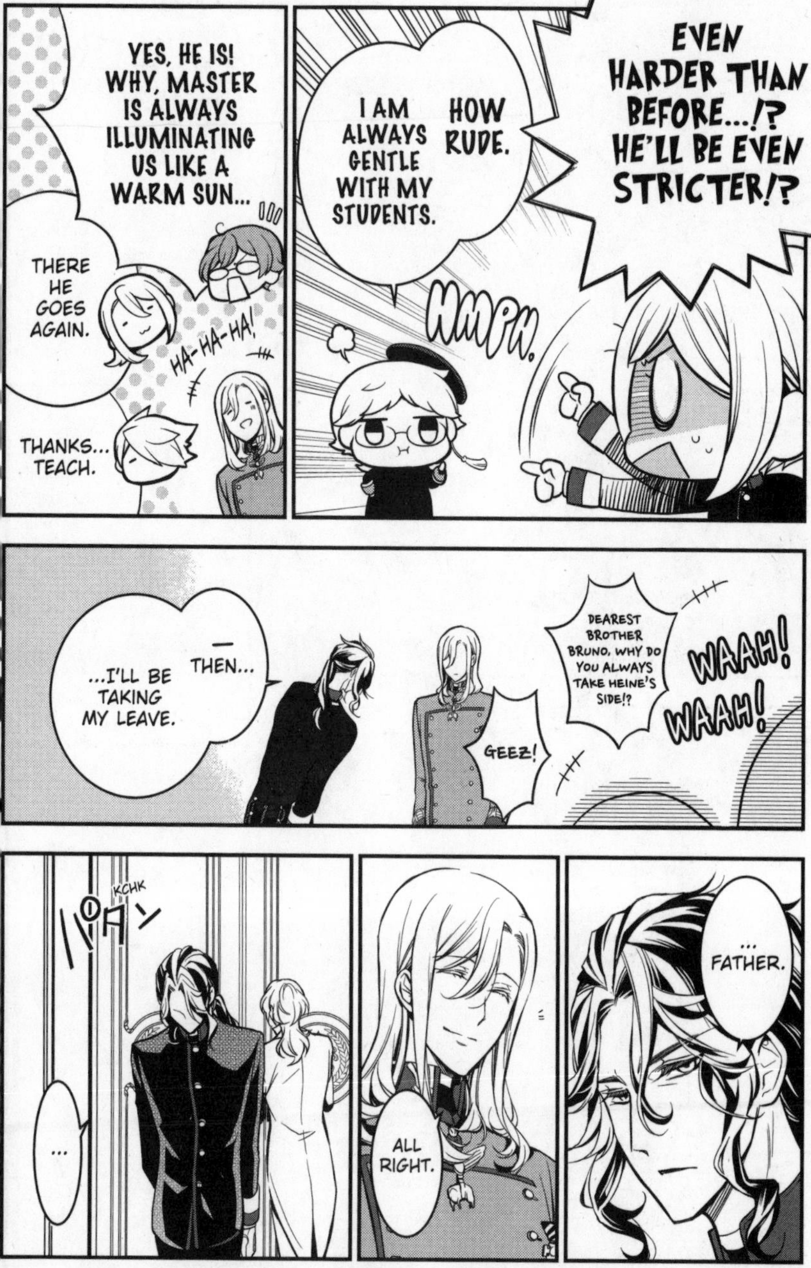
EVEN HARDER THAN BEFORE...!? HE'LL BE EVEN STRICTER!?
HOW RUDE.
I AM ALWAYS GENTLE WITH MY STUDENTS.
HMPH.
YES, HE IS! WHY, MASTER IS ALWAYS ILLUMINATING US LIKE A WARM SUN...
THERE HE GOES AGAIN.
HA-HA-HA!
THANKS... TEACH.
WAAH! WAAH!
DEAREST BROTHER BRUNO, WHY DO YOU ALWAYS TAKE HEINE'S SIDE!?
GEEZ!
—THEN...
...I'LL BE TAKING MY LEAVE.
... FATHER.
ALL RIGHT.
KCHK
...

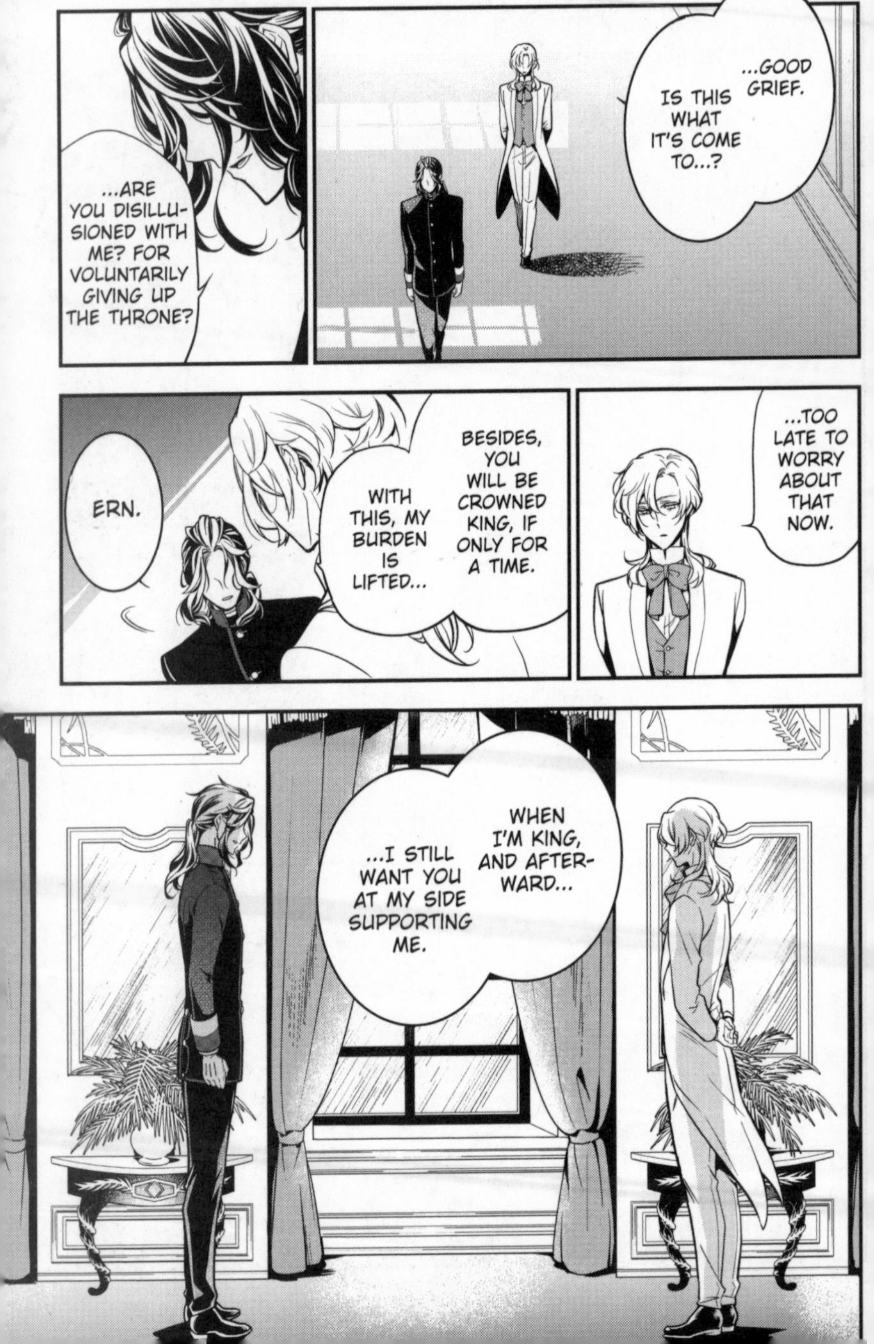
...GOOD GRIEF.
IS THIS WHAT IT'S COME TO...?
...ARE YOU DISILLUSIONED WITH ME? FOR VOLUNTARILY GIVING UP THE THRONE?
...TOO LATE TO WORRY ABOUT THAT NOW.
BESIDES, YOU WILL BE CROWNED KING, IF ONLY FOR A TIME.
WITH THIS, MY BURDEN IS LIFTED...
ERN.
WHEN I'M KING, AND AFTERWARD...
...I STILL WANT YOU AT MY SIDE SUPPORTING ME.

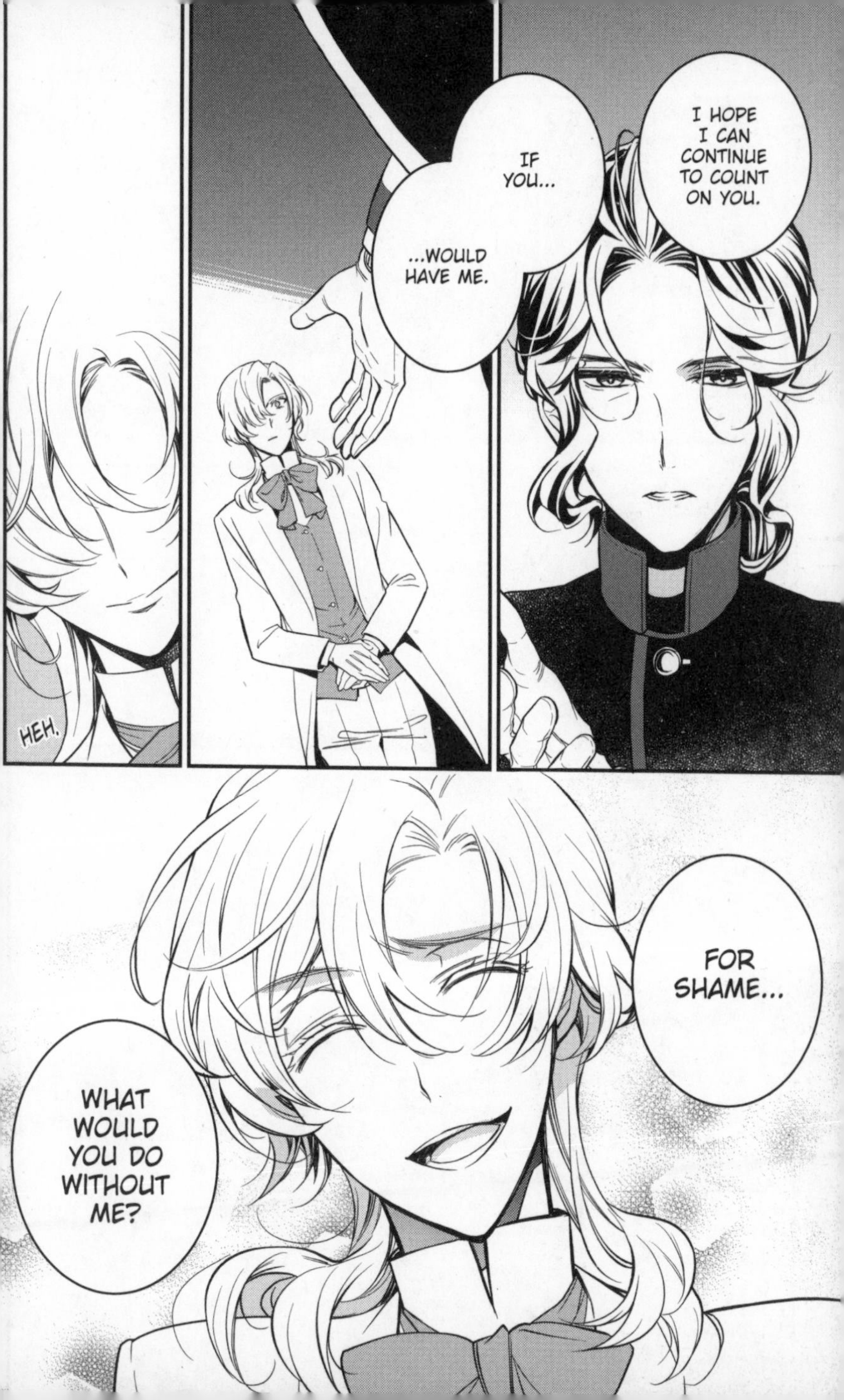
I HOPE I CAN CONTINUE TO COUNT ON YOU.
IF YOU...
...WOULD HAVE ME.
HEH.
FOR SHAME...
WHAT WOULD YOU DO WITHOUT ME?

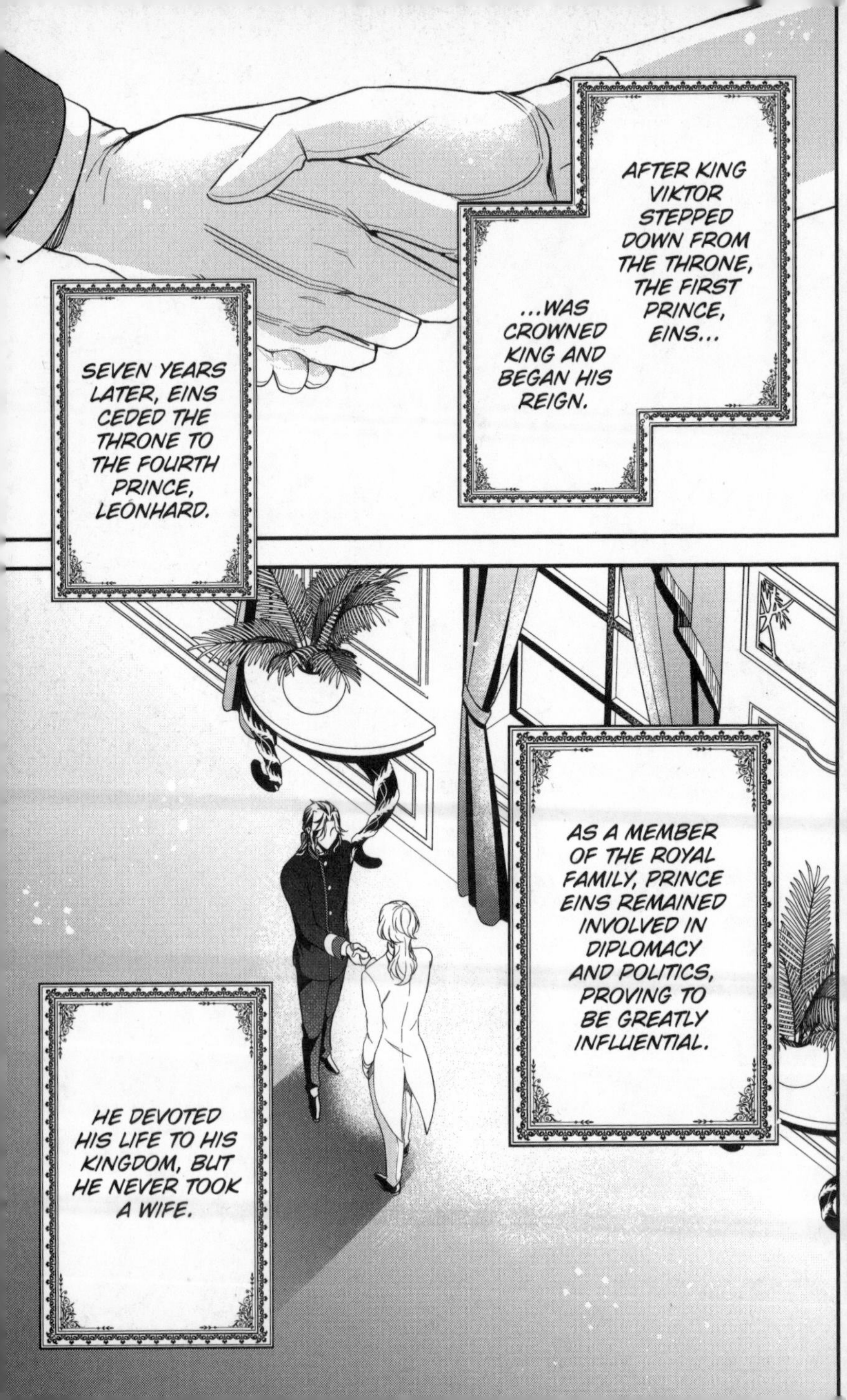
AFTER KING VIKTOR STEPPED DOWN FROM THE THRONE, THE FIRST PRINCE, EINS...
...WAS CROWNED KING AND BEGAN HIS REIGN.
SEVEN YEARS LATER, EINS CEDED THE THRONE TO THE FOURTH PRINCE, LEONHARD.
AS A MEMBER OF THE ROYAL FAMILY, PRINCE EINS REMAINED INVOLVED IN DIPLOMACY AND POLITICS, PROVING TO BE GREATLY INFLUENTIAL.
HE DEVOTED HIS LIFE TO HIS KINGDOM, BUT HE NEVER TOOK A WIFE.

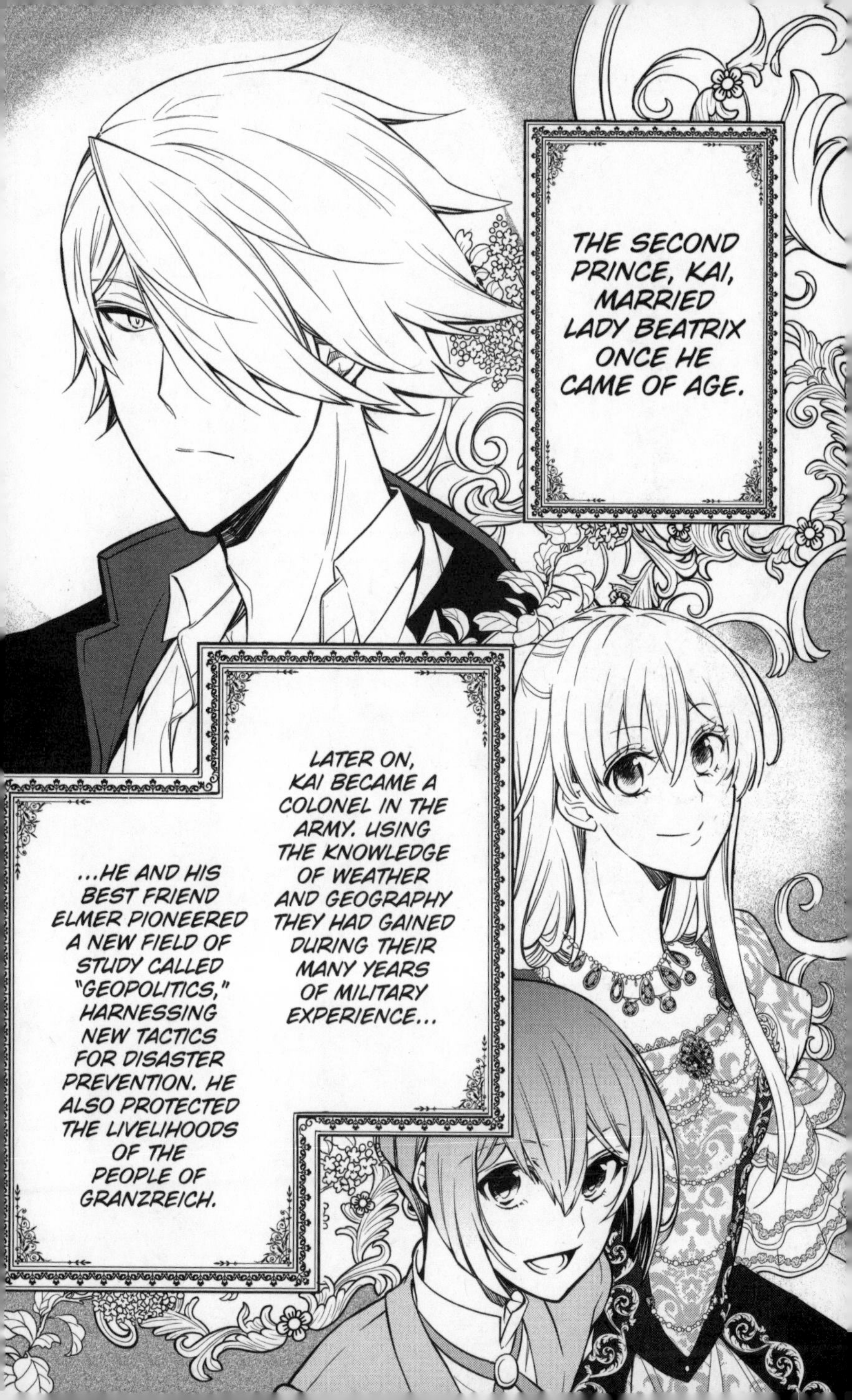
THE SECOND PRINCE, KAI, MARRIED LADY BEATRIX ONCE HE CAME OF AGE.
LATER ON, KAI BECAME A COLONEL IN THE ARMY. USING THE KNOWLEDGE OF WEATHER AND GEOGRAPHY THEY HAD GAINED DURING THEIR MANY YEARS OF MILITARY EXPERIENCE...
...HE AND HIS BEST FRIEND ELMER PIONEERED A NEW FIELD OF STUDY CALLED "GEOPOLITICS," HARNESSING NEW TACTICS FOR DISASTER PREVENTION. HE ALSO PROTECTED THE LIVELIHOODS OF THE PEOPLE OF GRANZREICH.

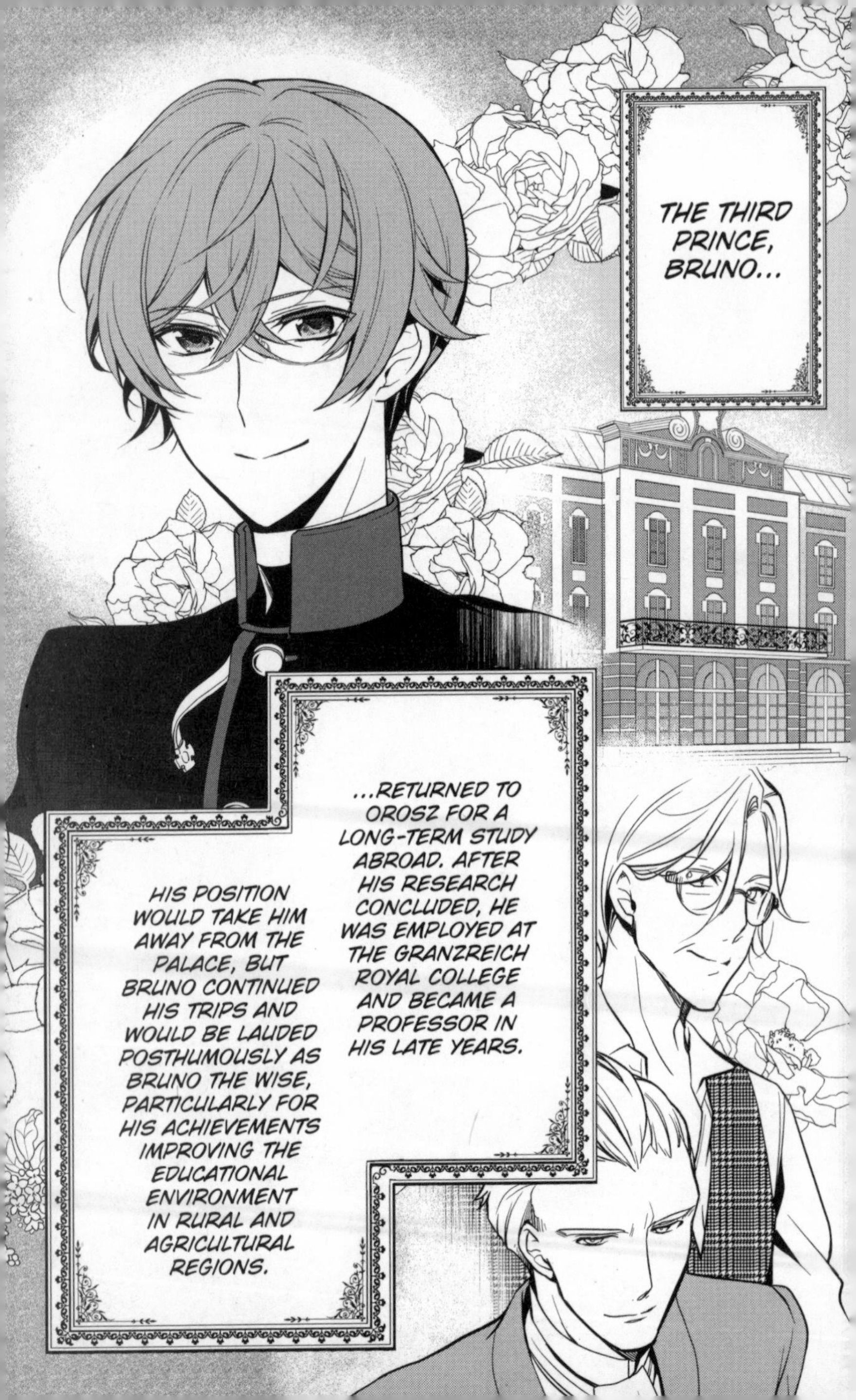
THE THIRD PRINCE, BRUNO...
...RETURNED TO OROSZ FOR A LONG-TERM STUDY ABROAD. AFTER HIS RESEARCH CONCLUDED, HE WAS EMPLOYED AT THE GRANZREICH ROYAL COLLEGE AND BECAME A PROFESSOR IN HIS LATE YEARS.
HIS POSITION WOULD TAKE HIM AWAY FROM THE PALACE, BUT BRUNO CONTINUED HIS TRIPS AND WOULD BE LAUDED POSTHUMOUSLY AS BRUNO THE WISE, PARTICULARLY FOR HIS ACHIEVEMENTS IMPROVING THE EDUCATIONAL ENVIRONMENT IN RURAL AND AGRICULTURAL REGIONS.

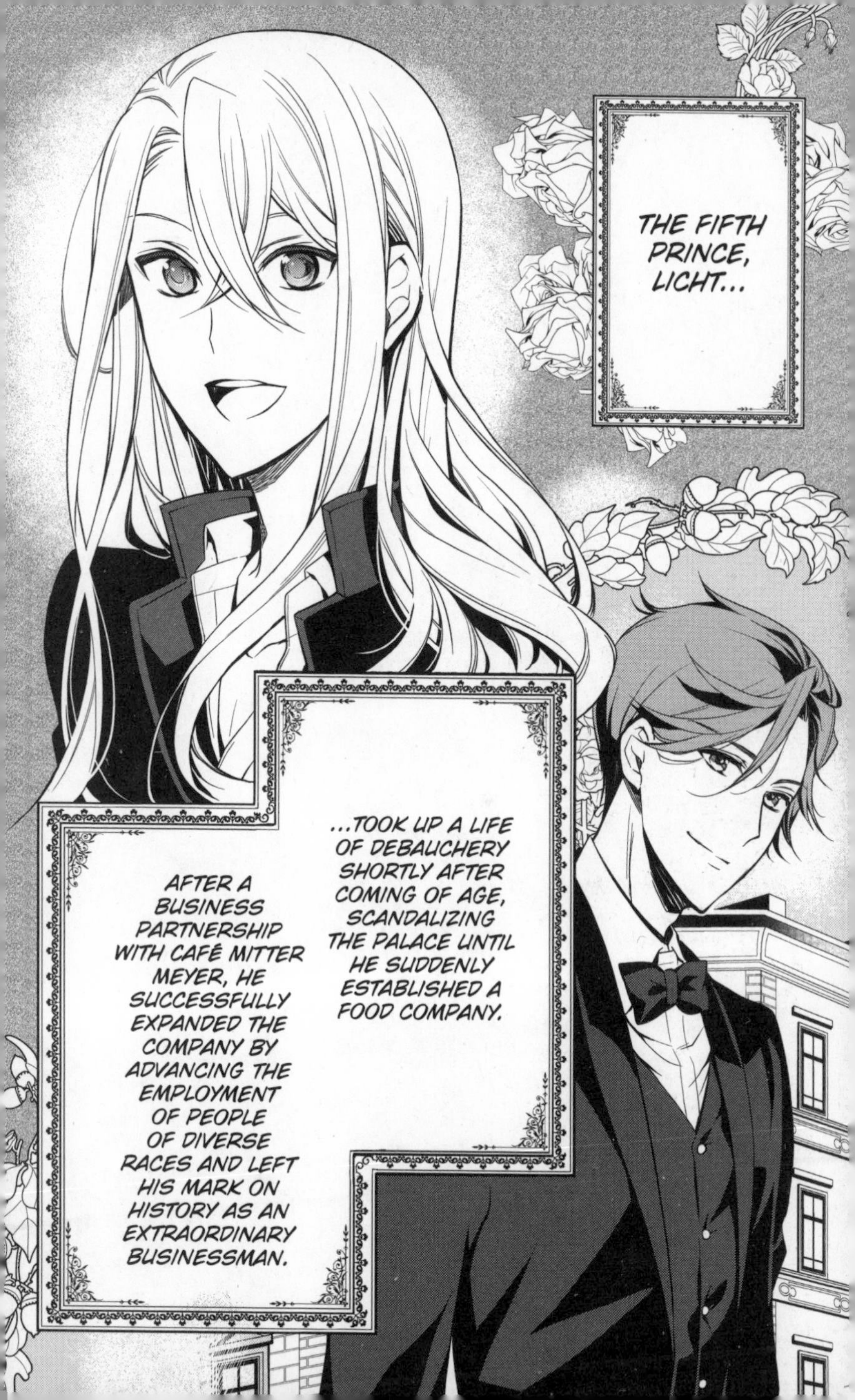
THE FIFTH PRINCE, LICHT...
...TOOK UP A LIFE OF DEBAUCHERY SHORTLY AFTER COMING OF AGE, SCANDALIZING THE PALACE UNTIL HE SUDDENLY ESTABLISHED A FOOD COMPANY.
AFTER A BUSINESS PARTNERSHIP WITH CAFÉ MITTER MEYER, HE SUCCESSFULLY EXPANDED THE COMPANY BY ADVANCING THE EMPLOYMENT OF PEOPLE OF DIVERSE RACES AND LEFT HIS MARK ON HISTORY AS AN EXTRAORDINARY BUSINESSMAN.

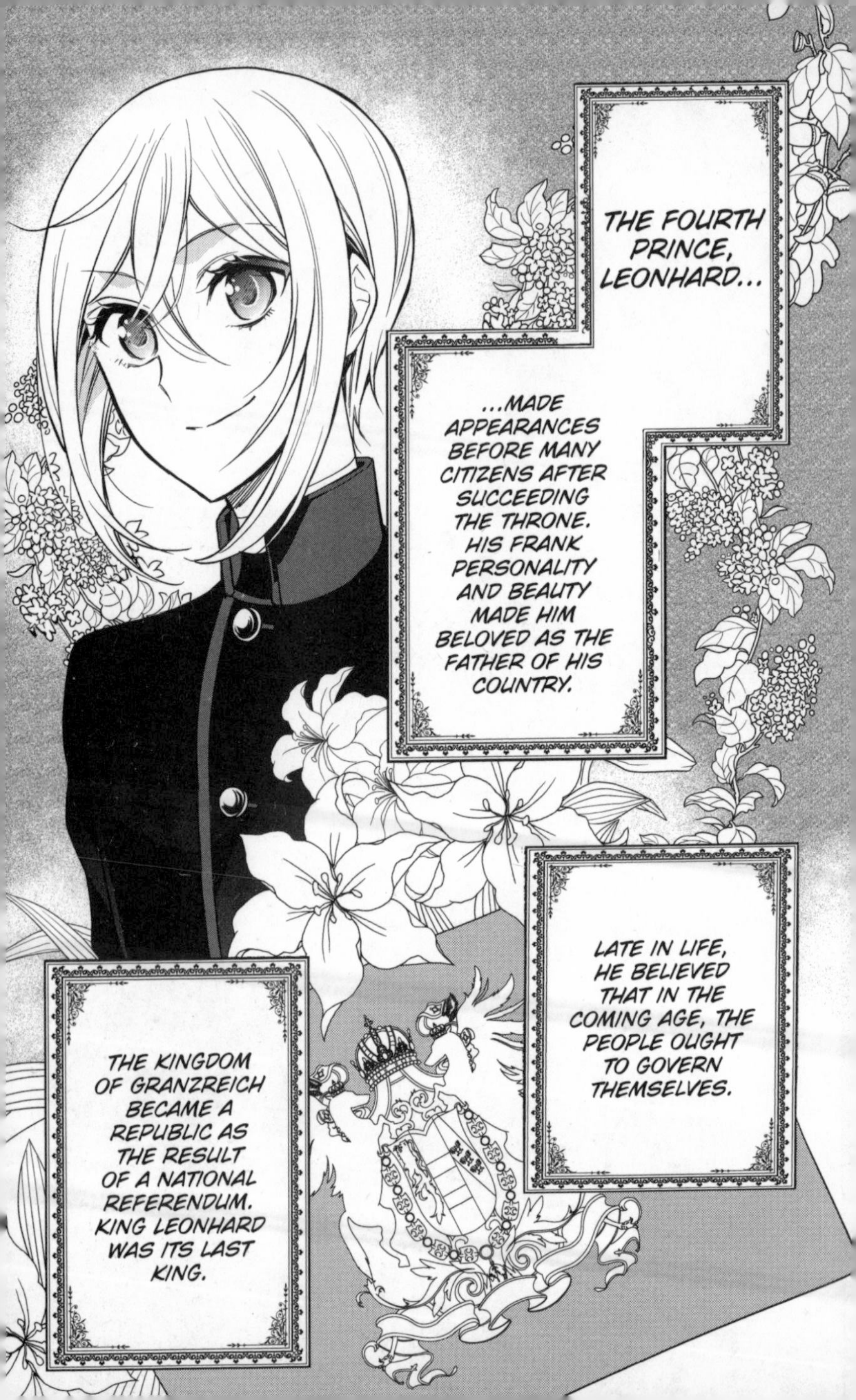
THE FOURTH PRINCE, LEONHARD...
...MADE APPEARANCES BEFORE MANY CITIZENS AFTER SUCCEEDING THE THRONE. HIS FRANK PERSONALITY AND BEAUTY MADE HIM BELOVED AS THE FATHER OF HIS COUNTRY.
LATE IN LIFE, HE BELIEVED THAT IN THE COMING AGE, THE PEOPLE OUGHT TO GOVERN THEMSELVES.
THE KINGDOM OF GRANZREICH BECAME A REPUBLIC AS THE RESULT OF A NATIONAL REFERENDUM. KING LEONHARD WAS ITS LAST KING.

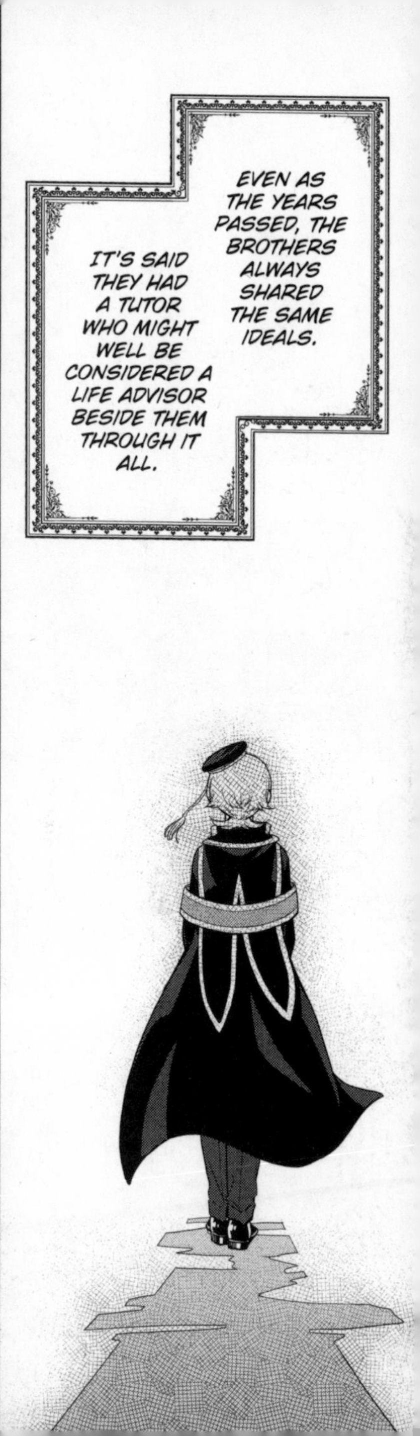
EVEN AS THE YEARS PASSED, THE BROTHERS ALWAYS SHARED THE SAME IDEALS.
IT'S SAID THEY HAD A TUTOR WHO MIGHT WELL BE CONSIDERED A LIFE ADVISOR BESIDE THEM THROUGH IT ALL.
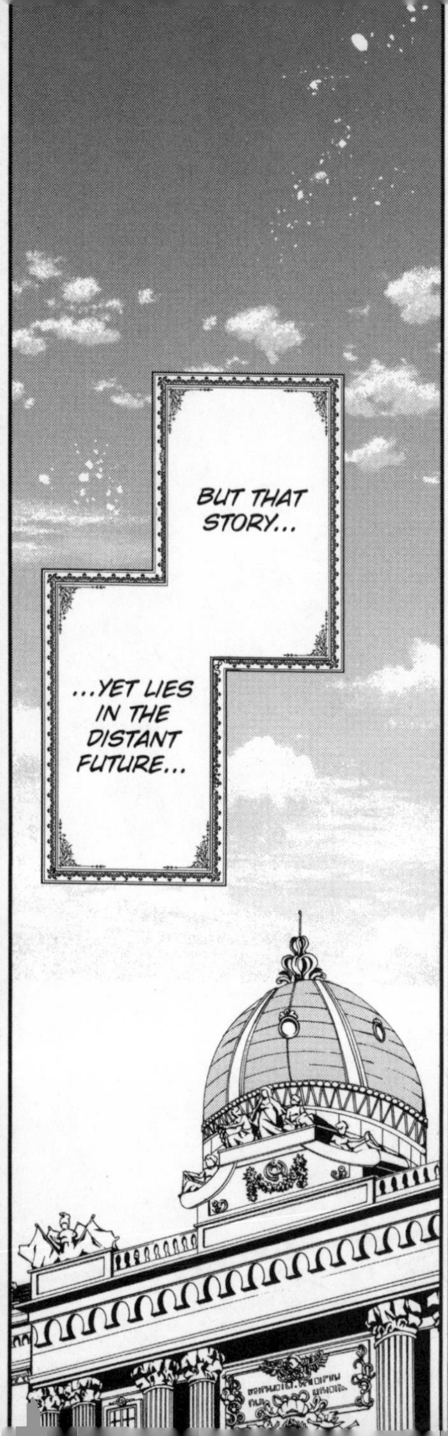
BUT THAT STORY...
...YET LIES IN THE DISTANT FUTURE...

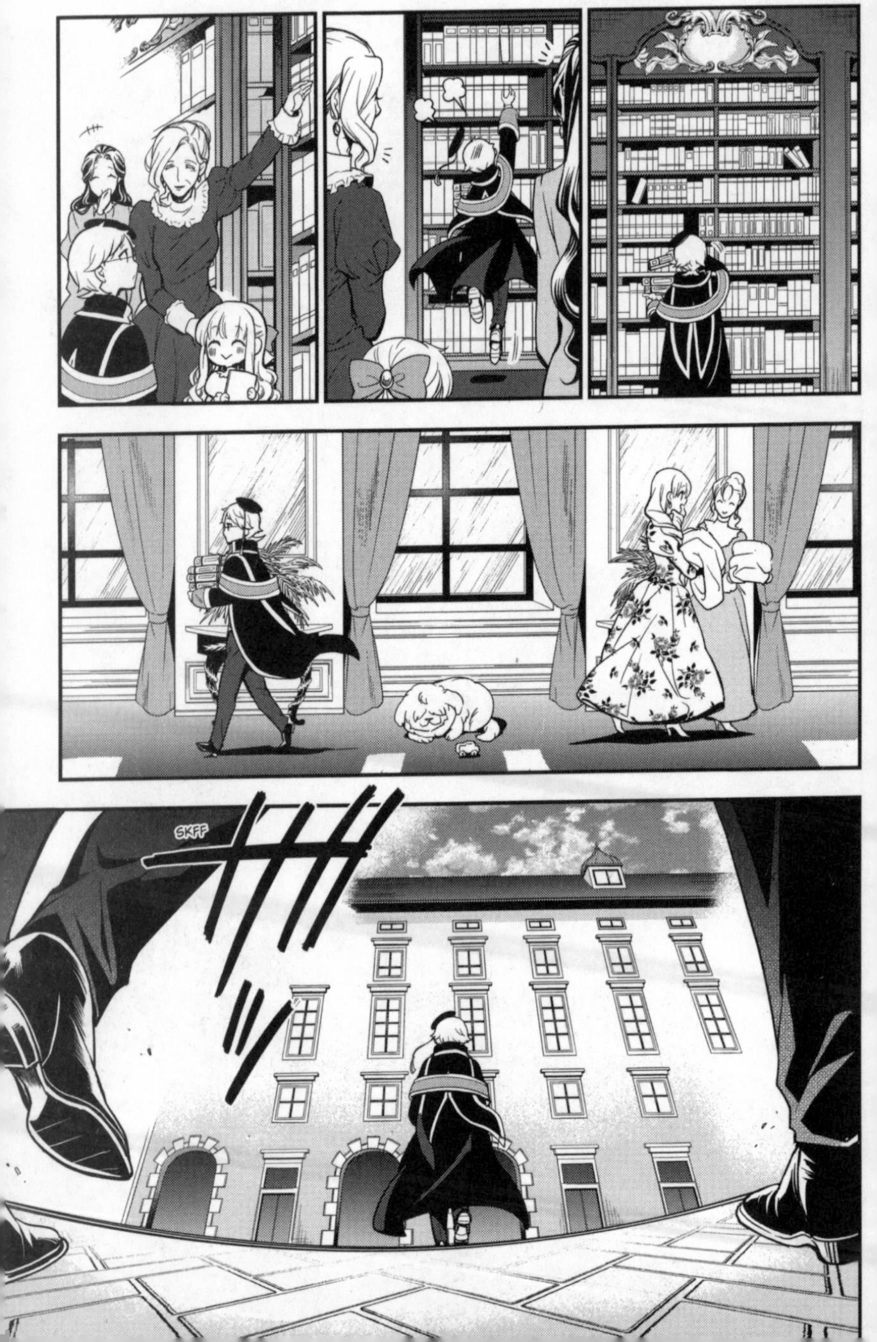
SKFF

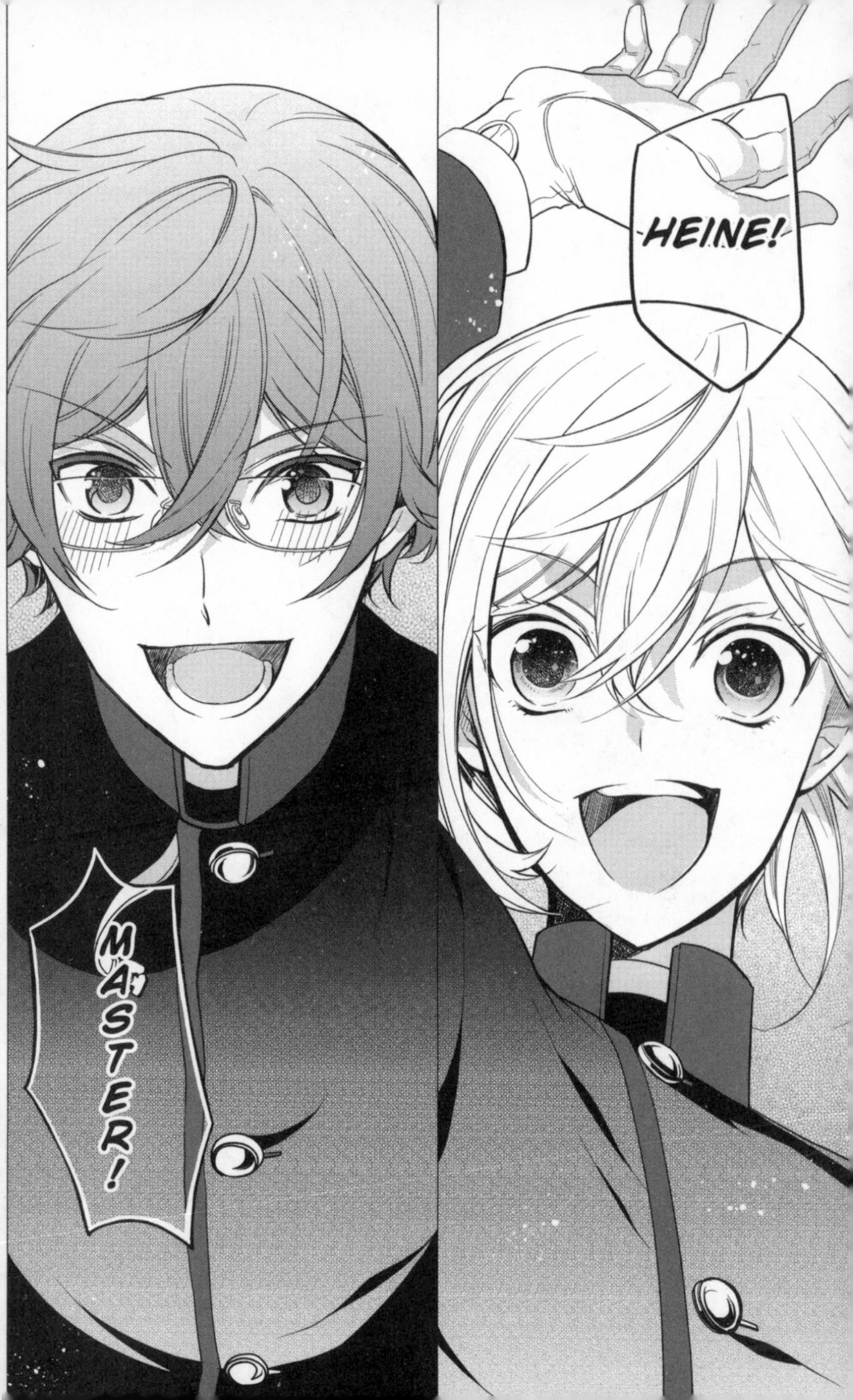
HEINE!
MASTER!

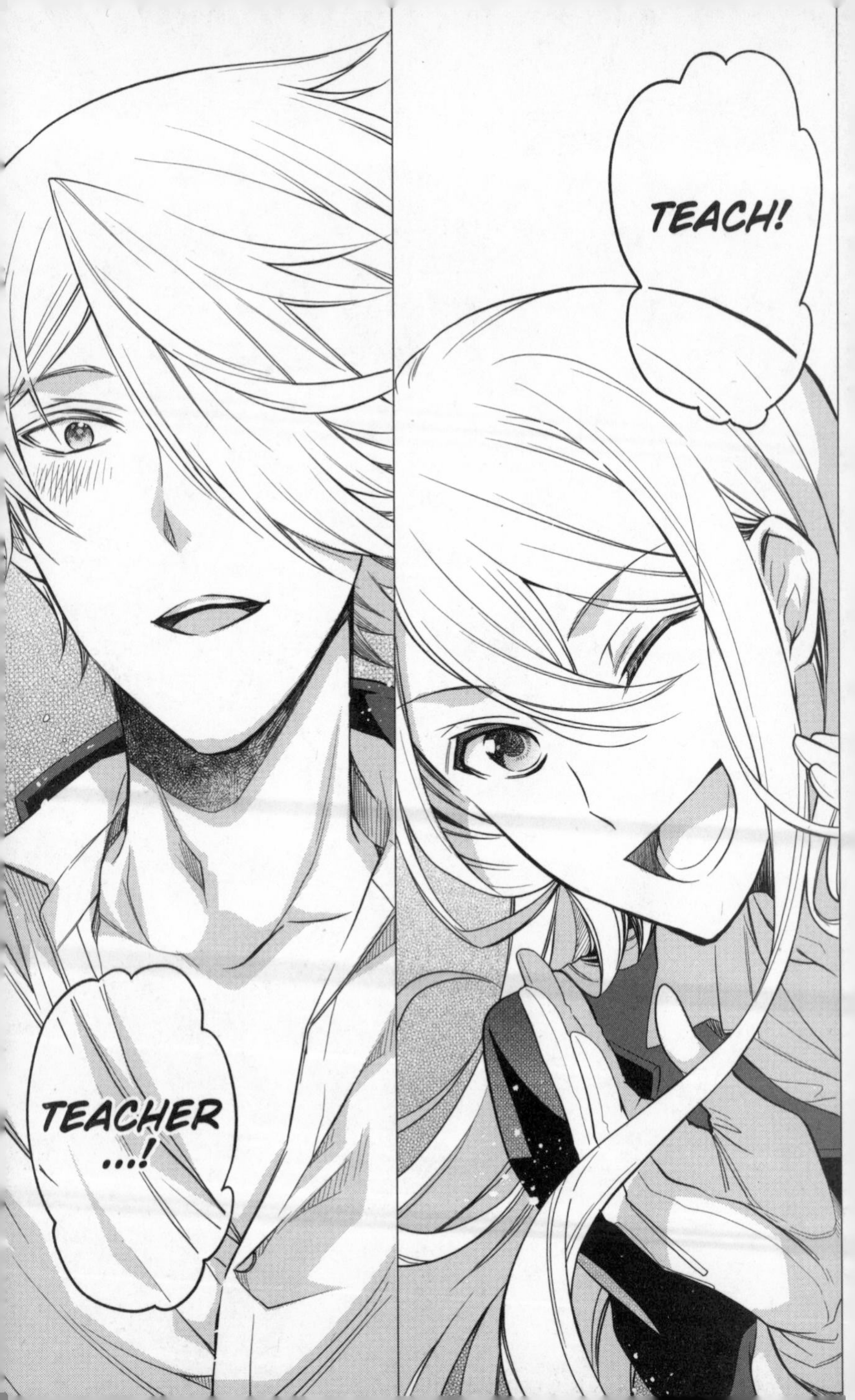
TEACH!
TEACHER ...!

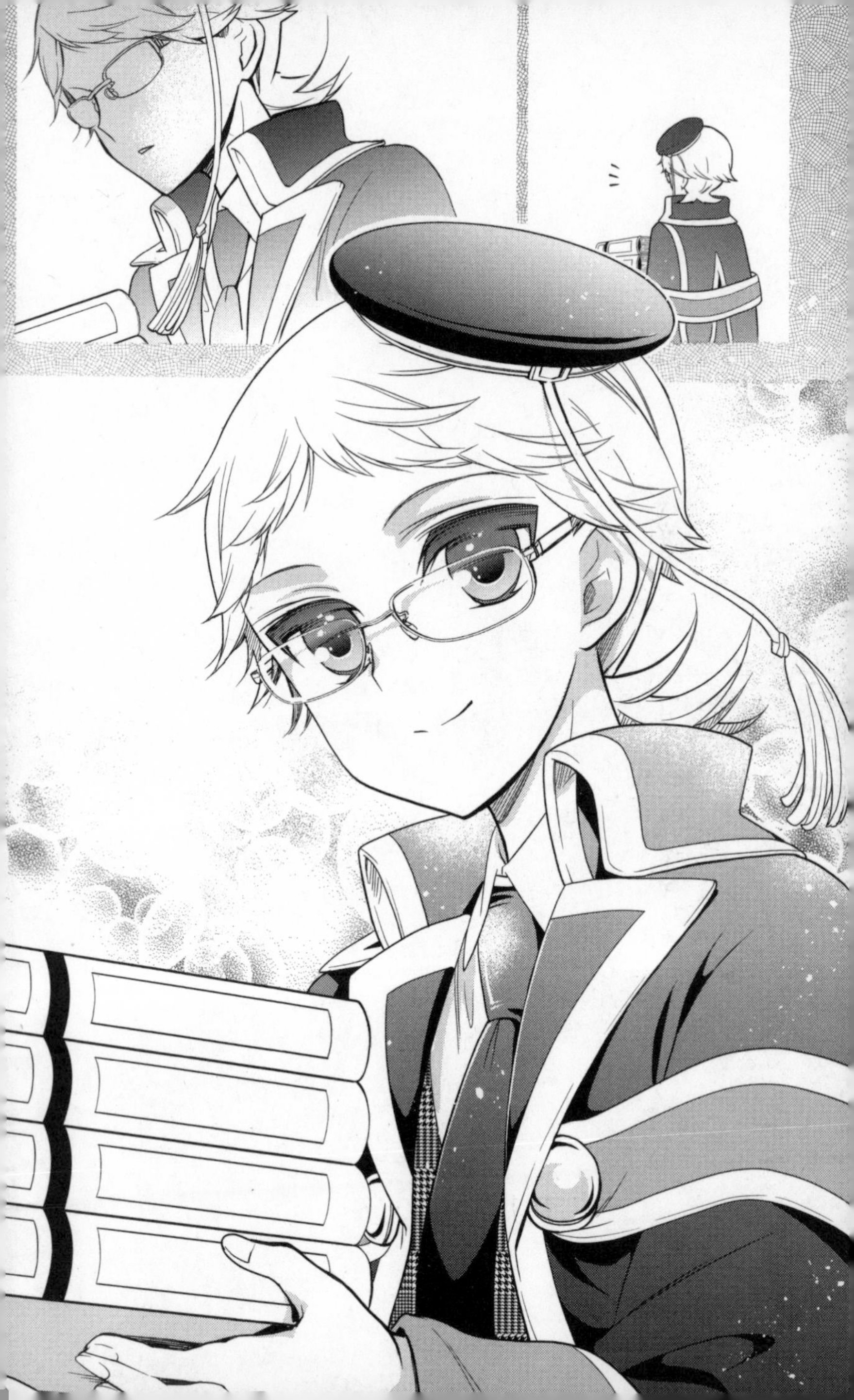

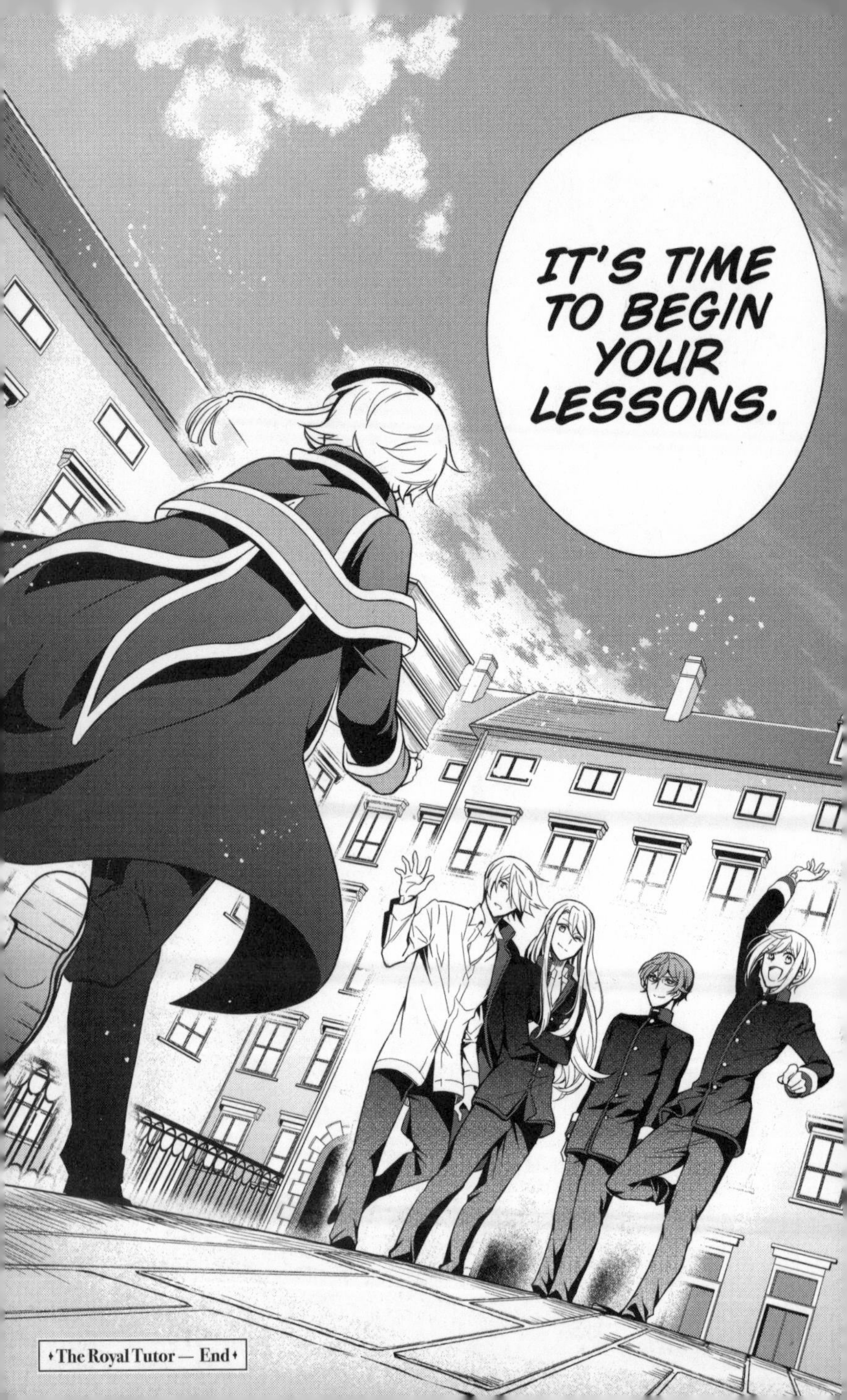
IT'S TIME TO BEGIN YOUR LESSONS.
•The Royal Tutor — End•

THE
ROYAL
TUTOR

Here it is, the final volume of *The Royal Tutor*. Thank you so much for reading this far! If I started recounting my memories of penning this series, I could go on and on. Out of all my manga, this is the one that reached the most people, which makes me very emotional. Thank you to my editor, everyone in the editorial department, the whole staff, the book designer, my assistants, and everyone else who was involved with *The Royal Tutor*. Most of all, thank you to all the readers. I was able to keep drawing to this point because of your support and cheering. Even though the manga is now complete, the characters and the world will continue to live on inside me and inside all of you who enjoy *The Royal Tutor*. Nothing would make me happier than for you to remember it fondly from time to time. I too have graduated from Heine's tutelage. I'll strive to use this experience as fuel to keep learning and growing so I can meet you all again in my next work.

Thank you so very much!

- SPECIAL THANKS -
    Tsuchiya-san,
    k-san, Ao-san,
My editor Akiyama-san,
    all my readers

Higasa Akai

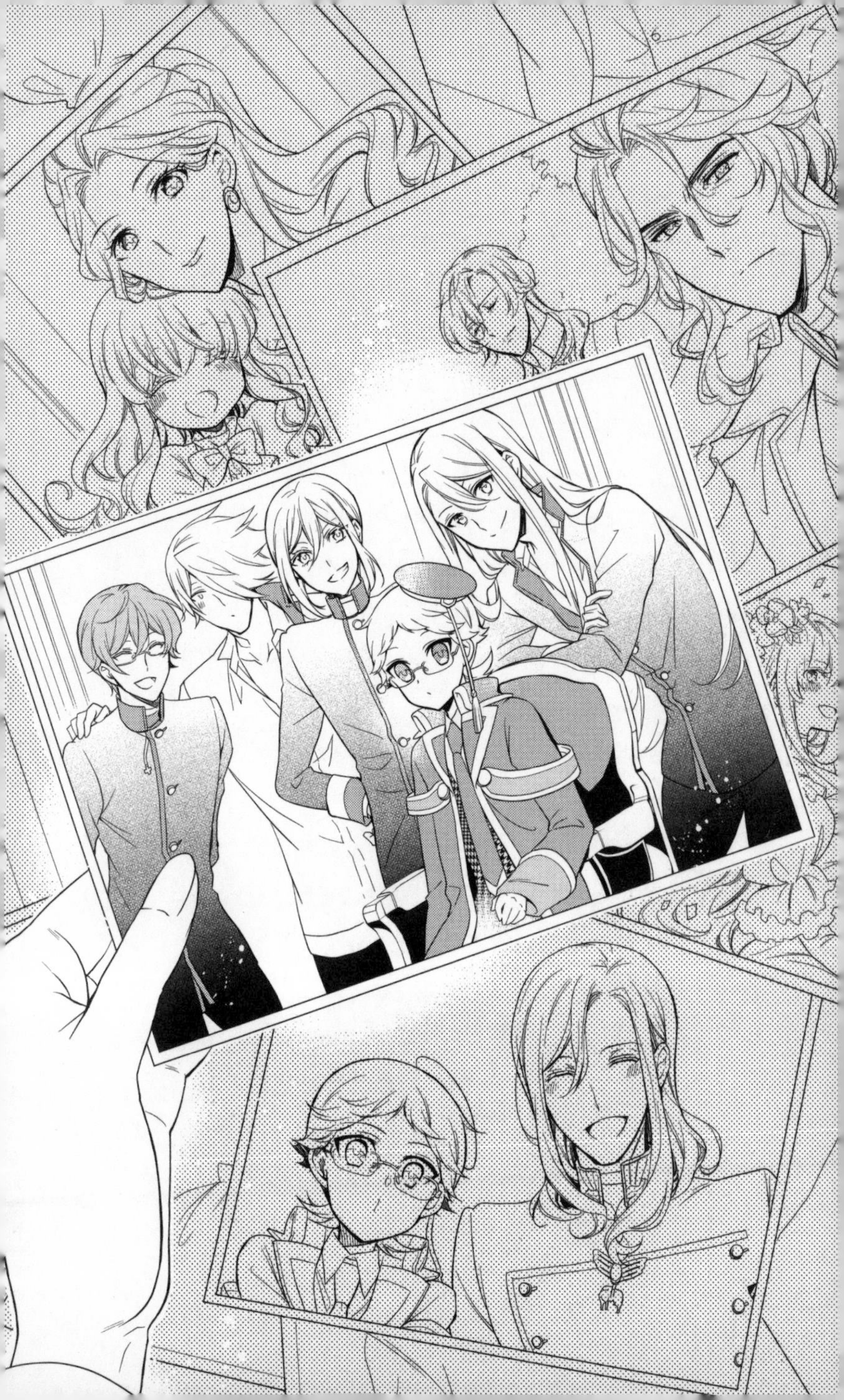

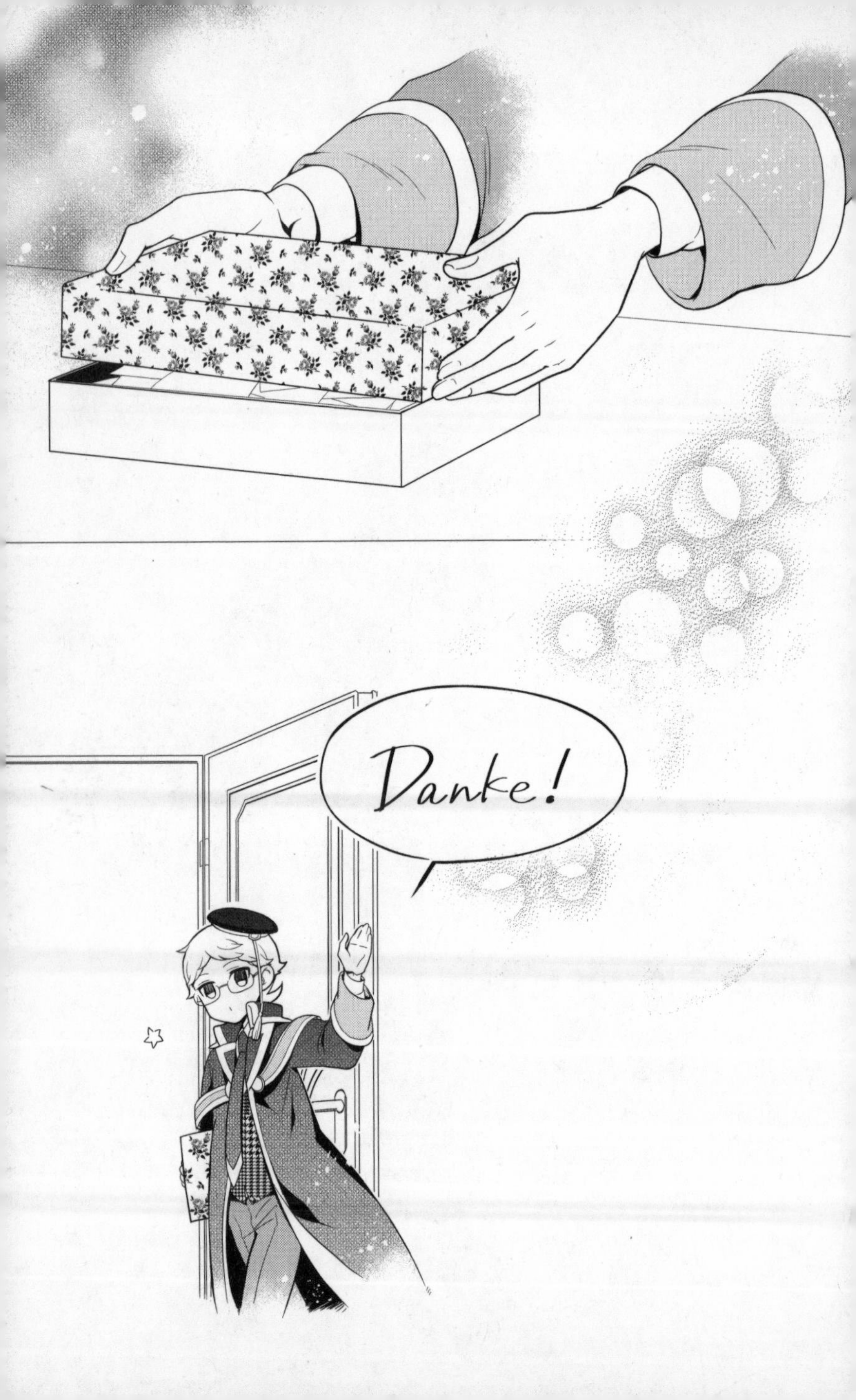
Danke!

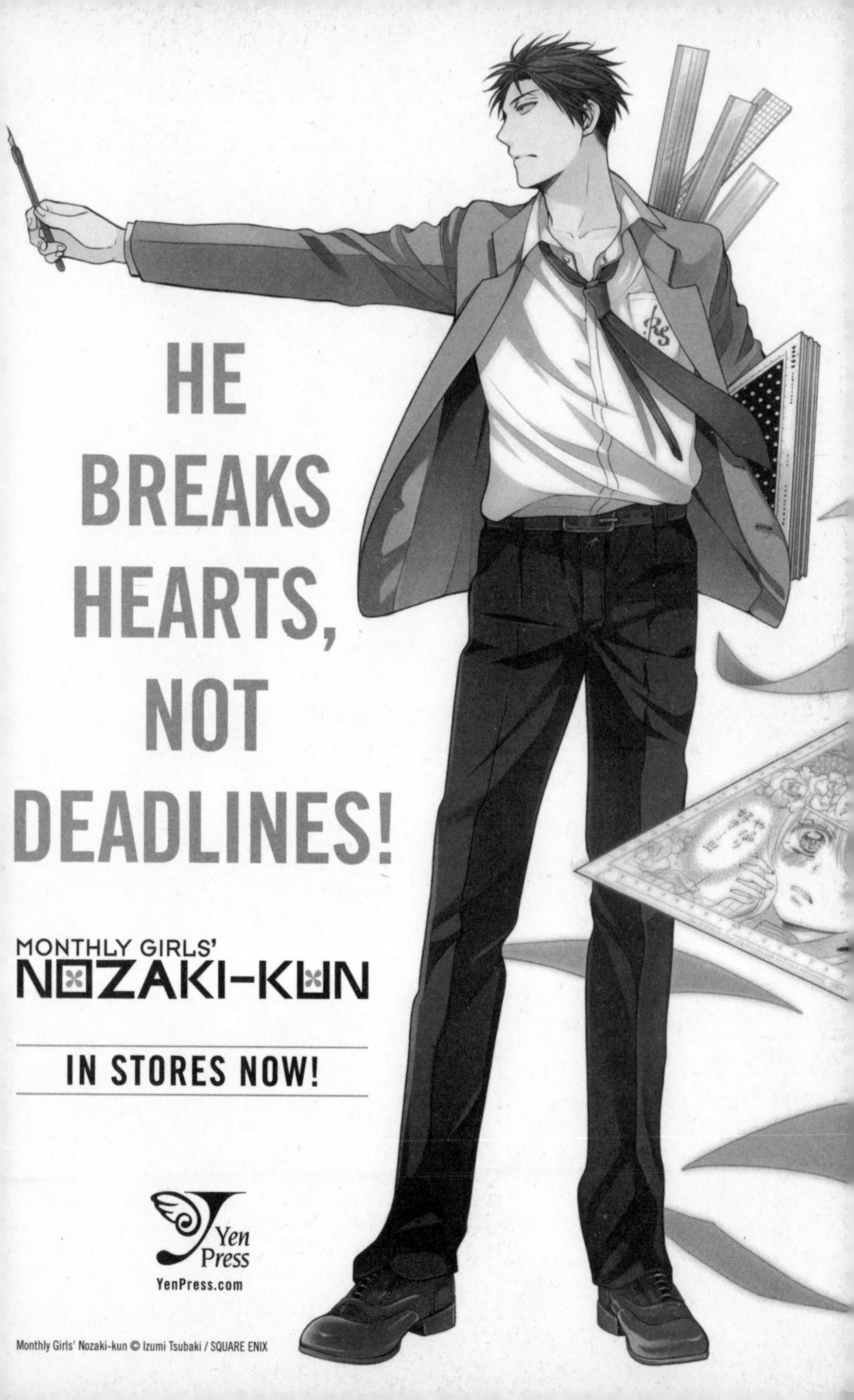

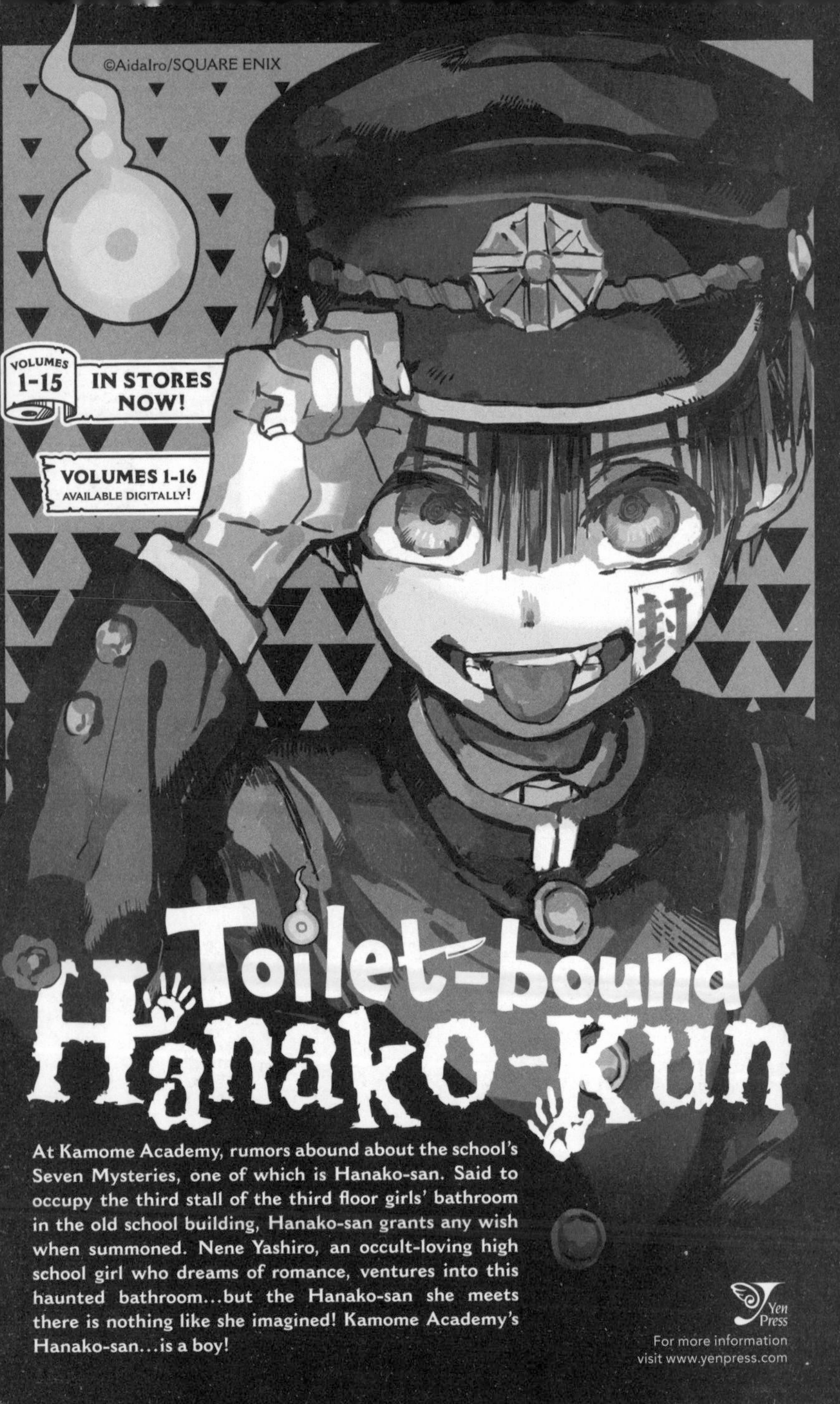
©AidaIro/SQUARE ENIX
VOLUMES 1-15 IN STORES NOW!
VOLUMES 1-16 AVAILABLE DIGITALLY!
Toilet-bound Hanako-Kun
At Kamome Academy, rumors abound about the school's Seven Mysteries, one of which is Hanako-san. Said to occupy the third stall of the third floor girls' bathroom in the old school building, Hanako-san grants any wish when summoned. Nene Yashiro, an occult-loving high school girl who dreams of romance, ventures into this haunted bathroom...but the Hanako-san she meets there is nothing like she imagined! Kamome Academy's Hanako-san...is a boy!
Yen Press
For more information visit www.yenpress.com

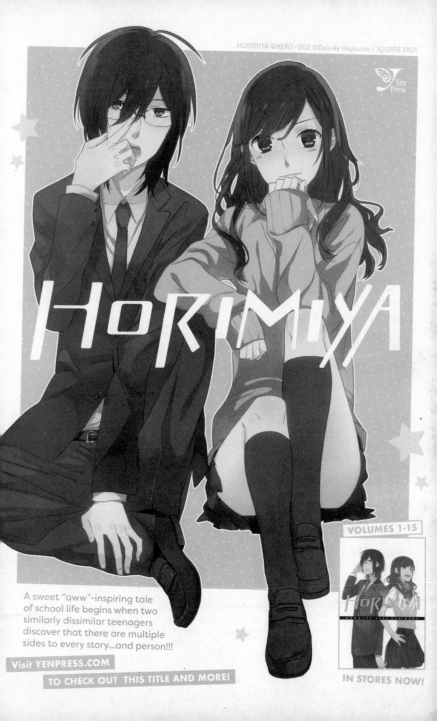

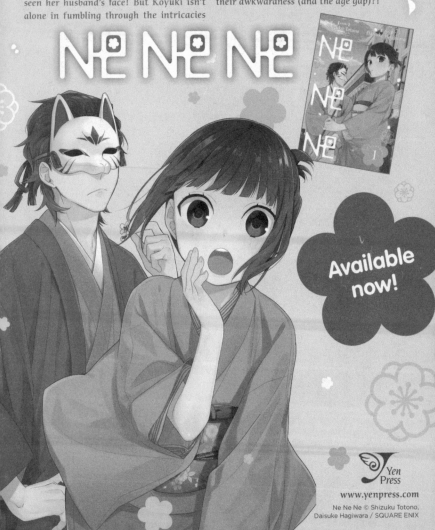

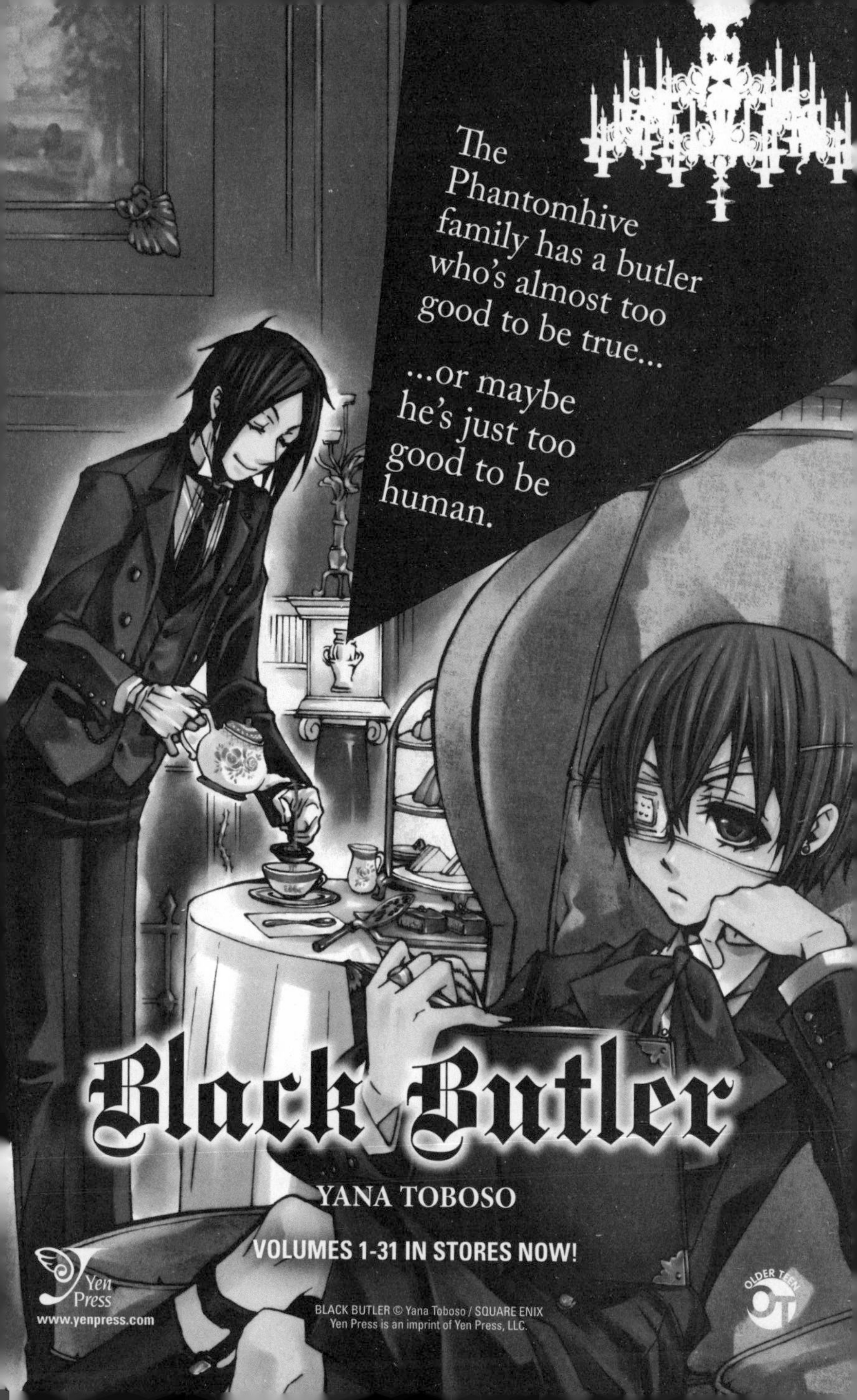
The Phantomhive family has a butler who's almost too good to be true...
...or maybe he's just too good to be human.
Black Butler
YANA TOBOSO
VOLUMES 1-31 IN STORES NOW!
Yen Press
www.yenpress.com
BLACK BUTLER © Yana Toboso / SQUARE ENIX
Yen Press is an imprint of Yen Press, LLC.
OLDER TEEN
OT

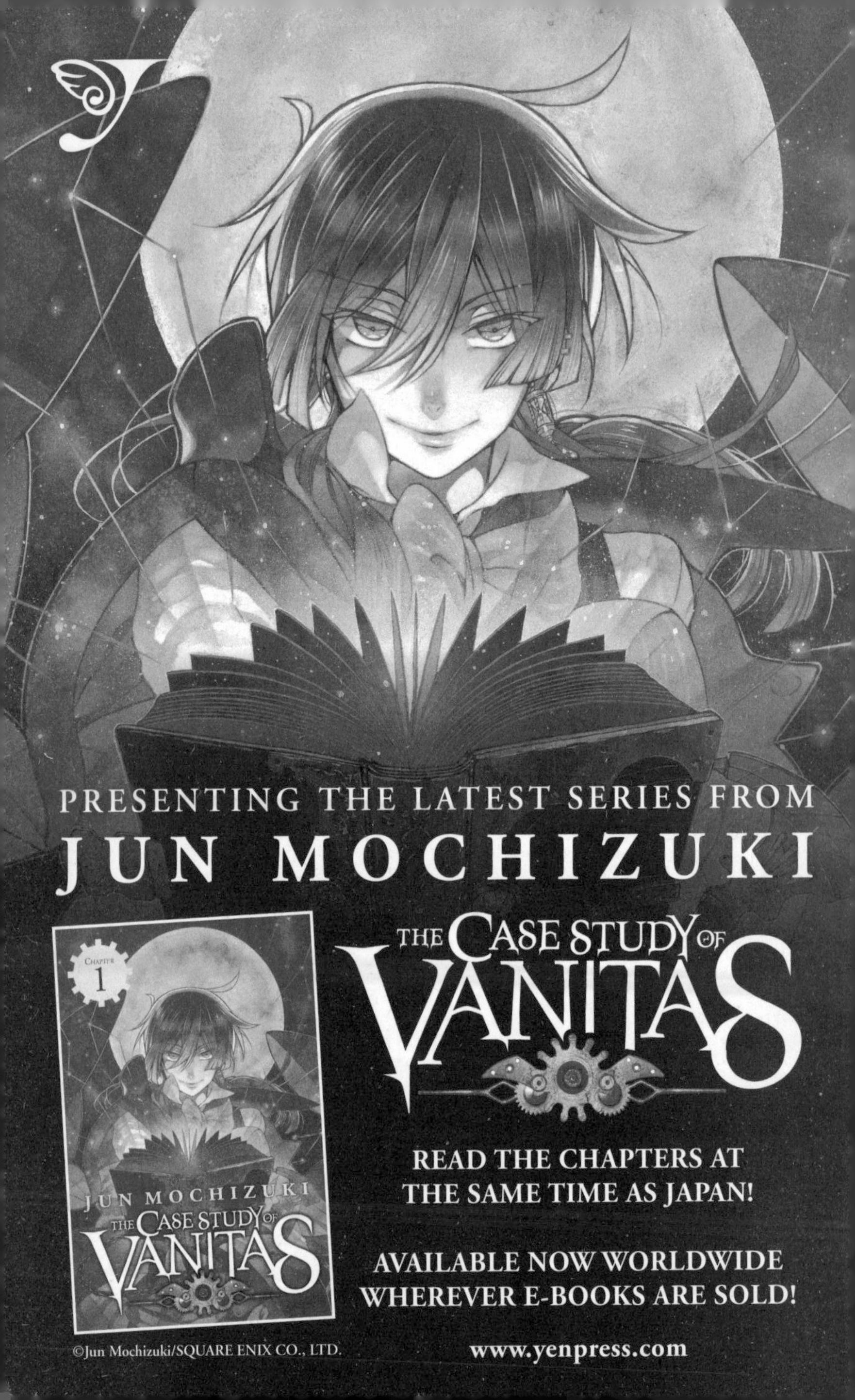
PRESENTING THE LATEST SERIES FROM
JUN MOCHIZUKI
CHAPTER 1
JUN MOCHIZUKI
THE CASE STUDY OF VANITAS
THE CASE STUDY OF VANITAS
READ THE CHAPTERS AT THE SAME TIME AS JAPAN!
AVAILABLE NOW WORLDWIDE WHEREVER E-BOOKS ARE SOLD!
©Jun Mochizuki/SQUARE ENIX CO., LTD.
www.yenpress.com

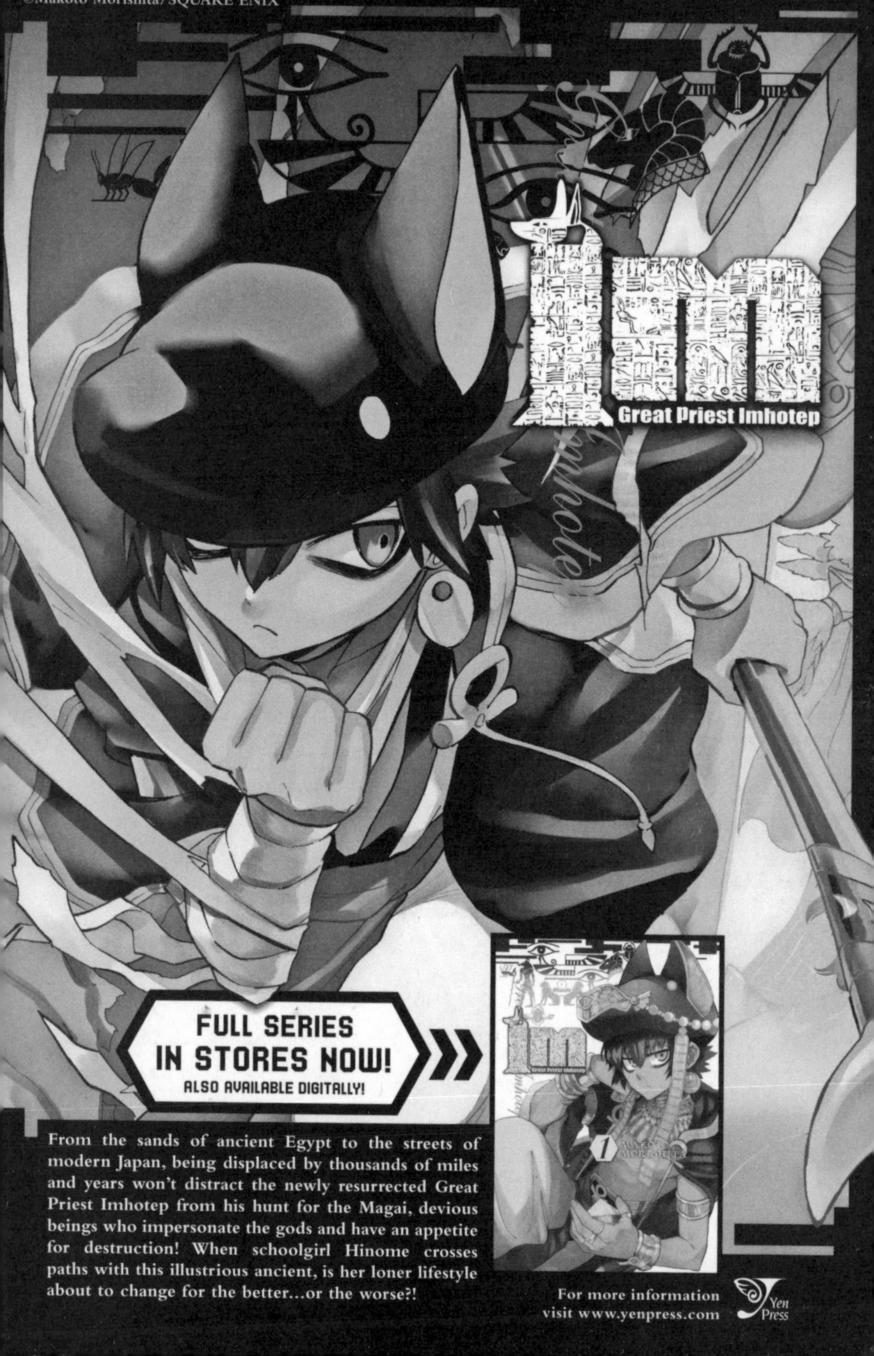
Im
Great Priest Imhotep
FULL SERIES
IN STORES NOW!
ALSO AVAILABLE DIGITALLY!
From the sands of ancient Egypt to the streets of modern Japan, being displaced by thousands of miles and years won't distract the newly resurrected Great Priest Imhotep from his hunt for the Magai, devious beings who impersonate the gods and have an appetite for destruction! When schoolgirl Hinome crosses paths with this illustrious ancient, is her loner lifestyle about to change for the better...or the worse?!
For more information
visit www.yenpress.com
Yen Press

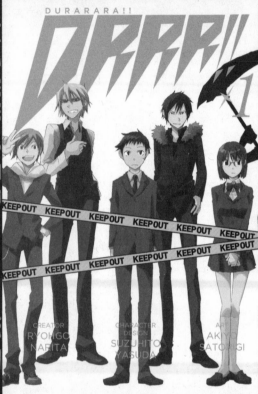

The Royal Tut

Translation: Amanda Haley • Lettering: Abigail Blackman

This book is a work of fiction. Names, characters, places, and incidents are the product of the author's imagination or are used fictitiously. Any resemblance to actual events, locales, or persons, living or dead, is coincidental.

THE ROYAL TUTOR Vol. 17 © 2021 Higasa Akai / SQUARE ENIX CO., LTD. First published in Japan in 2021 by SQUARE ENIX CO., LTD. English translation rights arranged with SQUARE ENIX CO., LTD. and Yen Press, LLC through Tuttle-Mori Agency, Inc., Tokyo.

English translation © 2022 by SQUARE ENIX CO., LTD.

Yen Press
150 West 30th Street, 19th Floor
New York, NY 10001

Visit us at yenpress.com
facebook.com/yenpress
twitter.com/yenpress
yenpress.tumblr.com
instagram.com/yenpress

First Yen Press Print Edition: July 2022
The chapters in this volume were originally published as ebooks by Yen Press.
Edited by Abigail Blackman & Yen Press Editorial: Won Young Seo, Kurt Hassler
Designed by Yen Press Design: Wendy Chan

Yen Press is an imprint of Yen Press, LLC.
The Yen Press name and logo are trademarks of Yen Press, LLC.

The publisher is not responsible for websites (or their content) that are not owned by the publisher.

Library of Congress Control Number: 2017938422

ISBNs: 978-1-9753-4743-7 (paperback)
       978-1-9753-4744-4 (ebook)

10 9 8 7 6 5 4 3 2 1

WOR

Printed in the United States of America